The
Nonverbal
Communication

The Nonverbal Communication Reader

Joseph A. DeVito
Michael L. Hecht

WAVELAND
PRESS, INC.

Prospect Heights, Illinois

For information about this book, write or call:

Waveland Press, Inc.
P.O. Box 400
Prospect Heights, Illinois 60070
(847) 634-0081

Printed in the United States of America

7

Consulting Editors

Joseph A. DeVito
Robert E. Denton, Jr.

Dedication

To my family

JDV

To my family

MLH

Contents in Brief

Contents

Part One ———————————
Beginning Perspectives   1

Part Two ─────────────────
Body Communication   **65**

Part Three
Facial and Eye Communication   113

Part Four
Artifactual Communication   149

Part Five

Spatial Communication
(Proxemics and Territoriality)   **181**

Part Six

Tactile Communication (Haptics)   **215**

Part Seven
Paralanguage and Silence   251

Part Eight
Smell (Olfactics)   277

Part Nine
Temporal Communication (Chronemics)   299

Appendix A
Deception and Deception Detection   329

Appendix B
Applications to Interpersonal Relationships 361

Appendix C
Researching Nonverbal Communication 413

Preface

Nonverbal communication is one of the fastest growing areas in the field of communication. This reader is in part a response to that rapid growth and the classroom needs that such growth creates. Currently, there are many excellent textbooks in nonverbal communication. There are, however, few places where the beginning student can go to read the research and theory first hand. We hope this reader will fulfill that need.

This reader is addressed to the student taking an introductory or intermediate course in nonverbal communication. It may be used in conjunction with *The Nonverbal Communication Workbook* (which follows a similar organizational pattern) or with any of the excellent textbooks. [A key coordinating these readings with the standard textbooks is contained in the *Instructor's Manual to Accompany the Nonverbal Communication Workbook* and is available from the publisher.] It may also, of course, be used as the primary text.

The Nonverbal Communication Reader covers the major areas of nonverbal communication. The first part covers beginning perspectives and approaches to nonverbal communication. Parts 2 through 9 cover the various areas of nonverbal communication: body, facial and eye, artifactual, spatial, tactile, paralanguage and silence, smell, and temporal communication. Each part contains theoretical and research studies so that the reader can more easily appreciate the richness in this field.

This reader also contains three appendices. These topics are placed in appendices because they do not fall into one of the areas of nonverbal communication. They do not appear as appendices because they are of lesser importance; quite the contrary. In many ways they are central to the entire reader. Appendix A covers the area of deception and deception detection and provides much practical insight into this exciting area. Perhaps more important, however, is that in this area we can see the individual areas of nonverbal communication coming together to bear on this one issue of lying and its detection. Appendix B also brings the areas of nonverbal communication together and focuses on interpersonal relationships. Appendix C covers research methods in nonverbal communication. We can best appreciate the research studies and findings when we know something of the ways in which research is conducted. This section should also prove helpful for students conducting a research project, a standard project in many nonverbal communication courses.

Unlike most readers, this text contains a variety of learning aids. An extensive introductory chapter, written by the editors, places the field of nonverbal communication in perspective and provides an orientation to the readings which follow. Each of the major parts of the reader begins with an overview to acquaint the reader with the articles contained in that part. Each of the articles is further placed in perspective by introductory headnotes. At the end of each part is a listing of "Key Terms and Concepts" arranged by article. These will provide convenient review guidelines. The index should further help identify the central concepts of nonverbal communication.

A unique feature of this reader is that the statistical explanations—of interest mainly to other researchers—have been deleted and the findings summarized "in English." This was done without damaging the integrity of the research and, in all cases, with the approval of the original researcher or publisher. We hope that this will make research studies more accessible to students beginning this study of nonverbal communication.

Another unique feature of this reader is its emphasis on the practical applications of nonverbal communication. Although we have in no way slighted research and theory—in fact, this reader contains many of the most significant research and theory papers by the field's leading contributors—many of the articles have important practical applications to a wide variety of situations. Increasing effectiveness in interviews, communicating power in an organization, establishing credibility, using touch to comfort and persuade, managing the impression one communicates to others, expressing rapport and empathy, using nonverbal communication to encourage others to "open up," and using eye contact to communicate relational messages are just some of the many practical issues addressed in this wide-ranging collection. In all cases, these practical applications are firmly based on findings from the very best nonverbal research we could find.

We enjoy teaching the nonverbal communication course and we want to share our enthusiasm with you. We hope this reader succeeds in doing that and more.

Acknowledgments

It is a pleasure to thank the many people who have contributed to this volume. Most importantly we thank those people who have allowed their work to be printed in this collection. They are clearly the writers of this book. Many of these authors spent time reviewing their original work and, in relevant cases, our summary of their statistical analyses and our adaptations. Their guidance was especially appreciated and is gratefully acknowledged. Brian Spitzberg, D. F. Gundersen, Stanley Jones, Sandra Petronio, John Bourhis, and Charlene Berquist took time from their busy schedules to write original papers especially for this volume. We owe these researchers a special thanks.

We would also like to thank Jason Sato and Jill Johnson for their help in obtaining the permissions.

As always Carol and Neil Rowe and the people at Waveland Press made working on this volume a pleasure. We thank them for their cooperation, their wise counsel, and their dedication to providing the field of communication with quality textbooks.

In addition to those already mentioned, Michael Hecht would like to thank Jim and Rebecca for keeping him young; Alan, Susan, and Bella for their support, and Mary and Sig for their memory.

Part One

Beginning Perspectives

Nonverbal communication is all around us in all our messages other than words themselves. We are expressing ourselves nonverbally when we smile, dress in a certain style, lean forward or back, stand close or far, or talk in a certain tone of voice. Nonverbal messages are important because they are generally more *believable* than verbal communication, are used to *express emotions*, and tell us a great deal about people and their relationships. However, nonverbal communication can be an illusive and ambiguous form of communication. You will interpret nonverbal messages more accurately if you avoid relying too heavily on a single nonverbal cue (for example, crossed arms as a sign of defensiveness) and, instead, look for groups or clusters of cues (for example, look for crossed arms, frowns, rigid posture, and leaning away as signs of defensiveness).

We have many ways of communicating nonverbally. We use our body, face and eyes, clothing and objects (for example, cars, jewelry, briefcases), space, touch, voice sounds and silence, smell, and time. These nonverbal messages communicate many different *meanings* and accomplish numerous *goals*.

We also have *expectations* about nonverbal behavior. We expect most people to keep their distance, face forward in elevators, look at us when they are talking, and wear appropriate clothes. We do not expect strangers to touch us without good reason (for example, nurses and hair stylists). These expectations play a major role in how we understand nonverbal communication.

Finally, *nonverbal skills* are crucial for successful communication. We use nonverbal messages to communicate that we are interested in other people, to start and end conversations, to express our feelings, and to influence others around us.

1 *This article provides an overview to nonverbal communication. Hecht and DeVito define nonverbal communication as all messages other than words. They explain how verbal and nonverbal communication are interrelated and describe the basic characteristics of nonverbal communication.*

Perspectives on Nonverbal Communication
The How, What, and Why of Nonverbal Communication

Michael L. Hecht
and Joseph A. DeVito

Nonverbal communication occurs in all areas of life. Note the role of nonverbal communication in business and personal relationships in these examples.

Pat is negotiating to buy an office building owned by Kelly. They have been negotiating for three weeks and now appear ready to complete the deal. "Five hundred thousand is my final offer!" asserts Pat. Kelly looks directly back at the other negotiator. Pat returns the gaze except for a brief glance and smile at the building they are discussing. Kelly also notices Pat's feet move nervously and thinks, "Pat really wants this property and is nervous about leaving without a deal." Kelly answers, "I won't take less than $510,000."

Jamie and Chris met two weeks ago at a party. Last week they went out for lunch and talked for three hours. Tonight they had their first date. After dinner and a drink at a quiet bar, they return to Chris' apartment. They talk for awhile and hold hands. Chris reaches over and softly touches Jamie's cheek. As their heartbeats quicken, Chris leans forward, slowly closing the distance between them until they kiss softly for the first time.

This article was written especially for this book.

These descriptions emphasize the nonverbal world in which we live (Frye, 1980). During the negotiation, Pat's words convey one meaning. Kelly, however, relies on nonverbal cues to make the last bid. In the romantic interaction, without speaking a word, a powerful message of attraction passes between two people and is acted upon. While most of our formal education focuses on verbal messages, our nonverbal skills often play the key role in our success or failure.

The Importance of Nonverbal Communication

Nonverbal communication plays an important role in our interactions (Mehrabian—Weiner, 1967). Some studies claim that most of the meaning we get from an interaction comes from the nonverbal part of the message. These studies show that people interpret messages by relying on nonverbal rather than verbal cues. For example, you may know what your boss is thinking from facial expressions, stance, and other nonverbal messages. From practical experience we know that verbal messages are important too. However, there are times when the nonverbal messages are more influential. In relating to our family, selling a product, or socializing at parties, nonverbal messages dominate. We communicate about 60% of our meaning nonverbally. In fact, it is likely that nonverbal messages are the primary means for communicating emotion, forming impressions, and communicating about relationships.

Nonverbal messages are usually more believable than verbal messages. When verbal and nonverbal messages contradict, most adults in the United States believe the nonverbal. Anyone who attempts to ignore nonverbal messages will surely be at a disadvantage.

A Definition of Nonverbal Communication

Nonverbal Communication means all the messages other than words that people exchange. This definition has three important parts. First, it says that nonverbal communication involves messages. Second, it says that nonverbal communication consists of all the aspects of communication not expressed in words. Third, it limits nonverbal communication to messages transmitted among people.

The definition states that nonverbal communication involves the exchange of *messages*. Messages are *symbolic*. They stand for something other than themselves. Many theorists use this difference to distinguish between nonverbal communication and nonverbal behavior. Communication occurs when we interpret as a message something which stands for something else. Behavior stands for itself. It just is. For example, consider the situation where someone hands you a paper to read and you lean away to get under a reading light. Your leaning away would be behavior, not communication. However, if you lean away because you do not like the person, then the leaning would *symbolize* or stand for your dislike. This would be communication.

The definition also distinguishes between verbal communication (involving words) and nonverbal communication (involving all the rest of the message). Nonverbal communication, therefore, involves all messages "other than words" including aspects of the voice, body movement, facial expressions, space, time, smell, and objects. This part of the definition also points to the complexity of nonverbal communication. It reminds us of all the different ways we communicate nonverbally. In interpreting the meaning of a message, therefore, we need to focus on the words and on the varied nonverbal messages from the eyes and facial expressions, the spatial distances, the body posture, and so on.

Finally, nonverbal communication occurs *among people*. This part of the definition excludes animal-human interactions and communication with oneself. Animal-human interactions, while certainly of interest, are inherently different from those among humans. Animals stress different senses than humans do (for example, smell). Further, they do not process the world symbolically, at least to the extent that people do.

Similarly, *intrapersonal communication* such as thought or other messages to ourselves, is best studied separately from what we call nonverbal communication. For example, research suggests that we display emotions nonverbally when other people are around, but rarely when we are alone. Other people seem to encourage us to display our emotions nonverbally. As we rarely talk to ourselves out loud, it is unusual to express nonverbal emotional messages just for our benefit.

The Relationship Between Verbal and Nonverbal Messages

When people communicate, they do not separate messages into verbal and nonverbal communication. If your friend says "I'm so sad" while crying, we do not consider the tears and the words separately. They act together to create a total impression. This occurs because communication is a single system. In sending and receiving, we combine all aspects of the message. "Verbal" and "nonverbal" name different aspects of the same message. The verbal element, words, cannot be used without some means for expressing them. As you read this sentence, the printing style and the paper are nonverbal parts of the overall message.

However, we separate verbal and nonverbal aspects of messages in our discussion to simplify our explanations. The distinction helps us to describe, understand, and explain nonverbal communication more effectively.

Since communication is a single system of which nonverbal and verbal messages are two components, there are many ways these two systems function together. Leading nonverbal researchers such as Paul Ekman (1965) and Mark Knapp (1978) discuss six such ways that nonverbal messages may relate to verbal messages:

1. Nonverbal messages *accent* when they stress or emphasize a particular part of the verbal message. We can highlight a key word or phrase by talking louder or banging a fist on the desk. In this manner, we call attention to a particular part of the message.

2. Nonverbal messages *complement* when they add to the verbal message. Complementary messages complete or supplement what is being communicated verbally. This is particularly true of emotional messages. For example, kissing complements saying "I like you" by adding the type of liking. Pushing someone complements expressions of dislike by showing how much dislike there is.

3. Nonverbal messages *contradict* verbal messages when they convey opposite meanings. Contradiction occurs when you get one interpretation from the verbal message and the opposite interpretation from the nonverbal message. For example, we have contradiction when you verbally express disinterest in a person while engaging in direct eye contact and smiling. Similarly, contradiction occurs when you say you are not angry about a decision through clinched jaws. Sarcasm is a clear example of contradiction. Here the verbal and nonverbal aspects of a message each give contradictory messages.

4. Nonverbal messages also *regulate* the flow of conversations. Such regulating messages tell you whose speaking turn it is, whether to continue or stop talking, and when the conversation is about to end. You may communicate that you want to get into a group conversation by leaning forward, gesturing in front of you, and inhaling. Or you may indicate that you want the speaker to say more by nodding approval and saying "uh huh!"

5. There are also instances in which nonverbal messages *repeat* the meanings of verbal messages. By restating or reinforcing the verbal messages, nonverbal communication fulfills this important function. For example, you may say "yes" and nod your head. You may say something is in the drawer and open the drawer or point to it.

6. Nonverbal messages can *substitute* for verbal messages. Substitution occurs when we use a nonverbal message instead of a verbal message. Shaking your head "no" or giving the "OK" sign substitute for specific words or phrases.

While verbal and nonverbal messages often go together, there are also important differences between them. The brain treats verbal and non-verbal messages differently. The brain processes most nonverbal messages holistically and synthetically. This means that the brain takes a nonverbal message as a whole and does not break it down into parts. Conversely, the brain processes verbal messages discreetly and analytically. It breaks verbal messages into their parts and analyzes each part.

There are also differences in the way we store in our brain the verbal and nonverbal memories (Woodall & Folger, 1981). Because of the immediate impact of nonverbal sensation, we recall these memories more easily and vividly. As a result, our recall of specific information is aided by the memory of the nonverbal sensations present at the time of our initial learning.

Nonverbal Behavior Versus Nonverbal Communication

In our definition we said that nonverbal *communication* consists of messages that are symbolic, that stand for something other than themselves. Nonverbal *behavior*, on the other hand, does not stand for something else. According to this viewpoint, then, actions would be considered nonverbal communication when the actor intends them to be symbolic or when the perceiver interprets the actions as symbolic. For example, if Jack leans forward while listening to Jan in order to show interest, this action is communication. If Jan interprets the forward lean to mean that Jack is expressing interest, it is also nonverbal communication. However, if Jack is leaning forward because it is hot and his shirt is sticking to the chair and if Jan doesn't notice him leaning forward or doesn't interpret it as meaningful, then the lean is nonverbal behavior not communication.

As a second example consider the distance between two people. Sometimes, people deliberately stand a certain distance from you. This is what we are calling nonverbal communication. At other times, distances are accidentally determined. This is what we are calling nonverbal behavior. Now let's see why this distinction is important.

Nonverbal actions that we intentionally send as messages are obviously communication. This type of action is usually very noticeable and easily interpreted. For example, when we give someone the "thumbs up" sign, it is clear that we are communicating a symbol that stands for something else.

There are also ways that people behave that another person can interpret as meaningful. For example, if a person begins unconsciously to stand farther away from a lover or spouse it may communicate a change in feelings. Or, imagine a business meeting conducted around a table. Two people sit in the exact same posture (called mirroring). These people may be on the same side of the issue and vote together. These actions are less obvious because we have to interpret something that is not intentionally sent as a message. However, in many cases we are able to interpret the action as a message because experience shows that such actions are usually meaningful. Yet these actions are not as easily interpreted as those nonverbal messages with intended meaning.

On the other hand, some nonverbal actions are neither intended nor interpreted as messages. This is nonverbal behavior, not communication. A person who scratches a mosquito bite may not be sending a message and we usually do not interpret these actions that way.

Some actions are ambiguous and we do not know if they are nonverbal behavior or nonverbal communication. This can be tricky to interpret. Suppose you go to a party and are talking to someone who is standing with arms crossed. Is this person uptight and defensive or just more comfortable in that position? We really have no way of knowing whether this is nonverbal behavior or communication. Did the person mean to send a message (stay away)? Should we assume there is a message here or that the action is not symbolic?

Probably the best strategy is to look for other nonverbal cues. Most often nonverbal behaviors that are meaningful come in groups or at least in pairs. Nonverbal researchers say that nonverbal communication is multichannelled because it comes in packages. This means that we send and receive messages through groups of cues. In the example above, we can assume that if the person with arms crossed is truly defensive, there should be other signs of this defensiveness. For example, the person might lean away, frown, show muscle tension in the jaws, shuffle feet, and talk in short sentences. In fact, it would be misleading to rely on a single nonverbal cue under the assumption that each action has one, clear meaning. Relying on single cues can result in stereotyping. For example, you stereotype if you assume that a heavy person is jolly or a person with glasses is intelligent.

The context or setting can also help us interpret nonverbal cues. Different types of nonverbal actions are appropriate in different settings. For example, we interpret laughter differently at parties, school, and funerals. The context or setting tells you what is appropriate or inappropriate and gives you hints about how to interpret nonverbal messages.

And so the distinction between nonverbal communication and nonverbal behavior is an important one which affects our everyday interactions. A person who treats all nonverbal behavior as communication will be reading too much into a situation. Research shows that paying too much attention to minor nonverbal actions can actually damage relationships. On the other hand, someone who treats most actions as nonverbal behavior (rather than as communication) would be naive. Striking a good balance is one of the keys to effective communication.

Characteristics of Nonverbal Communication

Here we continue our introduction to nonverbal communication by examining certain of its characteristics (DeVito, 1989; Pease, 1984). This section will introduce some of the terms and concepts that occur throughout the reader.

Nonverbal Communication Is Guided By Rules

Nonverbal communication is *rule-guided* activity (Smith & Williamson, 1985). Rules tell us how to behave nonverbally. Rules are statements of what you should or should not do, and what the consequences are for conforming and not conforming. These rules are not written anywhere. They are learned from observing others. While nonverbal rules are rarely discussed and rarely taught explicitly, they are costly to break. Staring at someone on a bus can result in hostility. Touching someone inappropriately can bring social censure. Even such mundane rules as facing the front in an elevator can result in discomfort when violated. In an organization, a young management trainee may be judged as pretentious for wearing a black suit, because black suits are reserved for people with greater power. Female executives who wear frilly blouses and tight, slitted skirts will probably have trouble getting promoted in most businesses in the United States because this attire is seen as inappropriate for executives. These rules are, of course, totally arbitrary. There is no reason, for example, why black suits should be reserved for upper management and blue and brown for lower management. This arbitrariness, however, should not blind us to the power of these rules. The rules are enforced and violators will have to face the consequences.

It is a good habit to discover the nonverbal rules before acting. One of the first things to do on a new job, for example, is to figure out the prevailing nonverbal rules. Does everyone dress the same way? Does it matter where you sit in the employee dining room? How are offices arranged? Similarly, observing nonverbal rules will make you a better sales person (where to sit for the first sales call?), more effective teacher (should chairs be in a circle or rows?), and a better date (should you arrive on time or a few minutes late?). In all these cases it is wise to determine the rules and to learn the hazards of nonconformity.

Nonverbal Communication Is Influenced By Culture

The rules of nonverbal communication vary from one culture to the next (Hecht, Andersen, & Ribeau, 1989). What one culture considers polite, another may consider offensive. View nonverbal communication—like verbal communication—as a "cultural event." Recognize that culture influences both the performance and the interpretation of nonverbal messages. In businesses in the United States, it is usually effective to get to the point quickly. The Japanese, however, may view this as rude and unfriendly.

Virtually all cultures interpret some nonverbal behaviors in the same way (for example, smiling). All cultures also, however, differ from each other in interpreting other nonverbal messages.

There are many examples of unsuccessful intercultural interactions to illustrate this principle. For example, one problem is the assumption that all people occupy the same nonverbal world. It is assumed that everyone feels the same way about crowding, smell, dress, and other nonverbal messages. Assumptions such as these are, of course, incorrect and have resulted in difficulties for American tourists in Middle Eastern countries where closer interpersonal distances are common. For example, many Middle-Easterners feel that to hide one's breath from the conversational partner is a sign of shame or deceit. Many feel that women who expose a great deal of skin wearing shorts or a mini-skirt are of low morals. Interestingly enough, this assumption and warnings against it were distributed in a booklet to all 37,000 United States volunteers working at the recent Pan American Games in Indianapolis (*Sports Illustrated*, Aug. 1987, p. 16):

> Realize that gestures can be significant. Hand motions which are innocent in one culture may be offensive in another. Keep your hands relatively still and refrain from pointing—instead use wide arm motions, turning your head in the desired direction. Avoid scratching your nose, indicating the number two by holding up two fingers, or making the thumbs up or the "O.K." sign.

The message is clear. When you are in a different culture, find out the nonverbal rules.

Nonverbal Messages Are Organized Into Codes

The nonverbal rules and practices of a culture are organized into *codes* (Knapp, 1978). Codes are organized message systems consisting of a set of symbols and the rules for their use. For example, our verbal language consists of words (a set of symbols) and the rules of grammar (the rules for combining). Other examples would include the Morse code for the telegraph, mathematics, any computer language, and fraternity or sorority initiation rituals.

We define the nonverbal codes by the means of expression we use. Each code is communicated by a different part of the nonverbal world—a part of your body, the environment, or the objects around you. The nonverbal codes we will discuss are: body communication, facial and eye communication, artifactual communication, spatial communication, tactile communication, paralanguage and silence, smell, and temporal communication.

Some researchers use the term *kinesics* to describe how our bodies communicate. Used this way, kinesics includes body, facial, and eye communication. We chose the more specific terms for purposes of clarity.

1. *Body communication*: This code deals with messages sent by our bodies. Included here are gestures, posture, body movement, body lean, and physical appearance. Body orientation or how directly we face other people is also an important cue.

2. *Facial and eye communication*: This code describes the movements of the face and eyes, and what they communicate to people. It includes facial expressions such as smiles, frowns, grimaces, yawns, and pouts. Also, it includes eye movements such as the length and type of eye contact, eye avoidance, and pupil dilation and constriction.

3. *Artifactual communication*: This code includes objects we associate with ourselves and other people, including clothing, hair style, jewelry, furniture, cars, colors, and the decorations in home and office. The expression "clothes make the person" and the prevalence of status symbols such as Rolex watches and Lamborghini cars emphasize the role of artifacts in social life. Popular books advise us to pay close attention to artifacts such as briefcases, ties, belts, and shoes in preparing for advancement up the corporate ladder.

4. *Spatial communication:* This code focuses on the space between and among people. *Personal space* refers to how far apart people are while engaged in various activities. *Territoriality* refers to the characteristics of our environment and deals with possessive or ownership-like reactions to fixed and moveable space. Territoriality includes home and public territories, how we use them, and how we react to encroachments. *Personal space* refers to the areas around and between people.

5. *Tactile communication:* This code deals with touch or the physical contact between two people. Different types of touches (for example, grabbing, stroking, patting, and punching) communicate different meanings. In addition, we have different rules for touching the various parts of the body. This code is also referred to as *haptics.*

6. *Paralanguage and Silence:* The paralanguage code includes the sounds of the voice when producing words. We are concerned with how we communicate through changes in speaking rate, volume, voice qualities and pitch, accents, pauses, and hesitations. Silence and the meanings attributed to it are also of interest.

7. *Smell:* This code, also called *olfactics*, deals with how odor communicates. Included here are body smells, perfume/cologne, and other smells. There are wide cultural differences in the reactions to smell. The perfume industry is larger in the United States than anywhere else in the world.

8. *Temporal communication:* This code describes how our use of time communicates. Time preferences, scheduling, perception of time (e.g., what it means to be "on time"), and biological cycles are all of interest here. This code is sometimes called *chronemics.*

These codes are useful in two ways. First, they describe and classify nonverbal communication. They tell us *how* nonverbal messages are communicated (for example, by the body, by the face, etc.). This allows us to separate nonverbal communication into smaller parts. It also helps us to organize messages into a meaningful whole.

Second, the codes call our attention to the ways we can communicate nonverbally. The eight codes remind us there are eight ways we can communicate nonverbally. They help us realize the many ways we send and receive messages, and they alert us to areas on which we should concentrate in communicating with and in understanding each other.

View these codes as working together because nonverbal communication is multichannelled (Andersen, 1985). When we communicate, we use many parts of our body at once. We cannot examine only one part; we must consider the others as well. For example, assume a physically attractive person smiled at you. Your interpretation and reaction may depend on whether or not the person is wearing a wedding ring.

One of the clearest clues that someone is lying is that different messages are communicated by different codes. For example, the face could say one thing and the body another. Similarly, if we want to know whether someone is tense, we need to look at more than gestures. The jaw, vocal pitch, and posture are important too. So, while these codes are useful in helping us describe nonverbal communication and understanding the many ways we have to express ourselves, we must be careful to consider the overall message. We must see the forest as well as the individual trees.

Some researchers have compared the relative importance of the codes and reached a number of conclusions. Here are a few examples:

1. The face is usually the most important channel, particularly when judging how positive or pleasant another person is. That importance decreases, however, when we suspect deception. When people expect deception they pay more attention to the voice and body.

2. We rely on the vocal channel for judgments of assertiveness, fearfulness, and sincerity. We also use the vocal channel to determine how intensely someone feels an emotion.

3. Women rely more on facial cues. In addition, both men and women are more likely to discount the positive facial expressions of women as unimportant.

Nonverbal Communication Is Meaningful

In addition to knowing how nonverbal messages are sent (the codes), we must also know *what* is being sent. Nonverbal messages are used to send three primary *meanings*: immediacy, power, and responsiveness (Mehrabian, 1971). These meanings answer the "what" question by telling us how nonverbal messages are interpreted.

1. *Immediacy*: This is an evaluative dimension which includes judgments such as good-bad, positive-negative, and close-far. Nonverbal messages tell us how people feel about the world. The more we like something, the more attentive we tend to be to it. We communicate immediacy by smiles, close distances, and

hugs. The immediacy principle, developed by Albert Mehrabian (1971), predicts that people will approach persons and things they like and avoid or move away from persons and things they dislike. A useful bibliography of immediacy is provided by Patterson, Reidhead, Gooch, and Stopka (1984).

2 *Power:* This dimension involves dominance and status. People have power to the degree that they can control the events around them. There are many nonverbal cues that communicate power, including having a large office, controlling and taking up space, and standing up and leaning over people who are seated.

3. *Responsiveness:* This describes the ways people react to the things, people, and events in their environment. Responsiveness refers to change and activity in response to a particular stimulus. People will see us as more responsive if we talk faster, gesture a lot, and have more eye contact.

Nonverbal messages, then, communicate these three meanings more frequently than any others. We can ask questions about immediacy, power, and responsiveness if we want to know how people are interpreting our nonverbal messages. These meanings provide a useful way of understanding how people interpret nonverbal messages.

Nonverbal Communication is Functional

Nonverbal *functions* tell us *why* nonverbal messages are sent. Once we know how nonverbal messages are communicated (codes) and what they say to us (meanings), we still need to know what they accomplish. Nonverbal functions refer to how nonverbal messages achieve goals and outcomes (Patterson, 1982, 1987). This helps us understand the ''why'' of nonverbal communication—why people use certain messages in order to obtain an outcome. The major functions served by nonverbal communication are as follows:

1. *Nonverbal messages provide information:* This function is fulfilled when nonverbal messages provide people with something they did not already know. When we point, or shake our head ''no,'' or hand someone a book, our actions provide information to others. If you reveal that you are lying by talking overly fast and in short sentences, you would also be providing information.

2. *Nonverbal messages regulate interaction:* Nonverbal messages that tell people how to conduct a conversation regulate the flow of the interaction. This includes when to begin a conversation,

whose turn it is to speak, how to get a chance to speak, how to signal others to talk more, and when the conversation is over.

Social rhythms, the synchronicity (coordination) and tempo (rate of speed) of conversations, are also significant. Cultures seem to have their own rhythms; individuals, too, can have their own unique "beats." These nonverbal messages tell us how to take turns and manage the give-and-take of conversations. For example, people often lean forward, gesture, and open their mouths slightly when they want a chance to talk in a group.

3. *Nonverbal messages express emotion:* As noted earlier, nonverbal communication is the primary means of expressing emotion. For example, smiles and wrinkles alongside the eyes are usually nonverbal displays of happiness. Frowns, on the other hand, are signs of displeasure. Nonverbal researchers have identified primary or basic emotions such as happiness, surprise, fear, anger, sadness, disgust, contempt, and interest. They have also identified the nonverbal cues we use in expressing these emotions. Researchers have also examined blends or mixes of more than one emotion at a time. There is some evidence showing that the expression and interpretation of emotions may cut across different cultures. If this is true, then the nonverbal expression of emotion is probably biologically determined.

4. *Nonverbal messages exercise social control*: Nonverbal messages of power and dominance can be used to control people and events. Think of the strong leaders you know. They probably have a distinctive nonverbal style. Powerful people touch others more than they are touched. They look at others less than they are looked at (but use eye gaze for a purpose such as "staring someone down"). Powerful people also take up more space than less powerful people.

Environments can also be used to control people. Take a look at your classroom. If it is like most others, the teacher will have a large share of the space and the chairs will be arranged so that students pay attention to the teacher and not to each other.

5. *Nonverbal messages facilitate service or task goals*: Nonverbal communication can also help accomplish a specific task. Nurses touch you in order to provide a medical examination. You use touch to help a friend get out of a car or hand a tool to a co-worker.

6. *Nonverbal communication metacommunicates*: Metacommunication is a "message about message." Verbal metacommunication consists of phrases such as "Just kidding," and "Don't take it so seriously." These messages tell your listener how to interpret your messages. Nonverbally, we signal sarcasm through voice tone. We communicate empathy while giving bad news by leaning forward and touching. We assure employees we still trust them through voice tone and eye contact even while giving them negative feedback on work performance. Many people would rather not talk about how their relationship is going. They may prefer instead to communicate this information nonverbally. They do not like explicit, verbal metacommunication about the nature of the relationship.

7. *Nonverbal messages present your self-image*: Some nonverbal messages present a person's image. These messages describe the type of personality. A person may behave in a caring way in order to be seen as a concerned person. Or someone may tell jokes and make wisecracks to be seen as exciting and fun. Nonverbal messages can contribute to our being seen as a loving spouse, an aggressive business person, or a scholarly professor.

Chapter Summary

In this chapter we defined nonverbal communication as involving all messages other than words that are used in our interactions. Nonverbal messages play a central role in communication and are interrelated with verbal messages in a variety of ways. A great deal of research has focused on nonverbal communication (Frye, 1980). In the remainder of this book we present articles that discuss these concepts in more detail.

This first part, Beginning Perspectives, presents readings that explain the basic concepts in nonverbal communication. Parts 2 through 9 discuss each of the codes in greater detail. Appendix A covers nonverbal deception. The applications of nonverbal communication in interpersonal communication are described in Appendix B. Nonverbal communication research is presented in Appendix C.

References

Andersen, P.A. (1985). Nonverbal immediacy in interpersonal communication. In A.W. Seigman & S. Feldstein (Eds.), *Multichannel integrations of nonverbal behavior*. Hillsdale, NJ: Lawrence Erlbaum Associates.

DeVito, Joseph A. (1989). *The Interpersonal Communication Book*, 5th ed. New York: Harper & Row.

Ekman, P. (1965). Communication through nonverbal behavior: A source of information about an interpersonal relationship. In S.S. Tompkins & C.E. Izard (Eds.), *Affect, Cognition, and Personality*. New York: Springer.

Frye, J.K. (1980). *Find: Frye's Index to Nonverbal Data*. Duluth, MN: University of Minnesota Computer Center.

Hecht, M.L., Andersen, P.A., and Ribeau, S. (1989). In Asante, M., and Gudykunst, W.B. (Eds.), *The Handbook of intercultural communication*. Beverly Hills, CA: Sage.

Knapp, M.L. (1978). *Nonverbal communication in human interaction*. New York: Holt, Rinehart, and Winston.

Mehrabian, A. (1971). *Silent Messages*. Belmont, CA: Wadsworth Publishing.

Mehrabian A., and Weiner, M. (1967). Decoding of inconsistent communications. *Journal of personality and social psychology, 6*, 108-114.

Patterson, M.L. (1982). A sequential functional model of nonverbal exchange. *Psychological review, 89*, 231-249.

Patterson, M. L. (1987). Presentational and affect-management functions of nonverbal involvement. *Journal of nonverbal behavior, 11*, 110-122.

Patterson, M.L., Reidhead, S.M., Gooch, M.V., and Stopka, S.J. (1984). A content-classified bibliography of research on the immediacy behavior: 1965-1982. *Journal of nonverbal behavior, 8*, 360-396.

Pease, Allan. *Signals*. New York: Bantam, 1984.

Smith, D.R., and Williamson, L.K. (1985). *Interpersonal communication: Roles, rules, strategies and games* (3rd Ed.). Dubuque, IA: Wm. C. Brown.

Woodall, W.G., and Folger, J.P. (1981). Encoding specificity and nonverbal cue context: An expansion of episodic memory research. *Communication monographs, 48*, 39-53.

Spitzberg describes nonverbal communication skills. He presents a measure of these skills and summarizes them in four fundamental categories: interaction management, other-orientation, composure, and expressiveness. The article shows how nonverbal communication is used to achieve success in conversations.

2

Perspectives on Nonverbal Communication Skills

Brian H. Spitzberg

For centuries, scholars and laypersons alike have pondered the nature of social skills. Why do some people seem so adept and competent at meeting people, initiating and maintaining conversations, and dealing with a variety of people in appropriate and successful ways? What skills and abilities are involved in socially skilled interaction?

Certainly, the search for these skills is an important one. An examination of over 300 studies and reviews conducted by Spitzberg and Cupach (1988) indicates that people who are less socially skilled are likely to be lower in self-esteem, academic success, occupational success, and higher in levels of loneliness, shyness, depression, mental illness, marital distress, hypertension, stress, and anxiety. There is even some evidence to suggest that less interpersonally skilled persons are more likely to become drug abusers, sexual offenders, and may experience higher mortality rates generally than those higher in social skills.

These conclusions should not be particularly surprising given how much of our everyday lives is centered around interpersonal interaction. Perlman and Rook (1987) review research indicating that approximately 70% of our waking time is spent in the presence of others. We grow up in family units, are educated in group systems, and some 90% of us will marry in our lifetimes. Many of us also communicate with other people while we work. As Rook's (1984) research reveals, our life satisfaction is

This article was written especially for this book.

strongly influenced by how positive or negative our interpersonal interactions are. Interpersonal skill is not simply a desirable commodity for a well-adjusted and satisfying life. It is virtually indispensable.

While it is impossible at this time to specify a comprehensive list of all the elements of interpersonal skill, there is some sound basis for identifying the most basic skills. For the most part, the basic interpersonal skills involve nonverbal forms of communication.

Many different skills have been associated with interpersonal effectiveness. In an attempt to verify the importance of many of these skills, Dillard and Spitzberg (1984) examined the results of sixteen studies of social skills. By looking at the results of several different studies, they were able to make more reliable and confident conclusions about which behaviors are most consistently perceived to be skillful or competent. Out of twelve behaviors studied, nine were nonverbal: *response latency* (the average or total amount of time it takes after one person stops talking before the other person begins talking), *eye gaze* (the average or total amount of time a conversant spends looking in the general region of the other person's face), *eye contact* (the average or total amount of time spent looking directly at the other person's eyes), *smiles (the frequency or total number of smiles in a conversation)*, *head movements* (generally, the number of head nods indicating understanding, agreement, or reinforcement), *adaptors* (e.g., finger tapping, hair-twirling, ring-twisting, etc.), *volume* (the average loudness of talk), and *talk time* (either the total amount of time a person spends talking or the average duration of speaking turns). All of these behaviors were related to perceptions of subject skillfulness; generally speaking, the more of each of these behaviors a person displayed, the more competent the person was perceived to be. The exception was the category of adaptors, such that the fewer adaptors displayed, the more competent the person was considered to be.

After examining this study, and the results of numerous other similar studies, Spitzberg and colleagues (Spitzberg and Hurt, 1987; Spitzberg, Brookshire, and Brunner, 1987) developed a measure of interpersonal skills. Over a thousand college students were asked to rate either a recent recalled conversation or a get-acquainted conversation they had just been involved in as part of an assignment. The ratings were on the questionnaire listed in Table 2.1. These behaviors, which are generally nonverbal in nature, were rated in terms of their competence or adequacy. Thus, the dimensions that result can be understood as the basic or essential skills of competent behavior.

Table 2.1

The Conversational Skills Rating Scale

Person being rated: _____

Person doing rating: _____

Rate the conversant according to the following responses:

1 = INADEQUATE   use was awkward, disruptive, or resulted in a negative impression of communicative skills)

2 = SOMEWHAT INADEQUATE

3 = ADEQUATE   (use was sufficient but neither very noticeable nor excellent. Produced neither positive nor negative impression)

4 = GOOD

5 = EXCELLENT   (use was smooth, controlled, and resulted in positive impression of communicative skills).

Circle the single most accurate response for each behavior:

1 2 3 4 5   (1) Use of eye contact

1 2 3 4 5   (2) Initiation of topics

1 2 3 4 5   (3) Maintenance of topics and follow-up comments

1 2 3 4 5   (4) Use of time speaking relative to partner

1 2 3 4 5   (5) Interruption of partner's speaking turns

1 2 3 4 5   (6) Speaking rate (neither too slow nor too fast)

1 2 3 4 5   (7) Speaking fluency (avoided pauses, silences, "uh"', etc.)

1 2 3 4 5   (8) Vocal confidence (neither tense nor nervous sounding)

1 2 3 4 5   (9) Articulation (language is clearly pronounced and understood

1 2 3 4 5   (10) Shaking or nervous twitches (weren't noticeable)

1 2 3 4 5   (11) Posture (neither too closed/formal nor too open/informal)

1 2 3 4 5   (12) Fidgeting (avoided swaying feet, finger-tapping, hair-twirling, etc.)

1 2 3 4 5   (13) Asking questions

1 2 3 4 5   (14) Nodding of head in response to partner's statements

1 2 3 4 5   (15) Lean toward partner (neither too far forward nor too far back)

1 2 3 4 5   (16) Speaking about partner (involved partner as topic of conversation)

1 2 3 4 5   (17) Speaking about self (didn't talk too much about self or own interests)

1 2 3 4 5   (18) Encouragements or agreements (encouraged partner to talk)

1 2 3 4 5   (19) Use of humor and/or stories

1 2 3 4 5   (20) Vocal variety (avoided monotone voice)

1 2 3 4 5   (21) Vocal volume (neither too loud nor too soft)

1 2 3 4 5   (22) Expression of personal opinions (neither too passive nor aggressive)

1 2 3 4 5   (23) Facial expressiveness (neither blank nor exaggerated)

1 2 3 4 5   (24) Use of gestures to emphasize what was being said

1 2 3 4 5   (25) Smiling and/or laughing

Extensive analyses indicated that these behaviors can be characterized according to four fundamental dimensions: *interaction management*, *other-orientation*, *composure*, and *expressiveness*. *Interaction management* concerns how well verbal speaking turns are managed, maintaining topical flow, and handling the initiation and termination of conversations. This dimension consists of behaviors such as "initiation of new topics," "maintenance of topics and follow-up comments," "use of time relative to partner," and "speaking fluency." *Other-orientation* represents the extent to which someone shows attention to, concern for, and interest in the other person in the conversation. It is exemplified by behaviors such as "use of eye contact," "nodding of head in response to partner's statements," "lean toward partner," and "speaking about self" and about "partner." *Composure* involves not only anxiety and nervousness, but also level of confidence and assertiveness. Composure (or lack thereof) is most clearly indicated by behaviors such as "vocal confidence," "shaking or nervous twitches," "posture," and "fidgeting." Finally, expressiveness concerns the level of animation and activity in the conversation and is identified by behavior such as "smiling and/or laughing," "use of gestures," "facial expressiveness," "volume," "vocal variety," and "speaking rate."

These components of competent interpersonal behavior, comprised as they are of primarily nonverbal behaviors, suggest a simple, understandable, and manageable model. Interactants, it seems, tend to assess and evaluate their own behavior and the behavior of their conversational partners in terms of a relatively small set of skills. Generally speaking, the more *expressive*, *other-oriented*, *composed*, and adept at *interaction management* an interactant is, the more likely this person will be viewed as a good interpersonal communicator. Of course, it is likely that there can be too much of a good thing. Obviously, someone who is overly expressive, confident, other-oriented, and smooth is likely to be seen as artificial or manipulative.

Furthermore, there are contextual or situational effects that can often alter this general advice. For example, while laughing and smiling are seen as skillful in most interactions, they are less likely to be seen as competent at a funeral or during a heated conflict. Behavior, to be seen as skillful, needs to be adapted to the cultural, interpersonal, and situational expectations.

These four skills seem intuitively appealing, yet they are not likely to be comprehensive. For example, skills such as self-disclosure, assertiveness, conflict management, deception, meeting people, etc. seem to be higher level abilities that may involve behaviors not represented in these dimensions. Still, the research seems very supportive at this point that the components of *interaction management, other-orientation, composure,* and *expressiveness* provide a useful and valid model of the basic skills of interpersonal behavior.

References

Dillard, J.P., and Spitzberg, B.H. (1984). Global impressions of social skills: Behavioral predictors. *Communication Yearbook, 8,* 446-463.

Perlman, D., and Rook, K.S. (1987). Social support, social deficits, and the family: Toward the enhancement of well-being. In S. Oskamp (Ed.), *Family processes and problems: Social psychological problems* (Applied Social Psychology Annual, Vol. 7, pp. 17-44). Newbury Park, CA: Sage.

Rook, K.S. (1984) The negative side of social interaction: Impact on psychological well-being. *Journal of Personality and Social Psychology, 46,* 1097-1108.

Spitzberg, B.H., Brookshire, R.G., and Brunner, C.C. (1987, November). *The factorial structure of competence evaluations of molecular interpersonal skills in naturalistic conversations.* Paper presented at the Speech Communication Association Conference, Boston, MA.

Spitzberg, B.H., and Cupach, W.R. (1988). *Handbook of interpersonal competence research.* New York: Springer-Verlag.

Spitzberg, B.H., and Hurt, H.T. (1987). The measurement of interpersonal skills in instructional contexts. *Communication Education, 36,* 28-45.

3
Mehrabian explains the role of nonverbal behavior in sales. The article explains how nonverbal cues are used to establish a relationship, and shows how different sales approaches are needed depending on the quality of the product.

Perspectives on Influence: Selling

Albert Mehrabian

Many subtleties in the use of actions rather than words become evident in the face-to-face promotion of a product. A salesman would certainly appear strange if he were to knock on a door and say, "I like you and therefore want to tell you something about our new product." It would seem inappropriate and insincere; and he might get the door slammed in his face. How can you meet someone and in the first moment, even before you get a good look at him, say that you like him? No one would believe it. Yet a good salesman does just this and gets away with it. He uses nonverbal behavior so cleverly that he does not need words to get this message across.

Why does a door-to-door salesman go to all this bother? He knows that to make a sale, he must not only show enthusiasm about his product but also somehow get the potential buyer to feel the same. This means getting someone to think differently about his product—acquire a new attitude toward it or change an existing one. Most salesmen intuitively, and quite correctly know that if you wish to influence someone, then it helps to have him get to like you. This is because people who like each other have a greater tendency to meet each others' demands. In the case of the salesman and his customer, the salesman must somehow elicit liking from the total stranger in a very short time. He does so by nonverbally showing positive feelings (Mehrabian & Williams, 1969). You have heard the expression "The customer is always right." He may assume a very respectful attitude and smile or be extra attentive when the customer talks. He

From *Silent Messages* by Albert Mehrabian, pp. 120-124. Copyright © 1971 by Wadsworth Publishing Company, Inc. Reprinted by permission of the publisher.

hopes that this will pay off through reciprocation and compliance from a customer who will buy the product.

This method of showing positive feelings toward the customer is necessary when the product will not sell itself, that is, when it is indeed necessary to bring about a change in the attitudes and behavior of a customer. On the other hand, a different method can be effective if the products are of high quality.

In sales rooms of prestigious stores in more affluent districts, usually nobody even approaches the shopper, who may feel lost to some degree because it is not clear where things are situated or whom to ask about prices and terms. There frequently are salespeople around who are casually talking to one another or to some other customer and seem to be ignoring the newcomer. Their aloofness implies "This furniture is good enough to sell itself; I don't have to sell it to you." In this situation when one asks for help, the salesman behaves in a very businesslike and matter-of-fact manner, with a good chance of making his sale.

Indeed, a shopper in one of these more expensive stores who is not well dressed may sometimes find the salesmen slightly disrespectful, with the implication that their products are not within the shopper's budget. Some such customers may be tempted to prove them wrong, even though they do not particularly like anything on display.

The same kind of situation can occur in an expensive restaurant if the diners are not "properly" dressed. The maître d' will seat them in "Siberia," where the waiter will take little care in serving them. Again the implicit communication is "You obviously do not belong here." The diner is thus challenged to prove that he does belong by buying an expensive meal he may not actually prefer.

Whether any of these sales methods succeeds depends on the quality of the product and the sophistication of the customer. When there is no obvious need for the product or when the product is of poor quality, the traditional selling approach is more effective: the salesman conveys liking and thereby elicits cooperation and buying behavior. When the product is of high quality, communication of positiveness is unnecessary and may even have an adverse effect. For instance, a well-known gourmet who made it a habit to remain anonymous once accidentally revealed his identity while in his favorite Chinese restaurant. The maître d' then tried excessively hard to please the man. He virtually ignored what was ordered and served special dishes he thought would be sure to please. He even went so far as to serve one of the most expensive champagnes available. The gourmet felt this was the worst meal he'd ever had at that restaurant. As far as the champagne was concerned, he just happened to prefer beer with Chinese food.

These examples of salesmanship have their analogues in the behavior of women who wish to attract the attention and interest of selected men. Feminine tactics also can be categorized into two classes: the straight-forward positive approach that is based on actions (smiles, proximity) as distinct from the aloof and unconcerned approach. Just as in the selling situation, the latter is more likely to imply, "You need me more than I need you," whereas the former says, "I like you, don't you want to be nice to me?" Indiscriminate reliance on either one of these two tactics, to the total exclusion of the other, is less effective than the ability to gauge and determine their usefulness according to the interest and level of sophistication of the other person in the situation.

References

Mehrabian, A. (1970). Some determinants of affiliation and conformity. *Psychological Reports, 27,* 19-29.

Mehrabian, A. & S. Ksionsky. (1970). Models for affiliation and conformity behavior. *Psychological Bulletin, 74,* 11-126.

Mehrabian, A. & M. Williams. (1969). Nonverbal concommitants of perceived and intended persuasiveness. *Journal of Personality and Social Psychology, 13,* 37-58.

Andersen and Andersen explain six different perspectives on nonverbal communication: affiliative conflict theory, expectancy norm models, an arousal-labeling model, an arousal-valence model, a discrepancy-arousal model, and a sequential-functional model. The authors review the empirical support for each perspective and discuss the advantages and limitations of each. This article is one of the more difficult ones because it discusses some rather complex theories.

4

Perspectives on Nonverbal Intimacy Theory

Peter A. Andersen and Janis F. Andersen

Scholars in a number of disciplines have dramatically increased our knowledge of nonverbal communication during the last decade. This research has established that a primary function of nonverbal behavior is the communication of affect through what commonly have been called intimacy behaviors (Argyle & Dean, 1965; Patterson, 1976, 1978), immediacy behaviors (J. Andersen, P. Andersen, & Jensen, 1979; P. Andersen, in press; Mehrabian, 1971; Patterson, 1973) or involvement (Cappella & Greene, 1982; Patterson, 1982, 1983). Even more recently, a number of attempts have been made to build models that explain the numerous empirical findings in this area. Indeed, three of the six sets of models reviewed in this report have been available in published form for just a few years. The purpose here is to summarize these six models briefly and to offer some insights into the strengths and weaknesses of each.

In different ways, each of these models attempts to account for the dyadic exchange of messages that communicate intimacy, immediacy, or involvement. While ·the authors recognize distinctions among these labels, they will be treated as functionally synonymous in the present paper. Discussions of the merits of these labels are available in a number

Edited with permission from: Andersen, P.A., and J.F. Andersen. (1984). The exchange of nonverbal intimacy: A critical review of dyadic models. *Journal of nonverbal behavior,* 8, 327-349.

of recent papers (J. Andersen, 1984; P. Andersen, in press; Cappella & Greene, 1982; Patterson, 1982). The models range from specific and narrow to broad and all-encompassing. The Burgoon (1978) model is an attempt to explain all of the functions of all nonverbal involvement behaviors. Thus the present authors recognize that these models are not entirely comparable. Nonetheless, each of these models examines the exchange of nonverbal intimacy messages in a dyadic setting. It is hoped that this review will contribute to better research and model building in the future.

Affiliative Conflict Theory

The first and most famous of the intimacy exchange theories is affiliative conflict theory, proposed two decades ago by Argyle and Dean (1965). Affiliative conflict theory, commonly referred to as equilibrium theory, proposes that interactants establish and maintain a comfortable intimacy equilibrium point for every interaction. If both interactants are comfortable with the overall amount of intimacy expressed, they will maintain this equilibrium by continuing to display the same overall amount of intimacy. If an interactant increases or decreases intimacy in one channel, he or she will compensate with an opposite increase or decrease in another channel. Similarly, if one interactant alters the amount of dyadic intimacy, the other interactant will restore equilibrium with a compensatory response.

Argyle and Dean posit that underlying, conflicting approach and avoidance drives are responsible for producing an equilibrium state. Too much approach creates anxiety, and too much avoidance makes it impossible to satisfy affiliation needs. Thus a balance or equilibrium point is maintained through compensatory responses. Patterson (1973) explains the compensatory process as operating like a hydraulic model where the total pressure must remain constant, but can differentially be distributed.

Because the affiliative conflict theory was the earliest of the models, it has been subjected to more scrutiny, both positive and negative, than any of the other models. On the positive side, affiliative conflict theory is an intuitively appealing, parsimonious, and testable explanation for intimacy exchange. The model has stimulated a great deal of research, and there is general support for the compensatory process (see reviews by P. Andersen, 1983, in press; Cappella, 1981; Patterson, 1973). However, many well-conducted studies have failed to support the theory's predictions, and these failures lead to the most damaging criticisms.

Several well-conducted investigations (Andersen, 1978; Coutts &

Schneider, 1976; Coutts, Irvine, & Schneider, 1977; Russo, 1975; Stephenson, Rutter, & Dore, 1972) have failed to find compensatory effects (see P. Andersen, in press; Firestone, 1977; Patterson, 1978, for reviews of these experiments). These failures are noteworthy in that a selection bias for publishing significant results probably means the number of nonsupportive findings is underestimated (Patterson, 1973; P. Andersen, in press). In addition, other researchers have found a reciprocity effect when the theory predicts compensatory effects (Bakken, 1978b; Breed, 1972; Rosenfeld, 1965; Word, Zanna & Cooper, 1974). Furthermore, affiliative conflict theory does not account for reciprocal processes that are both intuitively obvious and have been documented in intimacy exchange (Cappella & Greene, 1982; Patterson, 1982; Patterson, 1983).

Affiliative conflict theory is also vulnerable in its inability to explain individual differences in compensatory responses. For example, Aiello (1972, 1977a, 1977b) has found significant sex differences in compensatory behavior. These findings, together with the absence of an explanatory mechanism for how or why equilibrium levels change (Cappella & Greene, 1982), suggest that there may be numerous individual differences that explain intimacy exchange more fully than a single universal equilibrium response. (See the Rosenfeld, et al. paper in this volume for an example of individual and situational differences that affect compensatory reactions.)

In a strong critical stand against affiliative conflict theory's current usefulness, Cappella and Greene (1982) recommend "respectful internment." They acknowledge the theory's historic significance in spawning significant research, but suggest that three major weaknesses in the theory limit its present usefulness: (1) excessive modifications necessary to account for reciprocity, (2) its inapplicability to activity-related or involvement behaviors, and (3) the failure of approach and avoidance forces to provide a priori predictions and scientific understanding. Affiliative conflict theory is significant today because it was the first theory and, as such, provided the foundation for the other models discussed in this article.

Expectancy-Norm Models

One alternative to affiliative conflict theory may be seen in two theories based on interactants' expectancies for intimacy. The better formulated and more widely tested of these models is the model of personal space violations proposed by Burgoon and her colleagues (Burgoon & Jones, 1976; Burgoon, 1978; Burgoon, Stacks, & Woodall, 1979; Burgoon & Aho, 1982). Though presently limited to prediction about personal space and conversational distance, the model presents an intriguing alternative to some other approaches. This model proposes that people have well-established expectations about the interaction distances others will adopt. These expectations are primarily a function of cultural norms, but also a result of the known idiosyncrasies of others. Contrary to intuition, the model predicts that if persons are rewarding (high in status, credibility, attractiveness, etc.), they will be perceived more positively by deviating from the norm, unless a threat threshold is reached at close distances. On the other hand, a punishing interactant will create the most positive impressions in receivers at the expected distance and less positive perceptions at either close or farther distances.

A second expectancy-norm model has been offered by Bakken (1978a). Bakken suggests that norms are widely shared expectations about behavior resulting from the fact that most people experience regularity in others' behavior for specific types of interactions. Bakken (1978a) argues that the empirical research on intimacy regulation offers more support for intimacy being a function of social norms than for intrapsychic accounts such as equilibrium or arousal forces. While such intrapsychic forces are central in the Burgoon model, they are tangential to the Bakken model. The Bakken (1978a) model has not been as widely tested as the Burgoon model.

The Burgoon model is one of the best explicated models of intimacy regulation. Propositions, assumptions, and primitive terms are clearly specified, and empirical tests of the model are clearly derived (Burgoon, 1978; Burgoon & Jones, 1976). Thus it is probably the most testable of the intimacy regulation models. Moreover, it has been subjected to considerable empirical testing (e.g., Burgoon, 1978; Burgoon & Aho, 1982, Burgoon, Stacks, & Burch, 1982; Burgoon, Stacks, & Woodall, 1979; Stacks & Burgoon, 1979). Several tests of the model have established differential effects for the norm violations of low and high reward communicators (Burgoon, 1978; Burgoon, Stacks, & Burch, 1982). However, in a test of the model in a persuasive situation, Stacks and Burgoon (1979) generally failed to support the model. Recent tests of the model have shown patterns of mixed support (Burgoon and Aho, 1982; Burgoon, Stacks, & Woodall, 1979).

While the Burgoon model offers a promising approach to the study of intimacy, it has been limited to tests of distance violations. This is probably not an inherent limitation, but until other nonverbal variables are incorporated, it will remain a model of personal space violations rather than a general model of intimacy violation (P. Andersen, 1983, in press). Finally, recent research on the Burgoon model has found inconsistent patterns of support, numerous confounding or interacting variables, and more complex relationships than originally proposed.

These issues have caused Burgoon and Aho (1982) to conclude that the complexities of the communication process require a more complex predictive model than that originally proposed.

The Arousal-Labeling Model

A major revision and extension of affiliative conflict theory is Patterson's (1976) arousal model of interpersonal intimacy. It encompasses equilibrium theory and broadens it to explain reciprocity processes in addition to compensatory processes. Using arousal as the explanatory mechanism. Patterson's model proposes that expressed intimacy or immediacy behaviors create arousal change in a dyadic partner that is cognitively labeled as positive or negative. Schachter's (1964) theory of arousal labeling is incorporated into the model to explain how undifferentiated physiological arousal is cognitively interpreted as a positive or negative emotional state. Arousal-labeling theory posits that the cognitive interpretation of the arousal determines compensation or reciprocity. A negative emotional state such as one labeled anxiety, discomfort, or embarrassment will produce a compensatory response, whereas a positive emotion state such as one labeled liking, love, or relief will produce a reciprocity response. Arousal theory also holds that if the expressed intimacy behaviors of one person fail to produce arousal change in the other person, then a reactive behavioral change would not be predicted.

The arousal model can be considered an improvement over equilibrium theory in that it accounts for the compensatory process while also predicting two additional sets of empirical findings not accounted for by equilibrium theory. These findings not explained by equilibrium theory but accounted for by arousal labeling are reciprocity effects and those instances of intimacy manipulation that fail to produce any behavioral adjustments.

Several empirical studies support the predictions of the arousal-labeling model (Anderson, 1978; Chapman & Smith, 1977; Foot, Chapman, & Smith, 1977; Foot, Smith, & Chapman, 1977; Janik, 1980; Schaeffer & Patterson, 1980; Whitcher & Fisher, 1979; see P. Andersen, 1983, for a review of the support). In addition, Patterson's (1976) introduction of the model reviewed previous empirical studies that generally supported the model.

B's Reaction

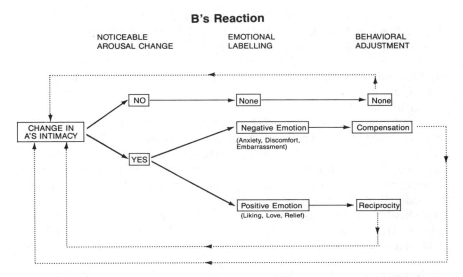

Figure 1. **The arousal-labeling model.** (From Patterson, M.L. (1976) An arousal model of interpersonal intimacy. *Psychological Review,* 1976, 83, 235-245).

Presently, the most severe critic of the model is Patterson (1983) himself. He claims the model is "too simplistic and mechanical in light of the complexity of nonverbal exchange" (p. 165). Patterson (1982, 1983) also criticizes this model for its focus on arousal as the primary mediator of nonverbal exchange and suggests the cognitive component may be inappropriately directed in typical interactions where people are more concerned with motives of others than they are with their own internal affective states. Cappella and Greene (1982) argue that the labeling component places too heavy a cognitive load and requires too long a reaction time to be compatible with the rapid changes that occur in speaker switches. Patterson (1982) also provides empirical evidence that fails to be explained by the model. Specifically, in one study, a lean-touch manipulation increased arousal when it occurred in the middle of an interaction, but failed to increase arousal as hypothesized in the beginning of an interaction (Patterson, Jordan, Hogan, & Frecker, 1981). The arousal model cannot easily explain why the same behavior would create different amounts of arousal in different stages of an interaction. In a related criticism, Cappella and Greene (1982) note that the arousal model is incapable of explaining intermittent periods of reciprocity and compensation.

The labeling process itself has attracted the most criticism because it is based on the questionable results of the Schachter and Singer (1962) studies (Cappella & Greene, 1982; Marshall & Zimbardo, 1979; Maslach, 1979; Schachter & Singer, 1979). However, P. Andersen (in press) suggests that other theories may explain this link in Patterson's model and, consequently, the arousal-labeling component should be evaluated on its own merit rather than on the merits or demerits of its theoretical grandparents.

Additional criticisms of the arousal model include the following observations by Cappella and Greene (1982): (1) the theory's restriction to affiliative behaviors rather than general involvement behavior, (2) the failure to indicate the conditions that produce positive or negative labeling, (3) the failure to specify an upward ceiling on the positive effects of arousal, and (4) the cognitive emphasis of arousal labeling that prevents its extension to infant-adult interaction. The model has also been criticized for beginning in the middle of the intimacy exchange process. That is, the model assumes that immediacy changes are perceived, and this may not always be the case (P. Andersen & Coussoule, 1980). This model and most of the other models of intimacy exchange would be improved by including a decoding component to the model (P. Andersen, in press). In this way, communicative actions that are unnoticed by a receiver would not be expected to trigger the arousal-labeling process.

As previously mentioned, Patterson now criticizes this model as being oversimplified. However, others have criticized the model as being too complex and have suggested that norm theories are more parsimonious explanations (Bakken, 1978a; LaFrance & Mayo, 1978). Despite these criticisms, the arousal model has provided an exciting theoretical framework that continues to stimulate research and controversy. Because the originator and major proponent (Patterson, 1976) is now a leading critic, the model is likely to fall on unfavorable times. However, the original model with appropriate modifications is testable and will continue to be tested. Its eventual worth is to be decided by the future weight of empirical evidence.

The Arousal-Valence Model

Another recent attempt to explain the exchange of nonverbal intimacy is the arousal-valence model (P. Andersen, 1983, 1984, in press). Like the other models discussed in this article, the arousal-valence model is an attempt to explain the variability in a receiver's responses to changes in the immediacy level of another interactant. The model suggests that when increased immediacy by person A is perceived by person B, arousal in person B occurs. The magnitude of person B's arousal will determine his/her reaction to person A. Very small changes in B's arousal require no changes in B's behavior. Very large changes, including both increases and decreases, in B's arousal are unpleasant and aversive (Berlyne, 1970; Eysenck, 1963, 1967, 1976, 1982; Mehrabian, 1976). Such highly aroused individuals are likely to become startled, fearful, or disoriented and engage in a fight or flight response. The behavioral consequence is withdrawal, compensation, and reduction of immediacy behaviors.

It is at moderate levels of arousal that the most complex and interesting affective and cognitive processes take place. Previous research has demonstrated that moderate arousal is perceived neutrally or positively (Berlyne, 1960; Eysenck, 1963, 1967, 1976; Mehrabian, 1976). At moderate levels of arousal, P. Andersen (1984) argues that six sets of variables positively or negatively valence the arousal. These valencers include: (1) social or cultural norms, (2) interpersonal relationship history, (3) perceptions of the other person, including interpersonal valence (Garrison, Sullivan, & Pate, 1976) and its components' credibility, attraction, and homophily, (4) environmental context, (5) the temporal, physical, or psychological state of a person, and (6) psychological or communication traits or predispositions. P. Andersen (1984) argues that the valencing process requires little decision-making or cognitive activity. The six valencers act as schemata (Smith, 1982a, 1982b) or scripts (Abelson, 1976, 1981; Berger & Roloff, 1980). Zajonc (1980) suggests these affective reactions can be invoked in a fraction of a second, sufficient time to produce the reciprocal or compensatory responses characteristic of interpersonal interaction. Thus positively valenced arousal results in reciprocity, whereas negatively valenced arousal results in compensation.

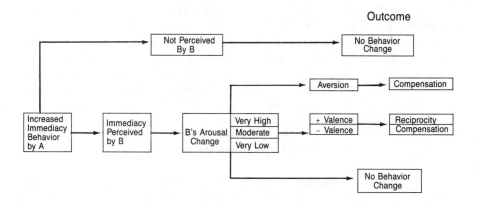

Figure 2. The Arousal-Valence Model.

The arousal-valence model represents an improvement over previous approaches in several ways. First it replaces the ambiguous labeling process characteristic of arousal-labeling theory with six clearly specified sets of valencers. Considerable empirical research in both social psychology and communication demonstrates that these valencers are employed by interactants in ongoing interpersonal communication. Second, it is argued that these six sets of valencers create cognitive schema or characteristic responses that can be quickly invoked and, consequently, fit the time demands of the sudden changes that occur in interpersonal interactions. Third, unlike many other models in this article, perception of the other interactant's behavior is included as an important step in the model. Perception is used in a broad sense to refer to the excitation of cells in the nervous system responsible for processing communication stimuli (Hebb, 1949; Pribram, 1971). If another's communication stimuli fails to evoke a significant neurological response and is not processed by the other interactant, no affective or behavioral changes will result. Finally, the arousal-valence model incorporates the principle that high arousal is perceived aversively. Excessive arousal acts as a warning system that circumvents cognitive processes and results in immediate compensation.

Several criticisms have been launched against the arousal-valence model. First, critics have charged that the arousal-valence model fails to specify clearly the nature of the perception phase of the model. Cappella (1983) argues that the model fails to address whether perception requires knowledge of the change or merely reaction to it. This argument is particularly important in light of research on "mindlessness." Langer's (1978) research on mindlessness demonstrates that behavior can be produced automatically with little or no cognitive activity. A second criticism offered by Cappella (1983) is that the valencing mechanism is unclear. In Andersen's (1984) more fully explicated model, cognitive scripts and schema are the mechanisms by which valencing occurs, but no empirical test of these mechanisms has been conducted. Moreover, the relative impact of these valencers in any interaction is unspecified. Although the arousal-valence model incorporates some of the best aspects of the earlier theories, it still waits the test of empirical research.

The Discrepancy-Arousal Model

An important alternative to previous models has recently been proposed by Cappella and Greene (1982). Their discrepancy-arousal theory is an attempt to explain patterns of exchange for all communication behaviors, both verbal and nonverbal. This model is an extension of Stern's (1974, 1977) explanation of infant-adult exchanges. Stern's theory proposes that infants develop a schema of objects, persons, and behaviors. When an infant encounters a novel stimulus that fails to conform to her/his expectation, arousal results. At low to moderate levels, Stern argues, this discrepancy becomes a source of stimulation and arousal that produces positive affect and attention. At some threshold, too great a discrepancy becomes unpleasant for the infant and results in avoidance or displeasure.

The Cappella and Greene model suggests that adults have cognitive expectations about other's expressive behavior that result from situational characteristics, social norms, individual's preferences, and past experiences. Increases or decreases in involvement by another individual that violate the person's expectations lead to arousal or cognitive activation. Following the research and theory of Berlyne (1960) and Eysenck (1967), Cappella and Greene (1982) propose that moderate arousal results in positive affect, whereas a large increase in arousal results in negative affect. In turn, the positivity or negativity of the affective response to this experience will determine whether an approach or avoidance response will ensue.

In a number of respects, discrepancy-arousal theory represents a theoretical advance over its predecessors. Perhaps its greatest virtue is its conceptual parsimony in eliminating the need for complex labeling processes or hypothetical equilibrium states as explanations. A second related advantage of the model is that the cognitive "work" occurs in perceiving the magnitude of discrepancy between expressed and expected behavior (P. Andersen, 1983, in press). Cappella and Greene (1982) argue that some accounts of mutual influence are cognitively "top-heavy" and cannot meet the requirements of rapid reaction times during ongoing interaction. For example, the labeling process is perhaps too ponderous a cognitive activity to occur during the rapid moment to moment approaches and withdrawals characteristic of communicative exchanges. The discrepancy-arousal model requires only a comparison between one's expectations and the displayed behavior, a much lighter cognitive load.

A third strength of the discrepancy arousal model is that it gives a strong role to arousal as a direct precursor of affect. The proposition that moderate arousal is perceived neutrally to positively has been repeatedly demonstrated in previous work (Berlyne, 1960; Eysenck, 1963, 1967, 1976, 1982; Mehrabian, 1976). This direct link between arousal and affect proposed in the discrepancy-arousal model replaces the labeling link between arousal and affect characteristic of other models. Indeed, in light of the recent doubts raised over the original research by Schachter and Singer (1962) on the self-labeling process, elimination of the labeling step may be advantageous (see Cappella & Greene, 1982; Marshall & Zimbardo, 1979; Schachter & Singer, 1979).

A final advantage of the discrepancy-arousal model is its comprehensiveness. The model is designed to incorporate a broad range of both verbal and nonverbal behaviors (Patterson, 1983, p. 19). It attempts to explain all involvement behaviors, not just expressions of immediacy and intimacy. Moreover, it provides explanations for expressive behavior for all phases of the life cycle, including infancy.

Despite the fact that discrepancy-arousal theory represents a fresh and promising approach to the question of intimacy exchange, it has also received its share of criticism. One criticism has been aimed at the linkages in the discrepancy-arousal model. The model assumes that discrepancy is a primary precursor of arousal, arousal causes affective states, and affective states cause a reciprocal or compensating response. It is entirely probable that other exogenous variables have substantial impact at each of these linkages. If so, what is the relative impact of these exogenous variables compared with the linkages proposed in the model? The answer to this question is unknown, but prior research has suggested several exogenous variables that may be as important as the links in the discrepancy-arousal model. For example, a number of variables other than discrepancy may produce arousal. Likewise, a number of exogenous precursors of affect other than arousal have been discussed in the psychological literature. Finally, one could easily argue that responses are the result of a number of exogenous variables such as habits or social rules quite independent of affect.

The first questionable link is the crucial discrepancy-arousal link. There is no empirical evidence that the discrepancy-arousal link actually exists, though there is evidence for an immediacy behavior-arousal relationship (P. Andersen, 1983, in press; Patterson, 1976). Moreover, as Andersen (1983, in press) suggests, one can quickly generate a list of arousing cognitions quite independent of discrepancy, including: (1) sexual arousal with a familiar other, (2) racial prejudice, (3) encountering a disliked other, (4) drug induced states, (5) environmental load, and (6) general trait anxiety. It is important to determine the impact of these other arousers relative to that of the discrepancy factor.

The second questionable link is the arousal-affect relationship. In this case, arousal has been empirically linked to affect, but it has been suggested that additional independent precursors of affect may attenuate this relationship (P. Andersen, 1983, in press). It can be argued that learned norms, relational histories, psychological states, and hedonic predispositions are independent, exogenous precursors of affect. If this is the case, the relative contribution of arousal versus those other variables must be ascertained.

The third questionable link is the affect-response relationship (see Figure 3). Although affect is certainly related to approach-avoidance responses, other variables may be antecedents of these responses quite independent of affect. For instance, social norms may require approach or avoidance rituals quite independent of true affective tone. Similarly, relationship or situational constraints may determine approach or avoidance responses that may supercede the effect of interpersonal affect.

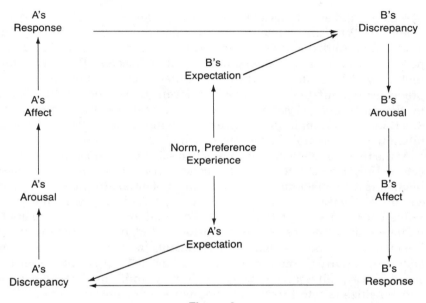

Figure 3.

A Schematic Representation of the linkages among variables for the discrepancy-arousal model. (From "A discrepancy-arousal explanation of mutual influence in expressive behavior for adult and infant adult interaction," by J.N. Cappella and J.O. Greene, 1982, *Communication Monographs, 49.*)

Two final criticisms of the discrepancy-arousal model have been reported elsewhere. First, the model assumes that one person's response is perceived by the interactant and accurately processed (P. Andersen, 1983, in press). Such an assusmption may be challenged. Some empirical evidence suggests that certain individuals are relatively oblivious to the immediacy and affect displays of others (P. Andersen & Coussoule, 1980; Rosenthal, Hall, DiMatteo, Rogers, & Archer 1979). Finally, though Cappella and Greene's discrepancy-arousal model is one of the broadest and most comprehensive, it has recently been criticized as insufficiently comprehensive (Patterson, 1983, p. 19). Compared to Patterson's (1982, 1983) sequential-functional model, it is true that the discrepancy-arousal model is less than comprehensive. Nevertheless, Cappella and Greene have presented an excellent, parsimonious model with great heuristic value for additional research and theorizing.

The Sequential-Functional Model

A recent and ambitious attempt to explain the process of intimacy exchange is Patterson's (1982, 1983) sequential-functional model. This model of nonverbal exchange starts with a set of antecedents, including personal, experiential, and relational-situational factors. Personal factors include variables such as culture, sex differences, and personality that predetermine differential involvement levels. Experiential factors relate to the influence of salient prior experiences on the interactions. Relational-situational influences are those interacting characteristics of relationship type and the setting in which the interaction occurs.

At the time an interaction is initiated, a set of preinteraction mediators acts as links between the antecedents and interaction behaviors. These mediators are behavioral predispositions, potential arousal change, and cognitive affective assessment. Behavioral predispositions are relatively stable characteristics of individuals. Potential arousal change refers to increases or decreases in arousal prior to and in anticipation of the interaction. Cognitive-affective assessments reflect the initiation of cognitive activity through schemas (Markus, 1977) or scripts (Abelson, 1981). These preinteraction mediators limit an individual's involvement and sensitize one to functional judgments about the interaction.

In the interaction phase, nonverbal involvement is a result of preferred involvement level, functional expectancies, and the perceived appropriateness of a behavior. A stable exchange is defined as one in which the discrepancy between the expected and actual involvement of the other person is minimal. When that discrepancy is large, a condition of cognitive instability results (Patterson, 1982). Instability leads to adjustments in nonverbal involvement that may or may not be accompanied by functional reassessment.

A primary advantage of Patterson's (1982) sequential-functional model is that it encompasses multiple functions for nonverbal involvement. Most other models concentrate primarily on exchange of affect or immediacy, to the exclusion of other involvement functions. Moreover, Patterson (1983) points out that the model is not only multifunctional, but provides for reassessments and shifts in the functions of involvement during ongoing interaction and as a result of interaction.

A second related strength of the model is the recognition of the fact that interactants may have incompatible perceptions of the particular function of an interaction. Additionally, these functional perceptions may be unstable within individuals, leading to fluctuating incompatibilities during a given interaction. For example, person A may become involved with another to provide information. During the course of the interaction A may begin to produce behaviors intended to express intimacy or exercise social control. These moment to moment changes in the primary function of A's communication will be different from the moment to moment changes in B's functional behaviors, leading to intermittent and fluctuating compatibilities and incompatibilities.

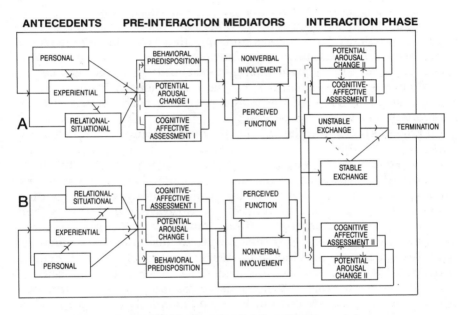

Figure 4 The sequential-functional model

(From Patterson, M.L. (1982). A sequential functional model of nonverbal exchange. *Psychological Review, 89* 231-249).

Another improvement over previous efforts is the recognition of antecedents and preinteraction mediators. Some previous models suggested that behavioral adjustments were simply the reactive product of the other interactant's behavior. The sequential-functional model recognized that other causes, such as predispositions and scripts, have an impact on the enactment of nonverbal displays.

A fourth strength of the model is Patterson's effort to incorporate rather than discard previous models. This is particularly true of both arousal-labeling theory and the discrepancy-arousal model. Important elements of both these approaches are retained and utilized in the sequential-functional approach.

Finally, the cognitive basis of the model is clearly a merit. The sequential-functional model recognizes that interactants have purposes and aims and attempt to direct the effects of their behavior. Patterson (1983) argues that this model is less mechanistic than its predecessors and that an individual's involvement behaviors are often part of a larger context of a meaningful coordinated behavioral sequence.

Despite the obvious merits of the sequential-functional model, it is not without problems. First, there is some question as to whether the model is fully testable or disconfirmable. Patterson (1983, p. 167) recognizes this issue and counters that deficiencies in testabliilty might be balanced by the functional model's comprehensiveness. Additionally, Patterson maintains that many parts of the model provide a basis for a variety of important and testable hypotheses.

It is certainly true that the functional model is relatively comprehensive when compared to other models. Nonetheless, it may be the case that it is not comprehensive enough to incorporate all of the relevant functions for nonverbal involvement. Patterson (1982) certainly specifies a number of important functions for nonverbal involvement, including providing information, regulation of interaction, expression of intimacy and involvement, social control, and facilitation of service or task goals. However, no rationale is provided for the exclusion of other functions of involvement behaviors including interactional synchrony and rhythms (Davis, 1982), culture and cultural pride (Hall, 1976), gender appropriateness (LaFrance & Mayo, 1978), inclusion (Schutz, 1960), confirmation (Waltzlawick, Beavin & Jackson, 1967), and manifestation of personality traits and self-definition (LaFrance & Mayo, 1978). Indeed, neither these additions nor Patterson's list is arguably comprehensive. Moreover, people's purposes in communication may be ideographic (Kelly, 1955; Delia, 1977) and individuals may generate numerous unique and ideosyncratic reasons for nonverbal involvement.

A second problem with the sequential-functional model is the lack of justification for the location of behavioral predispositions in the preinteraction phase but not in the interaction phase (P. Anderson, 1984). This gives the impression that behavioral predispositions cease to function during the interaction. The model also fails to distinguish between personal factors (personality) in the antecedent phase and behavioral predispositions (relatively stable characteristics of individuals) in the preinteraction phase. A futher distinction needs to be made between these variables, or they should be labeled the same.

Finally, Patterson, (1983, p. 166) recognizes that intentionality is still a controversial issue in communication and psychology. Some doubt exists as to whether individuals are consciously aware of their behavior as it is occurring or even whether they can retrospectively verbalize the cognitive processes that guided their behavior (Nisbett & Wilson, 1977). This is a crucial and testable aspect of the sequential-functional model. Future research should certainly address this issue.

Conclusion

At this stage in the development of these theories, it is necessary to issue the ubiquitous call for more empirical research on the models. Empirical research on the three most recent models (arousal-valence, discrepancy-arousal, sequential-functional) is certainly needed. Tests of the critical linkages need to be conducted for each of the models. This should culminate in an overall test of each model. This is not an easy task, due to the fact that a number of linkages exist in each model and the arousal cognitive processes are covert and difficult to measure.

Among the six models reviewed in this article, five of them incorporate arousal as an important construct. Both the Burgoon (1978) model of personal space violations and the Cappella and Greene (1982) discrepancy-arousal model suggest that deviations from expectations have arousal value. Burgoon maintains that these deviations activate observers' attention and arouse adaptive or defense mechanisms to cope with the deviation. Cappella and Greene (1982) follow others who believe that moderate arousal is pleasing and results in reciprocity whereas extreme arousal is aversive and results in compensation. The Andersen (1983, 1984, in press) arousal-valence model suggests that arousal is a function of changes, particularly increases in immediacy. Like the discrepancy-arousal model, an assumption of the arousal-valence model is that extreme arousal is aversive. However, moderate arousal simply signals a change in state that can be valenced based on one of the six valences described earlier. Arousal-labeling theory also holds that changes in immediacy can be arousing but the verbal labels are employed to determine whether positive or negative responses occur (Patterson, 1976). The sequential-functional (Patterson, 1982, 1983) model assigns a role to potential arousal changes at both the preinteraction phase and during the interaction phase. Patterson (1982) maintains that arousal changes may motivate behavior adjustment, differentially facilitate dominant adjustment patterns, or serve to initiate an analysis of the meaning associated with the changing circumstances.

As a result of the centrality of arousal as a construct in the the five most recent intimacy-exchange models, two research priorities are in order. First, the location or locations of arousal in each model need to be determined. Burgoon (1978) suggests arousal is a consequence of deviation from behavioral expectations and an antecedent of interpersonal evaluations. Cappella and Green (1982) purpose that arousal is a result of deviation from expectancy, but argue that the degree of arousal has a direct relationship with the positivity or negativity of the affective experience. Andersen (1983, 1984, in press) and Patterson (1976) argue that arousal is the result of changes in immediacy, though they differ on the effect of this arousal. Patterson's sequential-functional model (1982, 1983) employs arousal as a mediating variable prior to interaction and as a predictor of both adjustments in interpersonal involvement and functional reassessments. A priority for empirical research should be to assess the causal order between arousal and these other variables.

The second priority for empirical research is an unobtrusive or less reactive method of measuring arousal. Andersen (1983, in presss) reviews literature that examines behavioral immediacy effects on eight measures of arousal, including galvanic skin response, heart rate, electroencephalograph, nervous movements and self-manipulators, self-reports, palmar sweat, blood pressure, and duration and time to micturition. Similarly Cappella and Greene (1982) maintain that arousal may refer to a host of processes, including overt behavioral activity, physiological activity, autonomic arousal, or activation of the cortex.

In the discrepancy-arousal model and most likely the other theories as well, the construct of concern is cognitive activation or activation of the cortex, reticular activating system, and limbic system. It is assumed that most behavioral and physiological measures are indirect measures of cognitive arousal whereas the electroencephalogram and average evoked responses are direct indications of cognitive arousal (Cappella & Green, 1982, p. 98). Steinfatt and Roberts (1983) also criticize most arousal measures as being too indirect, difficult to interpret, and highly obtrusive. Indeed, prior research indicates arousal may be defined as metabolic activity that produces heat (Dabbs, 1975). Thus either caloric consumption or temperature would be a good index of arousal. Though the ideal location for such measurements would be a the hypothalamus, this procedure would be unethical and reactive. However, Dabbs (1975) and Steinfatt and Roberts (1983) maintain that hypothalamic temperature is associated with the temperature of the tympanic membrane. Steinfatt and Roberts (1983) report that research has successfully employed an ear probe of soft plastic that was both effective and unobtrusive, though Dabbs (1975) reports it is slightly uncomfortable for some subjects. Future research should examine tympanic temperature, electroencephalographic readings, measures of averaged evoked response, and other indices of cognitive arousal to measure the arousal construct more validly.

What is the present state of research and theory on intimacy exchange? Certainly there is reason for cautious optimism. In less than two decades, substantial strides have been made. The 1960s was a time of beginnings for research and theory in this area. The early 1970s produced a considerable quantity of empirical research but little theory to account for the findings. The late 1970s and 1980s produced a surge of new theoretical models as well as more empirical research. The viable second-generation models reviewed in this paper are now available for empirical testing. It is likely that none of the current models in its present form will eventually receive consensus as a superior explanation for the dyadic exchange of intimacy behavior. But it is equally likely that future models will incorporate a number of the critical components of the theoretical models discussed in this special issue.

References

Abelson, R.P. Script processing in attitude formation and decision making. In J.S. Carroll and J.W. Payne (Eds.). *Cognition and social behavior.* Potomac, Md.: Lawrence Erlbaum, 1976.

Abelson, R.P. Psychological status of the script concept. *American Psychologist,* 1981, *36,* 715-729.

Aiello, J.R. A test of equilibrium theory: Visual interaction in relation to orientation, distance and sex of interactants. *Psychonomic Science,* 1972, 27, 335-336.

Aiello, J.R. A further look at equilibrium theory: Visual interaction as a function of interpersonal distance. *Environmental Psychology and Nonverbal Behavior,* 1977a, 1, 122-140.

Aiello, J.R. Visual interaction at extended distances. *Personality and Social Psychology Bulletin,* 1977b, 3, 83-86.

Andersen, J.F., P.A. Andersen, & A.D. Jensen. The measurement of nonverbal immediacy. *Journal of Applied Communication Research,* 1979, 7, 153-180.

Andersen, P.A. Nonverbal immediacy in interpersonal communication. Paper presented at the annual meeting of the International Communication Association, Dallas, Tex., May 1983.

Andersen, P.A. An arousal-valence model of nonverbal immediacy exchange. Paper presented at the annual meeting of the Central States Speech Association, Chicago, Ill., April 1984.

Andersen, P.A. Nonverbal immediacy in interpersonal communication. In A. Seigman & S. Feldstein (Eds). *Nonverbal communication.* Hillsdale, N.J.: Lawrence Erlbaum, 1985, pp. 1-36.

Andersen, P.A., & A. Coussoule. The peception world of the communication apprehensive: The effect of communication apprehension and interpersonal gaze on interpersonal perception. *Communication Quarterly,* 1980, *28,* 44-53.

Andersen, D.R. Interpersonal relationship and intimacy of social interaction: Re-examining the intimacy-equilibrium model. (Doctoral dissertation, University of South Dakota, 1977). *Dissertation Abstracts International,* 1978, *38,* 4643B.

Argyle, M., & J. Dean. Eye contact, distance and affiliation. *Sociometry,* 1965, *28,* 289-304.

Bakken, D. Intimacy regulation in social encounters. Paper presented to the meeting of the Eastern Communication Association, Boston, Mass., April 1978(a).

Bakken, D. Nonverbal immediacy in dyadic interactions: The effects of sex and information about attitude similarity. Paper presented to the Eastern Psychological Association, April 1978b.

Berger, C.R., & M.E. Roloff. Social cognition, self-awareness, and interpersonal communication. In B. Dervin & M.J. Voight (Eds.). *Progress in communication sciences* (Volume II)(pp. 1-49). Norwood, N.J.: Ablex Publishing, 1980.

Berlyne, D.E. *Conflict, arousal, and curiosity.* New York: McGraw-Hill, 1960.

Breed, G. The effect of intimacy: Reciprocity or retreat? *British Journal of Social and Clinical Psychology,* 1972, *11,* 135-142.

Burgoon, J.K. A communication model of personal space violations: Explication and an initial test. *Human Communication Research,* 1978, *4,* 129-142.

Burgoon, J.K., & L. Aho. Three field experiments on the effects of violations of conversational distance. *Communication Monographs,* 1982, *49,* 71-88.

Burgoon, J.K., & S.B. Jones. Toward a theory of personal space expectations and their violations. *Human Communication Research,* 1976, *2,* 131-146.

Burgoon, J.K., D.W. Stacks, & S.A. Burch. The role of interpersonal rewards and violations of distancing expectations in achieving influence in small groups. *Communication,* 1982, *11,* 114-128.

Burgoon, J.K., D.W. Stacks, & W.G. Woodall. A communicative model of violations of distancing expectations. *Western Journal of Speech Communication,* 1979, *43,* 153-167.

Cappella, J.N. Mutual influence in expressive behavior: Adult-adult and infant-adult dyadic interaction. *Psychological Bulletin,* 1981, *89,* 101-132.

Cappella, J.N. Remarks on five functional approaches to nonverbal behavior. Paper presented at the annual meeting of the International Communication Association, Dallas, Tex., May 1983.

Cappella, J.N., & J.O. Greene. A discrepancy-arousal explanation of mutual influence in expressive behavior for adult and infant-adult interaction. *Communication Monographs,* 1982, *49,* 89-114.

Coutts, L.M., M. Irvine, & F.W. Schneider. Nonverbal adjustments to changes in gaze and orientation. *Psychology,* 1977, *14,* 28-32.

Coutts, L.M., & F. W. Schneider. Affiliative conflict theory: An investigation of intimacy equilibrium and compensation hypothesis. *Journal of Personality and Social Psychology,* 1976, *34,* 1135-1142.

Dabbs, J.M. Core body temperature and social arousal. *Personality and Social Psychology Bulletin,* 1975, *1,* 517-520.

Davis, M. (Ed.). *Interaction rhythms: Periodicity in communicative behavior.* New York: Human Sciences Press, 1982.

Delia, J.G. Constructivism and the study of human communication. *Quarterly Journal of Speech,* 1977, *63,* 66-83.

Eysenck, H.J. *Experiments with drugs.* Oxford: Pergamon Press, 1963.

Eysenck, H.J. *The biological basis of personality.* Springfield, Ill.: Charles Thomas Publisher, 1967.

Eysenck, H.J. Arousal, learning and memory. *Psychological Bulletin,* 1976, *83,* 389-404.

Eysenck, H.J. *Personality, genetics and behavior.* New York: Praeger, 1982.

Firestone, I.J. Reconciling verbal and nonverbal models of dyadic communication. *Environmental Psychology and Nonverbal Behavior,* 1977, *2,* 30-44.

Foot, H.C., A.J. Chapman, J.R. Smith. Friendship and social responsiveness in boys and girls. *Journal of Personality and Social Psychology,* 1977, *35,* 401-411.

Foot, H.C., J.R. Smith, & A.J. Chapman. Individual differences in children's responsiveness in humor situations. In A. J. Chapman & H. C. Foot (Eds.). *It's a funny thing, humor.* London: Pergamon, 1977.

Garrison, J.P., D.L. Sullivan, & L.E. Pate. Interpersonal valence dimensions as discriminators of communication contexts: An empirical assessment of dyadic linkages. Paper presented at the Speech Communication Association Convention, San Francisco, Cal., 1976.

Hall, E.T. *Beyond culture.* Garden City, N.Y.: Anchor Books, 1976.

Hebb, D.O. *The organization of behavior: A neuropsychological theory.* New York: John Wiley, 1949.

Janik, S.W. Visual adjustments to changes in apparent interactive distance: A test of Patterson's intimacy-arousal model. (Doctoral dissertation, University of Miami, 1979). *Dissertation Abstracts International,* 1980, *41,* 408B-409B.

Kelly, G.A. *The psychology of personal constructs.* New York: Norton, 1955.

LaFrance, M., & C. Mayo. *Moving bodies: Nonverbal communication in social relationships.* Monterey, Cal.: Brooks/Cole, 1978.

Langer, E.J. Rethinking the role of thought in social interaction. In J.H. Harvey, W. Ikes, & R.F. Kidd (Eds.). *New directions in attribution research* (Volume 2). Hillsdale, N.J.: Lawrence Erlbaum Associates, 1978.

Markus, H. Self-schemata and processing information about the self. *Journal of Personality and Social Psychology,* 1977, *35,* 63-78.

Marshall, G.D., & P.G. Zimbardo. Affective consequences of inadequately explained physiological arousal. *Journal of Personality and Social Psychology,* 1979, *37,* 970-988.

Maslach, C. Negative emotional biasing of unexplained arousal. *Journal of Personality and Social Psychology,* 1979, *37,* 953-969.

Mehrabian, A. *Silent messages.* Belmont, Cal.: Wadsworth Publishing Co., 1971.

Mehrabian, A. *Public places and private spaces.* New York: Basic Books, Inc., 1976.

Nisbett, R.E., & T.D. Wilson. Telling more than we can know. Verbal reports on mental processes. *Psychological Review,* 1977, *84,* 231-259.

Patterson, M.L. Compensation in nonverbal immediacy behaviors: A review. *Sociometry,* 1973, *36,* 237-252.

Patterson, M.L. An arousal model of interpersonal intimacy. *Psychological Review,* 1976, *83,* 235-245.

Patterson, M.L. Arousal change and cognitive labeling. Pursuing the mediators of intimacy exchange. *Environmental Psychology and Nonverbal Behavior,* 1978, *3,* 17-22.

Patterson, M.L. A sequential functional model of nonverbal exchange. *Psychological Review,* 1982, *89,* 231-249.

Patterson, M.L. *Nonverbal behavior: A functional perspective.* New York: Springer-Verlag, 1983.

Patterson, M.L., A. Jordan, M. Hogan, & D. Frerker. Effects of nonverbal intimacy on arousal and behavioral adjustment. *Journal of Nonverbal Behavior,* 1981, *5,* 184-198.

Pribram, K.H. *Languages of the brain: Experimental paradoxes and principles in neuropsychology.* Englewood Cliffs, N.J.: Prentice-Hall, 1971.

Rosenfeld, H. Effect of approval-seeking induction on interpersonal proximity. *Psychological Reports,* 1965, *17,* 120-122.

Rosenthal, R., J. A. Hall, M.R. DiMatteo, P.L. Rogers, & D. Archer. *Sensitivity to nonverbal communication: The pons test.* Baltimore, Md.: Johns Hopkins University Press, 1979.

Russo, N. Eye contact, distance and the equilibrium theory. *Journal of Personality and Social Psychology,* 1975, *31,* 497-502.

Schachter, S. The interaction of cognitive and physiological determinants of emotional state. In L. Berkowitz (Ed.). *Advances in experimental social psychology* (Volume 1). New York: Academic Press, 1964.

Schachter, S., & J. Singer. Cognitive, social, and physiological determinants of emotional state. *Psychological Review,* 1962, *69,* 379-399.

Schachter, S., & J.C. Singer. Comments on the Maslach and Marshall-Zimbardo Experiments. *Journal of Personality and Social Psychology,* 1979, *37,* 970-988.

Schaeffer, G.H., & M.L. Patterson. Intimacy, arousal, and small group crowding. *Journal of Personality and Social Psychology,* 1980, *38,* 283, 290.

Schutz, W.C. *FIRO: A three-dimension theory of interpersonal behavior.* New York: Holt, Rinehart, and Winston, 1960.

Smith, M.J. Cognitive schema theory and the perseverance and attenuation of unwarranted empirical beliefs. *Communication Monographs,* 1982a, *4,* 115-126.

Smith, M.J. *Persuasion and human action.* Belmont, Cal.: Wadsworth Publishing, 1982b.

Stacks, D.W., & J.K. Burgoon. The persuasive effects of violating spatial distance expectations in small groups. Paper presented at the annual convention of the Southern Speech Communication Association, Biloxi, Miss., April 1979.

Steinfatt, T.M., & C.V. Roberts. Source credibility and physiological arousal: An important variable in the credibility-information retention relationship. *Southern Speech Communication Journal,* 1983, *48,* 340-355.

Stephenson, G.M., D.R. Rutter, & S.R. Dore. Visual interaction and distance. *British Journal of Psychology,* 1972, *64,* 251-257.

Stern, D.N. Mother and infant at play: The dyadic interaction involving facial, vocal, and gaze behavior. In M. Lewis & L. A. Rosenblum (Eds.). *The effect of the infant on its caregiver* (pp. 187-213). New York: Wiley, 1974.

Stern, D. *The first relationship: Mother and infant.* Cambridge, Mass., Harvard University Press, 1977.

Storms, M.D., & G.C. Thomas. Reaction to physical closeness. *Journal of Personality and Social Psychology*, 1977, *35*, 412-415.

Watzlawick, P., J.H. Beavin, & D.D. Jackson. *Pragmatics of human communication.* New York: Norton and Company, 1967.

Whitcher, S.J., & J.D. Fisher. Multi-dimensional reaction to therapeutic touch in a hospital setting. *Journal of Personality and Social Psychology*, 1979, *37*, 87-96.

Word, C.O., M.P. Zanna, & J. Cooper. The nonverbal mediation of self-fulfilling prophecies in interracial interaction. *Journal of Experimental Social Psychology*, 1974, *10*, 109-120.

Zajonc, R.B. Feeling and thinking; preferences need no inferences. *American Psychologist*, 1980, *35*, 151-175.

In this article Burgoon and Hale explain nonverbal expectancy violations theory. This is one of the few theories specifically created to study nonverbal communication. The theory predicts that positive violations of expectations lead to successful interactions, while negative violations are unsuccessful. The theory also predicts that a "rewarding communicator" who violates expectations will be successful. Support for the theory is summarized.

5

Perspectives on Nonverbal Expectations

Judee K. Burgoon and Jerold L. Hale

Communication literature is rife with the assumption, and often the explicit dictum, that the road to success lies in conformity to social norms. One perspective that challenges that notion is nonverbal expectancy violations theory (Burgoon, 1978, 1983, 1985; Burgoon, Coker, & Coker, 1986; Burgoon & Jones, 1976; Burgoon, Stacks, & Woodall, 1979). The basic thesis of the model is that there are circumstances under which violations of social norms and expectations may be a superior strategy to conformity. Given the frequency with which we encounter others who deviate from expected behaviors in their daily transactions, it becomes an important communication issue to determine if and when such violations have favorable as opposed to detrimental consequences. The rise in interest in strategic communication behavior and communication competence also endorses the value of examining how violations may be used as strategic, goal-attaining acts.

Originally designed to explain terminal consequences of conversational distance changes during interpersonal interactions, the expectancy violations model has been revised and extended to apply to a greater range of nonverbal behaviors and communication outcomes (see Buller & Burgoon, 1986; Burgoon & Aho, 1982; Burgoon, Coker, & Coker, 1986; Burgoon, Manusov, Mineo, & Hale, 1985; Burgoon, Stacks, & Burch, 1982).

Adopted with permission from: Burgoon, J.K., and J.L. Hale. (1988). Nonverbal expectancy violations: Model elaboration and application to immediacy behaviors. *Communication Monographs*, 55, 58-79.

Numerous tests of the model, along with empirical results from other research that can be reinterpreted within the expectancy framework, have yielded support for many of the model's propositions (cf. Burgoon, 1983; Hale & Burgoon, 1984). At the same time, inconsistent findings across studies suggest a need for further elaboration and/or revision of the theory. Especially important is to distinguish how this model differs from others designed to predict the communication consequences of changes in nonverbal behavior. The scope of the model also remains indeterminate, having been applied primarily to manipulations of single nonverbal cues in interactions with strangers, but theoretically having the potential to apply to a wide range of cues and cue patterns and to interactions with familiar others as well as strangers.

The Nonverbal Expectancy Violations Model

In overview, the model posits that people hold expectations about the nonverbal behaviors of others. Violations of these expectations are posited to trigger a change in arousal, which heightens the salience of cognitions about the communicator and behavior. The valenced evaluation of the communicator, implicit messages associated with the violation behavior(s), and evaluations of the act combine to determine whether a violation is positive or negative, which in turn influences communication outcomes. The key elements in the process, then, are *expectancy violations, arousal, communicator reward valence, behavior interpretation and evaluation,* and *violation valence.*

At many junctures, the expectancy violations model shares assumptions with such other arousal and cognitive labeling approaches to nonverbal behavior as Andersen's (1985) arousal-valence model, Cappella and Greene's (1982) discrepancy-arousal model, Patterson's earlier (1976) arousal-labeling model, and his more recent (1982, 1983) sequential functional model. The model differs from these, however, in the underlying explanatory system that is advanced, in the directionality of its predictions, in the broader domain of nonverbal behaviors to which it is potentially applicable, and in its broader scope of applying to both the interaction exchange process and outcomes. A primary focus of the other models is predicting immediate, micro-level compensatory or reciprocal responses to changes in a partner's level of intimacy or involvement, with reciprocity predicted under nonaversive circumstances and compensation predicted under aversive ones. Not only does the expectancy violations model produce conflicting predictions and explanations for compensation and reciprocity exchange processes (see Hale & Burgoon, 1984), it attempts to predict and explain terminal communication consequences, such as attraction and persuasion, as well as more macro-level exchange patterns. It also has the potential to account for the effects of other nonverbal phenomena beyond intimacy and involvement signals.

Elements of the Model

Expectancies

The theoretical framework begins with the assumption that in interpersonal encounters, interactants develop expectancies and preferences about the nonverbal behaviors of others, an assumption that is also relatively central in the discrepancy-arousal, arousal-valence, and sequential functional models. The models differ in the extent to which they explain the origins of those expectancies and treat them as cognitive, affective, and/or behavioral.

According to the expectancy violations model, expectancies may include cognitive, affective, and conative components and are primarily a function of (1) social norms and (2) known idiosyncrasies of the other. With unknown others, the expectations are identical to the societal norms and standards for the particular type of communicator, relationship, and situation. That is, they include judgments of what behaviors are possible, feasible, appropriate, and typical for a particular setting, purpose, and set of participants (cf. Kreckel, 1981, for more detailed analysis of situational features that may impinge on expectations).

As illustration, conversational distance norms are based on a combination of communicator characteristics (e.g., gender, age, personality, style), relational characteristics (e.g., degree of acquaintance, status inequality, liking, relational history), and contextual factors (e.g., environmental constraints, definition of the situation or task, communication functions being accomplished). Thus, female friends in a social situation expect to interact at a closer distance than two males of different status and age in a work environment. All else being equal, interacting at moderately close range is also preferable to interacting at a greater distance because it heightens sensory involvement and carries such culturally approved meanings as equality and affiliation.

Although the pre-interactional and interactional factors dictating norms and preferences are complex in themselves, individuals appear to have little difficulty arriving at a net expectancy of how others should behave and recognizing deviations from that pattern. Research shows, for example, that people experience discomfort, compensate for, and rate as inappropriate and unexpected nonverbal interaction patterns that deviate from intermediate levels of distance, gaze, and sensory involvement

(Argyle & Cook, 1976; Burgoon, 1978; Burgoon & Coker, in press; Burgoon & Jones, 1976; Rosenfeld, Brack, Smith, & Kehoe, 1984; Smith & Knowles, 1979; Sundstrom & Altman, 1976; Thompson, Aiello, & Epstein, 1979). This ability to recognize violations of expected behaviors and sequences is evident even in infants (Gibson, Owsley, & Johnston, 1978; Haith, Kiesen, & Collins, 1969) and by adulthood becomes formalized into entire patterns of expected action—what some have labeled interaction scripts or behavioral programs (Abelson, 1981; Schank & Abelson, 1977; Scheflen, 1974; Street & Cappella, 1985)—that serve as standards against which to compare a given interaction.

Expectancies are not exclusively norm-based. Known idiosyncratic differences based on prior knowledge of the other, relational history, or observation may be factored in to yield person-specific expectations. For example, one may expect more vocal animation from a highly gregarious friend or closer conversational distance from someone who has impaired hearing. Idiosyncratic expectancies, then, reflect the extent to which the expectancies for a particular communicator deviate from the socially normative ones.

Expectancies also operate within a range, rather than representing some specific behavior. The expected distance for a personal conversation, for example, may range from two to four feet. This concept of range acknowledges that norms are not precise themselves but rather have some degree of variability associated with them. According to the original conceptualization of the expectancy violations model, there is a threshold or limen of recognition that must be passed before a deviation from the norm becomes a violation (Burgoon & Jones, 1976). Any discrepancies within the socially tolerated range of variability will be perceptually assimilated as part of the expected behavior pattern.

Based on one's own habitual behavior and that of others within a society, one comes not only to anticipate that others will behave in a particular fashion but also to assign evaluations, or *valences*, to these actions:

> People who interact develop expectations about each other's behavior, not only in the sense that they are able to predict the regularities, but also in the sense that they develop preferences about how others *should* behave under certain circumstances. (Jackson, 1964, p. 225)

This is the affective component of expectations. Jackson (1964, 1966) has shown that norms and role expectations can be scaled along two continua: a behavioral dimension (the frequency with which associated role behaviors might occur) and an approval dimension (subjective ratings of approval-disapproval, which Jackson equates with expectations). The same principle applies to communicative expectations. Although individual preferences color affective reactions to behaviors, valences are undoubtedly most strongly influenced by the society's standards or ideals for competent communication performance. Thus, one expects normal speakers to be reasonably fluent and coherent in their discourse, to refrain from erratic movements or emotional outbursts, and to adhere to politeness norms. Generally, normative behaviors are positively valued. If one keeps a polite distance and shows an appropriate level of interest in one's conversational partner, for instance, such behavior should be favorably received. In Jackson's (1966) terminology, the expected behaviors tend to be those that fall within the range of tolerable behavior (i.e., above the indifference threshold) and which become "crystallized" into consensually recognized norms.

The difficult question to answer is how deviations from expectations are evaluated. Most sociological writings on norms, rules, and roles implicitly assume that any form of violation is negative. While the nonverbal interaction models allow for the possibility of moderate deviations producing positive reactions, they also assume that extreme violations or extremely arousing events, which may be the result of violations, are negatively valenced. For example, the discrepancy-arousal model holds that large discrepancies produce large changes in arousal which in turn produce negative affect. As intuitively appealing as this position is, it may be incorrect. It is possible to imagine violations that are positively valenced, as in the case of a highly fluent, witty speaker or an intimate overture from the object of one's romantic fantasies. One form of positive violation is implicit in Aronson and Linder's (1965) gain-loss theory: Initially cold behavior from a communicator (which presumably sets the expectations), followed by reward behavior (a positive violation), is hypothesized to produce more favorable consequences than a warm-warm sequence (which entails no violation). Given the possibility that positive as well as negative violations may occur, what is needed is clarification of what qualifies as a positive versus a negative violation and how such violations compare to expectancy conformity in affecting communication processes and consequences.

According to the expectancy violations model, if one's interaction partner conforms to expectancies, the expectancies themselves and the nonverbal behaviors they govern should operate largely out of awareness, and communication outcomes should depend on such pre-interactional and interactional factors as communicator and relational characteristics, the definition of the situation, and the intrinsic meaning of the verbal and nonverbal behaviors being exchanged. This assumption parallels Patterson's (1983) argument in his functional model that behavior matching expectations serve to maintain stable exchanges. (The arousal-valence and discrepancy-arousal models make similar arguments.)

Violations and Arousal

If, however, the communicator violates expectancies to a sufficient degree for the deviation to be recognized (i.e., exceeds a limen of socially tolerated variability or receiver sensitivity), the violation is posited to heighten the violatee's arousal. All the models subscribe to the principle that noticeably deviant or discrepant behavior by a communicator produces a change in a partner's arousal level. All are also primarily focused on predicting and explaining how such deviations or instability-producing changes affect communication behaviors and evaluations. The expectancy violations, arousal-labeling, arousal-valence, and functional models contend that heightened arousal results in some cognitive-affective assessment of the situation and/or behavior. (The discrepancy-arousal theory moves cognitive processes to the role of antecedents to arousal change, but also treats affective changes as a consequent of arousal change.)

In the case of the violations model, the arousal change is posited to cause an alertness or orienting response that diverts attention away from the ostensive purpose of the interaction and focuses it toward the source of the arousal — the initiator of the violation. This position is consistent with Newtson's (1973) observation that introduction of an unexpected activity in the midst of a prolonged behavior episode results in finer-grained observations of behavior, that is, subsequent behavior is decomposed into smaller meaningful units. It is also consistent with the notion that deviant characteristics or behavior make people more mindful of specific details about the deviant (Lander, 1978; Langer & Imber, 1980). King and Sereno (1984) propose that unexpected language use shifts attention from the content level of an interaction to the relational implicature. The expectancy violations model makes essentially the same argument. It proposes that the attentional shift to the relational level makes communicator and message/behavior characteristics more salient, causing the violatee to engage in a two-stage interpretation and evaluation process that results in the violation act being defined as either a positive or negative violation of expectations. The explanation which follows separates expectancy violations from the other cognitive models, which fail to articulate precisely how the cognitive labeling process operates to yield a positive or negative valence.

Communicator Reward Valence

The first factor to influence the valencing of a violation as positive or negative is the reward value of the violator. Reward is a function of all those static and initial, or pre-interactional, communicator and relationship characteristics (such as gender, personality, physical attractiveness, reputation, status, and anticipated future interaction) and all those derived, interactional behaviors (such as possessing tangible rewards, having an amusing communication style, or giving positive feedback) that cause the communicator to be perceived, on balance, as someone with whom it is desirable to interact.[1] It is the net valence of all the relevant communicator and relationship characteristics that can be judged on an evaluative continuum. Put in exchange theory terms, it means the benefits of interacting with the communicator outweigh the costs.

Behavior Interpretation and Evaluation

Communicator reward value influences the valencing of a violation in two ways. First, it may affect *interpretation* of the violation. Many nonverbal behaviors carry implicit relational messages and other social meanings (Burgoon, Buller, Hale, & deTurck, 1984; Burgoon, et al., 1986; Burgoon, et al., 1985; Burgoon & Saine, 1978). Often a given act carries multiple interpretations among which several alternatives are plausible. Here is where regard for the communicator may influence selection of meaning. For example, increased proximity during conversation may be taken as a sign of affiliation if committed by a high reward person but as a sign of aggressiveness if committed by a low reward person. To the extent that multiple interpretations are possible, expectancy violations theory holds that more favorable ones will be given to the act when it is committed by a high reward than a low reward violator.

Where the meaning of the behavior is unequivocal, reward may mediate the *evaluation* of the violation. Although there are some nonverbal behaviors that may produce uniformly negative or positive evaluations regardless of who commits them (e.g., displaying an insulting gesture), the affective reaction to many behaviors depends on their source. For example, even if a behavior such as continuous gaze carries the same interpretation (e.g., high involvement) for both high and low reward violators, that level of gaze may be welcome from a high reward communicator and unwelcome from a low reward one. Thus, deviant gaze is favorably evaluated in the case of a high reward communicator and unfavorably evaluated in the case of a low reward one.

One other possibility is that the behavior is disregarded, either because it is seen as externally caused or because it has no discernible meaning. In both instances, the behavior is noncommunicative and is discounted.

Violation Valence

Positively evaluated behaviors, either because they originate from a positively valued communicator, are assigned positive interpretations, or have consensually assigned positive value within a speech community, should qualify as positive violations and produce favorable communication patterns and consequences. Negatively interpreted and evaluated deviations should qualify as negative violations and generate unfavorable interaction patterns and consequences. However, in contrast to the other nonverbal interaction models, the expectancy violations model predicts that an extreme violation, if committed by a high reward communicator, can be positively valenced, producing reciprocal communication patterns and positive outcomes such as higher credibility and attraction. The other models predict that an extreme violation produces compensatory interaction patterns. They do not address terminal communication outcomes (i.e., those resulting from an entire episode).

This interpretation and evaluation process as filtered through communicator reward is depicted in Figure 1. For simplicity, reward, expectancies, and violation valences have been dichotomized as positive or negative, although they should be understood as continua. In the case of a violation, the arousal change triggers the interpretive process. If the meaning of the behavior(s) is initially ambiguous, one must first decide if a positive or negative interpretation is to be selected. Once this decision is made, the interpreted message is evaluated—simply put, does the recipient like or dislike receiving it? The assignment of a behavior as a negative (or positive) violation can occur at either the interpretive or evaluative stage: At the interpretative stage, if the interpreted message is considered inappropriate or negatively valued *by society*, which results in an automatic unfavorable evaluation; at the evaluative stage, if the message is negatively valued *by the recipient* for this particular occasion or communicator. This valencing process need not entail cumbersome or lengthy cognitive effort. Indeed, to the extent that evaluations have been conditioned to the behaviors and interpretation is a habitual, overlearned activity, the valencing process may occur almost automatically.

Noteworthy is that a high reward communicator may commit a negative violation, either by engaging in an act which has an unambiguous negative interpretation (e.g., displaying complete disinterest in what one's partner has to say), or engaging in a positively interpreted act that the partner nevertheless finds unpleasant or undesirable (e.g., using too much affiliative touch). A low reward communicator may also engage in a positive violation, although the opportunities for such are more limited. A positive violation will be attributed to a poorly regarded communicator only when the violation carries an unambiguously positive interpretation *and* a socially positive evaluation.

The double pluses and minuses designate that violations produce more pronounced effects than conformity to expectations. A positive violation produces more favorable consequences, and a negative violation, more unfavorable ones, than adhering to the expected behavior pattern. This proposed intensification of response is bolstered by Langer and Imber's

(1980) finding that characteristics of deviants were perceived as more extreme and evaluated more extremely than those of "normal" individuals.

The foregoing discussion is not meant to imply that interpretations and evaluations are made in an absolute fashion. Rather, it is more likely that they are judged relative to the expectancy and can be placed with it along an evaluative continuum. Thus, ultimately the *direction* and *magnitude* of a violation dictate its type and consequences. If the actual (violation)

FIGURE 1
NONVERBAL EXPECTANCY VIOLATIONS MODEL

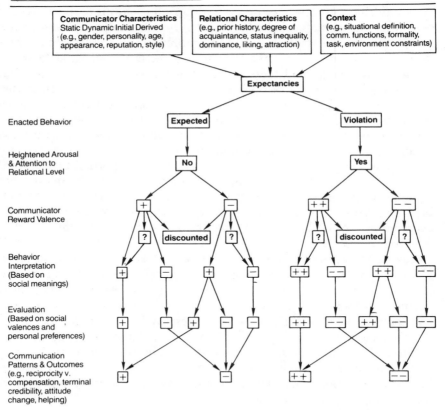

Note: For simplicity, communicator reward valence, behavior interpretation, and behavior evaluation valence have been dichotomized into positive and negative but should be understood to represent continua. Double pluses and minuses denote greater magnitude of effect.

behavior is more positively valenced than the expected behavior(s), a *positive violation* occurs and should produce more favorable communication outcomes than conforming to the expected (normative) pattern.[2] Conversely, if the actual behavior is more negatively valenced than the expected behavior, a *negative violation* is said to occur and should yield more negative consequences than conforming to expectations. The magnitude of discrepancy dictates whether a violation is actually perceived and how significant it is. The greater the magnitude of deviation from expectancy, the greater the impact on communication outcomes.

Because people may hold higher standards or more stringent expectations for a high reward person than for a low reward one, it is possible for a high reward person to commit a more grievous violation. For example, gaze aversion tends to carry uniformly negative interpretations and evaluations. If a well-liked person avoids gaze, this may be a more serious negative violation than if a disliked person does it, because one expects the well-liked person to reciprocate affiliative behavior but may hold no such expectations for the low reward communicator. Therefore, the gap between the actual and expected behavior could be much greater for the high than the low reward person.

Figure 2 illustrates several examples of small and large positive and negative violations. It should be noted that for strangers, the expected behavior is the same as the socially normative behavior. Otherwise, the relevant expectancy is the one held for the specific individual. The significance of the societal expectation is that it provides a basis for judging how large a violation is. For example, a low reward person, reputed to be a terrible speaker, who exhibits far greater fluency than is common, may be committing a large positive violation by not only exceeding the individual expectation but also the social norm (Case 2). Or a high reward person for whom one has high expectations may commit a small negative violation merely by conforming to the societal norm (Case 7).

Empirical Support for the Model

The accumulated research evidence relevant to the nonverbal expectancy model has produced support for the following conclusions:

1. *Interactants develop expectations about the distancing and immediacy behavior of others.* As noted earlier, people are most comfortable with, and regard as most appropriate and expected, intermediate levels of conversational distance, gaze, and sensory involvement.

FIGURE 2
EIGHT EXAMPLES OF POSITIVE AND NEGATIVE VIOLATIONS OF EXPECTATIONS

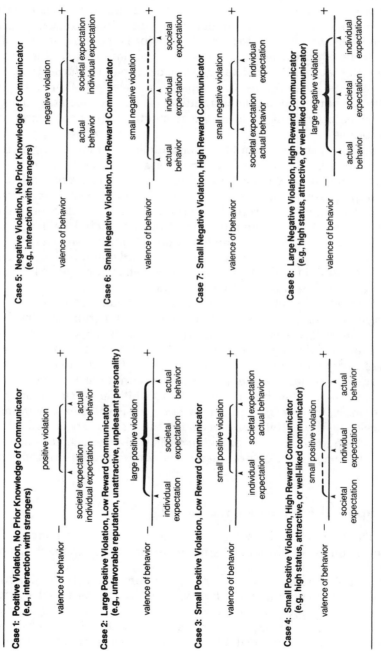

2. *Communicator behaviors and characteristics that contribute to interpersonal rewards mediate communication outcomes.* All of the following have been defined as bases for reward and shown to influence outcomes: positive and negative feedback, physical attractiveness, smiling, head nods, task competence, socioeconomic status, purchasing power, and attitudinal similarity (Burgoon, 1978; Burgoon & Aho, 1982; Burgoon, et al., 1982; Burgoon, et al., 1979; Schiffenbauer & Schiavo, 1976; Smith & Knowles, 1979; Stacks & Burgoon, 1981; Storms & Thomas, 1977).

3. *For conversational distance, rewarding communicators frequently accrue the most favorable communication outcomes by violating rather than conforming to expectancies.* The beneficial consequences result from both close and far violations and not only benefit the violator in an absolute sense but also relative to another, nondeviating interactant (Baron, 1978; Burgoon, 1978; Burgoon & Aho, 1982; Burgoon, et al., 1982; Burgoon, et al., 1979; Donohue, Diez, Stahle, & Burgoon, 1983; Ickes, Patterson, Rajecki, & Tanford, 1982; Imada & Hakel, 1977; Schiffenbauer & Schiavo, 1976; Smith & Knowles, 1979; Stacks & Burgoon, 1981; Storms & Thomas, 1977).

4. *For conversational distance, nonrewarding communicators frequently accrue their optimal communication outcomes by conforming to distance expectancies rather than violating them.* Violations by poorly regarded others tend to produce more negative consequences for the violator and have the effect of conferring greater credibility, attraction, and perceived influence on other, nonviolating interactants (Baron, 1978; Burgoon, 1978; Burgoon & Aho, 1982; Burgoon, et al., 1982; Burgoon, et al., 1979; Ickes, et al., 1982; Konecni, Libuser, Morton, & Ebbeson, 1973; Schiffenbauer & Schiavo, 1976; Smith & Knowles, 1979; Stacks & Burgoon, 1981; Storms & Thomas, 1977).

5. *For eye gaze, rewarding communicators achieve greatest attraction, credibility and endorsement for hiring by engaging in nearly continuous gaze or normal gaze; gaze aversion produces negative consequences.* A high degree of gaze is interpreted as expressing intimacy, affiliation, trust, interest, involvement, relaxation, composure, and possibly depth and similarity. These favorable

interpretations may qualify it as a positive violation when committed by a high reward person. Gaze aversion, by contrast, is interpreted as detached, cold, nonintimate, tense, untrustworthy, dissimilar and superficial, causing it to serve as a negative violation (Burgoon, et al., 1986; Burgoon, et al., 1985; Manusov, 1984).

6.   *Violations are arousing and distracting.* Distance violations and changes in nonverbal intimacy often produce physical manifestations of activation and discomfort and have been shown to shift attention away from the task or topic of discussion (Burgoon & Aho, 1982; Galle, Spratt, Chapman, & Smallbone, 1975; Konecni, et al., 1973; Smith & Knowles, 1979; Stacks & Burgoon, 1981).

References

Abelson, R.P. (1981). Psychological status of the script concept. *American Psychologist, 36,* 715-729.

Andersen, P.A. (1985). Nonverbal immediacy in interpersonal communication. In A.W. Siegman & S. Feldstein (Eds.). *Multichannel integrations of nonverbal behavior* (pp. 1-36). Hillsdale, NJ: Lawrence Erlbaum.

Argyle, M., & M. Cook. (1976). *Gaze and mutual gaze.* Cambridge: Cambridge University Press.

Aronson, E., & D. Linder. (1965). Gain and loss of esteem as determinants of interpersonal attractiveness. *Journal of Experimental Social Psychology, 1,* 156-171.

Baron, R.A. (1978). Invasions of personal space and helping: Mediating effects of invader's apparent need. *Journal of Experimental Social Psychology, 14,* 304-312.

Buller, D.B., & J.K. Burgoon. (1986). The effects of vocalics and nonverbal sensitivity on compliance: A replication and extension. *Human Communication Research, 13,* 126-144.

Burgoon, J.K. (1978). A communication model of personal space violations: Explication and an initial test. *Human Communication Research, 4,* 129-142.

Burgoon, J.K. (1983). Nonverbal violations of expectations. In J.M. Wiemann & R.P. Harrison (Eds.). *Nonverbal interaction* (pp. 77-111). Beverly Hills, CA: Sage.

Burgoon, J.K. (1985, May). *Expectancies, rewards, violations and outcomes: Applications to the instructional environment.* Paper presented at the annual meeting of the International Communication Association, Honolulu.

Burgoon, J.K. & L. Aho. (1982). Three field experiments on the effects of conversational distance. *Communication Monographs, 49,* 71-88.

Burgoon, J.K., D.B. Buller, J.L. Hale, & M.A. deTurck. (1984). Relational messages associated with nonverbal behaviors. *Human Communication Research, 10,* 351-378.

Burgoon, J.K. & D.A. Coker. (in press). Nonverbal expectancy violations and conversational involvement. *Journal of Nonverbal Behavior.*

Burgoon, J.K., D.A. Coker, & R.A. Coker. (1986). Communicative effects of gaze behavior: A test of two contrasting explanations. *Human Communication Research, 12,* 495-524.

Burgoon, J.K., & S.B. Jones. (1976). Toward a theory of personal space expectations and their violations. *Human Communication Research, 2,* 131-146.

Burgoon, J.K., V. Manusov, P. Mineo, & J.L. Hale. (1985). Effects of gaze on hiring, credibility, attraction and relational message interpretation. *Journal of Nonverbal Behavior, 9,* 133-146.

Burgoon, J.K., & T. Saine. (1978). *The unspoken dialogue: An introduction to nonverbal communication.* Boston: Houghton-Mifflin.

Burgoon, J.K., D.W. Stacks, & S.A. Burch. (1982). The role of interpersonal rewards and violations of distancing expectations in achieving influence in small groups. *Communication, 11,* 114-128.

Burgoon, J.K., D.W. Stacks, & G.W. Woodall. (1979). A communicative model of violations of distancing expectations. *Western Journal of Speech Communication, 43,* 153-167.

Cappella, J.N., & J.O. Greene. (1982). A discrepancy-arousal explanation of mutual influence in expressive behavior for adult-adult and infant-adult interaction. *Communication Monographs, 49,* 89-114.

Donohue, W.A., M.E. Diez, R. Stahle, & J.K. Burgoon. (1983, May). *The effects of distance violations on verbal immediacy: An exploration.* Paper presented at the annual meeting of the International Communication Association, Dallas.

Galle, A., G. Spratt, A.J. Chapman, & A. Smallbone. (1975). EEG correlates of eye contact and interpersonal distance. *Biological Psychology, 3,* 237-245.

Gibson, E.J., C.J. Owsley, & J. Johnston. (1978). Perception of invariants by five-month-old infants: Differentiation of two types of motion. *Developmental Psychology, 14,* 407-415.

Haith, M.M., W. Kiesen, & D. Collins. (1969). Response of the human infant to level of complexity of intermittent visual movement. *Journal of Experimental Child Psychology, 7,* 52-69.

Hale, J.L., & J.K. Burgoon. (1984). Models of reactions to changes in nonverbal immediacy. *Journal of Nonverbal Behavior, 8,* 287-314.

Ickes, W., M.L. Patterson, D.W. Rajecki, & S. Tanford. (1982). Behavioral and cognitive consequences of reciprocal versus compensatory responses to pre-interaction expectancies. *Social Cognition, 1,* 160-190.

Imada, A.S., & M.D. Hakel. (1977). Influence of nonverbal communication and rater proximity on impressions and decisions in simulated employment interviews. *Journal of Applied Psychology, 62,* 285-300.

Jackson, J. (1964). The normative regulation of authoritative behavior. In W.J. Gove & J.W. Dyson (Eds.). *The making of decisions: A reader in administrative behavior* (pp. 213-241). New York: Free Press.

Jackson, J. (1966). A conceptual and measurement model for norms and roles. *Pacific Sociological Review, 9,* 35-47.

King, S.W., & K.K. Sereno. (1984). Conversational appropriateness as a conversational imperative. *Quarterly Journal of Speech, 70,* 264-273.

Konecni, V.J., L. Libuser, H. Morton, & E.B. Ebbesen. (1973). Effects of a violation of personal space on escape and helping responses. *Journal of Experimental Social Psychology, 11,* 288-299.

Kreckel, M. (1981). *Communicative acts and shared knowledge as natural discourse.* New York: Academic Press.

Langer, E. (1978). Rethinking the role of thought in social interaction. In J.H. Harvey, W.J. Ickes & R.F. Kidd (Eds.). *New directions in attribution research* (Vol. 2, pp. 35-58). Hillsdale, NJ: Lawrence Erlbaum.

Langer, E.J., & L. Ember. (1980). Role of mindlessness in the perception of deviance. *Journal of Personality and Social Psychology, 39,* 360-367.

Manusov, V.L. (1984). *Nonverbal violations of expectations theory: A test of gaze behavior.* Unpublished master's thesis, Michigan State University.

Newtson, D. (1973). Attribution and the unit of perception of ongoing behavior. *Journal of Personality and Social Psychology, 28,* 28-38.

Patterson, M.L. (1976). An arousal model of interpersonal intimacy. *Psychological Review, 83,* 235-245.

Patterson, M.L. (1982). A sequential functional model of nonverbal exchange. *Psychological Review, 89,* 231-249.

Patterson, M.L. (1983). *Nonverbal behavior: A functional perspective.* New York: Springer-Verlag.

Rosenfeld, H.M., B.E. Breck, S.H. Smith, & S. Kehoe. (1984). Intimacy-mediators of the proximity-gaze compensation effect: Movement, conversational role, acquaintance, and gender. *Journal of Nonverbal Behavior, 8,* 235-249.

Schank, R.C., & R.P. Abelson. (1977). *Scripts, plans, goals and understanding.* Hillsdale, NJ: Erlbaum.

Scheflen, A.E. (1984). *How behavior means.* Garden City, NY: Anchor Books.

Schiffenbauer, A., & R.S. Schiavo. (1976). Physical distance and attention: An intensification effect. *Journal of Experimental Social Psychology, 26,* 332-346.

Smith, R.J., & E.S. Knowles. (1979). Affective and cognitive mediators of reactions to spatial invasions. *Journal of Experimental Social Psychology, 15,* 537-552.

Stacks, D.W., & J.K. Burgoon. (1981). The role of nonverbal behaviors as distractors in resistance to persuasion in interpersonal contexts. *Central States Speech Journal, 32,* 61-73.

Storms, M.D., & G.C. Thomas. (1977). Reactions to physical closeness. *Journal of Personality and Social Psychology, 35,* 412-418.

Street, R.L., Jr., & J.N. Cappella. (1985). Sequence and pattern in communicative behaviour: A model and commentary. In R.L. Street & J.N. Cappella (Eds.). *Sequence and pattern in communicative behaviour* (pp. 243-276). London: Edward Arnold.

Thompson, D.E., J.R. Aiello, & Y.M. Epstein. (1979). Interpersonal distance preferences. *Journal of Nonverbal Behavior, 4,* 113-118.

Key Terms and Concepts

Hecht and DeVito, *Perspectives on Nonverbal Communication*

importance of nonverbal communication	context
definition of nonverbal communication	rules
6 ways verbal and nonverbal messages are related	culture
memory	codes
nonverbal behavior versus nonverbal communication	meanings
multichannel	functions

Spitzberg, *Perspectives on Nonverbal Communication Skills*

skills	eye contact	interaction
competence	smiles	management
time in presence	head movements	other-orientation
of others	adaptors	composure
response latency	volume	expressiveness
eye gaze	talk time	

Mehrabian, *Perspectives on Influence: Selling*

liking and sales	customer dress
quality of product and sales	feminine tactics

Andersen and Andersen, *Perspectives on Nonverbal Intimacy Theory*

intimacy	rewardingness	schema
immediacy	arousal-labeling	novel stimulus
involvement	model	cognitive activation
affiliative conflict	arousal	sequential-functional
theory	compensation	model
equilibrium	reciprocity	behavioral
approach drive	arousal-valence	predispositions
avoidance drive	model	scripts
expectancy norms	amount of arousal	functions
models	discrepancy-arousal	
space violations	model	

Burgoon and Hale, *Perspectives on Nonverbal Expectations*

expectations	communicator characteristics
norms	relationship characteristics
idiosyncracies	contextual factors
reward and violation valence	

Part Two

Body Communication

We use our bodies to communicate in many ways. Our *posture* can express our feelings and attitudes. If we *lean* toward someone while talking, this may be a sign of interest and involvement, while leaning away is often interpreted as disinterest. Similarly, we tend to face friends *directly* and this may be a sign of interest, liking, or respect. It is also important to consider *postural relaxation* (more relaxed postures are found in higher status people), *mirroring* as in two or more people adopting the same or similar posture (this is often a sign of similarity or attraction), and *openness* (crossing of arms or legs may indicate defensiveness).

Physical appearance is also important. Our *body builds*, themselves, help form an impression. Appearance plays a surprising role in many areas of life, including grades, salary, and power, as well as the more obvious role in dating and marriage.

We are also interested in *body movement*. *Walking styles* are one way of forming an impression of people. An impression is conveyed by long confident strides, or short choppy steps, or heavy, rocking walks.

Finally, we can note when people *groom* themselves, for example, fixing their hair and clothes. We are more likely to groom when we are attracted to someone.

Our bodies are an important source of nonverbal information. In fact, research shows that we sometimes communicate unintentionally through this channel because we are frequently unaware of our body movements. This is called *leakage*. As a result the body provides extremely believable messages.

Cash, Cash, and Butters examined physical attractiveness. The article reports the results of a study testing the "contrast effect." Participants in the study saw pictures of either more or less attractive people. The participants gave lower ratings to their own physical attractiveness after seeing the pictures of attractive people due to the contrast effect.

"Mirror, Mirror, on the Wall . . . ?"
Contrast Effects and Self-Evaluations of Physical Attractiveness

Thomas F. Cash, Diane Walker Cash and Jonathan W. Butters

As the research on physical attractiveness has progressed in recent years (Cash, 1981), a few behavioral scientists have begun to examine factors that influence judgments of attractiveness. While one approach focuses on perceiver characteristics, a second approach considers the effects of contextual and situational factors on attractiveness judgments. One such contextual factor concerns the presence of other stimuli that vary in their levels of physical attractiveness. Melamed and Moss (1975) asked male and female college students to rate photographs of average-looking females presented in the context of other photographs of either attractive or unattractive females. The investigators observed the operation of a contrast effect—that is, targets were judged to be more physically attractive when viewed in the context of photos of unattractive females than in the context of attractive stimuli.

In a field study, Kenrick and Gutierres (1980) found that males downgraded the physical attractiveness of an average-looking female after having watched *Charlie's Angels* as compared to males who had watched

Adapted with permission from: Cash, T.F., D.W. Cash, & J.W. Butters. (1983). "Mirror, mirror, on the wall . . . ?": Contrast effects and self-evaluations of physical attractiveness. *Personality and social psychology bulletin*, (Vol. 9 No. 3) pp. 351-358, copyright © 1983 by the Society for Personality and Social Psychology, Inc. Reprinted by permission of Sage Publications, Inc.

Authors' Note: Appreciation is expressed to Douglas T. Kenrick, Brenda Major, Dan Walter, and Barbara A. Winstead for their helpful comments on this manuscript. Requests for reprints should be sent to Thomas F. Cash, Virginia Consortium for Professional Psychology, Department of Psychology, Old Dominion University, Norfolk, VA 23508.

another television program. These researchers also conducted two controlled laboratory experiments similar to that of Melamed and Moss (1975) and again confirmed the operation of a perceptual contrast effect on judgments of physical attractiveness.

Each of these investigations focused on the contrast effects of contextual factors on ratings of others' physical attractiveness. However, the influence of the level of physical attractiveness of comparison persons on self-evaluations of attractiveness has not been determined. The need for such research is underlined by the fact that the mass media constantly expose us to the upper extreme of the normal distribution of physical attractiveness. In their classic study extending the domain of Festinger's (1954) social comparison theory, Morse and Gergen (1970) did find that the casual exposure of subjects to persons whose manner and appearance conveyed either desirable or undesirable characteristics produced social comparison contrast effects on subjects' self-esteem. Since the stimulus persons varied on several dimensions, the role of their physical attractiveness per se is uncertain.

The principal purpose of the present experiment was to assess the effect of exposure to same-sexed peers of varying levels of physical attractiveness on self-perceptions of physical attractiveness. Derived from social comparison theory, our hypothesis was that of a contrast effect. Lower subjects' self-ratings were predicted under a more attractive than a less attractive stimulus context. Moreover, in lieu of a neutral comparison group to discriminate positive and negative contrast effects, we included a stimulus context that used professional models for the attractive stimulus persons (comparable to advertisements in "beauty magazines"). To the extent that models' status makes them dissimilar and less appropriate as comparison persons than peers (Festinger, 1954; Zanna, Goethals, & Hill, 1975), we would expect subjects to see themselves as less physically attractive following exposure to attractive peers as opposed to attractive advertising models. A secondary purpose of the study was to explore individual differences in self-evaluations of attractiveness, particularly differences related to personality variables derived from Buss's (1980) theory of self-consciousness.

Method

Subjects

A sample of 51 female college students was recruited from introductory psychology classes. All subjects were white Americans with a mean age of 22.7 years (sd=7.2).

Stimulus Materials

Three sets of 25 stimuli were constructed to represent the manipulation of social comparison conditions. All stimuli were pictures of 18- to 35-year-old women taken from magazine ads and articles and assembled with one per page in a booklet. In the not attractive condition, stimulus persons were determined by consensus of four student judges to reflect average to unattractive levels of physical attractiveness. Because of this range, the referent "not attractive" is more accurate than "unattractive." In the two attractive conditions, stimulus persons were consensually judged to be above-average in physical attractiveness. Stimuli included a range of picture sizes, both black-and-white and color pictures, as well as full-body, upper-body, and head-only photos. The not attractive and attractive conditions were matched on these factors. Photos of stimulus persons were cut out from their sources in a manner that eliminated information about their original contexts. The professionally attractive condition differed from the attractive only by the attachment of an advertiser's name (such as Calvin Klein, Cover Girl, Bloomingdale's) cut from magazines and randomly paired with each picture in order to emphasize the stimulus person's status as a professional model.

Procedure

Subjects arrived in small groups at the research laboratory, and the female experimenter explained the study's purpose as the development and evaluation of materials to be used in future research.

Subjects initially completed the Self-Consciousness Inventory (Buss, 1980; Fenigstein, Scheier, & Buss, 1975). This 23-item, factor-analyzed instrument contains three scales: private self-consciousness, public self-consciousness, and social anxiety. Subjects indicated on a 5-point scale the degree to which each item was characteristic of them. Persons who scored high on the Private Self-Consciousness Scale tended to engage in self-focused attention to inner processes and were more likely to possess clear and accurate knowledge of their personal feelings and motives. Persons who scored high on the Public Self-Consciousness Scale reported frequent awareness of themselves as social objects, including awareness of the impressions and appearance they convey to others in social situations. The Social Anxiety Scale measures feelings of discomfort and inhibition in social situations.

Next, subjects went to individual cubicles where they received all instructions by a standard tape-recording. Following a random groups design, each subject was assigned one of the three booklets of stimulus persons. In this manner, the three conditions were run simultaneously.

The subjects were instructed to look at the first picture for 15 seconds and to give tone-cued reactions on the Picture Rating Questionnaire provided. Thirty seconds were allowed for responses before instructions were given to turn the page, to observe the next picture for 15 seconds, and to give questionnaire ratings. This procedure was repeated until the subject had observed and rated all 25 pictures in her booklet. Ten-point ratings included an evaluation of each stimulus person's physical attractiveness embedded between evaluation of familiarity and noticeability.

Subsequent to their ratings of all stimulus persons, subjects were instructed to open an envelope and complete the enclosed self-evaluation scales as "a part of another research project." First, subjects rated their own physical attractiveness on a 10-point Likert scale. Second, subjects completed the Body Satisfaction Questionnaire (Berscheid, Walster, & Bohrnstedt, 1973; Bohrnstedt, Note 1)—making a 6-point rating of their satisfaction or dissatisfaction with each of 24 body parts and with overall appearance. Finally, subjects were debriefed and signed a "promise of nondisclosure" form, agreeing not to discuss the research with others until its completion.

Results and Discussion

Statistical analyses indicate subjects who observed pictures of more attractive persons rated their own physical attractiveness lower than those who had observed pictures of plainer persons.

Our pattern of results with self-perceived attractiveness are consistent with social comparison theory's proposition (Festinger, 1954; Zanna, et al., 1975) that people are more likely to compare themselves with others who are similar than with those who are dissimilar. Perhaps in the eyes of most of our subjects, peer beauty qualified as a more appropriate standard for social comparison than professional beauty. The differential effect between the two attractive conditions also serves to weaken the argument that the contrast effect is merely an artifact of using similar scales to measure social perception and self-perception.

Moreover, the pattern of mean differences suggests that this study's contrast effect was a negative one that occurred primarily for subjects exposed to photos of attractive peers. Viewed in a practical sense, our results further suggest that thumbing through popular magazines filled with beautiful models may have little immediate effect on the self-images of most women. Still, one clearly cannot rule out potential effects of long-term media exposure to cultural standards of beauty (Garner, Garfinkel, Schwartz, & Thompson, 1980; Kenrick & Gutierres, 1980).

While the contrast effect was evident for self-perceived attractiveness, the stimulus conditions had no significant overall effect on subjects' reports of satisfaction with various parts of their bodies. A number of possible explanations of the limited results with body satisfaction may be offered. As previously suggested (Cash & Cash, 1982), this particular index of body satisfaction may be a trait measure that is somewhat insensitive to transient situational influences and shows considerable stability even in the presence of more substantial interventions (Padin, Lerner, & Spiro, 1981). Another explanation entails the possible reactive effect of subjects' making discrete judgments about body parts, as opposed to evaluation of the gestalt of overall physical attractiveness. Differentiation of this global percept by focusing on individual components may have the effect of restoring subjects' gestalt to its precontrast level. Consistent with this possibility is the fact that no effect of stimulus conditions was apparent on the final, overall appearance item of the body satisfaction inventory. The use of symbolic stimuli (photographs) may also exert a weaker effect than stimulus persons who are actually present, and future research should examine the extent of the contrast effect with live confederates.

In order to examine cross-contextual individual differences in self-rated attractiveness, its correlation with each of the personality variables was computed across stimulus conditions. More attractive self-perceptions were reported by women who were less socially anxious, more privately self-conscious, and more satisfied with their body parts, lower torso, and overall appearance. The fact that persons who were socially anxious and more dissatisfied with their bodies also expressed less positive appraisals of their physical attractiveness replicates previous research findings (Berscheid, et al., 1973; Mitchell & Orr, 1976). We did not observe a significant relationship between self-perceived attractiveness and public self-consciousness, the disposition toward self-focused attention as a social object. Other studies have found that publicly self-conscious women are judged to be more attractive (McDonald & Eilenfield, 1980; Turner, Gilliland, & Klein, 1981), evaluate their own physical attributes more rapidly (Turner, et al., 1981), and are more likely to use facial cosmetics (Cash & Cash, 1982). Since public self-consciousness increases one's susceptibility to situational standards for self-evaluations (Buss, 1980), further research with a larger sample is needed to examine the possibility of an interactive effect of public self-consciousness and stimulus context on self-evaluation of physical appearance.[1]

The effect of context on perceivers' ratings of the physical attractiveness of others depends on the association between the targets and the context. A contrast effect occurs when the contiguous targets and context are not linked as friends (Kenrick & Gutierres, 1980; Melamed & Moss, 1975).

Physical attractiveness may radiate, producing an assimilation effect, when target and context are linked as friends or romantic partners (Bar-Tal & Saxe, 1976; Melamed & Moss, 1975; Sigall & Landy, 1973). Such data raise the interesting question of whether this assimilation effect also would occur for self-evaluation when the social context consists of friends as opposed to the strangers used in the present experiment.

Given the voluminous literature on the power of physical attractiveness as a social stimulus variable (Cash, 1981) and the fact that self-ratings of physical attractiveness often have weak correspondence with social reality (Berscheid & Walster, 1974; Cash & Soloway, 1975), we need further understanding of the determinants and the effects of these self-percepts. Indeed, while "objective" physical attractiveness seems only modestly related to a few personality attributes (Cash & Smith, 1982), "subjective" physical attractiveness represents a central dimension of self-concept for males and females across the life span (Adams, 1977; Berscheid, et al., 1973; Mendelsohn & White, 1982; Mitchell & Orr, 1976; Padin, et al., 1981; Sorell & Nowak, 1981).

Considered in the broader vein of Morse and Gergen's (1970) findings, our results suggest one process by which some attractive persons may have adverse effects on others. Depending on the situational and behavioral context, such a process may foster certain negative effects of beauty — prompting reactions of intimidation, jealousy, avoidance, or other negative attributions. Lest they themselves fall prey to the "what is beautiful is good" stereotype, researchers must investigate the liabilities as well as the benefits of beauty (Cash, Note 2). Therefore, further research should evaluate the generality of the present results across sex and age groups, and within a variety of more naturalistic social contexts.

Note

[1]Publicly self-conscious subjects expressed less satisfaction with their bodies only when exposed to stimulus persons who were attractive peers ($r=.57$, $p < .02$). Although the interactive effects of personality and stimulus context on self-evaluation of appearance represent a reasonable and interesting consideration, their thorough examination transcends the scope and sample size of the present study.

Reference Notes

1. Bohrnstedt, G.W. On measuring body satisfaction. Unpublished manuscript, Institute of Social Research, Indiana University, Bloomington, Indiana, 1977.
2. Cash, T.F. The interface of sexism and beautyism. Symposium paper (available from author) presented at the annual convention of the American Psychological Association, Los Angeles, August 28, 1981.

References

Adams, G.R. Physical attractiveness research: Toward a developmental social psychology of beauty. *Human Development,* 1970, *20,* 217-239.

Bar-Tal, D., & L. Saxe. Perceptions of similarly and dissimilarly attractive couples and individuals. *Journal of Personality and Social Psychology,* 1976, *33,* 772-781.

Berscheid, E., E. Walster, & G. Bohrnstedt. The happy American body: A survey report. *Psychology Today,* November 1973, 119-131.

Berscheid, E., & E. Walster. Physical attractiveness. In L. Berkowitz (Ed.). *Advances in experimental social psychology* (Vol. 7). New York: Academic Press, 1974.

Buss, A.H. *Self-consciousness and social anxiety.* San Francisco: W.H. Freeman, 1980.

Cash, T.F. Physical attractiveness: An annotated bibliography of theory and research in the behavioral sciences. *JSAS Catalog of Selected Documents in Psychology,* 1981, *11,* Ms. 2370.

Cash, T.F., & D.W. Cash. Women's use of cosmetics: Psychosocial correlates and consequences. *International Journal of Cosmetic Science,* 1982, *4,* 1-14.

Cash, T.F., & E. Smith. Physical attractiveness and personality among American college students. *Journal of Psychology,* 1982, *111,* 183-191.

Cash, T.F., & D. Soloway. Self-disclosure correlates of physical attractiveness: An exploratory study. *Psychological Reports,* 1975, *36,* 579-586.

Fenigstein, A., M. Scheier, & A. Buss. Public and private self-consciousness: Assessment and theory. *Journal of Consulting and Clinical Psychology,* 1975, *43,* 522-527.

Festinger, L. A theory of social comparison processes. *Human Relations,* 1954, *7,* 117-140.

Garner, D.M., P.E. Garfinkel, D. Schwartz, & M. Thompson. Cultural expectations of thinness in women. *Psychological Reports,* 1980, *47,* 483-491.

Kenrick, D.T., & S.E. Gutierres. Contrast effects and judgments of physical attractiveness: When beauty becomes a social problem. *Journal of Personality and Social Psychology,* 1980, *38,* 131-140.

McDonald, P.J., & V.C. Eilenfield. Physical attractiveness and the approach/avoidance of self-awareness. *Personality and Social Psychology Bulletin,* 1980, *6,* 391-395.

Melamed, L., & M.K. Moss. The effect of context on ratings of attractiveness of photographs. *Journal of Psychology,* 1975, *90,* 129-136.

Mendelson, B.K., & D.R. White. Relation between body-esteem and self-esteem of obese and normal children. *Perceptual and Motor Skills,* 1982, *54,* 899-905.

Mitchell, K.R., & F.E. Orr. Heterosexual social competence, anxiety, avoidance, and self-judged physical attractiveness. *Perceptual and Motor Skills,* 1976, *43,* 553-554.

Morse, S. & K.J. Gergen. Social comparison, self-consistency, and the concept of self. *Journal of Personality and Social Psychology,* 1970, *16,* 148-156.

Padin, M.A., R.M. Lerner, & A. Spiro. Stability of body attitudes and self-esteem in late adolescents. *Adolescence,* 1981, *16,* 371-384.

Sigall, H., & D. Landy. Radiating beauty: Effects of having a physically attractive partner on person perception. *Journal of Personality and Social Psychology*, 1973, *28*, 218-224.

Sorell, G.T., & C.A. Nowak. The role of physical attractiveness as a contributor to individual development. In R.M. Lerner & N.A. Bush-Rossnagel (Eds.). *Individuals as producers of their development: A life-span perspective*. New York: Academic Press, 1981.

Turner, R.G., L. Gilliland, & H.M. Klein. Self-consciousness, evaluation of physical characteristics and physical attractiveness. *Journal of Research in Personality*, 1981, *15*, 182-190.

Zanna, M.P., G.R. Goethals, & J.F. Hill. Evaluating a sex-related ability: Social comparison with similar others and standard setters. *Journal of Experimental Social Psychology*, 1975, *11*, 86-93.

7

Wells and Siegel examined the stereotypes associated with body builds. Ectomorphs, who are long and thin, were perceived to be tense and quiet. Endomorphs, who are short and round, were perceived to be lazy, jolly, and talkative. Finally, mesomorphs, who are athletic or "V" shaped, were perceived to be stronger and more adventurous.

Stereotyped Somatotypes

William D. Wells and Bertram Siegel

It has often been suggested that social stereotypes may account for a major share of the correlation between physique and temperament. Those who take this point of view argue that reactions to body build are likely to be important features of the individual's social environment, both in terms of the way the individual is treated by others and in terms of the personality and character traits others expect of him. It is also argued that social stereotypes may influence research results in a less direct and more artificial manner. Whenever research designs permit contamination of temperament ratings by knowledge of bodily characteristics, such contamination may increase correlation between physique and temperament artificially, or even produce correlations which otherwise would not be found at all (Anastasi, 1958).

Although these arguments have face validity, whether either must be taken seriously depends upon whether clearly defined and generally accepted physique-temperament stereotypes actually do exist. The purpose of this study was to test for the presence of such stereotypes among members of the general population.

Ss were 120 adults selected to fill sex and economic class quotas from the metropolitan area surrounding Newark, New Jersey. Half were male, half were female. Of the two sex groups, one-third were from the middle, one-third from the lower-middle, and one-third from the upper-lower economic classes as defined by Warner, et al. (1949). None had attended college, and none expressed familiarity with any formal theory linking physique and personality.

Ss were shown four silhouette drawings. One of the drawings pictured a man of "average" physique; the remaining three pictured the three body

Reprinted with permission of authors and publishers from: Wells, W.D., & Siegel, B. Stereotyped somatotypes. *Psychological Reports, 8,* 77-78.

types described by Sheldon (1954). Ss were asked to rate each of the pictured persons on a set of 24 bipolar rating scales. The scales (with poles like ambitious—lazy, dependent—self-reliant, intelligent—unintelligent, fat—thin, and short—tall) were designed to tap the psychological and physical characteristics most likely to be evident in ordinary social interaction (Wells, 1959). The following stereotypes emerged.[1]

Compared with the others, the *endomorph* was rated: fatter, older, shorter (even though the silhouettes were all the same height), more old-fashioned, lazier, less strong (physically), less good looking, more talkative, more warm-hearted anad sympathetic, more good-natured and agreeable, more dependent on others, and more trusting of others. The *mesomorph* was rated: stronger, more masculine, better looking, more adventurous, younger, taller, more mature (in behavior), and more self-reliant. And the *ectomorph* was rated: thinner, younger, more ambitious, taller, more suspicious of others, more tense and nervous, less masculine, more stubborn and inclined to be difficult, more pessimistic, and quieter.

These stereotypes, obtained from persons who had no contact with formal theory, are so clear and so close to what Sheldon and others have found, that they would seem to be a potential influence in any study of the correlation between physique and temperament. People believe that different temperaments go with different body builds. Even when research designs have ruled out the obvious sources of contamination, the subtle, long-term effects of these beliefs may still be present.

Existence of the stereotypes defined above suggests a further question. Perhaps because stereotypes have played so large a role in studies of race prejudice, psychologists have been inclined to assume that stereotypes are gross distortions of the truth, if not false altogether. From this point of view, stereotypes of somatotypes are dismissible along with other folk lore as not worth serious consideration. Yet it is equally reasonable to assume that stereotypes of somatotypes represent a distillation of ages of social experience; that even if they are not determined by developments in the embryo, they are self-perpetuating and effective forces in the social environment. If this latter assumption is correct, they cannot be dismissed as fiction.

Summary.—One hundred and twenty adults who had no knowledge of Sheldon's work were asked to rate silhouettes representing endomorphic, mesomorphic, ectomorphic, and average physique on a set of personality rating scales. The ratings showed clear stereotypes linking physique and personality.

Note

[1]The differences among ratings of body types were tested for statistical significance by the Friedman two-way analysis of variance by ranks (Siegel, 1956). Differences significant at the .01 level appeared on 18 of the 24 rating scales. Only these differences were used in the stereotypes outlined above. A table showing first, second, and third quartile scores for each body type on each rating scale may be obtained on request from the senior author. This table has also been deposited with the American Documentation Institute, Photoduplication Service, Auxiliary Publications Office, Library of Congress, Washington 25, D.C. Order Document No. 6446, remitting $1.25 for 35-mm. microfilm or $1.25 for 6- by 8-in. photocopies.

References

Anastasi, A. *Differential psychology.* New York: MacMillan, 1958.

Sheldon, W.H. *Atlas of men.* New York: Harper, 1954.

Siegel, S. *Nonparametric statistics for the behavioral sciences.* New York: McGraw-Hill, 1956.

Warner, W.L., M. Meeker, & K. Eells. *Social class in America: a manual of procedure for the measurement of social status.* Chicago: Science Research Assoc., 1949.

Wells, W.D. *The Rutgers social attribute inventory.* Chicago: Psychometric Affiliates, 1959.

The data analyses revealed that observers could accurately identify sadness, anger, happiness, and pride from the walkers' gaits. However, proud gaits were more difficult to identify than were other gaits, and the gaits of some walkers were more difficult to identify than those of others. In addition, several gait characteristics were associated with particular emotion displays. Angry gaits showed more heavyfootedness than other gaits, sad gaits showed less arm swing than the others, and proud gaits showed longer strides. Finally, variations in the erectness of the walkers' posture appeared to have little impact on observers' perceptions of emotions in the walkers' gaits.

8

The Identification of Emotions from Gait Information

Joann M. Montepare, Sabra B. Goldstein and Annmarie Clausen

Theorists interested in the information value of nonverbal behaviors have long recognized that a person's gait can provide useful social knowledge to observers. James (1890), for example, believed that walking alongside a person and observing or mimicking the walker's gait would reveal what the walker was feeling. German Expression psychologists of the early 1900s furthermore maintained that a person's character could be ascertained from a person's style of walking (Wallbott, 1982). More recently, theorists such as Birdwhistell (1972) and Henley (1977) have argued that walking patterns serve as potent sources of gender information. Although gait has been acknowledged as a useful source of social information, the amount of empirical research devoted to documenting its utility has been relatively scarce compared to that which has examined the information value of other sources of nonverbal information such as facial or vocal characteristics.

Adapted with permission from: Montepare, J.M., S.B. Goldstein, & A. Clausen. (1987). "The identification of emotions from gait information." *Journal of nonverbal behavior*, 11, 33-42.

Portions of this paper were presented at the 26th meeting of the New England Psychological Association, Boston, MA, November, 1986.

Although limited, the research which has been done on gait lends strong support to the claim that a person's gait reveals useful social information. For example, it has been shown that individuals can readily identify themselves (Beardsworth & Buckner, 1981), as well as their friends (Cutting, 1977), solely on the basis of gait information. Several researchers have also shown that observers can accurately identify a person's sex, and to some extent age, from characteristics of a person's gait (Barclay, Cutting, & Kozlowski, 1978; Montepare, McArthur, & Amgott-Kwan, 1984). In addition, variations in gait have been found to exert a strong impact on trait impressions (Montepare, 1985; Montepare & McArthur, 1986; Montepare, McArthur, & Amgott-Kwan, 1984; Wolff, 1943).

The purpose of the present study was to document further the information value of gait by examining the extent to which observers can identify specific emotions from variations in walking styles. To achieve this goal, subjects viewed videotaped displays of walkers and judged which of four emotions, happiness, sadness, anger, and pride, walkers were expressing. Walkers read brief scenarios describing emotional situations and were instructed to imagine themselves in the situations and to walk accordingly. The scenarios described situations likely to be encountered by the research participants in their daily lives and were ones in which walking was the primary overt behavioral act. The four emotions selected for study were ones shown by other researchers to be readily detected from nonverbal information (Ekman & Freisen, 1975; Davitz & Davitz, 1959) and were ones thought to be most easily revealed in particular situations by variations in gait. In addition to making emotion identifications, subjects rated the gait displays on several gait characteristic scales in an attempt to identify what specific gait characteristics convey emotion information.

Method

Subjects

Ten female undergraduates volunteered to serve as subjects in the present study. Subjects were randomly assigned to one of two viewing groups with five individuals in each group.

Independent Variables

Five female undergraduates served as targets in the creation of the gait stimulus displays. All walkers appeared to have normal gaits and were within average height and weight ranges for their age and gender group.

Stimulus displays depicting gait patterns were created by videotaping walkers from the neck down as they walked in an L-shaped path in front of a stationary black and white video camera while imagining themselves in each of four emotion situations. Walkers' heads were not filmed to reduce the possibility of confounding gait with facial information. Walkers first walked toward and away from the camera in a straight path and then across to the left of the viewing field. All walkers were dressed similarly in comfortable clothing which included jeans and a sweatshirt to minimize potential biasing effects due to differences in apparel.

Prior to the videotaping of each of the four emotion displays, the filming procedure was explained in detail to each walker. Each walker was then given a written copy of a scenario and told to imagine how she would feel in the situation. Each walker was allowed the opportunity to ask questions for clarification, however, none did so and all indicated that the context and intended emotion was clearly understood. When the walker was ready to be filmed, one of the experimenters read the scenario out loud and when she finished, the walker began walking. Videotaping of the four emotion displays for each walker was done in a single session. All walkers were filmed individually. The order in which walkers enacted the four emotion scenarios was randomized for each walker.

The scenario depicting happiness was: "Pretend you are walking down to your friend's room to tell her that you just got a job offer from your first choice firm." The sadness scenario was: "Pretend you are walking down the corridor of a hospital after having just visited a friend who was in a serious car accident." The anger scenario was: "Pretend you are walking away from friend with whom you have just had an argument because she ruined the new blouse you let her borrow." The pride scenario was: "Pretend you are walking out of class after the teacher handed back an exam and told you that you got the highest grade in the class." Prior to the onset of the study, the scenarios were reviewed by 10 members of a seminar in nonverbal behavior for their appropriateness as descriptions of situations associated with the intended emotions. All members concurred that the scenarios were realistic and valid exemplars of the intended emotions.

Dependent Variables

Subjects were familiarized with the four scenarios and intended emotions and they identified each emotion by recording whether "happiness," "sadness," "anger," or "pride" was being expressed while they watched each display. Subjects were told that each of the four emotions would appear only once for each walker. Subjects were further told that they could record the same emotion more than once if they felt it applicable; however, they were instructed not to change any of their answers once recorded. This procedure was used in order to determine the extent to which certain emotions might be confused with others. It also reduced the possibility of subjects making correct or incorrect judgments by the process of elimination. Correct judgments were scored as a 1 and incorrect judgments were scored as a 0.

After making emotion identification, subjects viewed the displays a second time and judged four characteristics of walkers' gait patterns on seven point bipolar scales. The characteristics were similar to those used in previous gait research (Montepare, 1985; Montepare & McArthur, 1986; Montepare, et al., 1984) and included: uses short strides / uses long strides, doesn't swing arms / swings arms alot, lightfooted / heavyfooted, and slouches / stands up straight. In addition to making scaled responses, subjects were asked to write down any additional gait characteristics they noticed.

Procedure

Subjects were run in two viewing groups with five subjects in each group. The order of presentation of the stimulus displays was the same for each group. Subjects in each viewing group sat at a table in front of a videomonitor used for presenting the gait displays. Each subject was given an instruction sheet which described the types of judgments to be made and the scenarios and emotions being portrayed by walkers. The initial wording of the scenarios was modified slightly for subjects. More specifically, subjects' scenarios began "This person is. . . ." rather than "Pretend you are. . . ." Before the emotion identifications were made, subjects were shown a sample display of a walker to acquaint them with the nature of the information they would be using to make their judgments. Subjects were then shown each of the four emotion displays, one at a time, for each of the five walkers and made their identifications on an answer sheet provided.

After the emotion identifications were completed, the videotape was rewound and subjects made the gait characteristic ratings. Subjects were instructed not to turn back to their emotion identifications and to concentrate on the movements of each target. Finally, for each display, subjects were asked to record in the space provided on the rating sheet any additional movement characteristics they noticed.

Results

Statistical analyses indicated that:

1. Observers could accurately identify sadness, anger, happiness, and pride from the walkers' gait.
2. Anger and sadness were the most easily identified. Pride was the most difficult to identify.
3. The following summarizes the findings for specific cues:

Cue	Emotion
Heavyfootedness	Anger
Less Arm Swing	Sadness
Longer strides	Anger or Pride

4. Standing up straight (posture) did not have any affect.

Discussion

The present study has demonstrated that observers can identify specific emotions from variations in walking styles. More specifically, subjects were able to identify, at better than chance levels, whether a person was expressing sadness, anger, happiness, or pride from watching a brief sample of the person's gait. Moreover, the present study has identified several gait characteristics which differentiate sadness, anger, happiness, and pride revealed by gait. In particular, angry gaits were found to be relatively more heavyfooted than the other gaits, and sad gaits were found to have less arm swing than the other gaits. It was also observed that proud and angry gaits have longer stride lengths than happy or sad gaits. Finally, happy gaits appeared to subjects to be faster paced than the other gaits.

The present study also revealed that some emotions are more difficult to identify on the basis of gait information than are other emotions. Specifically, subjects were less proficient at identifying pride compared to sadness or anger. Previous research on emotion detection from nongait nonverbal channels has also found differences in the ease of detection of these emotions (Davitz & Davitz, 1959). Similarities between the present findings and those of past research suggest that there may be important reasons why some emotions are more easily identified than others. McArthur and Baron's (1983) ecological approach to social perception provides one clue to explain these differences. Based on the notion that emotions serve as social affordances which guide important interpersonal behaviors, the ecological position argues that it may be socially and biologically adaptive to detect certain emotions more quickly and accurately than others. For example, the expression of sadness may indicate to observers that a person is ill and in need of immediate care. The expression of anger may signal danger or threat to observers and encourage their necessary attention or avoidance. While the detection of pride may serve to communicate positive affect, failure to identify this emotion may not carry with it the negative consequences the failure to detect emotions such as anger or sadness might. Surely, other theoretical explanations are possible, and have been discussed in detail elsewhere (see for example, Ekman, 1971; Ekman & Freisen, 1975).

Another possible explanation for subjects' poor performance in identifying pride is that important gait information for the detection of this emotion may have been lacking in the stimulus displays. In particular, in keeping with the common assumption that a proud person is "one who holds one's head up high," the detection of pride may require information about the placement of the head in relation to the rest of the body while walking. Since the neck-down gait displays used in the present study do not provide such information, the absence of posture effects may be due to the nature of the stimulus displays rather than indicating that posture does not convey emotion information. This argument may also account for lack of effects on the posture ratings which was noted earlier. Other researchers using neck-down displays have also failed to find systematic effects for posture. For example, research by Montepare and colleagues (Montepare, McArthur, & Amgott-Kwan, 1984; Montepare, 1985; Montepare and McArthur, 1986), which employed neck-down point-light gait displays, failed to find any relationship between subjects' ratings of walkers' posture and their judgments of walkers' age, sex, or personality.[1] Moreover, these findings cannot be attributed to the fact that subjective rather than objective posture measures were used insofar as objective measures of the degree of walkers' body lean obtained from static point-light displays were highly correlated with subjects' ratings and produced similar effects. Using total-body gait information sources, however, other researchers have found that erectness of posture is a strong indicator of emotional state. For example, Weisfeld and Beresford (1982) found that after being handed examination grades, those students who had received the highest grades also walked with the most erect posture (as judged by two blind judges). Thus, before concluding that posture is not an important gait information cue in the communication of emotion, additional research using total-body stimulus displays is clearly needed.

In addition to demonstrating that some emotions are more difficult than others to identify from gait information, the present study indicated that some walkers are better at encoding certain emotions than are others. Differences in the walkers' ability to communicate particular emotions are consistent with encoder differences noted in other nonverbal research (Davitz & Davitz, 1959). Encoder differences may reflect a number of factors. One such factor might be that the situations described to the walkers were more meaningful to some than others. Indeed, one of the walkers whose display of pride was not correctly identified, remarked to the experimenters that "Pretending that I got the highest grade in class will take a lot of imagination." To equate task meaningful across encoders, future research may consider an alternative emotion manipulation technique such as allowing targets to think of a personal situation in which they have experienced a particular emotion. This technique has been used successfully by researchers interested in facial sources of emotion information (Malatesta & Izard, 1984).

While the present study lends strong support to the claim that important social information is revealed in gait, one may question the extent to which this is true when other sources of information are available such as vocal or facial information. Research comparing the relative impact of body, facial, and vocal characteristics on personality and affect judgments has suggested that the importance of a cue depends on the attribute being judged (Ekman, Freisen, O'Sullivan, & Scherer, 1980). Research is not needed to ascertain if these effects hold true when gait and other nonverbal information are simultaneously available as information sources for social judgments.

Another question of interest which arises is whether women and men differ in their abilities to display and identify emotions on the basis of gait. Only female participants were used in the present study because of availability and because research on the impact of gait information on trait impressions has failed to find systematic sex differences in ratings of or by men and women (Montepare, 1985). However, there is some evidence that men and women differ in their sensitivity to emotion messages via nonverbal channels such as the face (see for example, Buck, Miller, & Caul, 1974). Thus, future research may wish to examine more closely possible sex differences in the use of gait information to communicate emotions.

Day-to-day situations often require people to make social judgments on the basis of gait information. For example, identifying people and arriving at judgments about their goals, attitudes, or emotional state when they are viewed at distances or in positions such that their faces are not easily visible or their voices cannot be heard must rely in large part on body movement information such as gait. It is hoped that the present study will encourage greater attention to observers' skill at making social judgments based on gait and a fuller understanding of the nature of the stimulus information which influences these judgments.

Note

[1]A point-light gait display is created by attaching small pieces of reflecting tape to the major limb joints of a walker who is filmed on videotape while walking in front of a dark wall. The display is then played back on a video monitor adjusted such that the brightness is reduced and the contrast is maximized. The resultant display consists of small luminous dots moving across a black background from which only the walker's movement patterns are visible.

References

Barclay, C.D., J.E. Cutting, & L.T. Kozlowski. (1978). Temporal and spatial factors in gait perceptions that influence gender recognition. *Perception and Psychophysics, 23,* 145-152.

Beardsworth T., & T. Buckner. (1981). The ability to recognize oneself from a video recording of one's movements without seeing one's body. *Bulletin of the Psychonomic Society, 18,* 19-22.

Birdwhistell, R.L. (1970). *Kinesics and context.* Philadelphia, P.A.: University of Pennsylvania Press.

Buck, R.W., R.E. Miller, & W.F. Caul. (1974). Sex, personality, and psychological variables in the communication of affect via facial expression. *Journal of Personality and Social Psychology, 30,* 587-596.

Cutting, J.E. (1977). Recognizing friends by their walk: Gait perception without familiarity cues. *Bulletin of the Psychonomic Society, 9,* 353-356.

Davitz, J.R. & L.J. Davitz. (1959). The communication of feelings by content-free speech. *Journal of Communication, 9,* 6-13.

Ekman, P. (1971). Universals and cultural differences in facial expressions of emotion. *Nebraska Symposium on Motivation, 18,* 207-283.

Ekman, P., & V.W. Freisen. (1975). *Unmasking the face.* Englewood Cliffs, N.J.: Prentice-Hall.

Ekman, P., W.V. Freisen, M. O'Sullivan, & K.R. Scherer. (1980). Relative importance of face, body, and speech in judgments of personality and affect. *Journal of Personality and Social Psychology, 38,* 270-277.

Henley, N.M. (1977). *Body politics: Power, sex, and nonverbal communication.* Englewood Cliffs, N.J.: Prentice-Hall.

James, W. (1890). *Principles of psychology.* New York: Henry Holt.

Kozlowski, L.T., & J.E. Cutting. (1977). Recognizing the sex of a walker from dynamic point-light displays. *Perception and Psychophysics, 21,* 575-580.

Malatesta, C.Z., & C.E. Izard. (1984). The facial display of emotion: Young, middle-aged, and older adult expressions. In C.Z. Malatesta and C.E. Izard (Eds.). *Emotion in adult development.* Beverly Hills, C.A.: Sage Publications.

McArthur, L.Z., & R.M. Baron. (1983). Toward an ecological theory of social perception. *Psychological Review, 90,* 215-238.

Montepare, J.M., & L.Z. McArthur. (1986). *Impressions of people created by age-related qualities of their gaits.* Unpublished manuscript.

Montepare, J.M. (1985). *Dynamic sources of age and gender information: Influences of voice and gait.* Unpublished doctoral dissertation: Brandeis University.

Montepare, J.M., L.Z. McArthur, & T. Amgott-Kwan. (1984, April). *Variations in gait as a source of age and gender information.* Paper presented at the 55th meeting of the Eastern Psychological Association, Baltimore, MD.

Walbott, H.C. (1982). Gait, gestures, and body movement. *Journal of Nonverbal Behavior, 7,* 20-32.

Walbott, H.C., & K.R. Scherer. (1896). Cues and channels in emotion recognition. *Journal of Personality and Social Psychology, 51,* 690-699.

Weisfeld, G.E., & J.M. Beresford. (1982). Erectness of posture as an indicator of dominance and success in humans. *Motivation and Emotion, 6,* 113-131.

Wolff, W. (1943). *The expression of personality.* New York: Harper & Row.

9

Daly, Hogg, Sacks, Smith, and Zimring studied self-grooming. They observed preening or self-grooming (fixing hair, straightening clothes, looking at self in mirror) and found that females preen more than men and that people who are just beginning a relationship preen more than those in an established relationship.

Sex and Relationship Affect Social Self-Grooming

John A. Daly, Elizabeth Hogg, David Sacks, Marcy Smith and Lori Zimring

Given the ubiquity of self-grooming or preening in everyday life it is surprising that the activity receives so little attention from behavioral scientists. While a number of ethological studies of grooming among birds and primates exist (Eibl-Eibesfeldt, 1975; Lawick-Goodall, 1968; Sparks, 1967; Yerkes, 1933) only Scheflen (1965) and Given (1978) have directly considered the role of preening in human social activities. Among humans, preening may serve a number of functions including boosting self-esteem, relieving boredom, reducing physical discomfort, and managing positive impressions in the presence of others. This investigation examined some correlates of preening as an impression management activity: a pattern of behaviors oriented towards improving one's physical appearance in social environments. More specifically, two potential mediators of the amount of social preening a person engages in were investigated. The first was the person's sex; the second, who he or she was with in the social setting where observations took place.

The first variable considered in this study was the sex of the person. Women were expected to engage in more preening than men. In many cultures standards for feminine beauty receive more explicit recognition than those for males (Ford & Beach, 1951). Empirical evidence suggests that females emphasize appearance more than males. Adolescent women are more concerned about positive social impressions, one of which may be appearance, than their male counterparts (Rosenberg & Simmons, 1975) and both males and females consider attractiveness more central for

Adapted with permission from: Daly, J.A., E. Hogg, D. Sacks, M. Smith, & L. Zimring. (1983). Sex and relationship affect social self-grooming. *Journal of nonverbal behavior, 7*, 183-189.

females than for males (Williams & Bennett, 1975). This greater emphasis by females on attractiveness may be a function, in part, of the importance it plays in judgments made of them by others. Bar-Tal and Sax (1976) found that appearance serves as a more important cue in evaluations of females than of males. Among college students Stroebe, Insko, Thompson and Layton (1971) demonstrated that physical attractiveness was a more important determinant of opposite-sex attraction for males than for females. Further, while females are comparatively unconcerned with the attractiveness of men, males perceive their roles as being attracted to females' physical appearance (Lerner, Karabenick & Stuart, 1973) and often consider it more important in dating choices than do females (Bersheid & Walster, 1974).

The sort of relationship between a person and those he or she is with in a social environment was the second mediating variable in this study. The amount of preening was expected to vary as a function of the permanence of the association between the people. As relationships progress from the first meeting to stable, permanent, and enduring associations physical appearance may become less important (Schlenker, 1980). Physical appearance seems to play its most crucial role in initial impression formation; familiarity lessens its impact (Bersheid & Walster, 1974). Consequently, physical appearance has a greater effect on dating choices than on marrying ones with college students (Stroebe, Insko, Thompson & Layton, 1971). Insofar as physical attractiveness is especially important in initial encounters more preening was expected among people who were involved in relatively new relationships than among those in extended relationships.

The purpose of this study was to explore preening as an impression management technique used by people in a social setting. Two variables were hypothesized to affect the amount of preening that occurs. The first was the sex of the person. Females were hypothesized to preen more than males. The second was the nature of the relationship between the person and those he or she is with. The more established the relationship the less preening was expected.

Method

Subjects

Seventy-seven individuals (32 males and 43 females), all in their early to mid-twenties, served as subjects in this study. Subjects were randomly selected from an estimated 500 potential participants available during the observational phase of this investigation.

Procedures

Data collection took place in two stages. The first was the observation of preening behaviors. Preening by subjects (defined as hair grooming, clothes straightening, and gazing at self in mirror) was unobtrusively observed and timed in the restrooms of five restaurants and bars located within the university community.[1] Four different observers were used to time preening activities during various observation sessions. However, only one observer timed the preening of any individual subject. Prior to data collection, high reliability among the four observers had been established in terms of identifying and timing preening actions. The observers worked together in identifying preening behaviors and then practice-coded examples until high reliability (percent agreement > 90 percent) was established. Reliable timing of preening was obtained in the same fashion with a similar level of reliability established during practice sessions. The procedures used in any of the settings by any observer were identical. The observer, positioned in the restroom so that he or she could observe preening behavior but at the same time not be overly noticeable, timed each subject's preening. Observers were trained to avoid standing unusually close to subjects, preening themselves while observing subjects, or engaging in behaviors that would attract undue attention from subjects. These cautions were designed to reduce possible confounding among distraction, facilitation, or modeling.

The second phase was the interview phase. As a subject left the bathroom the observer followed and identified the subject to a person who served as an interviewer. After identifying the subject to the interviewer the observer recorded the subject's sex and amount of preening. The interviewer, unaware of how much preening the subject had done, approached him or her and asked if he or she would mind answering three questions for a class survey. No subject refused. The interviewer proceeded to ask (1) how long the subject had been in the establishment, (2) the nature of the relationship between the subject and the person(s) sitting with him or her, and (3) how long the subject had known the other person(s) with him or her.[2] Responses to the second question were coded into four categories: (1) long-term, stable relationships which included married couples and long-term same sex friends who had no intentions of meeting new people that evening, (2) couples who were dating and who had dated for more than four dates, (3) couples who were in the early stages of the relationship: the date was one of their first four with each other, and (4) individuals and groups who were specifically in the establishment trying to meet new people. After the subject answered the questions the interviewer explained the investigation and asked subject about his or her awareness and reactions to it.

No subject reported being aware of the observations that had occurred or experiencing any adverse reactions to the project.

Results

Statistical tests indicated that:

1. Females preen for longer periods of time than males.
2. People who are married or close friends preen less than other groups.
3. Couples on their first, second, third, or fourth date preen more than those who have been dating longer.
4. The longer people knew one another, the less time they spend preening.

Discussion

This study is one of the very few investigations to explore self-grooming among humans. It provides an empirical demonstration of human social preening and some of its mediators. The results of the investigation are consistent with an impression management interpretation of social preening. Females, for whom physical appearance may be a more important impression management strategy than it is for males, preened significantly more than males. Further, impression management via preening was hypothesized to be more critical in early stages of relationships than in later ones. The data supported this expectation in two ways. First, there was a significant and inverse correlation between the length of a relationship and the time its member(s) spent preening. Second, a significant main effect for relationship type was found in an analysis of variance of preening as a function of relationship. The pattern of means supported the hypothesis: members of more established relationships preened less than early relationship members. In short, women preened more than men and the more extensive the relationship, the less preening its members engaged in.

Aside from the impression management function it would be interesting to examine other potential functions of preening among humans and their mediators. Further, it would be interesting to examine the presentation strategies that people choose to use as relationships develop. In this study physical appearance via preening was found to be differentially important as a function of sex and relationship. Simply because appearance may become less salient as a relationship develops doesn't imply that impression management becomes less important.

Rather, other strategies gain salience. Research to date has mostly focused on the strategies used in initial encounters. It seems important to identify how strategies people select as central to a positive impression change across the life of relationships.

Notes

[1]Concern might arise about the potential privacy invasion involved in this study. A number of procedures were completed in an attempt to minimize any actual or perceived invasion of privacy. First, a number of undergraduates were polled in a classroom setting about how they would feel if such an activity were to take place and they were to be observed. Not one of over 150 indicated it would be a source of concern. Second, managers of each establishment where observations were completed were asked about the potential reactions of patrons. None indicated any particular concern. Third, when the interviewer explained the project to participants none evidenced any concern. A few, in fact, responded in quite positive ways saying, for example, how "neat" and interesting the project was and they wished they had class projects like this one. Finally, each subject was told that if he or she had any objections to the study his or her data would be excluded.

[2]Both observer and interviewer attempted to estimate how sober each subject was. While reliable (r=.76) in their estimates, soberness ratings were not significantly related to any of the other variables.

References

Bar-Tal, D., & L. Saxe. Physical attractiveness and its relationship to sex role stereotyping. *Sex Roles*, 1976, *2*, 123-133.

Berscheid, E., & E. Walster. Physical attractiveness. In L. Berkowitz (ed.), *Advances in Experimental Social Psychology*, Vol. 7, New York: Academic Press, 1974, 158-216.

Eibl-Eibesfeldt, I. *Ethology: The biology of behavior.* New York: Holt, Rinehart & Winston, 1975.

Ford, C.S., & F.A. Beach. *Patterns of sexual behavior.* New York: Harper, 1951.

Given, D.B. The nonverbal basis of attraction: Flirtation, courtship, and seduction. *Psychiatry*, 1978, *41*, 346-359.

Kirk, R.E. *Experimental design: Procedures for the behavioral sciences.* Monterey, California: Brooks/Cole, 1968.

Lawick-Goodall, J. van. The behavior of free living chimpanzees in the Gombe Stream Reserve. *Animal Behavior Monographs*, 1968, *1*, 161-311.

Lerner, D., J.A. Karabenich, & J.L. Stuart. Relations among physical attractiveness, body attitudes, and self-concept in male and female college students, *Journal of Psychology*, 1973, *85*, 119-121.

Rosenberg, F.R. & R.G. Simmons. Sex differences in the self-concept of adolescence. *Sex Roles*, 1975, *1*, 147-160.

Scheflin, A.E. Quasi-courtship behavior in psychotherapy. *Psychiatry*, 1965, *28*, 245-251.

Schlenker, B.R. *Impression Management.* Monterey, CA, Brooks Cole, 1980.

Sparks, J. *Allogrooming in primates: A review.* In D. Morris (ed.) Primate Ethology. Chicago: Aldine, 1967.

Stroebe, W., C.A. Insho, V.D. Thompson, & B.D. Layton. Effects of physical attractiveness, attitude similarity, and sex on various aspects of interpersonal attraction. *JPSP,* 1971, *18,* 79-91.

Williams, J.E., & S.M. Bennet. The definition of sex stereotypes via the Adjective Check List. *Sex Roles,* 1975, *1,* 327-337.

Yerkes, R.M. Genetic aspects of grooming, a socially important behavior pattern. *Journal of Social Psychology,* 1933, *4,* 4-25.

10 *We have different expectations for the nonverbal communication of men and women. Rubinstein demonstrates many of these differences in sitting and standing postures, and explains how failing to conform to the stereotypes can affect impressions.*

Body Politics

Gwen Rubinstein

Professor Janet Mills has transformed the great urban pastime — and her great love — of people watching into a career. Primarily, she has observed, men speak a body language that is high in status, power, and dominance, while women speak a language of submission, affiliation, and passivity. These differences often create chaos in the workplace.

By realizing their differences and striving more toward blending the best of masculine and feminine traits, however, men and women can improve their organizations and themselves, Mills has contended in presentations to countless civic, professional, and business groups, including the Ohio Hospital Association, Columbus, Altrusa International, Chicago, and the Chamber of Commerce of the United States, Washington, D.C. On leave from her position as a professor of human relations at the University of Oklahoma, Norman, Mills has been a visiting professor of management at Northern Arizona University, Flagstaff, since last August.

Men and women learn their body languages unconsciously as they grow up, she says. So by the time they reach adulthood, they send and receive their signals relatively unconsciously. Only when someone breaks the unspoken rules do the differences — and the discord — rise to the surface of relationships.

Managerial and professional women face a particularly difficult struggle in their everyday communication, according to Mills. Expected to be feminine as women and powerful as managers, women simultaneously play two roles with different sets of often-contradictory rules.

Managerial and professional men are not exempt from the confusion, Mills adds. Expected to be the dominant and powerful protectors of women, many find themselves reporting to women executives and competing with women peers—the very women they were raised to protect.

Because one picture is supposed to be worth 1,000 words, *Association Management* offers this photographic essay for your education—and amusement. *Warning: By seeing traditional sex roles reversed in these poses, differences between men's and women's nonverbal behavior may become shockingly apparent.*

Women learn to sit with legs together, crossed at the ankles or knees, toes pointed in the same direction, feet tucked under the chair, as Mills demonstrates. Women also hold their arms close to their bodies, their hands together in their lap.

What's wrong with this picture? Volunteer model William D. Coughlan, CAE, executive vice president of the American Physical Therapy Association, Alexandria, Virginia, offers a man's interpretation of how a woman sits.

In what Mills calls the "power spread," men sit with their legs in the "broken four"—at a 5- to 15-degree angle and crossed ankle to knee—with their hands behind their head and their elbows away from the body.

How would you feel sitting across from this woman at a conference table, over lunch, or in your office? Notice that Mills leans back into the chair in her interpretation of this classic male pose.

In a typical office scene, ASAE Foundation Manager Eric Johnson portrays the dominant man—feet shoulder-width apart, hands in pockets, weight shifting side to side or back and forth, indirect gaze straight ahead.

Right: In reverse, it's easy to notice how a man posing as a woman balances his weight on one hip, lowers his shoulders, and stands in a "bashful knee bend," with his hands "placed gingerly together."

Bottom: In a typical scene from a convention general session: Between two men, a woman sits at attention, looking straight ahead, constricting her body, and yielding her space to those around her.

In a mirror pose, Mills spreads out and intrudes on the space the two men have yielded to her. Notice the men have leaned their bodies tensely to the side; she is relaxed, "laid back," and comfortable.

In an ordinary conversation with men or other women, whether in the workplace or somewhere else, women smile, open their eyes wide, arch their brows, lift and lower their heads, and nod more often than men.

Acting out a man's role in a one-on-one conversation, Mills sits back in her chair, sets her shoulders square, stares directly ahead, keeps her head erect, and gestures forcefully.

To pick something up from the floor "femininely," women keep their knees together, their back straight, their arms close to their body, and approach the object from the side.

To pick an object up from the floor "masculinely," men generally squat, keep their back flexible, extend their arms from their body, and approach the object from the front.

11

Nonverbal communication is one of the key factors in successful job interviews. Gifford, Ng, and Wilkinson studied interviews and found that applicants who dressed more formally, gestured more, and talked more were perceived to be more skilled by the interviewer.

Nonverbal Cues in the Employment Interview
Links Between Applicant Qualities and Interviewer Judgments

Robert Gifford, Cheuk Fan Ng and Margaret Wilkinson

Not much empirical evidence supports the validity of the employment interview as a means of personnel selection (Ulrich & Trumbo, 1965). However, as the interview is considered by most employers to be an important part of the hiring process, investigators have examined various components of the interview process to discover what distinguishes an unsuccessful interview from a successful interview. The applicant's nonverbal behaviors are often assumed by interviewers to provide useful information that is not likely to be expressed verbally (Schlenker, 1980).

Recent research has demonstrated the importance of nonverbal behaviors in the interview situation (Edinger & Patterson, 1983). Unfortunately, most previous research focuses on only half the role of nonverbal behaviors—connections between the job applicant's behavior and the interviewer's attributions. The present study investigates the full role of nonverbal behaviors in job interviews, that is, the connections between the applicant's job-related qualities and nonverbal behaviors, as well as connections between nonverbal behaviors and interviewer judgments.

Gifford, R., C. Fan Ng, & M. Wilkinson. (1985). Nonverbal cues in the employment interview: Links between applicant qualities and interviewer judgments. *Journal of applied psychology,* 70, 729-736. Copyright © 1985 by the American Psychological Asociation. Adapted by permission.

Interviewer Judgments

Several studies have examined the effects of the applicant's nonverbal behaviors on the interviewer's impression and hiring decision. The pattern of results suggests that increased eye contact, smiling, gestures, and head nods by an applicant produce favorable outcomes (Edinger & Patterson, 1983). For example, in McGovern's (1976) study, only applicants who displayed such nonverbal behaviors as above-average amount of eye contact, high energy level, speech fluency, and voice modulation were evaluated as worth seeing for a second interview. In Amalfitano and Kalt's (1977) study, applicants who engaged in more eye contact were judged more alert, assertive, dependable, confident, responsible, and as having more initiative. Applicants rated highly on these attributes were also evaluated most likely to be hired. Young and Beier (1977) and Forbes and Jackson (1980) also showed that applicants were most favorably rated when they engaged in more eye contact, smiling, and head movement.

A modified Brunswik lens model (Brunswik, 1956) was used to assess the correspondence between judges' decoding of applicant nonverbal behaviors and applicants' encoding of self-appraised attributes (see Figure 1). This model has three components: applicant qualities, nonverbal cues, and interviewer perceptions of applicant qualities.. The left half of the lens represents the relation between nonverbal cues and the applicant's qualities ("ecological validity"), and the right half represents the relation between nonverbal cues and the interviewer's attributions (cue utilization). Achievement refers to the relationship between applicant qualities and interviewer attributions. Correlation coefficients are used to measure the relationships. We place the term *ecological validity* in quotes because applicant qualities are self-assessed. Obviously, an applicant's *actual* qualities are difficult or impossible to measure. In this study, we assume that the applicant's self-assessments are reasonably valid measures of their actual attributes. We use the term *ecological validity* in this article to refer to the relation between an applicant's self-assessed qualities and their nonverbal cues recognizing that, ideally, the applicant's actual qualities should be measured.

The purpose of the present study is to understand the full role of nonverbal behaviors in actual job interviews, using this modified Brunswik lens model to examine the ecological validity, cue utilization, and achievement of attributions made about job-related qualities of job applicants. We believe the lens model can provide a useful basis from which interviewers could make more accurate assessments of job applicants.

Method

Subjects

Thirty-eight applicants (7 male and 31 female) responded to an advertisement in the local newspaper for a temporary, part-time position as research assistant in the Psychology Department of a medium-sized Canadian university. Their ages ranged from 18 to 67, and their background in education and work experience varied considerably. Four of the 38 applicants arrived for the interview but were excluded from the study due to technical problems with the videotape ($n=2$), pre-existing friendship with the interviewer ($n=1$), or refusal to be viodetaped ($n=1$).

The interviews were actually used for selection. One applicant was hired for the job. Eighteen judges (13 male and 5 female), each with training and several years' experience in interviewing, watched all the videotaped interviews and evaluated the applicants.

Measures

Social skill and motivation to work. The two applicant qualities selected for study were motivation and social skill. They were chosen because (a) they have often been shown to be major criteria by which applicants are judged by employers (Landy & Trumbo, 1980, p. 212) and (b) they were required for the research assistant position.

Questionnaires were constructed to measure work motivation and social skill. On the work motivation questionnaire, applicants indicated how willing they were to accept each of 10 nonstandard work situations. For example, two items queried how willing the applicant was to work at unusual hours or to accept a lower-than-average wage. Responses, on 5-point scales, ranged from *this is unacceptable to me* to *fine—no problem*. On the social skill questionnaire, applicants reported (a) how they had actually handled and (b) how they felt about handling each of 12 difficult social situations at work. For example, two items asked applicants whether they had apologized without embarrassment when they were wrong or initiated contact with a stranger who was important to their work. Responses, on a 5-point scale, ranged from *always* to *never*. Parallel items asked how they would feel about handling such a situation. Responses, on a 5-point scale, ranged from *no discomfort at all* to *very uncomfortable*.

Nonverbal cues. Seven nonverbal cues were chosen, based on previous studies (Edinger & Patterson, 1983). Dynamic behaviors included time spent talking, facial regard, smiling, gesturing, trunk recline, self-manipulation, and object-manipulation. Static cues included age, sex, formality of dress, and physical attractiveness.

An event recorder was used to measure the dynamic cues. Time talked was scored as the total number of minutes the applicant spent responding to the interviewer's questions. Gesturing, self-manipulation, object-manipulation, and facial regard (looking toward the interviewer's face) were measured as the proportion of the interview spent in these activities. Smiles were measured as the weighted average of time spent in each of five categories of facial pleasantness (from full smile to negative expression). Recline was measured as the weighted average of time spent in each of four positions (from a slight back lean to a very forward lean). Formality of dress was coded on a 3-point scale (informal to formal). Physical attractiveness was coded on a 7-point scale (from *very ugly* to *suitable for a fashion magazine cover*).

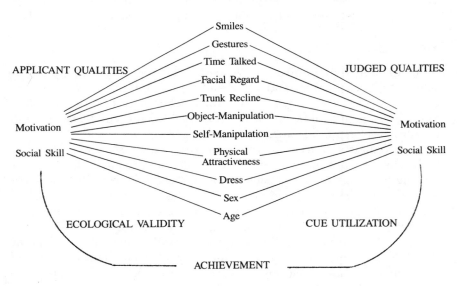

Figure 1. A modified Brunswik lens model. The inference of job applicant qualities through nonverbal cues.

Procedure

Appointments were made with job applicants when they telephoned in response to an advertisement in the local newspaper. Upon arrival at the interview, held in the laboratory office, the interviewer, a female laboratory employee, asked applicants for permission to videotape their interviews so the employer could view them later because he could not be present at all the interviews. The interviewer asked a standard set of 10 typical interview questions, offered brief acknowledgments to responses, and attempted in all interviews to maintain a consistent pattern of nonverbal behavior.

The camera was placed in a smoked-glass cabinet just behind and over the shoulder of the interviewer so that viewers of the videotape saw the applicant very much as the interviewer did. After the interview, applicants asked any questions they wished to about the job and completed the motivation and social skill questionnaires. Finally, applicants were told that the job interview was part of a study as well as a real interview and asked for the experimental use of the visual channel of their interviews.

The second phase of the study involved the scoring of applicants' nonverbal behaviors. Two scorers were trained; they measured the nonverbal behaviors from the videotapes.

In the third phase of the study, one or two judges at a time viewed the interviews on tapes in five approximately 45-min. sessions. To counteract order effects, five different orders of interviews were presented to the judges. They reviewed blank social skill and motivation-to-work questionnaires identical to those completed by the job applicants, then watched the videotaped interviews (which ranged from 2.5 min. to 23 min. in length) with the sound turned off. Then the judges rated the applicants on motivation and social skill on 1-to-10 scales. On the motivation scale, high ratings indicated that the judges believed the applicant would have responded *fine — no problem* to most or all of the 12 nonstandard conditions. On the social skill scale, high ratings indicated that the judge believed the applicant would have responded *always* and *no discomfort at all* to most or all of the 10 difficult social situations. Judges also rated the applicants' hireability, on a 1-to-10 scale, on which higher ratings indicated greater likelihood that the judge would hire the applicant.

Results

Statistical analyses indicated that:

1. Applicant answers were each about 6 minutes long. They gazed at the interviewer 41% of the time, and gestured 7% of the time.
2. Applicants who said they were more highly motivated leaned back more and dressed more formally. Males said they were more motivated than females.

3. Applicants are perceived by interviewers to be more motivated if they smile more, gesture more, and talk more. These cues differ from those associated with applicant's self-reported motivation.

4. Applicants who gave themselves high social skill ratings gestured more, talked more, and dressed more formally. Older people rated their skills more highly than younger people.

5. Applicants are perceived by interviewers to be more socially skilled if they dress more formally, gesture more, and talk more. These cues are the same as those associated with applicant's self-rated skill.

6. Interviewers are better at perceiving applicant social skill than applicant motivation. Both skill and motivation are highly related to "hireability."

Discussion

The value of the lens model in elucidating the full role of nonverbal behaviors in the job interview process is clear. Social skill, desirable for most job positions, is shown in this study to have been reasonably accurately inferred by interviewers through these applicant nonverbal cues in the interview: rate of gesturing, time spent talking, and formality of dress. Applicant motivation, however, was poorly inferred or, more precisely, was mis-inferred by judges.

One probable explanation for this pattern of results is that social skill is encoded more clearly in nonverbal behavior than is motivation. As Harriot (1971) suggested, the job interview itself is a social interaction in which both the applicant and the interviewer are expected to follow their role behaviors. Applicants who have acquired appropriate role behaviors through past experience apparently demonstrate their social skill through nonverbal behaviors and the way they dress for the interview. Interviewers seem to pick up these same cues because they are the expected role behaviors of applicants.

However, it may be more difficult for applicant motivation to be inferred accurately from nonverbal behaviors. Other information, such as the applicant's preparation for the interview or the applicant's verbal statements, may be more accurate indicators of applicants' motivation for a job position. Whether applicants arrive early for their interviews, their verbal responses to the questions or, perhaps, the questions they ask at the interview might be better indicators of their degree of motivation than is nonverbal behavior.

Perhaps when judges are restricted to nonverbal cues, their inability to perceive valid indicators of applicant motivation leads them to rely on their judgment of social skill as an indicator of motivation. The pattern of results indicating that social skills are more accurately inferred and that judges' estimates of motivation are closely tied to their estimates of social skills support this notion. If so, this reliance is unfortunate, because applicant social skill is only slightly related to applicant motivation.

Findings based on the lens model might be used to foster a better relationship between ecological validity and cue utilization. Greater accuracy (or, in lens model terminology, achievement) in the employment interview inference process might be obtained with an improved match between ecological validity and cue utilization and selection of the appropriate nonverbal cue predictors (Hammond, et al., 1964). It would be useful to examine the inference process for other job-related qualities.

Our own research is now also directed toward investigating the role of verbal behaviors in the inference of applicants' qualities. As mentioned earlier, 40% to 50% of the variance is unaccounted for by the nonverbal cues examined in this study. Obviously, verbal behavior also plays an important role in job interviewing.

Social Implications

The results of this study could have practical implications for job interview training. More lens model-based research is necessary before firm conclusions may be drawn, but eventually applicants might be taught to exhibit particular nonverbal behaviors that reflect job-related qualities valued by interviewers in the attribution process. Interviewers, on the other hand, might focus on nonverbal cues that truly reflect applicants' job-related qualities. A more immediate goal is to attain a better match between cues used by interviewers in their attributions and those representative of applicants' actual attributes. In any case, more attention to the full role of nonverbal behavior is warranted. The lens model seems an appropriate and promising tool for this purpose.

References

Amalfitano, J.G., & N.C. Kalt. (1977). Effects of eye contact on the evaluation of job applicants. *Journal of Employment Counseling, 14,* 46-48.

Brunswik, E. (1956). *Perception and the representative design of psychological experiments.* Berkeley: University of California Press.

Edinger, J.A., & M.L. Patterson. (1983). Nonverbal involvement and social control. *Psychological Bulletin, 93,* 30-56.

Forbes, R.J., & P.R. Jackson. (1980). Nonverbal behavior and the outcome of selection interviews. *Journal of Occupational Psychology, 53,* 65-72.

Hammond, K.R., C.J. Hursch, & F.J. Todd. (1964). Analyzing the components of clinical inference. *Psychological Review, 71,* 438-456.

Harriot, P. (1981). Towards an attributional theory of the selection interview. *Journal of Occupational Psychology, 54,* 165-173.

Hollandsworth, J.G., Jr., R. Kazelskis, J. Stevens, & M.E. Dressel. (1979). Relative contributions of verbal, articulative, and nonverbal communication to employment decisions in the job interview setting. *Personnel Psychology, 32,* 359-367.

Hursch, C.J., K.R. Hammond, & J.L. Hursch. (1964). Some methodological considerations in multiple-cue probability studies. *Psychological Review, 71,* 42-60.

Imada, A.S., & M.D. Hakel. (1977). Influence of nonverbal communication and rater proximity on impressions and decisions in simulated employment interviews. *Journal of Applied Psychology, 62,* 295-300.

Keenan, A. (1976). Effects of the nonverbal behavior of interviewers on candidates' performance. *Journal of Occupational Psychology, 49,* 171-176.

Keenan, A., & A.A.I. Wedderburn. (1975). Effects of the non-verbal behavior of interviewers on candidates' impressions. *Journal of Occupational Psychology, 48,* 129-132.

Landy, F.J., & D.A. Trumbo. (1980). *Psychology of work behavior* (Rev. ed.). Homewood, IL: The Dorsey Press.

McGovern, T.V. (1976). The making of a job interviewee: the effect of nonverbal behavior on an interviewer's evaluations during a selection interview. *Dissertation Abstracts International,* 4740B.

Schlenker, B.R. (1980). *Impression management.* Monterey, CA: Brooks/Cole.

Ulrich, L., & D. Trumbo. (1965). The selection interview since 1949. *Psychological Bulletin, 63,* 100-116.

Washburn, P.V., & M.D. Hakel. (1973). Visual cues and verbal content as influences on impressions formed after simulated employment interviews. *Journal of Applied Psychology, 58,* 137-141.

Wexley, K.N., S.S. Fugita, & M.P. Malone. (1975). An applicant's nonverbal behavior and student-evaluators' judgments in a structured interview setting. *Psychological Reports, 36,* 391-394.

Young, D.M., & E.G. Beier. (1977). The role of applicant nonverbal communication in the employment interview. *Journal of Employment Counseling, 14,* 154-165.

12

It is important to establish rapport when communicating. Research suggests this is particularly important when doctors communicate with their patients. In this chapter Harrigan, Oxman, and Rosenthal identify the nonverbal cues that patients interpret as empathic.

Rapport Expressed Through Nonverbal Behavior

Jinni Harrigan, Thomas Oxman and Robert Rosenthal

Harrigan, Oxman, and Rosenthal studied how doctors establish relationships with their patients. Previous research demonstrates the importance of communication skills. Effective doctor-patient communication generally leads to better treatment. One of the key elements is the doctor's ability to express *empathy* or concern for the patient. In this study, the authors identified the nonverbal behaviors which communicate empathy or *rapport* to a patient.

Nine physicians participated in the study. These physicians were first-year residents beginning their clinical training in Family Medicine at the University of Cincinnati. Each was videotaped twice; once interacting with a new patient and once interacting with a returning patient. The study focused on the interview phase of the visit, not the physical examination which followed. Coders viewed the tapes and used the category system in Table 1 to analyze the interactions.

Adapted with permission from: Harrigan, J., T. Oxman, & R. Rosenthal. (1985). Rapport expressed through nonverbal behavior. *Journal of nonverbal behavior, 9,* 95-110.

Table 1

Nonverbal Behavior Categories and Acts

Category	Type	Measurement
Proximity	Distance	— overall mean distance between doctor and patient, and frequency of shifts
	Orientation	— % of time doctor faces toward or away from patient; 0°, 45°, and 90° orientations coded — overall means and frequencies of shifts
Body Posture	Trunk Angle	— % of time in forward, upright, and backward positions — overall means and frequencies of shifts
	Arm Position	— % of time in open and crossed (hands together) symmetrical, and asymmetrical arm positions
	Leg Position	— % of time legs were crossed (knee over knee or ankle over knee)
Gaze Orientation	Mutual Gaze	— % of time eye contact with patient
	Gaze at Patient	— % of time doctor looks at patient when patient is not looking at doctor
	Gaze at Chart	— % of time doctor looks at chart
	Gaze at Other Objects	— % of time doctor looks at other objects
Hand Movements	Gestures	— % of time doctor gestured with hand
	Self-Adaptors	— % of time doctor's hand came in contact with own body for purposes of rubbing, scratching, picking, or grooming activities
	Object-Adaptors	— % of time doctor was involved in non-goal oriented manipulation of objects such as paper clips, pens, etc.
	Chart Actions	— % of time doctor was engaged in reading or writing in the chart
Head & Face Movements	Head Nodding	— % of time doctor nodded head
	Head Shaking	— % of time doctor shook head
	Head Cocking	— % of time doctor tilted head to side
	Positional Head Movements	— % of time doctor repositioned head which was not considered as a head action listed above or which did not involve change in gaze direction
	Smiling	— % of time doctor smiled

The categories listed in Table 1 were identified from previous research. The two *proxemic* or spatial categories were distance and orientation. Coders estimated the distance between the doctor and the patient during the interview and counted the number of times this distance changed. They also assessed how directly the doctor faced the patient (orientation).

Three *body posture* categories were identified: trunk angle, arm position, and leg position. Trunk angle refers to body lean; whether the doctor leaned forward or backward or sat upright. Arm and leg position concerned openness or closedness. A position is open if the arms or legs are *not* crossed, and closed if they are crossed (for example, one leg crossed over the other). Researchers also coded arm and leg symmetry or asymmetry. Arms are said to be symmetrical when both are in the same position (for example, both resting on the table) or asymmetrical when they are in different position (for example, one arm on the table, the other in the lap). Similarly leg positions can be symmetrical or asymmetrical.

Gaze orientation measures the direction of the doctor's eyes. Mutual gaze when the doctor and patient look into each other's eyes. The doctor's gaze at the patient, chart, and other objects was also recorded.

The researchers were also concerned with *hand movements*, including gestures, self-adaptors, object adaptors, and chart actions. The researchers recorded the number of times the doctors gestured with hands, rubbed, scratched, picked or groomed their own body (self adaptor), handled objects in the room (object adaptor), or used the chart. Adaptors are behaviors that are learned for one purpose and then "adapted" or used for other purposes. Because they are used unconsciously, adaptors often communicate a great deal.

The final category was *head and face movements* and included nodding, shaking, and cocking (tilting sideways) the head, smiling, and positional head movements (any head movement not described above.

The videotapes were then shown to 10 nurses who rated them on 18 scales listed in Table 2. These scales measured the amount of rapport established in the interview. For example, on the first scale the nurse would rate how close or distant the doctor and patient were.

Table 2

Rapport Variables

1. distant—close	10. closed—open
2. negative—positive	11. not attentive—attentive
3. tenacious—yielding	12. submissive—dominant
4. severe—lenient	13. cold—hot
5. not interested—interested	14. passive—active
6. excited—calm	15. tense—relaxed
7. not friendly—friendly	16. unpleasant—pleasant
8. rejecting—accepting	17. weak—strong
9. bad—good	18. not empathic—empathic

Statistical analyses indicated that:

1. Doctors were consistent in their nonverbal behavior. They behaved the same way with different patients and at different times.
2. Doctors who establish rapport sit slightly closer to their patients and lean forward or move closer during the interview. Low rapport doctors tend to sit in a more erect posture or lean backward.
3. Doctors establish more rapport when they face their patients more directly (body orientation is more direct).
4. Doctors establish greater rapport when they sit with their arms and legs uncrossed (open posture), and with both arms in the same position (symmetrical). Low rapport doctors often sit with their legs and arms crossed (closed posture) and with one arm resting on a table (asymmetrical).
5. Doctors who achieve more rapport have less mutual gaze with their patients (looking at each other's eyes) than low rapport doctors. Instead, high rapport doctors look at the patient's chart and around the room more frequently.

The authors concluded that they had successfully identified a pattern of behaviors which communicate rapport or empathy. These deal primarily with body positions (orientation, arm and leg position) rather than nonverbal actions (smiles, gestures, head nods). Further, behaviors which convey dominance or status such as sideways or backward lean, asymmetrical arm and leg positions, hand relaxation, and less direct orientation detracted from rapport. Finally, while doctors who achieved more rapport had less mutual gaze with patients (looking at each other's eyes), they used more varied gaze behaviors. This minimized dominance aspects (staring) and made the doctors appear to be conscientious.

Key Terms and Concepts

Cash, Cash, and Butters, *"Mirror, Mirror, on the Wall...?"*

attractiveness
contrast effect
social comparison theory

objective and subjective physical
attractiveness
"what is beautiful is good" stereotype

Wells and Siegel, *Stereotyped Somatotypes*

somatotypes   endomorph   ectomorph   mesomorph

Montepare, Goldstein, and Clausen, *The Identification of Emotions from Gait Information*

gait   gender information   emotion detection

Daly, Hogg, Sacks, Smith, and Zimring, *Sex and Relationship Affect Social Self-Grooming*

self-grooming/preening
impression management
presentation strategies

Rubinstein, *Body Politics*

traditional sex roles   power spread   bashful knee bend

Gifford, Ng, and Wilkinson, *Nonverbal Cues in the Employment Interview*

validity of employment interview
favorable nonverbal behaviors
Brunswik lens model

inferences about motivation
and social skill
hireability

Harrigan, Oxman, and Rosenthal, *Rapport Expressed Through Nonverbal Behavior*

rapport
empathy
nonverbal behavior categories
open positions

body orientation
symmetry
mutual gaze
body lean
immediacy

relaxation
gender
dominance
status

Part Three

Facial and Eye Communication

Your face and eyes provide the most visible nonverbal messages. During conversations we spend a great deal of time looking at the other person's face, particularly while we are listening to that person speak. Looking at their face helps clarify what they mean in their words. This is called *metacommunication*—messages about messages. Facial expressions and eye movements tell us how to interpret verbal messages.

We look at the other person less often while talking than listening. These messages, however, are no less meaningful. We look at the listener for signs of interest, to know if we should go on talking or stop, and to see if further explanation is needed.

Facial and eye communication fulfills many *functions*, including *emotional expression* and *coordinating conversations*. Our faces and eyes are the primary means for expressing emotions and researchers have identified typical patterns of expression. Probably the clearest example is the smile which expresses happiness, the easiest emotion to recognize for most people. Other emotions like anger are not clear unless communicated by all parts of the face.

We also use our face and eyes to coordinate conversations. Think about what happens when you see someone with whom you want to talk. One of the most obvious cues is *mutual eye contact*—you catch each other's eyes. Conversely, eye contact decreases when the conversation is about to end. If we don't want to talk to someone we also signal this with eye contact. Two people can be in the same room (for example a medical doctor's office), be aware of each other, and agree not to focus their attention on each other. This is called *civil inattention*.

We also use facial and eye communication to coordinate *speaking turns* — to tell each other when we are stopping and starting our turn at speaking. A person who is nearing the end of a speaking turn and about to become a listener will often look at the other person more than earlier in the speaking turn.

Gender plays an important role in facial and eye communication. Women tend to smile more often than men and, in general, express more positive emotions. As a result it is easier to know when many women are feeling negatively — it is such a contrast to their typical expression. Men, on the other hand, tend to be less expressive.

So it is apparent that facial and eye communication play an important role in our lives. The face is probably the one thing you remember best about a person and it is the nonverbal communication channel we control the most consciously.

13

Women tend to smile more than men, according to Jacqueline Shannon, and this may be a critical mistake. In this article, Shannon discusses how women's tendency to smile most of the time can work against them if it communicates a mixed message, makes them appear less assertive or weak, costs them respect, or is inappropriate. The article provides/suggests ways that women can learn to smile less often.

Don't Smile When You Say That

Jacqueline Shannon

Veterans of strict grammar schools may remember that, in class, seriousness was the order of the day. "Take that smile off your face, or I'll wipe it off!" was the teachers' battle cry in their fight for scholarly sobriety. In the corporate world, it's equally important to know when to keep a straight face. And, as your teachers may have told you, it's *for your own good.*

When you get down to business, smiling can take the punch out of your most powerful statements. Anna, a marketing director, committed this kind of cheery hara-kiri at her company's monthly staff-meeting-cum-gripe-session. "How are things going?" the division vice president asked her. "Not too well," she said. "It took me six weeks to get my raise — the one that was supposed to be retroactive to February 1. The bureaucratic nonsense that I had to go through was unbelievable." She recounted the details. Around the table, people murmured, "That's terrible," and similar words of sympathy. Even the vice president shook his head. "This never should have happened," he said.

Then, just as Anna wrapped up her story and began to sit down, she smiled.

"All of a sudden, we didn't know how seriously to take her," says Audrey Nelson-Schneider, Ph.D., who was at the meeting. "We all started wondering just how upset Anna really was."

Reprinted from: Shannon, J. (1987). Don't smile when you say that. *Executive female, 10,* 33, 43.

Nelson-Schneider, a national trainer and communication consultant with her own firm, Nelson and Associates, in Boulder, Colorado, says that inappropriate smiling is the most common example of the way women's nonverbal behavior discounts their verbal messages.

"When we are angry or we are trying to sell something, we want to be taken seriously," she says. "But then we smile. Since communication research like that cited in UCLA professor Albert Mehrabian's book, *Silent Messages*, shows that nonverbal communication is more potent than verbal" — that actions really do speak louder than words — "a smile can be a critical mistake. At the very least, as in Anna's case, the mixed messages can leave the audience very confused."

Why do women do this? Nelson-Schneider says that unlike males, who are taught to mask their feelings, females in our culture learn early that they are expected to be always-happy, always-smiling "pleasers."

"As a result, women will smile at anybody, anywhere, any time, judging by almost a decade of my research on their smiling behavior," says Nelson-Schneider. "According to my surveys and informal experiments, a stranger can elicit a smile from a woman much more readily than from a man. Ninety percent of the time, to be exact."

Nelson-Schneider tags women's knee-jerk-smiling habit "The Howdy Doody Syndrome," and says its danger on the job is that it's viewed by both men and women as nonassertive, low-power behavior. Women instinctively rely on a smile to soften their presentations; they use it to make assertive, "unfeminine" behavior, such as making a demand, more socially acceptable.

"In my communication seminars, I'm always asked, 'Won't my coworkers and business associates find my behavior *unacceptable* if I stop smiling?'" says Nelson-Schneider. "And the answer is yes, some people won't like you, especially those who have a vested interest in your remaining powerless. Unlike your sobersided male colleagues, you'll risk being labeled hard-nosed, pushy, humorless or 'in your time of the month.'"

But the price of playing Howdy Doody is much higher, says Nelson-Schneider. "Sure, you want people at work to like you; that's part of success. The problem is that they might like you so much — and respect you so little — that you'll always be shut out of power position."

The answer is not to swear off smiling at work. "When humor is appropriate, so is a smile. Just be sure your smiles are suited to the occasion or conversation," Nelson-Schneider says. "Smiling is inappropriate just about any time you want to persuade or influence, to make a claim to power. A simple rule of thumb: When you want to be taken seriously, wear an expression to match." (Nelson-Schneider has observed that a serious face enhances the perceived credibility of a speaker's words.)

How can you undo 25, 35, 45 or more years of smile-reflex conditioning? Nelson-Schneider has some suggestions: "Pay attention to what your face does and when it does it. Spend some time studying your expressions in a mirror, perhaps mentallly "replaying" a recent meeting. Better still, act it out on videotape, to become aware of your facial expressions. Many people just aren't aware of how their faces look to others. Some, for example, have no idea that when they think their faces are expressionless, others see a half-smirk, because their features are arranged that way."

When you catch yourself in the Howdy Doody act, try to put on a not-so-happy face. At first, of course, you'll only realize your mistake *after* you've smiled inappropriately. But Nelson-Schneider says that the longer you monitor yourself, the shorter the time lapse between smiling and changing your expression will get. Eventually, you'll be able to recall your smile before it travels from your brain to your lips. Then you can substitute an expression that's serious, angry, aggressive or whatever the situation requires.

Nelson-Schneider also recommends asking a sympathetic colleague to watch your nonverbal behavior during a meeting or presentation. Ask her later, "Did my face ever conflict with my words?"

As you learn to coordinate the two, the change in your behavior will almost certainly be noticed, and may even evoke the question that is never asked of grown men: "Where's your smile today?"

That's the time to remember "not to slip back into the grinning, subservient Howdy Doody role," says Nelson-Schneider. "Instead, try an honest but good-natured reply, such as, 'I'm just thinking about serious things — like how I'm going to finish all this work by Friday.'"

And don't smile when you say that.

This chart summarizes the primary emotions and the facial cues that typically express them. These descriptions are based on the work of Paul Ekman.

14

Primary Affect Displays

Abstracted from the work of Paul Ekman

The table below describes primary affect displays based on the works of Paul Ekman listed at the end of this chapter. Primary affect displays are the ways people express the basic emotions. Researchers identify six primary or basic emotions: sadness, happiness, anger, surprise, disgust, and fear. Ekman's research describes the way people commonly reveal or display each emotion. While he presents the most typical expressions, Ekman has identified over 1,000 variations for each basic emotion using his Facial Affect Scoring Technique (FAST).

Emotion	**Facial Expression**
Sadness	Indicated by raised eyebrows (inner corner) with forehead wrinkles sloping down and out from the center and a downward turn to the corner of the lips or trembling lips.
Happiness	Involves muscles Ekman calls the "lip corner puller," the "dimpler," and the "cheek raiser." Raised cheeks and lip corners (smile) cause folds or dimples to appear in two locations: from the nose to the outer edges of the lips, and out from the eyes (crows-feet). This is the easiest emotion to recognize.
Anger	Expressed by eyebrows that are lowered and drawn together, vertical lines between the brows, a hard stare, tense eyelids, and lips either tightly pressed together or in a slightly open, square-shaped mouth. Nostrils may be dilated. Tight lips may appear before the person is aware of feeling anger and this may "leak" or give away the feeling of anger. Anger is ambiguous unless expressed in all parts of the face.

Surprise   Appears very quickly on the face. Typical signs are raised
               eyebrows, skin below the brow is stretched, horizontal
               wrinkles across the forehead, slightly raised upper
               eyelids, the white of the eye (sclera) shows above the iris
               (and often below), and an open mouth. The jaw is open
               so that the lips and teeth are parted without tension or
               stretching of the mouth. If the upper eyelids are raised
               all the way, the expression will look like fear.

Disgust   Revealed by a wrinkling of the nose, lowering of the brow,
               and raising the upper lip. In extreme disgust the cheeks
               also rise and the mouth curls with the corners of the lips
               pulled back and down. This is one of the easier emotions
               to recognize.

Fear   Expressed by an open mouth with lips tensed and drawn
               back, brows raised and drawn together, wrinkles in the
               center of the forehead (not across the entire forehead),
               upper eyelid is raised showing the white of the eye
               (sclera), and lower eyelid is drawn up and tense.

For further discussion of Ekman's work see:

Ekman, P., W.V. Friesen, & S.S. Tomkins. (1971). Facial affect scoring technique:
     A validity study. *Semiotica, 3.*
Ekman, P. (1980). *The Faces of Man.* Garland STPN Press.
Ekman, P., W. Friesen, and S. Ancoli. (1980). Facial signs of emotional experience.
     Journal of Personality and Social Psychology, 39, 1125-1134.
Goleman, D. (1981). The 7,000 faces of Dr. Ekman. *Psychology Today, 15,* 42-49.

Some people are particularly skilled at getting others to "open up" and talk more freely. They are called skilled conversational openers. Purvis, Dabbs, and Hopper studied this conversational skill and found that certain nonverbal behaviors were used to convey warmth, responsiveness, and interest in order to encourage people to express themselves more openly.

15

The "Opener"
Skilled Use of Facial Expression and Speech Pattern

James A. Purvis, James M. Dabbs, Jr. and Charles H. Hopper

Some people are able to encourage conversation and promote their partner's self-disclosure, while others lack this skill. Those people who can "open up" others in conversation may do so by conveying warmth, responsiveness, and an interest in their partners' utterances. It seems more is involved than simple verbal content. Interested facial expressions and brief responsive utterances should also encourage conversation. The present research asked whether such visual displays and speech patterns would characterize the conversation of persons who are better able to get others to open up and talk.

We studied the conversations of high and low opener subjects, selected by their responses to the Opener Scale of Miller, Berg, and Archer (1983). This self-report inventory measures the ability to get others to talk about themselves and has been shown to identify reliably those individuals skilled in promoting self-disclosure by their partners. Subjects knew that their interactions were being recorded. We examined the conversations

Adapted with permission from: Purvis, J.A., J.M. Dabbs, Jr., & C.H. Hopper. The "Opener": Skilled User of Facial Expression and Speech Pattern. *Personality and Social Psychology Bulletin, 10* (2), pp. 61-66, © 1984. Reprinted by permission of Sage Publications, Inc.

in detail, analyzing the temporal patterning of speech and gaze (see Dabbs, Evans, Hopper, & Purvis, 1980) and the facial expressions of the participants.

We expected high openers, in contrast to low openers, to display more eye contact, more facial expressions of positive affect, and speech patterns indicating more interest in the conversation.

Method

One hundred males and 138 females completed the Opener Scale. Thirty males and 30 females were selected to participate in the study, 10 each from the upper, middle, and lower thirds of each respective sex. The experiment included 30 pairs of subjects, with the partners in each pair similar in sex and opener score, producing 6 groups with 5 pairs in each group.

Upon arriving for the experiment, subjects were introduced to each other and seated on opposite sides of a small table. On the table was a 2 foot X 2 foot (.6m X .6m) wooden box with an opening in the center, through which subjects could see each other (Dabbs, 1979). A videotape camera was mounted inside the box to record the subjects' images. Lapel microphones were used to record the subjects' voices on two audio channels on the videotape. The operation of the box was briefly explained, and the subjects were left alone for 10 minutes to converse. It was suggested that the subjects get to know each other, which they might accomplish by talking about their backgrounds, activities in school, or things outside of school.

Gaze and Speech Patterns

The 30 conversations were later scored for speech and gaze, using the procedure described by Dabbs, et al. (1980). Speech was scored electronically. An electronic device assigned each voice signal to the proper subject and converted the signals into on-off binary codes (Dabbs & Evans, 1982). Gaze was scored by two judges observing a videotape monitor, each judge watching one subject. Judges depressed a button whenever their assigned subject appeared to look directly forward at the judge from the monitor. A subject who looked directly forward would have been looking directly at his or her partner during the original conversation (Dabbs, 1979). The gaze button was depressed by the judge until the subject looked away.

While judges scored gaze, a microcomputer sampled the on-off states of the voice signals and the judges' gaze buttons every 250 msec during the 10-minute conversation. This information was later transferred to a large computer where the basic speech codes were expanded into the codes described by Jaffe and Feldstein (1970). Other investigators have employed different sampling rates. Jaffe and Feldstein (1970) compared the data from their 300 msec studies with the results of Brady's (1968) 5 msec study and found no marked difference in speech code average values per time interval. From their comparison, they concluded that sampling rates between 5 and 300 msec should produce comparable results.

Jaffe and Feldstein divide conversation into alternating "turns," each turn beginning when one subject speaks alone and ending when the partner speaks alone. Turns are made up of "vocalizations" (speech or sound uttered by the subject who has the floor) and "pauses" (silences between these vocalizations). If a turn ends with silence, that silence is called a "switching pause." Vocalizations, pauses, and switching pauses are credited to the turn taker. Sound interjected by one partner while the other is already talking is "simultaneous speech" and is credited to the person who interjected it. Simultaneous speech is usually quite brief (average duration in the present study was 0.05 sec.); either the person interjecting falls silent, or the original speaker falls silent and the other continues, at which point a change of turn occurs. Feldstein and Welkowitz (1978) discuss a distinction between noninterruptive and interruptive simultaneous speech. In our own data, however, this distinction was not followed. Either form of simultaneous speech, interruptive or noninterruptive, represents responsive behavior on the part of the person who does not have the turn, and we chose to combine the codes in our own analyses.

In the present study, the conversation of each pair of subjects was reduced to a continuous record of the on-off states of each subject's gaze and each subject's Jaffe and Feldstein speech codes. The percent of total dyadic conversation time occupied by each code was computed for each subject. The overall percentage of a code's occurrence has been found to be a useful measure in a previous investigation of dyadic conversation (Dabbs, et al., 1980).

Visual Displays of Interest/Attentiveness

The 30 conversations were later scored separately by a third judge for expressions of interest in and attentiveness to the partner. Each videotaped conversation was observed at twice normal speed, without sound, to accentuate the display of nodding, responsive facial expression, and brief lip movement. Attention of the judge shifted during the interaction to focus upon the partner who currently was the listener of the pair. Interest/attentiveness was scored by having the judge press a button whenever the listener appeared interested in and attentive to the partner (rather than, say, thoughtful or distracted). This judgement was recorded continuously, and a percentage of the total time interest/attentiveness was coded was calculated for each pair.

Subsequently, each of the authors examined the videotaped conversations to try to pick out observable features of the subject behavior that might vary among the three opener levels. The authors felt, from this examination, that it was likely that subjects' appearance of enjoyment, interest, comfort, and nervousness differed among the three opener levels. Seventeen undergraduate judges then viewed the tapes to provide systematic rating of these behaviors. The judges sat in groups of 4 or 5 separated by partitions to avoid interjudge influence, and viewed the first 30 seconds of each conversation. Conversations were viewed without sound. Three different orders of presenting the conversations were used with different subgroups of the judges. After viewing each conversation, the judges marked four 5-point Likert scales to indicate their ratings of the apparent enjoyment, interest, comfort, and nervousness of the pair as a whole.

Results

Statistical analyses indicated that:

1. The judges were able to effectively rate the conversations.
2. Females look at their partners more than males.
3. Males who are good openers talk at the same time as their partner (simultaneous speech). This is not true for females who are good openers or for poor openers in general.
4. Good openers are rated as more interested and attentive to their partner than poor openers.
5. Good openers show greater enjoyment, interest, and comfort than poor openers.
6. Females show more enjoyment, interest, and comfort than males.

Discussion

Those individuals able to promote conversation and self-disclosure in their partners apparently use an identifiable set of behaviors that may serve to reinforce their partners' participation. Simultaneous speech, that is, the addition of various brief responsive utterances, seems to be used by high opener males to stimulate their partners during conversation.

This verbal tactic does not appear to be used by high opener females, however, who may depend more on components of their visual display than do their high opener male counterparts. Females, in general, were found to spend more time gazing at their partners than males. This is a common finding in the literature.

The appearance of comfort, enjoyment, and an attentive facial expression form a composite visual display that the higher opener presents to his or her partner during conversation. We do not know how our judges would have scored the content of the subjects' conversation, nor do we know what the subject actually felt about his or her partner's contribution, but the higher opener appeared to be genuinely interested, attentive, and engaged with his or her partner. The higher opener gave the appearance of being comfortable and at ease in the conversation. Those behavioral skills could contribute in large part to the ability of higher openers to promote conversation and self-disclosure in others. This set of behaviors has long been considered important to the success of counselors, therapists, and others dealing with the emotional needs of people. An awareness of and training in these skills would seem to be a critical facet of such a worker's education. It may also be that doctors, lawyers, teachers — those dealing with the public in general — would be well-advised to cultivate such skills.

The present study suggests that those who listen may use visual display and speech behavior to actively influence the course of their partners' conversational contribution. The relative importance of visual and verbal displays may differ between the sexes. Future research should investigate how such a set of behaviors is learned and how it affects overall social competence. Efforts should also be made to explore the possibility of training individuals to be more aware of and tactful in the use of their visual displays and patterns of speech behavior.

References

BMD biomedical computer programs. (1974). Los Angeles: University of California Press.

Brady, P. T. (1968). A model for generating on-off speech patterns in 16 conversations. *Bell System Technical Journal, 47,* 73-91.

Cohen, J. A. (1960). A coefficient of agreement for nominal scales. *Educational and Psychological Measurement, 20,* 37-46.

Dabbs, J. M., Jr. (1979). Portable apparatus for recording direct frontal views of conversing subjects' faces. *Behavioral Research Methods and Instrumentation, 11,* 531-532.

Dabbs, J. M., Jr., (1983). Patterns of speech and gaze in social and intellectual conversation. In H. Giles & R. N. St. Clair (Eds.), *Recent advances in language, communication, and social psychology.* London: Erlbaum.

Dabbs, J. M., Jr., & Evans, M. S. (1982). Electronic AVTA: Signal processing for automatic vocal transaction analysis, *Behavior Research Methods and Instrumentation*, 14, 461-462.

Dabbs, J. M. Jr., Evans, M. S., Hopper, C. H., & Purvis, J. A. (1980). Self-monitors in conversation: What do they monitor? *Journal of Personality and Social Psychology*, 39, 278-284.

Feldstein, S., & Welkowitz, J. (1978). A chronography of conversation: In defense of an objective approach. In A. W. Siegman & S. Feldstein (Eds.). *Nonverbal behavior and communication.* Hillsdale, NJ: Erbaum.

Jaffe, J., & Feldstein, S. (1970). *Rhythms of dialogue.* New York: Academic.

Miller, L. C., Berg, J. H., & Archer, R. L. (1983). Openers: Individuals who elicit intimate self-disclosure. *Journal of Personality, and Social Psychology*, 44, 1234-1244.

Shrout, P. E., & Fleiss, J. L. (1979). Intraclass correlations: Uses in assessing rater reliability. *Psychological Bulletin*, 86, 420-428.

In this article Grumet provides an overview of eye contact. First,
Grumet explains the physiology of the eyes — the nerves and
organs associated with vision. Next, Grumet describes how eye
contact affects relationships. Finally, the article concludes with
a discussion of the functions of eye contact.

16

Eye Contact
The Core of Interpersonal Relatedness

Gerald W. Grumet

Look into a person's pupils; he cannot hide himself.
—Confucius (551-478 B.C.)

In about 450 B.C. the Greek philosopher Empedocles explained vision
as resulting from a stream of fiery corpuscles passing first from the eye
to the object of vision and returning to the eye. Plato later wrote, "They
set the face in front . . . and constructed light-bearing eyes, and caused
pure fire to flow through the eyes" (Siegel 1970, p. 24). Such ancient
theories reflect the sense of power ascribed to sight and bedeviled
scientific thought until the 17th century, when Kepler correctly proposed
that the eye was an optical instrument able to form an image on its own
retina. Vision has always carried with it a sense of graphic truth and
authenticity, placing it in a position of prominence among the senses.
Soltis (1966, p. 111) notes, "One of our firmest ordinary beliefs is that
whatever objects we take to be visually perceived by us do exist." Gibson
(1960, p. 220) adds, "visual perceiving often enough does not feel like
knowing; instead it feels like an immediate acquaintance or a direct
contact." Freese (1977, p. 72) points out that if discrepant sensory

Reprinted by special permission of the William Alanson White Psychiatric Foundation,
Inc. Adapted from *Psychiatry*, 48, pp. 172-180. © 1983 by William Alanson White Psychiatric
Foundation.

information is received, the influence of sight is likely to predominate: "visual perception is capable of overriding all other information should any of it conflict with the visual sense."

The Impact of Direct Vision

The old axiom, "I'll believe it when I see it," is readily understood in reviewing the impressive neuroanatomical substrates of human vision. Of the 3,000,000 or so sensory fibers entering the primate brain, about two-thirds arise from the eye, and of the 12 cranial nerves, 6 are involved with ocular performance. The complexity and capacity of the human visual cortex is reflected in its enormous size: about 20 square feet by 1/10 inch if flattened out (Newell 1978). The extraocular muscles, which have the highest innervation of any muscles of the body, may contract 100,000 times a day. As Llewellyn-Thomas (1981, p. 319) notes, "We have extraocular muscles which, like the wing muscles of insects, do not fatigue. Muscles that keep my eyes jumping constantly while I'm awake and much of the time I'm asleep, forever seeking information from the world around me or following events in the world of my imagination."

The eyes serve a scanning function, and their inputs are subjected to a variety of secondary perceptual processes by which salient stimuli are differentiated from less important ones. The fovea or point of central vision is directed to scrutinize the most significant. William James wrote in 1892 (p. 73), "The main function of the peripheral parts of the retina is that of sentinels which when beams of light move over them cry 'Who goes there?' and call the fovea to the spot." Excitation of cells within the tiny fovea, 1½ millimeters in diameter, is thought to cause neurons within a region 10,000 times the original area to respond (Kaufman 1974). If one sees in the retinal periphery a face pointed in his direction, it demands foveal attention and the extraocular muscles move the eyeball so that the image falls upon the point of central vision. Certainly, the visual perception of another individual looking at us carries with it considerable importance for survival and mating behavior. It is reasonable to assume that evolutionary selection pressures developed brains which stored generalized representations of salient environmental stimuli, such as visual interest of other parties, coloring it with rich emotional significance. The critical importance of eye contact for lower animals is quite literally emblazoned on the bodies of butterflies, birds, snakes, fish and peacocks, whose eye-shaped patterns are thought to mimic the eyes of predators and thus induce an avoidance response. In many species a common effect of staring eyes is physiological arousal (Argyle and Cook

1976). In monkeys with permanently implanted electrodes, a maximum alerting response is elicited when their gaze meets that of the experimenter (Wada 1961). In human subjects, EEG recordings reveal signs of increased arousal when eye contact is established (Gale, et al. 1972), and direct eye-to-eye engagement has been shown to generate significantly more excitation in galvanic skin responses than does unreciprocated gaze (Nichols and Champness 1971).

Eye contact is usually a first step in interpersonal engagement, beginning a train of action that develops and defines the relationship between the gazer and gazed upon. As Garrison and Arensberg (1976, p. 292) note, "On eye contact, predator and prey, or rival and rival, or lover and loved, are alerted, tensed for what may come next, and a move follows: predator or rival to the attack, lover to tactile approach. . . ."

Survival Implications

A remarkable feature of ocular contact is its ability to transmit instant and meaningful information within new relationships. A pedestrian, crossing the street in front of an automobile halted for a "Stop" sign, will likely attempt to establish eye contact with the driver before beginning to cross in front of him. In doing so, he makes sure that the motorist is cognizant of his presence and will allow him to cross safely. There are other situations where the opposite rule prevails, and avoiding eye contact is more likely to assure safety. Russell Baker of the *New York Times* writes,

> Veterans of New York's guerilla life know better than to make eye contact with other people on the streets. For the criminal, eye contact is an invitation to produce his knife. . . . The rule of survival is never look anyone in the eye, and it is a hard, hard rule to follow at times. . . . Among outlanders there is an embittered old saying about New York that there are a million people on every street corner and not one of them will give you so much as a glance. Those million people are not being coldblooded. Just surviving. [1981, p. 17A]

The ability of interocular contact to convey menace is an outgrowth of man's instinctive fear of predatory gaze, a sinister legacy of Darwinian evolution. Roberts (1976), in a cross-cultural analysis of 186 past and present societies, found evidence for evil-eye beliefs in 67 cultures. Versions of the evil eye are embedded in legends, folklore, mythology and superstitions from antiquity to the present, dating as far back as the 3rd millennium B.C. (Tomkins 1963). In Euroopean folk versions, themes of oral aggression and oral jealousy predominate, with old women held chiefly responsible for the "hostile devouring glance," which is usually directed at infants, children and nursing mothers (Roheim 1953). A reversal of the evil-eye superstition is found in the Japanese neurotic disorder *taijin kyofu*, in which a person avoids others for fear he will injure them if their eyes meet (Gutheil 1979).

It should be noted that there is a difference between "looking" and "staring." The former is dynamically tied to the subject's behavior and is influenced by it, whereas the latter is not responsive to the other person's behavior and persists regardless of it. The fear engendered by a stare was well depicted in a study by Ellsworth and coworkers (1972), who had an experimenter on a motorbike stare at motorists stopped for a red light at an intersection. Not surprisingly, these motorists' departure from the intersection was significantly more rapid when the light changed, paralleling the flight behavior of animals. The authors note that "gazing at a person's face is an exceedingly salient stimulus with interpersonal implications which cannot be ignored" (p. 311). This phenomenon was well demonstrated in the World Chess Championship between Viktor Korchnoi and Anatoly Karpov in 1978. The Russian entourage supporting Karpov included Vladimir Zukhar, a parapsychologist and hypnotist: "His only job seemed to be to sit up front and stare at Korchnoi with his bulging, scary eyes. By the third game, Korchnoi was convinced he was being hypnotized. . . . At game 7, Korchnoi, a nervous wreck by that time— and with Karpov way ahead in the match—started to yell, saying he would descend from the stage and poke Zukhar in the nose. Zukhar was moved to a seventh-row seat." (Schonberg 1981, p. 37).

Couriers of Affection

In amorous behavior, eye contact again plays a pivotal role, this time as a messenger and inspirer of love. As expected, Rubin (1970) found that couples in love spend more time gazing into each other's eyes. Eye imagery in poetry and song has for centuries proven an effective and economical way of describing the power and suddenness of passion and the tyranny which love exercises over its victim. Donaldson-Evans (1980, pp. 8, 21) has made an excursion into what he calls "the dangerous territory of Renaissance love poetry where one glance from a Lady's eye can bring love, suffering and death." He notes that romantic poets preferred the ancient efflux theory of vision: "the eyes shoot arrows, daggers or swords, project fiery beams which burn the soul and kindle love's flame." Direct eye contact between strangers may, on occasion, be described as "love at first sight," which is implied in the lyrics of "Some Enchanted Evening" by Oscar Hammerstein II:

> Some enchanted evening, you may see a stranger;
> You may see a stranger across a crowded room;
> And somehow you know, you know even then,
> That somewhere you'll see her again and again.

The song suggests that a single glance at an unfamiliar person can produce an enormous emotional impact. While a one-way glance signifies one person's interest in another, a mutual glance signifies the inception of a relationship or what has been variously called "shared interocular intimacy" (Tomkins, p. 157), "participation in a wordless exchange" (Exline 1963, p. 3), or "consciousness of consciousness" (Sartre 1953, p. 363).

A naive woman, writing to the medical column of a Philadelphia newspaper, communicates the intense and unexpected amorous impact of an ocular exchange (Steincrohn 1975, p. 67):

> Question: I blame my problem on eyes — mine and those of another. I am a married woman with children and was absolutely not looking for another man. But — BOOM! — there it is. My age is 35. . . . I experience this feeling whenever our eyes meet. . . . Of this feeling, we have never spoken, but I sense that he is experiencing the same as I am. . . . How does one turn this off? This must be the way many extramarital affairs begin. Where does it come from? What sets it off? Please try to explain it medically. Just what is there in the eye contact to produce such a problem?
>
> Answer: . . . I wish I knew the answer. . . . All I can offer as a doctor is the fact that the eyes themselves are not to blame. If you really want the problem resolved, better discuss it with your family doctor or with a marriage counselor. . . .

That romantic love can be obsessional in nature and visually-based is depicted in Al Dubin's 1934 lyrics, "I Only Have Eyes for You":

> My love must be a kind of blind love,
> I can't see anyone but you.
> And dear, I wonder if you find love
> An optical illusion too?
> Are the stars out tonight?
> I don't know if it's cloudy or bright —
> 'cause I only have eyes for you. . . .

The Search for Meaning

Visual perception is an active process in which incoming stimuli are combined with learned information in order to make deductions which go far beyond the immediate sensory evidence. What we "see" is actually a mental construction built upon visual inputs, along with information from other senses and from previous experience. Soltis writes of "successful seeing," i.e., adequately interpreting the optical stimulus. He notes that our knowledge about things in the world if "threaded" into the process of visual perception, and visual inputs are "capped" with interpretations that are both economical and comprehensible to the viewer. An example of how the brain searches for meaning from the visual information presented to it is provided by the transparent "Necker" cube, which spontaneously reverses itself in depth as one looks at it. This reversal results from alternating cerebral explanations of what the ambiguous retinal image represents. Similarly, in the more complex interpretative tasks of interpersonal communication, eye contact is an essential avenue in the quest for comprehension. In dyadic encounters, people look at their conversational partners a large percentage of the time, especially while listening; in one study, women looked at their partners 94% of the time while they were listening, and men, 82% of the time (Exline and Winters 1966). Yarbus (1967) notes that experimental subjects direct foveal attention primarily to the eyes and lips of photographed faces, as these provide the most information to the observer. As Argyle and Dean (1965, p. 289) note, "Without eye-contact, people do not feel that they are fully in communication."

The reliance upon vision for extracting supplementary meaning even in an established personal relationship is exemplified by the Senate testimony of Herbert W. Kalmbach, one of President Nixon's personal attorneys. Kalmbach had been instructed to make secret payments to the Watergate burglars and sought assurance from Nixon aide John Ehrlichman that the payments were proper:

> Kalmbach: I can remember it very vividly because I looked at him, and I said, "John, I am looking right into your eyes. I know Jeanne and your family, you know Barbara and my family. You know that my family and my reputation mean everything to me, and it is just absolutely necessary, John, that you tell me, first that John Dean has the authority to direct me in this assignment, that it is a proper assignment, and that I am to go forward on it."
>
> Dash[1]: And did he look at you in the eyes?
>
> Kalmbach: Yes, he did.
>
> Dash: What did he say to you?
>
> Kalmbach: He said, "Herb, John Dean does have the authority, it is proper, and you are to go forward." [Hearings Before the Select Committee on Presidential Campaign Activities 1973, p. 2106]

Kalmbach, apparently suspicious that he was being drawn into unsavory activities, had attempted to prod Ehrlichman into a truthful disclosure by establishing interocular contact and reminding him of their family ties. He reportedly could never get over the fact that Ehrlichman later denied that this conversation had ever taken place (Miller 1974). Although it is a general perception that persons with high ocular contact are more sincere than those who tend to avert their gaze (Kleinke, et al. 1973), people occasionally reveal increased eye-to-eye contact while being deceptive. This was demonstrated in an elaborate experimental study by Exline and coworkers (1970), who contrasted the visual performance of subjects identified as high or low in "Machiavellianism" while implicated in cheating. They noted that those with high Machiavellian tendencies increased their direct eye contact after being accused of cheating as if to project an image of innocence, whereas those with low Machiavellian qualities tended to avert their gaze, being less able to conceal their shame.

A Multiplicity of Functions

Further evidence of the prominence of vision in interpersonal relations is the exceptional number of psychological influences which impinge upon visual interaction and ocular performance. A few of the main features follow.

Social Position: Persons in positions of leadership tend to gravitate toward locations where they are the visual focus of attention, such as the head of a table (Howells and Becker 1962; Lott and Sommer 1967). This is similar to the behavior of lower primates where a single dominant animal attains a position of visual command while subordinate members of the pack remain around him, glancing periodically, but carefully refraining from encroaching upon his territory (Chance and Jolly 1970).

Positive vs. Negative Emotions: Positive emotions, such as surprise, delight or interest, are associated with increased gaze, while negative emotions, such as horror or disgust, are associated with gaze aversion (Kendon 1967). During periods of high anxiety, eye movements are deployed in an avoidant manner with shorter eye fixations and shifts of gaze away from threatening areas (Luborsky, Blinder, and Mackworth 1963). Similarly, pupillometric studies reveal that the pupils enlarge when people look at things they like and get smaller when the subjects viewed are uninteresting or distasteful (Hess 1975). Both gaze direction and pupil size combine to welcome more positive stimuli and avoid more negative ones.

Willingness to Relate: A person's decision to look back into the eyes of someone who is already looking at him is one of the principal signals by which one denotes a willingness to begin an encounter, for ocular engagement reflects human engagement. Mutual gaze or "catching someone's eye" indicates the entrance into a relationship and may be consciously manipulated toward this end. Common examples are efforts to establish ocular contact with a waiter in a restaurant or to avoid establishing eye contact with a beggar on the street.

Women vs. Men: Women tend to look at their conversational partners somewhat more than men (Exline, Gray, and Schuette 1965; Exline and Winters). Women also appear to engage more readily in mutual gazing, while men show a greater tendency toward one-way ("stolen") glances (Exline).

Cultural Factors: Culturally prescribed norms of visual engagement exert a profound effect on gazing patterns (Hall 1963). Certain groups — such as Americans, Japanese and Navaho Indians — are taught not to stare at others, whereas Arabs, Greeks and South Americans emphasize intense eye contact as evidence of sincerity and interest.

Synchrony of Speech: Analysis of eye contacts during speech reveals typical patterns for listening and for speaking. Listeners glance more frequently than talkers (Kendon), and gaze aversion among talkers is more pronounced during periods of unfluent speech, presumably to limit distracting sensory input while difficult verbal production is in progress (Goldman-Eisler 1961). These patterns are believed to assist conversationalists in synchronizing their speech by supplementing auditory information with an interchange of facial expressions and body kinesics.

Character Traits: A direct gaze is more likely to be returned by the person with aggressive and assertive character traits (Moore and Gilliland 1921). Extroverts also tend to exchange eye contact more readily than introverts (Argyle and Ingham 1972), and hysterics have been found to avert their gazes more often than obsessives when confronted by a sexually evocative stimulus (Luborsky, et al. 1965). People with a high degree of eye contact are judged by their associates to be more "friendly," "natural," "self-confident" and "sincere," while those with little eye contact are perceived as "cold," "defensive," "evasive," "submissive" or "inattentive" (Kleck and Nuessle 1968; Kleinke, et al.).

Thus, visual interactive styles are a final common pathway for a multiplicity of social, psychological and cultural influences, resting ultimately upon a balance of approach and avoidance forces. With direct eye contact, we allow our ocular partner to witness our emotions as we witness his or hers and to mutually acknowledge affective engagement; in gaze aversion, we indicate a desire to maintain psychological distance and to avoid receiving or sending messages of affective arousal.

Note

[1]Samuel Dash, Chief Counsel for the Senate Watergate Committee.

References

Abraham, L. "Restrictions and Transformations of Scoptophilia in Psycho-
    Neurotics: With Remarks on Analogous Phenomena in Folk-Psychology"
    (1913) in K. Abraham, *Selected Papers.* Hogarth, 1927.
Argyle, M., and M. Cook. *Gaze and Mutual Gaze.* Cambridge University Press,
    1976.
Argyle, M., and J. Dean. "Eye Contact, Distance and Affiliation," *Sociometry*
    (1965) 28:289-304.
Argyle, M., and R. Ingham. "Gaze, Mutual Gaze and Proximity," *Semiotica* (1972)
    6:32-49.
Baker, R. "Survival Reflects Reflexes," *Sunday Democrat and Chronicle* (Rochester,
    NY), July 26, 1981.
Callan, H.M.W., M.R.A. Chance, and T.K. Pitcairn. "Attention and Advertence
    in Human Groups," *Social Science Information* (1973) 12:27-41.
Chance, M.R.A., and C.J. Jolly. *Social Groups of Monkeys, Apes and Men.* London:
    Cape, 1970.
Donaldson-Evans, L. *Love's Fatal Glance: A Study of Eye Imagery in the Poets
    of The Ecole Lyonnaise.* University, MS: Romance Monographs, 1980.
Ellsworth, P.C., J.M. Carlsmith, and A. Henson. "The Stare as a Stimulus to Flight
    in Human Subjects: A Series of Field Experiments," *Journal of Personality
    and Social Psychology* (1972) 21:302-11.
Exline, R. "Explorations in the Process of Person Perception: Visual Interaction
    in Relation to Competition, Sex and Need for Affiliation," *Journal of
    Personality* (1963) 31:1-20.
Exline, R., D. Gray, and D. Schuette. "Visual Behavior in a Dyad as Affected by
    Interview Content and Sex of Respondent," *Journal of Personality and Social
    Psychology* (1965) 1:201-9.
Exline, R., J. Thibaut, C. Hickey, and P. Gumpert. "Visual Interaction in Relation
    to Machiavellianism and an Unethical Act," in R. Christie and F. Geis, eds.,
    Studies in Machiavellianism. Academic Press, 1970.
Exline, R., and L. Winters. "Affective Relations and Mutual Glances in Dyads,"
    in S.S. Tomkins and C. Izard, eds., *Affect, Cognition and Personality.*
    Tavistock, 1966.
Fenichel, O. *The Psychoanalytic Theory of Neurosis.* Norton, 1945.
Freese, A.S. *The Miracle of Vision.* Harper & Row, 1977.
Freud, S. *Standard Edition of the Complete Psychological Works.* Hogarth, 1953-74.
    The Interpretation of Dreams (1900), Vol. 4. "On Beginning the Treatment"
    (1913), Vol. 12.

Gale, A., B. Lucas, R. Nissim, and B. Harpham. "Some EEG Correlates of Face-to-Face Contact," *British Journal of Social and Clinical Psychology* (1972) 11:326-32.

Garrison, V., and C.M. Arensberg. "The Evil Eye: Envy or Risk of Seizure? Paranoia or Patronal Dependency?" in C. Maloney, ed., *The Evil Eye*. Columbia University Press, 1976.

Gibson, J.J. "Pictures, Perspective and Perception," *Daedalus* (1960) 89:216-17.

Goldman-Eisler, F. "The Distribution of Pause Durations in Speech," *Language and Speech* (1961) 4:232-37.

Grumet, G.W. "Telephone Therapy: A Review and Case Report," *American Journal of Orthopsychiatry* (1979) 49:574-84.

Gutheil, T.G. "Anxiety and the Eye," in Harvard Medical School, Department of Psychiatry, ed., *Differential Diagnosis of Anxiety*. New York: Audio Visual Medical Marketing, 1979 (audiotape).

Hall, E.T. "A System for the Notation of Proxemic Behavior," *American Anthropologist* (1963) 65:1003-26.

Hearings Before the Select Committee on Presidential Campaign Activities of the United States Senate, Ninety-third Congress. Watergate and Related Activities. July 11, 12, 13, 16 and 17, 1973. Book 5. Government Printing Office, 1973.

Hess, E.H. *The Tell-Tale Eye: How Your Eyes Reveal Hidden Thoughts and Emotions*. Van Nostrand Reinhold, 1975.

Hinchliffe, M.K., M. Lancashire, and F.J. Roberts. "A Study of Eye-Contact Changes in Depressed and Recovered Psychiatric Patients," *British Journal of Psychiatry* (1971) 119:213-15.

Howells, L.T., and S.W. Becker. "Seating Arrangement and Leadership Emergence," *Journal of Abnormal and Social Psychology* (1962) 64:148-50.

Hutt, C., and C. Ounsted. "The Biological Significance of Gaze Aversion with Particular Reference to the Syndrome of Infantile Autism," *Behavioral Science* (1966) 11:346-56.

James, W. *Psychology*. Henry Holt, 1892.

Kaufman, L. *Sight and Mind: An Introduction to Visual Perception*. Oxford University Press, 1974.

Kendon, A. "Some Functions of Gaze-Direction in Social Interaction," *Acta Psychologica* (1967) 26:22-63.

Kleck, R.E., and W. Nuessle. "Congruence Between the Indicative and Communicative Functions of Eye Contact in Interpersonal Relations," *British Journal of Social and Clinical Psychology* (1968) 7:241-46.

Kleinke, C.L., A.A. Buston, F.B. Meeker, and R.A. Staneski. "Effects of Self-Attributed and Other-Attributed Gaze on Interpersonal Evaluations Between Males and Females," *Journal of Experimental Social Psychology* (1973) 9:154-63.

Kramer, M. "Anxiety and Sleep Disorders," in M. Kramer, ed., *Anxiety: The Therapeutic Dilemma*, #4. Chicago: Abbott Laboratories, 1982.

Laing, R.D. *The Divided Self*, Penguin, 1965.

Llewellyn-Thomas, E. "Can Eye Movements Save the Earth?" in D.F. Fisher, R.A. Monty, and J.W. Senders, eds., *Eye Movements: Cognition and Visual Perception*. Hillsdale, N.J.: Lawrence Erlbaum Associates, 1981.

Lott, D.F., and R. Sommer. "Seating Arrangements and Status," *Journal of Personality and Social Psychology* (1967) 7:90-95.

Luborsky, L., B. Blinder, and N. Mackworth. "Eye Fixation and Recall of Pictures as a Function of GSR Responsivity," *Perceptual and Motor Skills* (1963) 16:469-83.

Luborsky, L., B. Blinder, and J. Schimer. "Looking, Recalling and GSR as a Function of Defense," *Journal of Abnormal Psychology* (1965) 70:270-80.

MacCurdy, E., Ed. *The Notebooks of Leonardo da Vinci*, Vol. 1. New York: Reynal and Hitchcock, 1938.

Miller, M. *The Breaking of a President 1974*, Vol. 2. Los Angeles: Therapy Productions, 1974.

Miller, W. "The Telephone in Outpatient Psychotherapy," *American Journal of Psychotherapy* (1973) 27:15-26.

Moore, H.T., and A.R. Gilliland. "The Measurement of Aggressiveness," *Journal of Applied Psychology* (1921) 5:97-118.

Newell, F.W. *Ophthalmology: Principles and Concepts*, 4th ed. St. Louis: Mosby, 1978.

Nichols, K.A., and B.G. Champness. "Eye Gaze and the GSR," *Journal of Experimental Social Psychology* (1971) 7:623-26.

Reimer, M.D. "The Averted Gaze," *Psychiatric Quarterly* (1949) 23:108-15.

Roberts, J.M. "Belief in the Evil Eye in World Perspective," in C. Maloney, ed., *The Evil Eye*. Columbia University Press, 1976.

Roheim, G. "The Evil Eye," *Year Book of Psychoanalysis* (1953) 9:283-91.

Rubin, Z. "Measurement of Romantic Love," *Journal of Personality and Social Psychology* (1970) 16:265-73.

Rutter, D.R., and G.M. Stephenson. "Visual Interaction in a Group of Schizophrenic and Depressive Patients," *British Journal of Social and Clinical Psychology* (1972) 11:57-65.

Sartre, J. *Being and Nothingness*. Washington Sqare Press, 1953.

Schonberg, H.C. "Cold War in the World of Chess," *New York Times Magazine*, September 27, 1981.

Schooler, C., and J. Silverman. "Perceptual Styles and Their Correlates among Schizophrenic Patients," *Journal of Abnormal Psychology* (1969) 74:459-70.

Schooler, C., and J. Silverman. "Differences Between Correlates of Perceptual Style and Petrie Task Performance in Chronic and Acute Schizophrenics," *Perceptual and Motor Skills* (1971) 32:595-601.

Siegel, R.E. *Galen on Sense Perception*. S. Karger, 1970.

Soltis, J.F. *Seeing, Knowing and Believing: A Study of the Language of Visual Perception*. Addison-Wesley, 1966.

Steincrohn, P. "Doctor Says," *The Evening Bulletin* (Philadelphia), October 8, 1975.

Strachey, J. Introduction to "Freud's Psycho-Analytic Procedure," in *Standard Edition of the Complete Psychological Works of Sigmund Freud*, Vol. 7, Hogarth, 1953.

Sullivan, H.S. *The Psychiatric Interview.* Norton, 1954.

Tomkins, S.S. *Affect, Imagery and Consciousness,* Vol. 2, Springer, 1963.

Venables, P.H. "The Relation of Two-flash and Two-click Thresholds to Withdrawal in paranoid and Non-paranoid Schizophrenics," *British Journal of Social and Clinical Psychology* (1967) 6:60-62.

Wada, J.A. "Modification of Cortically Induced Responses in Brain Stem by Shift of Attention in Monkeys," *Science* (1961) 133:40-42.

Williams, E. "An Analysis of Gaze in Schizophrenics," *British Journal of Social and Clinical Psychology* (1974) 13:1-8.

Wolff, S., and S. Chess. "A Behavioural Study of Schizophrenic Children," *Acta Psychiatrica Scandinavica* (1964) 40:438-66.

Yarbus, A.L. *Eye Movements and Vision.* Plenum, 1967.

Zahn, T.P., B.C. Little, and P.H. Wender. "Pupillary and Heart Rate Reactivity in Children with Minimal Brain Dysfunction," *Journal of Abnormal Child Psychology* (1978) 6:135-47.

Zuckerman, Miserandino, and Bernieri explain a phenomenon called civil inattention. Civil inattention occurs when two people are together in a space, notice each other, and agree not to pay attention to each other. The process, which was first discussed by Erving Goffman, is almost exclusively a nonverbal one.

17

Civil Inattention Exists —in Elevators

Miron Zuckerman, Marianne Miserandino and Frank Bernieri

According to Goffman (1963), "civil inattention" is a behavioral ritual enacted when two or more persons are mutually present but not involved in any form of interaction. This ritual involves the exchange of glances between the persons in question followed by gaze aversion. The function of the glance is to acknowledge each other's presence; the subsequent aversion of gaze serves to assure the other person that he or she is not an object of curiosity or attention. By enacting this ritual, "the individual implies that he has no reason to suspect the intention of the others present and no reason to fear the others, be hostile to them, or wish to avoid them" (Goffman, 1963, p. 84). The two possible violations of civil inattention are an open stare, indicating a search for information as well as a reaction to this information; or a complete gaze aversion, indicating that the other person is not worthy of even minimal attention.

Goffman (1963) proposed that civil inattention is likely to occur when pedestrians encounter one another on the street. When separated by a

Adapted with permission from: Zuckerman, M., M. Miserandino, & F. Bernieri. (1983). Civil inattention exists — in elevators. *Personality and social psychology bulletin, 9,* (41), © 1983. Reprinted by permission of Sage Publications, Inc., 578-586.

Authors' Note: The present research was conducted when Marianne Miserandino and Frank Bernieri were students at the University of Rochester. Requests for reprints should be sent to Miron Zuckerman, Department of Psychology, University of Rochester, Rochester, NY 14627.

distance of about eight feet, the pedestrians eye each other and then cast their eyes down until they pass, "a kind of dimming of the lights" (p. 84). Surprisingly, it was not until recently that a series of studies by Cary (1978a) examined this ritual. Unexpectedly, the results failed to support predictions derived from Goffman's model. Specifically, two film studies of naturally occurring behavior showed that people did not avoid or use less direct gaze when passing another person. A third study indicated that behavior consistent with the rule of civil inattention — looking and then looking away — was rated less favorably than behaviors inconsistent with civil inattention — a continuous stare, and no looking followed by a sudden look. In a fourth study, confederates found that pedestrians on the street neither lowered their heads nor averted their gaze as they approached and passed them.

Cary suggested that the rule of civil inattention may not apply to the population of students participating in his studies; or that civil inattention could be conveyed by more subtle cues than those examined in these studies — for example, eyeblinks or facial microexpressions (compare Ekman & Friesen, 1975). It is also possible, of course, that the rule of civil inattention does not exist — at least not for pedestrian passing.

Actually, there is a good reason why pedestrians can easily break the rule of civil inattention. First, it takes very little time for two people to close an eight foot distance while walking toward one another. Second, after the pedestrians pass one another, they are not likely to meet again. Thus both the duration and the likelihood of punishment (embarrassment, difficulty in interaction, etc.) are minimal. From this perspective, Cary's failure to find support for civil inattention appears less surprising. On the other hand, civil inattention may exert greater influence on visual behavior in settings other than those he has examined.

One setting that appears particularly suitable for circumstances leading to Goffman's description of civil inattention is the elevator. During an elevator ride, passengers share a limited amount of space usually without being involved in any interaction. Also, unlike pedestrians on the street, they are forced to remain in proximity, at least for the duration of the ride. Consequently, the need arises to acknowledge the presence of others without turning them into targets of attention. In short, it appears probable that at the beginning of an elevator ride there will be an exchange of glances followed by gaze aversion lasting the length of the ride.

The present series of studies was designed to examine the existence of civil inattention in elevators. Two complementary procedures were used: observation of natural behavior in Study 1 and controlled experimental manipulation in Studies 2 and 3. In Study 1, experimenter-observers recorded the frequency of glances they received as well as the latency and length of the first glance during elevator rides. In Studies

2 and 3, confederates behaved in a manner consistent or inconsistent with the rule of civil inattention; the effects of these behavioral patterns on other riders' impressions of the confederate as well as of the ride were measured.

Study 1

Method

The visual behavior of 320 elevator riders was observed by two experimenters, one male and one female. Half of the subjects were males and half females; half were observed in elevators of a downtown department store or office building, and half in elevators of a large apartment building serving the university and its medical school; finally, half of the subjects were already in the elevator when the experimenter arrived and entered (Enter condition) whereas the other half met a waiting experimenter as they themselves entered the elevator (Wait condition). The various observation conditions formed a 2 (sex of experimenter) × 2 (sex of subject) × 2 (location: downtown or university) × 2 (experimental condition: Enter/Wait) factorial design with 20 subjects in each cell. Only single elevator riders were observed.

The experimenters trained extensively to standardize the procedure for observations, timing, and recording of the data. Only looks that were oriented toward the experimenters' face or upper body were recorded, looks that were oriented toward the experimenters' feet did not count. The experimenters used two stopwatches, one to record the latency and the other to record the length of the subject's first look. Stopwatches were held in the experimenters' pockets and could not be heard. Timing of latency started when either the subject or the experimenter crossed the threshold of the elevator door. During the ride, the experimenters maintained neutral expressions and directed their gaze somewhat away from the subject. Thus they were able to observe the subject without staring at him or her.

On completion of a trial, the experimenter recorded the number of glances received from the subject, latency and length of first glance, location and length of the ride (first recorded as number of floors and later translated into time units), and the estimated age and sex of the subject.

Results and Discussion

The elevator rides ranged in length from 10 to 29 seconds, with a mean of 16.1 seconds. Within this time span, 50.3% of the subjects looked at the confederate once, 25% looked twice, 10.0% looked three times, and

4.1% looked four or five times; 10.6% did not look at all. It can be seen that, in general, subjects let very little time pass before looking at the experimenter (median latency=.56 sec.); in fact, latency of 73% of all first looks was less than 1 second. Similarly, first looks were short (median length=.35 sec.); 88% of all first looks lasted less than 1 second.

Overall, the above results are consistent with predictions of the civil inattention rule. The only exception was that a substantial number of subjects engaged in more than one glance. Although the duration of these additional glances was not recorded, they did not seem longer or different in any other way (e.g., direction, the accompanying facial expression) when compared to the first glance. Perhaps some of the subjects needed to renew their acknowledgement of the confederate as the ride progressed; a second glance may also be a ritualized display of interest in the other person.[1] Consistent with this latter notion, Cary (1978b) reported that the occurrence of mutual glances predicted the initiation of conversation between two strangers.

The extent to which people tend to follow the rule of civil inattention may be influenced by other variables. In the present study we were able to examine effects of sex experimenter, sex of subject, location of observation, and experimental condition. These four variables served as between-subjects factors in three separate analyses of variance; number of looks, latency of first look, and length of first look served as the dependent variables.[2]

Analysis of the number of looks showed that subjects glanced more at an experimenter who entered the elevator than at an experimenter who waited for them; perhaps the waiting experimenter was perceived as part of the situation, whereas the entering experimenter was considered an intrusion deserving more visual notice. Females looked more at a male experimenter and less at a female experimenter in the university apartment building relative to the downtown location; males showed the opposite pattern, thus looks were relatively more common between mixed-sex pairs at the university building than downtown. This finding may simply indicate greater interest in the opposite sex at the university.

Latency of first look was greater in the downtown location than at the university building. This difference may indicate a greater reluctance to accord recognition to others at the more public downtown location. In addition, the Enter condition induced greater latency when experimenter and subject were of mixed sex, whereas the Wait condition induced greater latency when experimenter and subjects were of the same sex. We are not sure how to interpret this interaction.

The first look lasted longer when the experimenter was male rather than female, when subjects were males rather than females, and when subjects and experimenter were of same sex. It appears as if the rule of only a brief glance is more relaxed when the looker or the person looked at is male or if same-sex pairs are involved. Finally, the university building induced longer looks than the downtown location. This latter result is consistent with the previously reported finding of shorter latency at the university, indicating a stronger tendency to create contact with others at this location.

None of the effects reported above was predicted and some are hard to interpret. Furthermore, the obtained differences between the single male and single female experimenters may be due to other factors besides gender, and the same may be true for differences between the university and the downtown location. Thus the only possible inference at this point is that there may be systematic variation in the enactment of civil inattention. It should be noted, however, that the absolute magnitude of this variation was very small. That is, these results do not suggest any exceptions to the general rule of civil inattention.

If civil inattention is the customary and expected behavior in elevators, people should look unfavorably on those who choose not to practice it. Furthermore, infraction of the rule may lead not only to negative impressions regarding the violators but to negative impressions regarding the elevator ride itself. These predictions were examined in Studies 2 and 3.

Studies 2 and 3

Method

Study 2 was designed to examine subjects' reactions to violation of the rule of civil inattention. Study 3 was an exact replication, conducted two years later with different experimenters and a different subject population.

Subjects (144 in Study 2 and 240 in Study 3) were single riders in elevators in university buildings. Half were males and half were females; half were run with a male confederate and half with a female confederate; as in Study 1, the confederate either entered an elevator already occupied by a subject (Enter condition) or waited in the elevator until a subject entered (Wait condition). During the ride, the confederate behaved in a manner that was either consistent or inconsistent with the civil inattention rule. In the former case, he or she glanced at the subject as soon as the two met and then avoided eye contact for the rest of the ride (Glance condition); in the latter case, the confederate either avoided eye contact (Ignore condition) or stared at the subject (Stare condition) for the duration of the ride. It should be noted that compared to Study 1, the confederate's body orientation in the Ignore condition was further away from the subject, reducing any possibility of eye contact. Equal numbers of subjects were assigned to the Ignore, Glance and Stare conditions. Thus, the experimental design consisted of a 2 (sex of subject) × 2 (sex of confederate) × 2 (Enter/Wait condition) × 3 (Ignore/Glance/Stare) factorial. There were six subjects in each cell in Study 2 and 10 subjects in each cell in Study 3.

Subjects' reactions to the manipulation of civil inattention were measured by an experimenter who was unaware of the condition to which a specific subject was assigned. This experimenter waited at ground or other exit floors and administered a short questionnaire to every person leaving the elevator in the company of the confederate. Specifically, subjects were asked to fill out a short questionnaire as part of a survey about reactions to elevator rides. The questionnaire consisted of three items, each answered on a 9-point scale: (1) Did you have a pleasant ride? 1=ride was extremely unpleasant, 9=ride was extremely pleasant. If there was another person with you in the elevator—what was your overall impression of him or her? (2a) 1=person was extremely impolite, 9=person was extremely polite; (2b) 1=person was extremely unpleasant, 9=person was extremely pleasant. On completion of the questionnaire, the subjects were thanked for their participation.

Results

Responses to each question were examined in an analysis of variance with sex of subject, sex of confederate, Wait/Enter conditions, Ignore/Glance/Stare conditions, and Study 2/Study 3 as the between-subjects factors. For each question, the mean scores associated with the three experimental conditions, F of the contrast between behavior consistent with civil inattention (Glance condition) and behaviors inconsistent with civil inattention (Ignore and Stare conditions) and the d, or effect size associated with this contrast were analyzed. It was evident that violations of civil inattention were rated less favorably than behavior consistent with civil inattention. Not surprisingly the magnitude of this effect was almost twice as large for ratings of the violators (how polite and how pleasant was the confederate) than for ratings of the ride (how pleasant was the ride).

The difference between the Glance and Ignore conditions for ratings of the ride only approached significance, $F(1,224)=3.36$, $p < .07$, whereas all other differences were significant. It appears that the two violations of the rule of civil inattention were frowned on equally.

Of the 45 possible interactions between the manipulation of civil inattention and other variables, only two were significant and thus could have been due to chance alone.

General Discussion

The present series of studies provides strong support for the existence of civil inattention. Study 1 showed that about half of all elevator riders tended to eye a fellow passenger briefly at the beginning of the ride and subsequently avoid contact for the remainder of the ride. Of the riders, 35% added to the initial look one or two glances, indicating perhaps a renewal of acknowledgement or a certain interest in the other person. Studies 2 and 3 indicated that behaviors inconsistent with the rule of civil inattention—continuous gaze aversion or continuous stare—were rated less favorably than behaviors consistent with the civil inattention rule—a glance followed by gaze aversion. The fact that gaze aversion and staring were equally unwelcome is of particular importance, since there have been previous reports indicating that staring alone can be negatively interpreted by subjects. Specifically, Ellsworth, Carlsmith, and Henson (1972) in a field study composed of five experiments, found that subjects exposed to a continuous stare moved away from the person staring faster than did those exposed to a fleeting glance. However, the setting in the Ellsworth, et al. (1972) study was not particularly appropriate for the enactment of the civil inattention ritual. Consequently, it was found that an Ignore manipulation in Experiment 5 (a condition labeled incongruous because the confederate was engaged in an unusual activity) did not produce more negative reactions than the fleeting glance. In short, the relatively negative reactions to both gaze aversion and staring in the present experiment indicate that the normative behavior in an elevator must have two components—acknowledgement of another's presence followed by a withdrawal of attention.

It could be argued that the pattern of behavior that was found reflects situational demands rather than the ritual of civil inattention. Specifically, one glances at another passenger in order to orient oneself in the confined space of an elevator, but one does not stare so as to avoid intruding on another's personal space. However, an explanation of glancing in terms of orientation in space cannot account for the lower pleasantness and politeness rating obtained in the Ignore condition. If anything, the person who does not glance may be considered more polite, since he or she avoids exploration of space so as not to inconvenience the other passenger. Staring, on the other hand, can certainly be conceptualized as an intrusion, but this is almost identical to Goffman's explanation of gaze aversion. According to his model, people do not stare at an individual so as to avoid an expression of too much curiosity. Stated differently, staring is avoided so that the other person's privacy is maintained and his or her personal space not violated. Thus civil inattention consists of acknowledging the other's presence without making him or her an object of inquiry.

Once the existence of civil inattention is established, it is interesting to speculate on variations and exceptions to the rule. For example, it was found in Study 1 that about a third of the subjects looked more than once at the confederate. It is possible then, that elevator riders would not react negatively to a small increase in the number of glances given them. Furthermore, although the most frequent behavioral pattern observed in the elevator involved an initial glance followed by gaze aversion, this temporal order may not be that important. Thus riders on elevators may rate aversion followed by a glance more favorably than continuous gaze aversion or staring, although perhaps less favorably than a glance followed by gaze aversion. One may also wonder about the point at which staring becomes aversive. Perhaps longer and/or more frequent looks than the single glance practiced in the present study will not be rated unfavorably. Of course, there must be a point where the interest shown by longer and/or more frequent looks is no longer welcome. However, the temporal location of this point is unknown to us.

Civil inattention may also be modified by the size of the group that is involved. It is possible that in groups consisting of three or more persons, there is less need to acknowledge any particular person's presence. Thus diffusion of responsibility, anonymity, and practical difficulties (one can look at only so may people) may lead to a shift from civil inattention to complete inattention in public places (e.g., crowded elevators, waiting lines, subways).

The visual behavior of civil inattention may be replaced or modified by other forms of nonverbal displays. For example, a person standing adjacent to a fellow rider in an elevator cannot establish eye contact, and yet the small distance between the pair and the "cooperative posture" (the two standing side by side) may already suggest some kind of acknowledgement. Finally, the extent to which civil inattention is expected and practiced may vary across cultures. Perhaps in cultures mandating close physical contact among interactants, civil inattention would be considered a cold and relatively impolite behavior; conversely, there may be cultures in which civil inattention implies too much intimacy between strangers.

Notes

[1]This possibility was suggested to us by Mark S. Lay, whose help is gratefully acknowledged.
[2]Analysis of covariance, with estimated age of subjects and length of ride as covariates, were also performed. However, neither covariate was related to any of the dependent variables. Specifially, of six partial correlations (all independent variables, sex of

experimenter, sex of subject, and so on were held constant), only the correlation between length of ride and number of looks approached significance, r=.10, < .10. Consequently, the covariance analyses did not change any of the results obtained by the analyses of variance.

References

Cary, M.S. Does civil inattention exist in pedestrian passing? *Journal of Personality and Social Psychology*, 1978, 36, 1185-1193. (a)

Cary, M.S. The role of gaze in the initiation of conversation. *Social Psychology*, 1978, 41, 269-271. (b)

Ekman, P., & W.V. Friesen. *Unmasking the face: A guide to recognizing emotions from facial expressions*. Englewood Cliffs, NJ: Prentice-Hall, 1975.

Ellsworth, P.C., J.M. Carlsmith, & A. Henson. The stare as a stimulus of flight in human subjects: A series of field experiments. *Journal of Personality and Social Psychology*, 1972, 21, 802-811.

Goffman, E. *Behavior in public places*. New York: Free Press, 1963.

Rosenthal, R. Combining results of independent studies. *Psychological Bulletin*, 1978, 85, 185-193.

Key Terms and Concepts

Shannon, *Don't Smile When You Say That*

> inappropriate smiling
> gender
> child development

Ekman, *Primary Affect Displays*

> sadness
> happiness
> anger
> surprise

> disgust
> facial affect scoring
>   technique

Purvis, Dabbs, and Hopper, *The "Opener"*

> openers
> self-disclosure
> simultaneous speech
> gender

> turns
> vocalizations
> pause
> switching pause

Grumet, *Eye Contact*

> scanning function
> interpersonal engagement
> instant information
> rules
> avoiding eye contact
> predatory gaze
> looking
> staring
> love
> deception

> functions
> social power
> positive emotions
> negative emotions
> willingness to relate
> gender
> culture
> synchrony
> character traits
>   (personality)

Zuckerman, Miserandino, and Bernieri, *Civil Inattention Exists — In Elevators*

> civil inattention
> ritual
> rule of civil inattention

> gender
> exceptions
> nonverbal displays

Part Four

Artifactual Communication

Artifacts are the objects in our lives. They include clothing, jewelry, accessories, cars, furniture, and briefcases. These objects are not only functional; they create images and shape perceptions.

Clothing is one of the most influential artifacts. Clothing styles tell us a lot about people. Often there is a written or unwritten *dress code.* Many companies expect their employees to dress in a certain style. Other groups have their own dress norms. Is there a fraternity or sorority on your campus which is noted for particularly "trendy" clothing?

Those in the popular press have been quick to note that there is more to dressing than clothing. *Accessories* are also important. It is easier to buy a gray, pin striped Brooks Brothers suit than to pick out the appropriate belt, tie, and shoes to accompany it. Other objects such as briefcases and pens also create an image for us.

Uniforms are a type of clothing that can call attention to someone or make them inconspicuous. The uniform also can be a source of power. Think of all the people you encounter in a uniform — police, mail carriers, soldiers, nurses, surgeons. Can you imagine how they would look doing their job without uniforms?

Color is one of the most important characteristics of artifacts. Colors can create moods and communicate about a person's personality. Recent styles have allowed for greater variation in the use of color in homes and clothes. This is changing how we react to colors.

Think about the objects that are most important to you. Some people will think about their car. What does your car say about you? Others will own a special ring, necklace, or earrings. Still others will focus on something they inherited from a special relative. All of these artifacts communicate about you.

18   *Gross writes about dress policies and the role of dress in U.S. corporations. He talks about the "uniform" of business executives and, while noting regional and industry variation, sees a great deal of uniformity in this dress style. The dress styles of various industries are discussed in this article.*

Admit It or Not, Work Dress Codes Are a Fact of Life

Michael Gross

When Jeff Leston was a salesman at International Business Machines, no one told him the company had an unwritten dress code, but, he said, "You got the message." So he dressed in dark suits, conservative ties and white shirts with button-down collars. "Your collar couldn't be too long or too short," Mr. Leston said.

Then one day he rebelled. His boss eyed the blue shirt Mr. Leston had chosen to wear and asked, "Jeff, are you selling to the Air Force this morning?"

"There are ways to apply pressure to people," said Mr. Leston, who is now a financial management consultant.

Maxine Yee, a spokesman for I.B.M., insisted, "We do not have a dress code policy. We have never had a dress code." But unwritten rules like those Mr. Leston believed were in effect at I.B.M. are an acknowledged act of urban professional life.

"If you are in a service business, the client wants to feel you can be trusted," said Jerry Fields, president of Jerry Fields Associates, an advertising and executive search company. "In business in general, in banks, insurance, steel, automobiles, the image is set by top management, not by writing, not by edict, but by everyone saying 'Do as they do. Let's not make waves.'"

"All people with money and power act, walk, talk and dress in the same style," said John Molloy, the author of "Dress for Success" (Wyden,

1975), columnist, researcher and self-described corporate image engineer. "There's very little difference at the top," he said. "The men who run CBS don't dress differently from the men who run I.B.M." And their style, Mr. Molloy insists, is by no means arbitrary. "Research shows a blue suit, white shirt and maroon tie project honesty," he said. "That's why it's the politician's uniform."

That uniform is the garb of choice for most male business executives today. "There's something about the importance of being proper," said Patricia Grodd, merchandise coordinator for Paul Stuart. "We sell more navy and gray suits for that reason. There is a code, but it shouldn't be thought of as a uniform."

While Mr. Molloy says dress codes vary region by region and industry by industry, he still insists on the uniform's universality. Recently, he was hired as a consultant by a small San Diego accounting firm that was opening a Los Angeles office. Its principals firmly believed potential entertainment business clients would distrust accountants in suits. "They even call them 'suits,'" Mr. Molloy said.

But at his urging, the accountants donned the uniform. "Now they have 19 offices," Mr. Molloy said, "and they only have one rule: suits." The moral of the story? "People who wear gold chains won't give their money to people who wear gold chains."

Those who strive for corporate gold, however, do well to follow the lead of those who already have it. "Style and dress filter down from the top," said Jerry Fields.

Lee Niedringhaus, who worked for the Marine Midland Bank in New York, London and the Far East before becoming a vice president of the McLean Group, a financial management consulting firm, agreed. Banking dress codes are communicated through "osmosis," Mr. Niedringhaus said. "You look around," he said. "You look at the chairman's picture in the annual report. Good fashion is not a ticket to the top. But it's a secure means whereby you won't be criticized."

The uniform is the banking norm. But the banker's code is more detailed than that. Tassel loafers are acceptable footwear, Mr. Niedringhaus said, though they should almost always be black. "Never brown shoes," he said. "Always black socks. Always boxer underwear. Polka-dotted if you want," he added, laughing. The only exception is in summer, when bankers may wear tan suits. "But in July and August only," Mr. Niedringhaus said, "at which point you are also allowed to wear brown shoes. Never a blazer, though. You *always* wear a suit."

Price Waterhouse, the accounting firm, has similar unwritten rules. "You wear a suit," said Arthur Jenks, a recruitment partner. "That's just common sense."

Professionals ignore the rules at their peril. "To dress in what would be considered a flashy mode is a ticket to a nonsuccessful career," Mr. Niedringhaus said.

In creative areas of businesses such as film, music, publishing and advertising, flashy and even eccentric dress can be a plus. But flash is proscribed for those dealing with corporate clients and particularly for corporate job-seekers. "There are standards we look for," said Barry Nathanson, president of Richards Consultants, an executive search company. "A certain kind of image, not overdone. A certain kind of shoe, not beaten up." Brown suits are verboten. "Brown just isn't done," Mr. Nathanson said. "It shows a lack of sensitivity," as do "wrong-colored, short socks" or "tight sweaters and plunging blouses" on women. Those indicate "she's trying to sell herself on some other level than she should," Mr. Nathanson said.

Business dress codes for women are "a tough subject" said Mr. Niedringhaus, who believes the banking standard for women is still "a suit with a little bow tie and a white or occasionally striped shirt." But today's businesswomen seem to have more freedom to dress than do men.

"It's dramatically changed," said Christine Sheppard, a registered nurse and assistant director of clinical services at Lenox Hill Hospital. "In the past," she said, "nurses were viewed as subservient, so they were in uniform. A person in uniform has less autonomy." Today's nurses have more education and independence, she said, "so we no longer dress the same."

Karen Shatzkin, an entertainment lawyer, worked for a large Wall Street firm while attending law school. "I wore dramatically short skirts," she said, "and they treated me like a professional despite dress, which was not appropriate. Now I care about appropriate." Still, she disdains the "success suit," with its demure blouse and bow tie, even when meeting her most formal Wall Street clients. "Women have more leeway," she said, pointing to the combination of colors she was wearing, a green corduroy skirt and brown jacket. "A man couldn't wear this."

"In life, women have more choices," said Jacalyn F. Barnett, a partner at Shea & Gould, a major New York law firm. "In our closets, we do too." She wore tailored suits during her first year at the firm, she said, because "I was insecure professionally." Now she tends to dress more fashionably. "When you have confidence, you feel more comfortable wearing what you want," she said. Still, Miss Barnett keeps her dress appropriate to the occasion; she compared going to court in pants, for example, to "playing Russian roulette with your client."

Appropriateness also guides Linda Stein, a real-estate agent with Edward Lee Cave, whose clients range from heirs to rock stars like Madonna. "If I'm out with Hollywood types, I wear leather and suede," she said. "For old money, I'm understated."

The same unwritten code of appropriateness guides her in matching clients with dwellings. "People looking in 'A' buildings are usually comfortable in 'A' buildings and know how to dress appropriately when they meet the boards," she said. "People who are creative, who dress creatively, feel comfortable in an environment where creative people are welcomed."

Feeling comfortable is, finally, what unwritten dress codes are all about. Served by uniformed professionals, clients feel secure. Surrounded by lookalikes, so do corporate leaders. But some successful professionals still cast an iconoclast's eye on dress restrictions. Jerry Simon Chasen, an entertainment attorney, wore plaid shirts and bow ties, even when he practiced at stuffy midtown law firms. "It's always struck me as amazing," he said, "that people entrusted with advising corporations on multimillion-dollar deals are also the ones who lack the good sense to take off a necktie in 90-degree heat."

19

Gorden, Tengler, and Infante conducted a survey to determine if women's tastes in clothing influenced their actual dress choices at work and their job satisfaction. They found that women who were more clothing conscious tended to dress more conservatively and be more satisfied with their job.

Women's Clothing Predispositions as Predictors of Dress at Work, Job Satisfaction, and Career Advancement

William I. Gorden, Craig D. Tengler and Dominic A. Infante

Beyond protection from the elements, humans cover their bodies for many symbolic reasons. Clothing is instrumental in perpetuation of traditions and religious ceremony; in self-beautification, real or imagined; in fostering cultural values regarding sexual identity and practice; in differentiating authority and roles; and in display of and acquisition of status.[1] The symbolic worth of apparel in Hartman's view is "proportionate to its contribution to some sort of extension or differentiation or enrichment of the self."[2] Clothing may be our human effort, in Fromm's words, "to address man's need to rise above his animal nature, to become a creative person instead of remaining a creature."[3]

The language of dress provides considerable information about a person, and how a person feels about him or herself in a particular setting.[4] Clothing is an aspect of impression formation over which a person has some control, enabling others to gather cues prior to and/ or during verbal transactions. Attire is assigned meaning. In varied

Adapted with permission from: Gorden, W.I., C.D. Tengler, & D.A. Infante. (1982). Women's clothing predispositions as predictors of dress at work, job satisfaction, and career advancement. *Southern Speech Communication Journal, 47*, 422-434.

experimental tests, dressing well has proven rewarding: the well-dressed individual is picked up more often when hitchhiking,[5] receives help more readily,[6] obtains directions more easily,[7] has space invaded less,[8] receives more tips,[9] and is followed more when crossing a street against the light.[10] Well-dressed people tend to create first impressions of success, power, positive habits and the ability to earn money.[11] Social class and status of working women were found by Rosencrantz to be related to clothing awareness.[12] Aiken, found that decoration in dress correlated positively with such traits as conformity, sociality, and nonintellectualism; preference for comfort in dress correlated positively with self-control and extroversion; interest in dress correlated with compliance, stereotypic thinking, social consciousness and insecurity; and conformity in dress correlated positively with responsibility, alertness, efficiency and precision.[13]

Rosenfeld and Plax recognized the impact of dress and developed a measure of clothing predispositions.[14] Their instrument contains four dimensions: clothing consciousness, exhibitionism, practicality, and designer. An assumption of research such as this is that attitudes toward clothing have consequences. This idea was explored in the present study for female employees in organizations.

Michael Korda argues that women who rise in an organization wear "a simple, rather formal dress or suit" and take care to "dress unobtrusively and conservatively."[15] Rosabeth Moss Kanter, in her prize-winning work *Men and Women of the Corporation*, suggests that the "packaging of a secretary (97% of which are women) is very important to her success.[16] In a study by Form and Stone, men who were asked to comment on a woman's promotion from typist to receptionist rated good appearance more important than ability.[17] They also reasoned that a woman who could dress attractively, thus enhancing the company's public image, usually would have other positive personality traits.

We reasoned that women's clothing predispositions should matter in the office situation. A woman who is clothing-conscious and practical should be more likely to recognize the constraints of the situation and dress accordingly.[18] In the office situation this would constitute conservative dress, avoiding dress which is intended more for sport, leisure, or pleasure. If she accepts the constraints of the situation, this may be because she is satisfied with her job and career advancement. On the other hand, a female employee who is less clothing-conscious and practical but more exhibitionistic in clothing predispositions would be more prone to violate the dress expectations in an office situation. She would tend to dress less conservatively and more for comfort and pleasure. Such clothing predispositions should also predict less job satisfaction and career advancement since conformity in dress is a necessary requisite for career success.[19]

These ideas represent expectations which may be summarized by the following hypothesis which was tested in the present study: Female office employees whose clothing predispositions indicate higher clothing-consciousness and practicality and lower exhibitionism will dress more conservatively and experience more career advancement and job satisfaction.

Method

The subjects of the study were 300 women employees in approximately 200 organizations of employment in three widely separated regions: a large city in the West, a large city in the South and an urban area in the Midwest. All subjects were women office personnel employed in secretarial and clerical positions. The first two groups were participants in annual seminars sponsored by the National Secretaries Association. For each of the two groups, 100 women were asked to participate in the study. No one asked refused to participate in the project. The third group of 100 participants was administered the instruments for the study in their offices in a large urban area of the Midwest.

The Rosenfeld and Plax Clothing Questionnaire[20] was selected to ascertain general clothing predispositions. This scale contains four dimensions: clothing-consciousness (eight items), exhibitionism (four items), practicality (three items), and designer (two items). Three additional items were added in our investigation to the 17 in order to increase the number of items for the designer and practicality dimensions. The items added to the design factor read "I dress the way I want to regardless of how different I am." and "I like to wear clothes that are really different." The one item added for practicality read "People spend too much on clothing to impress other people." A five-point scale which spanned from "strongly agree" to "strongly disagree" was used for each of these 20 items.

Since no scale was available to measure how women dress on the job, the "always" and "nevers" in John Molloy's *Women's Dress for Success Book*[21] were worded into 22 items. Molloy's general thesis is that women should wear a business "uniform," and the closest apparel to a uniform available for a woman is the skirted suit. Therefore a skirted suit heads his "always" list and also includes such items as "wear upper middle class clothing," along with guidelines such as "ask yourself who you are going to meet and what you are going to do before you get dressed." His "never" list includes such items as "wear knit polyester slack suits to work" and "I wear blue jeans or sweaters." A five-point scale which ranged from "almost always" to "almost never" was used for these items.

Eleven items to measure satisfaction with job outcomes were taken from the International Communication Association audit.[22] Examples of the items from the ICA audit are satisfaction with ''your relationship(s) with people in your department or work group,'' and ''your progress in your organization up to this point in time.'' We added a question to measure the degree of satisfaction with career advancement. A five-point scale with ''very satisfied'' and ''very dissatisfied'' endpoints was used for these items. Several additional items asked for the number of promotions, sex of superior, whether the superior was at the upper, middle, or lower

---

Table 1

Clothing Predisposition Questionnaire

Clothing Consciousness

I like to ''dress up'' and I usually spend a lot of time doing so.
There's nothing like a new item of clothing to improve my morale.
The people I know always notice what I wear.
I think most men notice what a woman is wearing.
It is very important to be in style.
I would love to be a clothes designer.
I like to try out new ''effects'' in my clothing which others will
    admire and envy.
I spend a lot of time reading about style and fashions.
I would like to be a clothes model.
If I had more money I would spend it on clothes.

Practicality

I usually dress for warmth or coolness rather than for fashion.
When buying clothes, I am more interested in practicality than in
    beauty.
I buy clothes for comfort rather than appearance.
People spend too much on clothing to impress other people.

Exhibitionism

I like close-fitting figure-revealing clothes.
I approve of skimpy bathing suits and wouldn't mind wearing one
    myself.
I like to wear clothes that are really different.
I see nothing wrong with wearing clothes which reveal a lot of skin.

---

level of management, and years of employment. The number of promotions was considered a measure of "career advancement."

Prior to the opening of educational seminars conducted by the senior author, the 60-item questionnaire was completed by the subjects in the South and Southwest. The subjects from the Midwest completed the questionnaires at their place of work.

Statistical analyses indicated that:

1. People's clothing predispositions consist of their clothing consciousness, practicality, and exhibitionism. The measure of these predispositions is presented in Table 1. This measure is fairly effective.
2. There are two considerations in dressing on the job: conservatism and fun. A measure of dress behavior on the job is presented in Table 2. This measure is fairly effective.
3. People who are more clothing conscious tend to dress more conservatively and be more satisfied with their job.
4. Women are more exhibitionist in dress with a male boss.
5. People who have been on the job a shorter period of time are more exhibitionist in dress.

Table 2
Dressing Behaviors on the Job

Conservative Dress on the Job

I wear a dark colored blazer-cut jacket with matching skirt to work.
I consider what I must do and who I will meet in selecting what I will
  wear to work.
I wear wool, linen and natural blends to work.
I wear plain pumps on the job.
When I wear dresses to work, the sleeves are full or three-quarter length.
To help my career I dress well but conservatively.
I dress as well or better than my boss.
What I wear at work conveys the impression that I take my job seriously.
I endeavor to groom my body into the best physical appearance possible.

Dressing for Fun on the Job

I wear dresses to work that would be great at a party.
I wear sexy outfits and lots of jewelry to work.

Discussion

The attempt of this investigation was to discover to what degree clothing predispositions are related to reported dress practices on the job, to satisfaction with job outcomes and career advancement. Previous research could be found to support the general notion that those who dress well fare well, but, other than John Molloy's[23] experiments'' for which the data is sparsely reported, no research could be found which examines these relationships. We reasoned that those who were more clothing-conscious would also report dressing more conservatively, be more satisfied with job outcomes and would be more upwardly bound. We sought to test this relationship by first finding clothing predispositions, next measuring dress practices on the job, and finally rating satisfaction with a variety of job outcomes and promotions.

Clothing-consciousness, defined by Rosenfeld and Plax as the degree to which an individual is concerned with his or her clothes, for the tested sample of women in clerical and secretarial roles did predict self-reports of conservative dress behavior. The nature of their jobs for the most part demands a concern for clothing. Those individuals less concerned about their clothes were not as satisfied with the jobs and had fewer promotions.

The profile of the clothing-conscious person is one who likes to dress up, believes that people notice what she wears, and likes to read about and spend money on clothes. Our clothing-conscious respondents enjoyed clothing design, fashion, and modeling, yet they saw themselves as choosing rather conservative business outfits. They avoided dress in the office that was inappropriate and frivolous. Dressing for fun, indeed, was secondary when on the job. The clothing-conscious woman, however, was not unaware of her body nor was she entirely lacking practicality.

These women who feel good about their jobs are not so stoic or dull as Molloy would suggest. Dressing appropriately means dressing well and attending to fashion, but avoiding extremes on the job. A post hoc analysis discovered a greater predisposition for exhibitionism in clothing for women employees with male than with female superiors; also these women had been employed for a short time, and therefore possibly were younger. Length of employment was related to whether women employees dressed for "fun" on the job, another clue that the socialization process was working to tell what was appropriate and inappropriate in the work place. In Goffman's terms, "dress carries much of the burden of expressing orientation within a situation."[24]

As would be expected, those who were closer to power (they worked for a superior in upper as opposed to lower level of management) were more satisfied with the rewards of their employment, and those who had been employed longer were more satisfied than those of shorter employment and likely had better jobs, and they chose to dress more conservatively.

Although this study did not investigate the effect of self-concept and clothing, previous work by Gorden and Infante[25] found that self-esteem and clothing-consciousness are related, and Ryan[26] discovered a relationship between "dressing well" and positive personality ratings of self and by others. Satisfactions with job outcomes do appear to be rewards for clothing-conscious, conservatively dressed women employees. Dressing up for the job to which one aspires, as Korda[27] suggests, is in a sense similar behavior to those who dress up for an initial job interview. Gardner Murphy put it succinctly when he said that clothing "makes real the role one plays."[28]

The present study may be interpreted as supporting the notion that organizations have expectations for dressing behavior and employees tend to be most satisfied with their jobs when their clothing predispositions and actual dress behavior are consistent with those organizational expectations. This idea might be explored in a variety of ways in future research. For instance, does a violation of organizational dress expectations have consistent negative consequences even though the violation is positive (i.e., the person dresses "better" than expected)? What personality and attitude attributions are made for violators? Are there sex differences in the consequences of violating dress expectations in organizations? While not denying the importance of other communication behaviors in the organizational setting, it seems reasonable to speculate that dressing behavior may be particularly significant with regard to a variety of organizational outcomes.

Notes

[1]Adamson E. Hoebel, *Man in the Primitive World* (New York: McGraw-Hill, 1958), 239-51; F.E. Sterling, "Net Positive Social Approaches of Young Psychiatric Inpatients as Influenced by Nurses' Attire," *Journal of Consulting and Clinical Psychology*, 48 (1980), 58-62; Stephen Amira and Stephen I. Abramowitz, "Therapeutic Attraction as a Function of Therapist Attire and Office Furnishings," *Journal of Consulting and Clinical Psychology*, 47 (1979), 198-200; Janice Lee Wood, "The Effects of Teacher Dress upon Ratings of Status, Credibility, and Physical Attractiveness in the Initial Impression Situation," unpub. M.A. thesis, Kent State University, 1979; Thomas J. Long, "Influence of Uniform and Religious Status on Interviewees," *Journal of Counseling Psychology*, 25 (1978), 405-409; Marvin L. Bouska and Patricia A. Beatty, "Clothing as a Symbol of Status: Its Effect on Control of Interaction," *Bulletin of the Psychonomic Society*, 11 (1978), 235-38; R.D. Coursey, "Clothes Doth Make the Man, In the Eye of the Beholder," *Perceptual and Motor Skills*, 36 (1973), 1259-64; H. Resnick and S. Stillman, "Does Counselor Attire Matter?" *Journal of Counseling Psychology*, 19 (1972), 347-48.

[2]George W. Hartman, "Clothing Personal Problem and Social Issues," *Journal of Home Economics*, 41 (1949), 296.

[3]Eric Fromm, *The Sane Society*, (New York: Holt, Rinehart and Winston, 1955), 36.

[4]Thomas Ford Hoult, "Experimental Measurement of Clothing as a Factor in Some Social Ratings of Selected American Men," *American Sociological Review*, 19 (1954), 324-28.

[5]Peter Crassweller, Mary Alice Gordon, and W.H. Tedrods, "An Experimental Investigation of Hitchhiking," *Journal of Psychology*, 82 (1972), 43-47.

[6]Mary Barbara Harris and Gail Bays, "Altruism and Sex Roles," *Psychological Reports*, 32 (1973), 1002.

[7]Steven R. Schiavo, Barbara Sherlock, and Gail Wicklund, "Effect of Attire on Obtaining Directions," *Psychological Reports*, 34 (1974), 245-46.

[8]James H. Fortenberry, Joyce McLean, Pricillia Morris, and Michael O'Connell, "Mode of Dress as a Perception Cue to Deference," *Journal of Social Psychology*, 104 (1978), 139-40.

[9]Jeri Jayne W. Stillman and Wayne E. Hensley, "She Wore a Flower in Her Hair," Paper presented at the Central States Speech Association Convention, 1980 and; "What Tips Tippers to Tip," *Psychology Today*, 14 (May, 1980), 98, Stillman and Hensley's summary of research on the impact of dress guided a portion of our literature search.

[10]M. Lefkowitz, Robert Blake and Jane Mouton, "Status Factors in Pedestrial Violation of Traffic Signals," *Journal of Abnormal and Social Psychology*, 51 (1955), 704-706.

[11]Leonard Bickman, "Clothes Make the Person," *Psychology Today*, 7 (April, 1974), 49-54; Mary Lou Rosencrantz, *Clothing Concepts* (New York: MacMillan Co., 1969), 53.

[12]Rosencrantz.

[13]Lewis R. Aiken, "The Relationship of Dress to Selected Measures of Personality in Undergraduate Women," *Journal of Social Psychology*, 59 (1963), 119-28; Norma H. Compton, "Personal Attributes of Color and Design Preferences in Clothing Fabrics," *Journal of Psychology*, 54 (1962), 191-95.

[14]Lawrence B. Rosenfeld and Timothy G. Plax, "Clothing as Consciousness," *Journal of Communication*, 27 (1977), 24-31.

[15]Michael Korda, *Power and How to Achieve Success*, (New York: Ballantine Books, 1977), 166.

[16]Rosabeth Moss Kanter, *Men and Women of the Corporation*, (New York: Baasic Books, 1977).

[17]William H. Form and Gregory P. Stone, *The Social Significance of Clothing in Occupational Life* (East Lansing, Michigan: Michigan State University Agricultural Bulletin 262, November, 1957).

[18]John T. Molloy, *The Women's Dress for Success Book*, (Chicago: Follett Publishing Co., 1977).

[19]Edward Gross and Gregory P. Stone, "Embarrassment and the Analysis of Role Requirements," *The American Journal of Sociology*, 70 (1964), 4.

[20]Rosenfeld and Plax.

[21]Molloy.

[22]Gerald Goldhaber, "The ICA Audit: Rationale and Development," Paper presented at Academy of Management, Kansas City, 1976.

[23]Molloy.

[24]Erving Goffman, *Behavior in Public Press*, (New York: Free Press of Glenco, 1963), 213.

[25]William I. Gorden and Dominic A. Infante, "System Involvement for Women Subordinates: Relations with Communication and Personality Variables," paper presented at the International Communication Association, Acapulco, 1980.

[26]Mary S. Ryan, "Perception of Self in Relation to Clothing," *Dress, Adornment and the Social Order*, eds. Mary Ellen Roach and Joanne Bubolz Eichler (New York: John Wiley, 1965), 247-49.

[27]Korda.

[28]Gardner Murphy, *Personality*, (New York: Harper and Row, 1947), 495.

20

Smith and Malandro provide four checklists summarizing the effects of appearance on credibility and approachability. The authors describe the clothing, colors, jewelry, eyeglasses, hair and fingernail styles needed for men and women to be perceived as believable and likeable.

Personal Appearance Factors Which Influence Perceptions of Credibility and Approachability of Men and Women

Lawrence J. Smith and Loretta A. Malandro

Checklist: Male personal appearance factors which increase the perception of credibility

1. *Clothing*

    ____classic, conservative clothing

    ____traditional two-piece suit (avoid three-piece suits, especially in rural areas; avoid trendy suits; avoid poor quality suits; avoid sports jacket)

    ____acceptable fabrics for suits include wools and wool blends (avoid silk, ultrasuede, or any other less traditional fabric)

    ____acceptable suit patterns include small pinstripes, solids, subtle and small plaids, subtle and small striped patterns (avoid all unusual patterns or very pronounced patterns)

    ____have suit pants and coat sleeves tailored to appropriate length (lengths which are too short reduce credibility; lengths which are too long project a look of being "overwhelmed" and "submissive")

    ____conservative tie (avoid unusual designs and patterns)

Smith, L.J., & L.A. Malandro (eds.). (1985). *Courtroom communication strategies.* NY: Kluwer Book Publishers. Reprinted with permission by the Michie Company.

____solid long sleeved white shirt with classic collar (avoid open buttons and button-down collar)

____acceptable fabric for shirts is cotton (avoid silk and polyester shirts)

____conservative well-polished shoes (avoid casual shoes such as penny loafers)

____conservative leather belt (avoid unusual belt buckles and designs)

2. *Colors*

____acceptable colors for suits include colors in the gray and navy blue families (avoid browns, tans, beiges, and unusual suit colors)

____acceptable color for shirts is white (highest perception of credibility); light blue can also be worn (avoid shirts with designs and patterns; stay with solid colors)

3. *Jewelry*

____wear limited jewelry such as one ring, watch, tie bar or tie pin (avoid bracelets, necklaces, pocket watch, extra rings, garish jewelry, and belts with large buckles or jeweled belt buckles)

____acceptable rings include wedding ring, class ring, or a conservative ring (avoid large, expensive, and sparkling stones as well as unusual rings)

____wear rings only on the ring finger of either hand (avoid rings on any other finger)

4. *Eyeglasses*

____eyeglasses, in general, increase the perception of credibility

____wear conservative frames (avoid round wire-rim frames and unusual colored frames; avoid black frames, acceptable frames include tortoise shell, neutral colors, some wire-rimmed frames; avoid all fashionable and trendy types of eyeglasses)

____wear clear lenses (avoid all tinted lenses and photo-sensitive lenses)

5. *Hair*

____short, conservative hairstyle (keep hair well-groomed and neat; avoid hair over the ears and hair hitting the collar area; avoid sideburns)

____classic, traditional hairstyle (avoid unusual or fashionable hairstyles) _____use natural hair (avoid hair pieces and toupees; avoid combing hair to cover balding or thinning area; if hair is colored, have it done professionally)

_____clean-shaven look (if beards and moustaches are worn they should be well trimmed and conservative; avoid all unusual looks including handlebar moustaches)

6. _Fingernails_

_____nails should be short, well-groomed, and clean

_____nails should be healthy and natural looking (avoid nail polish)

Checklist: Male personal appearance factors which increase the perception of approachability and likeability

1. _Clothing_

_____conservative clothing

_____sports jacket (avoid two- and three-piece suits)

_____acceptable suit patterns include tweeds, small plaids, and solids (avoid pinstriped suits)

_____acceptable fabrics for suits include cashmere, wools, and wool blends (avoid silks, ultrasuede materials and other less traditional fabrics)

_____acceptable fabric for shirts is cotton (avoid silk and polyester shirts)

_____have suit pants and coat sleeves tailored to appropriate lengths (avoid lengths which are too short or too long)

_____conservative or leather belt (avoid unusual belt buckles and designs)

_____solid or subtle patterned long-sleeved shirt (short-sleeved shirt is acceptable only in very informal settings; button-down collar is acceptable; shirt can have small design, such as stripes)

_____conservative, well-polished shoes (avoid shoes that are too casual; loafers are acceptable in informal setting)

2. _Colors_

_____acceptable colors for suits include colors in the brown family — tans, beiges, browns (avoid gray and navy if jacket and pants match; gray and navy can be used for either jacket or pants)

_____acceptable colors for shirts are light blue or light pink/rose (avoid white shirts)

3. *Jewelry*

___wear jewelry such as a ring and/or watch (avoid tie bar, tie pins, bracelets, necklaces, pocket watch, extra rings, garish jewelry, and belts with large buckles or jeweled belt buckles)

___acceptable rings include a wedding ring, class ring, or a conservative ring (avoid large, expensive, and sparkling stones as well as unusual rings)

___wear rings on the ring finger of left or right hand only (avoid rings on any other finger)

4. *Eyeglasses*

___eyeglasses are acceptable; they should be removed occasionally to increase perception of approachability

___wear conservative frames (avoid round wire-rim frames, unusual colored frames; avoid black frames; acceptable frames include tortoise shell, neutral colors, and some wire-rimmed frames; avoid all fashionable and trendy types of eyeglasses)

5. *Hair*

___short, conservative hairstyle (keep hair well-groomed and neat; avoid hair over the ears and hair hitting the collar area; avoid sideburns)

___classic, traditional hairstyle (avoid unusual or fashionable hair styles)

___use natural hair (avoid hair pieces and toupees; avoid combing hair to cover balding or thinning area; if hair is colored, have it done professionally)

___clean-shaven look (avoid beards and moustaches)

6. *Fingernails*

___nails should be short, well-groomed, and clean

___nails should be healthy and natural looking (avoid nail polish)

Checklist: Female personal appearance factors which increase the perception of credibility

1. *Clothing*

___classic, conservative clothing

___traditional, two-piece suit with matching skirt and jacket (avoid pantsuits, trendy suits, poor quality suits, and suits with contrasting jacket and skirt) _____avoid three-piece suits (avoid all types of vests, either cloth or sweater vests)

_____acceptable suit patterns include solids, subtle and small plaids, subtle and small striped patterns (avoid the classical pinstriped pattern; avoid all unusual patterns or very pronounced patterns)

_____acceptable fabrics for suits include wools and wool blends; lighter weight spring and summer fabrics are acceptable (avoid fabrics which wrinkle, such as silk suits; avoid ultrasuede and other less traditional fabrics)

_____acceptable fabrics for blouses are cotton and silk (avoid shiny and polyester blouses)

_____bows and pleated blouses are acceptable (avoid male-looking ties; avoid ruffles)

_____have coat sleeve length tailored to appropriate length (a sleeve length which is too long will result in the perception of submissiveness and being overwhelmed)

_____skirt length should fall from just below the knee to two inches below the knee (avoid all extremes in skirt lengths such as above-the-knee and mid-calf lengths)

_____if a belt is worn, it should be conservative and understated

_____avoid all designer clothing and accessories

2. _Shoes_

_____wear heels of 2½ inches or less (avoid high heels and flat heels)

_____wear closed-toe and closed-heel shoes (avoid open-toe and sling-back shoes)

_____wear classic and traditional shoes (avoid all designs, jewelry or bows on shoes; avoid unusual and fashionable shoes)

3. _Colors_

_____acceptable colors for suits include colors in the gray, white, off-white, beige, and navy blue families (avoid browns and unusual suit colors)

_____acceptable blouse colors include white (for the higher perception of credibility); light blue can also be worn (avoid blouses with designs and patterns; stay with solid colors)

4. _Jewelry_

_____wear limited jewelry, up to five points; this may include earrings, a ring, a necklace, and a pin on jacket (avoid "male-type" accessories such as a tie bar or a tie pin; avoid bracelets that dangle, move, or make a noise; avoid garish jewelry and belts with large buckles or jeweled belt buckles) _____wear small- to medium-sized earrings (avoid all dangling and oversized earrings; select conservative earrings and avoid fashion trends)

_____acceptable rings include wedding ring, class ring, or a conservative ring (avoid large, expensive, and sparkling stones as well as unusual rings)

_____wear rings on the ring finger of the left or right hand only (avoid rings on any other finger; a ring on each hand is acceptable)

_____wear a necklace that falls in upper chest area (avoid long dangling necklaces or necklaces with unusual designs and patterns; the most acceptable necklaces are conservative, such as a strand of pearls or a gold necklace)

_____wear moderately-priced jewelry (avoid extremes in high-priced or low-priced jewelry; avoid costume jewelry)

_____watches are acceptable and count as a piece of jewelry

5. *Eyeglasses*

_____eyeglasses, in general, increase the perception of credibility

_____wear conservative frames (avoid high fashion look in glasses; avoid round wire-rim frames; acceptable frames include tortoise shell, neutral or pastel colors, some wire-rimmed frames; wear wider, more open lenses as opposed to small glass lenses)

6. *Hair*

_____conservative and classic hairstyle; wear hair shoulder length or shorter or pull hair on top of head (avoid long hair below the shoulder line or hair that is extreme in shortness and appears to be a male-imitation look)

_____classic, traditional hairstyle (avoid unusual or fashionable hairstyles; avoid bouffants, ponytails, and braids)

_____hair should appear to be a natural color (avoid "colored" looks, such as bleached blond or streaked hair; keep coloring subtle)

_____hair should be well-groomed and neat

7. *Fingernails*

_____nails should be a moderate length, well-groomed and clean (avoid long nails; short nails are acceptable)

_____nails should be healthy and natural looking (avoid colored nail polish, such as red and fuchsia; acceptable nail polish colors include clear, buff, and opaque colors such as light pink; avoid all decals and decorations on fingernails)

8. *Makeup*

_____wear little to moderate makeup (avoid extremes of too much makeup or no makeup; makeup should look very natural in sunlight)

_____wear soft colors (avoid eyeshadows with definite colors such as blues, greens, and purples)

Checklist: Female personal appearance factors which increase the perception of approachability and likeability

1. *Clothing*

_____classic, conservative clothing

_____traditional, two-piece suit with contrasting skirt and jacket (for example, a solid jacket with a plaid skirt)

_____dress with or without a jacket (dress should be tailored and conservative; absence of jacket reduces "authority" look)

_____acceptable suit patterns include solids, subtle and small plaids, subtle and small striped patterns (avoid the classic pinstriped pattern)

_____acceptable fabrics for suits include cashmere, wool and wool blends (avoid silks, ultrasuede, and other less traditional fabrics)

_____acceptable fabrics for blouses are cotton and silk

_____wear blouse with bow, pleats, slight ruffle or soft tie (avoid male-looking tie and blouses which are plain: a necklace can be substituted for a tie)

_____wear blouses with jewel or normal neckline (avoid high-collared blouses)

_____avoid all designer clothing and accessories

2. *Shoes*

_____wear heels of 2½ inches or less (avoid high heels and flat heels)

_____wear closed-toe and closed-heel shoes (avoid open-toe shoes and sling back shoes)

_____wear classic and traditional shoes (avoid all designs, jewelry, or bows on shoes; avoid unusual and fashionable shoes)

3. *Colors*

_____acceptable colors for suits include colors in the brown, gray, and blue family; a wider choice of colors can be used including pinks and roses (avoid gray or navy if jacket and skirt match; gray and navy can be used for either jacket or skirt) ____acceptable blouse colors include all pastels such as blue, pink, light rose, green, and so forth (avoid very bright colors and white blouses)

4. *Jewelry*

____wear limited jewelry, up to five points; this may include earrings, a ring, a necklace, and a pin on jacket (avoid "male-type" accessories such as a tie bar or tie pin; avoid bracelets that dangle, move, or make a noise; avoid garish jewelry and belts with large buckles or jeweled belt buckles)

____wear small- to medium-sized earrings (avoid all dangling and oversized earrings; select conservative earrings and avoid fashion trends)

____acceptable rings include wedding ring, class ring, or a conservative ring (avoid large, expensive, and sparking stones as well as unusual rings)

____wear rings on the ring finger of the left or right hand only (avoid rings on any other finger; a ring on each hand is acceptable)

____wear a necklace that falls in upper chest area (avoid long dangling necklaces or necklaces with unusual designs and patterns; the most acceptable necklaces are conservative, such as a strand of pearls or a gold necklace)

____wear moderately-priced jewelry (avoid extremes in high-priced jewelry and low-priced jewelry; avoid costume jewelry)

____watches are acceptable and count as a piece of jewelry

5. *Eyeglasses*

____eyeglasses, in general, increase the perception of approachability

____wear conservative frames (avoid high fashion look in glasses; avoid round wire-rim frames; acceptable frames include tortoise shell, neutral or pastel colors, some wire-rimmed frames; wear wider, more open lenses as opposed to small glass lenses)

6. *Hair*

____Soften the hairstyle, bring hair around the face in soft curls or waves (avoid severe hairstyles, such as pulling the hair back too tight)

____conservative and classic hairstyle; wear hair shoulder length or shorter or pull hair on top of head (avoid long hair below the shoulder line or hair that is extreme in shortness and appears to be a male-imitation look) _____classic, traditional hairstyle (avoid unusual or fashionable hairstyles; avoid bouffants, ponytails, and braids)

_____hair should appear to be a natural color (avoid "colored" looks such as bleached blonde or streaked hair; keep coloring subtle)

_____hair should be well-groomed and neat

7. _Fingernails_

_____nails should be a moderate length, well-groomed and clean (avoid long nails; short nails are acceptable)

_____nails should be healthy and natural looking (avoid colored nail polish, such as red and fuchsia; acceptable nail polish colors include clear, buff, and opaque colors such as light pink; avoid all decals and decorations on fingernails)

8. _Makeup_

_____wear little to moderate makeup (avoid extremes of too much makeup or no makeup; makeup should look very natural in sunlight)

_____wear soft colors (avoid eyeshadows with definite colors, such as blues, greens, and purples)

This chapter discusses the role of uniforms. Gundersen says that uniforms are symbolic and establish a role stereotype. He argues that uniforms give people conspicuous invisibility because we see the uniform but not the person in it.

21

Uniforms: Conspicuous Invisibility

D. F. Gundersen

The purposes of uniforms are fairly obvious at first glance. People wear uniforms to signify specific functions, and the public links an expectation of a function to a uniform. Medical personnel rely on being recognized and given control in emergency situations. Law enforcement officers need to be visible both to other officers and to those who need their assistance (officers who don't have these needs, don't wear uniforms). Uniformed custodians and grounds keepers find the public is more understanding of the small intrusions necessary in their work.

We put military recruits in identical fatigues and give them short hair cuts as a leveling tactic, to make them all look and feel equal. We make them feel less individual—more members of a class—and almost instantly they begin to act more like soldiers. Soon the class to which they belong becomes more important than individual identities, and the group can accomplish things that would be impossible for the individuals. This class can also do things as a group that would be repellant to each individual, for the individuals do not bear the guilt. I need not give examples, they are all too common in history and in the daily newspapers. An armed force cannot run by consensus of the soldiers. The unit must work as a group, and uniforms are a major communicator in fostering this attitude.

We put many school children, girl scouts, and boy scouts in uniforms for similar reasons. There is a time for children to learn to give up a bit of individual identity for the good of the group and to learn to accomplish things that would be virtually impossible working as individuals. Uniforms are usually worn in schools that stress equality among students.

This article was written especially for this book.

No longer can the best dressed student command the admiration of less fortunate classmates. When all students dress alike, individuality is expressed in less obvious forms, and some students who might otherwise be relegated to the fringes of interaction are given the opportunity to excel. So on occasion, the use of uniforms simply makes people be a little more creative (and perhaps more genuine) in their individuality.

The Uniform as a Symbol

A uniform is a nonverbal artifact, something that adds to one's appearance and communicates to those who see it. Uniforms alter the perceptions of those who see them. What would you do if a stranger asked you to do some small favor such as picking up a paper bag in the street, putting a coin in a parking meter, or not standing in a bus stop zone? Would you do it? Would you think the person odd to have asked you? Leonard Bickman (1974) did a study in which he had an experimenter ask passersby on the street to do such favors for him. The experimenter was dressed in some cases in a coat and tie, in others as a milkman or a guard. It was assumed that the "civilian" had no more authority than any other person on the street. The milkman had a low authority identity, and the guard looked very much like a police officer.

Though Bickman varied the procedure in several fashions, the overall finding of his study was that people complied with the requests quite often when they were made by the guard, less often when they came from the milkman, and least often when asked by a "civilian." Bickman's findings suggest that nearly any uniform has more authority than attire that is not recognizable as a uniform and that some uniforms have more authority than others (depending on the role or identity signified). Although a uniform confers authority, some uniforms are stereotyped as greater in authority than others.

The Uniform as a Role

Law enforcement officers and researchers in the field of law enforcement are aware of the mixture of positive and negative stereotypes elicited by police uniforms. In the last two decades, some departments have radically changed their uniforms in the hope that the public would alter some of the unfortunate stereotypes associated with the traditional uniform. These departments changed to a blazer and slacks uniform, forsaking the traditional paramilitary officers' garb (a uniform that has changed little in over a century). The paramilitary uniform is the one you see on most officers, it is a near copy of an army dress uniform but has the badge and gun belt to make it look even more fearsome. The findings have been mixed. Initially, these departments reported more congenial relations with the public and more positive attitudes on the part of their officers (Tenzel and Cizanckas, 1973), but this may have been merely a product of the novelty of the change. Over time, the positive aspects of the change seemed fewer and fewer (Mauro, 1984). At this time about half of the departments that adopted the blazer and slacks uniform have returned to the traditional garb. In some few cases, officers quit the force rather than adopt the new uniform. I know of one officer who took a lower paying job on another force, but in the force "where he could look like a cop." Another officer, wearing the blazer and slacks uniform, was approached by an elderly citizen who said, "Sonny, you look like a fast young man. There's a robbery going on at the gas station. Run and get a policeman."

In an attempt to determine some of the effects of these new uniforms both on the public and on the police officers wearing them, two police forces, similar in size, constituency, and geography, cooperated in a comparative study (Gundersen and Summerlin, 1978). The only obvious difference between these departments was that one wore the traditional uniform, gun belt, and insignia, while the other had been wearing the blazer and slacks (no badges or firearms obvious) for nearly a decade. Members of the communities served by these two forces were queried concerning their perceptions of the local police force. The officers on each force were similarly queried concerning their perceptions of themselves. The findings exhibited some predictable and some surprising insights.

The traditionally attired officers were seen by the public as quite dynamic, while only moderately professional, objective and trustworthy. The non-traditionally dressed officers were seen as highly trustworthy, objective, and professional, yet lacking in dynamism. This is a mixed set of findings since one would hope that officers would receive high marks in all, not just some of these categories. More startling was the finding that the officers themselves mirrored the reports of the public. They saw themselves as more professional, trustworthy, objective, and less dynamic, if they wore the blazer and slacks.

In another study (Gundersen, 1987), three types of police uniforms were drawn by a skilled artist. Each was drawn in the same pose, yet in isolation. These line drawings showed the uniforms in a standing position, as though they were being worn by an invisible officer. One was a standard paramilitary uniform, the second was a modified paramilitary (Eisenhower jacket and slacks), and the third was the blazer and slacks. Separate drawings designated male and female officers. These six drawings were presented to subjects who were asked to make judgments based solely on the clothing they were seeing (the word uniform was never used).

Even when subjects dealt with such sterile stimuli, differences in their judgments were evident. The blazer and slacks uniform was rated as more professional than the other two uniforms. No differences were evident in the measures of objectivity, trustworthiness, or dynamism. A disquieting, yet predictable, sidelight was that any female uniform was judged to be less dynamic and professional than any male uniform. This is likely related to stereotyped assumptions that police officers need to be large and muscular and probably has little to do with the uniform styles.

The Uniform as a Trap

Perhaps you begin to see how seemingly simple things like uniforms can trigger complex interactions between the public and the uniformed individuals, as well as cause changes within the person who wears the uniform. The role that the uniform defines becomes the role that the public expects, and it becomes shocking to see a police officer acting like a civilian. If you see a middle-aged woman kissing a younger man as he gets into a taxi, you may raise an eyebrow but are not apt to think much of the occurrence. When this middle-aged woman was a uniformed police officer, it led to complaints from the public and disciplinary action against her. In truth, the young man was her son, and he was leaving for the army. In many ways, the uniformed person becomes trapped in a role and locked away from her or his actual identity by the expectations the uniform fosters.

The chances are quite good that you saw an officer in the last few hours. What did the officer look like? Did she have long or short hair? Did he have glasses? Or is it possible that you can't remember? You may recall seeing an officer, but remember very little else about the person. All you saw was an officer. The aspects of this person's appearance that make for individuality were obscured by the uniform and the role identity it forces on you.

Officers report that this phenomenon is particularly vexing on the receiving end. They feel stigmatized. They feel like members of a highly visible, impersonally stereotyped minority. They are rarely remembered as persons, but merely as officers. They are rarely treated as persons, but rather as objects. People in uniforms are pretty obvious if you need their help or if you are trying to avoid them, but they tend to blend into the woodwork when your attention is elsewhere. To a lost child an officer may look like a gallant knight. To a victim of a crime an officer may look like John Wayne. To someone from out of town the officer may look like an information booth. To someone looking for a place to get some film developed, the officer may look like nothing at all—the officer may not even be noticed.

"There's Never a Cop Around When You Need One."

A uniformed person may be simultaneously obvious and unobtrusive. In uniform, a person becomes assigned to a class, and individual identity diminishes. If the role/class is important to you at that time (do you need an officer at this moment?), then the class is noticed, but if not, the officer becomes an object and joins that preponderance of things in the world that you simply don't see. Just as you pay little attention to mailboxes or pay phones until you need them, you don't notice how often you see law enforcement officers until you have reason to look for one. The cliche states, "There's never a cop around when you need one," suggesting that you rarely notice the *presence* or *absence* of a uniformed person without good reason. This can lead to some interesting problems.

The power of a uniform to depersonalize yet lend authority is evident in the recurring phenomenon of the uniformed criminal. Criminals find easy access to the homes of their victims if they are dressed as police officers. A criminal dressed in white has virtually unlimited access in a hospital (this very problem has led to identification badges for medical staff in many hospitals, reinstating individual identity among the uniformed personnel). Even a set of coveralls may "uniform" a criminal as a janitor or grounds keeper and provide ready access to victims and property.

Some years ago a small town in Arizona had a rash of baffling daylight burglaries. These crimes were committed regularly in neighborhoods while people were mowing lawns, children were playing on the sidewalks, and garments were being hung on clotheslines in backyards. Investigating officers could get no eye witness descriptions of the burglars. It was as though they were invisible.

The solution to the case, and to many similar crimes over the years, involved a tactic noted by G.K. Chesterton in 1911 in his short story "The Invisible Man." In this story, an apparently invisible person is responsible for leaving threatening notes in crowded places, as well as leaving a prominent message on a window while a couple is having tea just inside the pane. People even hear the criminal's voice on deserted streets. Finally, a murder is committed in a house that has four men guarding its only entrance. The invisible murderer leaves the reader to ponder a pool of blood in the house, footprints in the snow that wind among the men who were guarding the door and the body of the victim found at some distance from the crime. The culprit turns out to be a postman, a uniformed person who is so common in everyday British life as to be virtually invisible.

In the small town burglaries, the culprits were a couple of men who had a nondescript panel truck and who wore neat blue work uniforms—the kind worn by appliance repairmen. They would drive brazenly up to a house and carry out appliances (as well as many unseen smaller articles) without being noticed. The neighbors rarely recalled seeing anything out of the ordinary because the appearance of such a truck and such workmen is so common in suburban life that it is unremarkable.

Summary

There are contradictions evident in the ways uniforms affect people, and these contradictions have been explored in this chapter. The effects of a uniform are rather predictable. Put an eight-year-old in a fireman's hat, and you will get stereotyped firefighter behavior. Put a cowboy outfit on him and expect a similar (if behaviorally different) response. Moreover, the other children around him will treat him as though he really were a firefighter or a cowboy. In this fashion, a uniform (with its stereotypic role expectations) changes the behavior of the one wearing it and the behavior of those with whom contact is made. Whether the change takes place because of the uniform itself or because of the decision to wear it, is a matter of conjecture.

Remember the primary purpose for a uniform is to identify the wearer (to assign a role). In so doing, uniforms communicate in two directions—outward to those viewing them and inward to those wearing them. They create role expectations that lead to selective perception by both parties. Either party may be misunderstood if the other's expectations aren't met. Uniforms allow instant identification of the class of the uniformed person while obscuring the identity of the individual beneath the uniform. Insofar as the viewer treats the wearer as a member of a class, the one wearing the uniform feels more a member of that class and less an individual. Being treated as an object may make the uniformed person feel less human and less responsible for individual actions.

Uniforms are powerful nonverbal symbols that create and define roles. These roles usually become stereotyped and can become traps for both the uniformed person and those with whom he or she comes in contact.

References

Bickman, L. (1974). The social power of a uniform. *Journal of Applied Social Psychology*, 4, 47-61.

Chesterton, G.K. (1911). The invisible man. In *The innocence of Father Brown*. New York: Dodd, Mead & Co., Inc.

Gundersen, D.F. (1987). Credibility and the police uniform. *Journal of Police Science and Administration*, 15, 192-95.

Gundersen, D.F., and Summerlin, R.E. (1978). The police uniform: A study of change, *FBI Law Enforcement Bulletin*, 47 (4), 13-15.

Mauro, R. (1984). The constable's new clothes: Effects of uniforms on perceptions and problems of police officers. *Journal of Applied Social Psychology*, 14, 42-56.

Tenzel, J.H., and Cizanckas, V. (1973). Uniform experiment. *Journal of Police Science and Administration*, 1, 421-24.

22

Colors create an impression and can be used to establish an image or a mood. Research shows that people have specific associations with colors. This chart lists the various colors and the moods and meanings associated with them.

Color in the Environment
Judee K. Burgoon and Thomas J. Saine

Color	Moods	Symbolic Meanings
Red	Hot, affectionate, angry, defiant, contrary, hostile, full of vitality, calm, tender	Happiness, lust, intimacy, love, restlessness, agitation, royalty, rage, sin, blood
Blue	Cool, pleasant, leisurely, distant, infinite, secure, transcendent, calm, tender	Dignity, sadness, tenderness, truth
Yellow	Unpleasant, exciting, hostile, cheerful, joyful, jovial	Superficial glamor, sun, light, wisdom, masculinity, royalty (in China), age (in Greece), prostitution (in Italy), famine (in Egypt)
Orange	Unpleasant, exciting, disturbed, distressed, upset, defiant, contrary, hostile, stimulating	Sun, fruitfulness, harvest, thoughtfulness
Purple	Depressed, sad, dignified, stately	Wisdom, victory, pomp, wealth, humility, tragedy
Green	Cool, pleasant, leisurely, in control	Security, peace, jealousy, hate, aggressiveness, calm
Black	Sad, intense, anxiety, fear, despondent, dejected, melancholy, unhappy	Darkness, power, mastery, protection, decay, mystery, wisdom, death, atonement
Brown	Sad, not tender, despondent, dejected, melancholy, unhappy	Melancholy, protection, autumn, decay, humility, atonement
White	Joy, lightness, neutral, cold	Solemnity, purity, femininity, humility, joy, light, innocence, fidelity, cowardice

Key Terms and Concepts

Gross, *Admit It or Not, Dress Codes Are a Fact of Life*

unwritten rules
success suit

gender differences
appropriateness

Gorden, Tengler, and Infante, *Women's Clothing Predispositions as Predictors of Dress at Work, Job Satisfaction, and Career Advancement*

language of dress
impression formation
clothing predispositions

clothing-consciousness
self-concept
self esteem

Smith and Malandro, *Personal Appearance Factors Which Influence Perceptions of Credibility and Approachability of Men and Women*

credibility and clothing
approachability and clothing
gender

Gundersen, *Uniforms: Conspicuous Invisibility*

expectations
leveling tactic
depersonalize

uniform as a symbol,
role, and trap
obvious and unobtrusive

Burgoon and Saine, *Color in the Environment*

meanings of colors
moods
symbolic meanings

Part Five

Spatial Communication
(Proxemics and Territoriality)

Spatial communication, also called *proxemics*, is concerned with the perception and use of space. Here we are concerned with how space is organized, objects in space, and distances between and among people.

The use of space involves the complicated balancing of *affiliative* and *privacy* needs. People have the need to affiliate or to be in contact with other people. Very few of us can survive in isolation for extended periods of time. People offer us the stimulation, support, and contact needed for psychological and physical health.

On the other hand, we also need our privacy. People prefer to have space around them and to be alone for certain periods of time. Privacy needs are met in different ways depending on whether you live in a crowded city, a suburb, or a rural environment.

And so people must balance their conflicting needs for affiliation and privacy. This is done through controlling our *territories* and *personal space*. Territory is a geographic area. Animals exhibit an innate need for territory called *territoriality*. Some territories are clearly private. These include your home, your room, and your office. Other territories are more public and may include your seat in a classroom, a table in the library, or a booth in a restaurant.

People mark their territory by placing personal objects there to communicate to others that the space is taken. For example, you may enter a classroom, place your books on a chair to mark it, and then go out for a drink of water before class begins. You would probably be surprised and disturbed to return and find your books moved and someone else occupying your marked space.

One of the most important features of territories is *crowding*. Crowding is defined as the perception of the number of people in a space. If there are too many people, the space will be perceived as overcrowded. Continuous overcrowding causes mental and physical health problems.

It is important to distinguish between crowding and *density*. Density is the actual number of people in a space while crowding involves the *perception* of the number of people. A person who has been raised in a large city such as New York may feel less crowded at a large meeting than someone raised on a large ranch in Texas.

While territory refers to a geographic area, personal space refers to the area around you. This area moves with you and is sometimes referred to as your *personal space bubble* because it involves a "bubble" of space on all sides of you. Your personal space will expand and contract depending upon the situation. It will be larger in a formal situation among strangers. Here you want more space between you and others. Your personal space will contract, however, when a close friend approaches.

Spatial communication plays an important role in our lives. We refer to developing friendships as "getting close" to someone. We use space to dominate and manipulate people, or to put them at ease. Space is used in many different ways in our lives and its effects, while subtle, are profound.

23

Hall discusses the importance of distance. He explains the situational influence on the use of space, and differentiates and describes four spatial zones: intimate, personal, social, and public distances. Each zone is used for different purposes and the system has become a basis for the study of spatial communication.

Distances in Man

Edward T. Hall

Birds and mammals not only have territories which they occupy and defend against their own kind but they have a series of uniform distances which they maintain from each other. Hediger has classified these as flight distance, critical distance, and personal and social distance. Man, too, has a uniform way of handling distance from the fellows. With very few exceptions, flight distance and critical distance have been eliminated from human reactions. Personal distance and social distance, however, are obviously still present.

How many distances do human beings have and how do we distinguish them? What is it that differentiates one distance from the other? The answer to this question was not obvious at first when I began my investigation of distances in man. Gradually, however, evidence began to accumulate indicating that the regularity of distances observed for humans is the consequence of sensory shifts — the type cited in Chapters VII and VIII.

One common source of information about the distance separating two people is the loudness of the voice. Working with the linguistic scientist George Trager, I began by observing shifts in the voice associated with changes in distance. Since the whisper is used when people are very close, and the shout is used to span great distances, the question Trager and I posed was, How many vocal shifts are sandwiched between these two extremes? Our procedure for discovering these patterns was for Trager to stand still while I talked to him at different distances. If both of us agreed that a vocal shift had occurred, we would then measure the distance and note down a general description. The result was the eight distances described at the end of Chapter Ten in *The Silent Language*.

Further observation of human beings in social situations convinced me that these eight distances were overly complex. Four were sufficient; these I have termed intimate, personal, social, and public (each with its close and far phase). My choice of terms to describe various distances was deliberate. Not only was it influenced by Hediger's work with animals indicating the continuity between *infraculture* and culture but also by a desire to provide a clue as to the types of activities and relationships associated with each distance, thereby linking them to peoples' minds with specific inventories of relationships and activities. It should be noted at this point that *how people are feeling toward each other* at the time is a decisive factor in the distance used. Thus people who are very angry or emphatic about the point they are making will move in close, they "turn up the volume," as it were, by shouting. Similarly—as any woman knows—one of the first signs that a man is beginning to feel amorous is his move closer to her. If the woman does not feel similarly disposed she signals this by moving back.

The Dynamism of Space

In Chapter VII we saw that man's sense of space and distance is not static, that it has very little to do with the single-viewpoint linear perspective developed by the Renaissance artists and still taught in most schools of art and architecture. Instead, man senses distance as other animals do. His perception of space is dynamic because it is related to action—what can be done in a given space—rather than what is seen by passive viewing.

The general failure to grasp the significance of the many elements that contribute to man's sense of space may be due to two mistaken notions: (1) that for every effect there is a single and identifiable cause; and (2) that man's boundary begins and ends with his skin. If we can rid ourselves of the need for a single explanation, and if we can think of man as surrounded by a series of expanding and contracting fields which provide information of many kinds, we shall begin to see him in an entirely different light. We can then begin to learn about human behavior, including personality types. Not only are there introverts and extroverts, authoritarian and egalitarian, Apollonian and Dionysian types and all the other shades and grades of personality, but each one of us has a number of learned *situational* personalities. The simplest form of the situational personality is that associated with responses to intimate, personal, social, and public transactions. Some individuals never develop the public phase of their personalities and, therefore, cannot fill public spaces; they make very poor speakers or moderators. As many psychiatrists know, other people have trouble with the intimate and personal zones and cannot endure closeness to others.

Concepts such as these are not always easy to grasp, because most of the distance-sensing process occurs outside awareness. We sense other people as close or distant, but we cannot always put our finger on what it is that enables us to characterize them as such. So many different things are happening at once it is difficult to sort out the sources of information on which we base our reactions. Is it tone of voice or stance or distance? This sorting process can be accomplished only by careful observation over a long period of time in a wide variety of situations, making a note of each small shift in information received. For example, the presence or absence of the sensation of warmth from the body of another person marks the line between intimate and non-intimate space. The smell of freshly washed hair and the blurring of another person's features seen close up combine with the sensation of warmth to create intimacy. By using one's self as a control and recording changing patterns of sensory input it is possible to identify structure points in the distance-sensing system. In effect, one identifies, one by one, the isolates making up the sets that constitute the intimate, personal, social, and public zones.

The following descriptions of the four distance zones have been compiled from observations and interviews with non-contact, middle-class, healthy adults, mainly natives of the northeastern seaboard of the United States. A high percentage of the subjects were men and women from business and the professions; many could be classified as intellectuals. The interviews were effectively neutral; that is, the subjects were not noticeably excited, depressed, or angry. There were no unusual environmental factors, such as extremes of temperature or noise. These descriptions represent only a first approximation. They will doubtless seem crude when more is known about proxemic observation and how people distinguish one distance from another. It should be emphasized that these generalizations are not representative of human behavior in general—or even of American behavior in general—but only of the group included in the sample. Negroes and Spanish Americans as well as persons who come from southern European cultures have very different proxemic patterns.

Each of the four distance zones described below has a near and a far phase, which will be discussed after short introductory remarks. It should be noted that the measured distances vary somewhat with differences in personality and environmental factors. For example, a high noise level or low illumination will ordinarily bring people closer together.

Intimate Distance

At intimate distance, the presence of the other person is unmistakable and may at times be overwhelming because of the greatly stepped-up sensory inputs. Sight (often distorted), olfaction, heat from the other person's body, sound, smell, and feel of the breath all combine to signal unmistakable involvement with another body.

Intimate Distance—Close Phase

This is the distance of love-making and wrestling, comforting and protecting. Physical contact or the high possibility of physical involvement is uppermost in the awareness of both persons. The use of their distance receptors is greatly reduced except for olfaction and sensation of radiant heat, both of which are stepped up. In the maximum contact phase, the muscles and skin communicate. Pelvis, thighs, and head can be brought into play; arms can encircle. Except at the outer limits, sharp vision is blurred. When close vision is possible within the intimate range—as with children—the image is greatly enlarged and stimulates much, if not all, of the retina. The detail that can be seen at this distance is extraordinary. This detail plus the cross-eyed pull of the eye muscles provide a visual experience that cannot be confused with any other distance. Vocalization at intimate distance plays a very minor part in the communication process, which is carried mainly by other channels. A whisper has the effect of expanding the distance. The vocalizations that do occur are largely involuntary.

Intimate Distance—Far Phase

(Distance: six to eighteen inches)

Heads, thighs, and pelvis are not easily brought into contact, but hands can reach and grasp extremities. The head is seen as enlarged in size, and its features are distorted. Ability to focus the eye easily is an important feature of this distance for Americans. The iris of the other person's eye seen at about six to nine inches is enlarged to more than life-size. Small blood vessels in the sclera are clearly perceived, pores are enlarged. Clear vision (15 degrees) includes the upper or lower portion of the face, which is perceived as enlarged. The nose is seen as over-large and may look distorted, as will other features such as lips, teeth, and tongue. Peripheral vision (30 to 180 degrees) includes the outline of head and shoulders and very often the hands.

Much of the physical discomfort that Americans experience when foreigners are inappropriately inside the intimate sphere is expressed as a distortion of the visual system. One subject said, "These people get so close, you're cross-eyed. It really makes me nervous. They put their face so close it feels like they're *inside you*." At the point where sharp focus is lost, one feels the uncomfortable muscular sensation of being cross-eyed from looking at something too close. The expressions "Get your face *out* of mine" and "He shook his fist *in* my face" apparently express how many Americans perceive their body boundaries.

At six to eighteen inches the voice is used but is normally held at a very low level or even a whisper. As Martin Joos, the linguist, describes it, "An intimate utterance pointedly avoids giving the addressee information from outside of the speaker's skin. The point . . . is simply to remind (hardly 'inform') the addressee of some feeling . . . inside the speaker's skin." The heat and odor of the other person's breath may be detected, even though it is directed away from subject's face. Heat loss or gain from other person's body begins to be noticed by some subjects.

The use of intimate distance in public is not considered proper by adult, middle-class Americans even though their young may be observed intimately involved with each other in automobiles and on beaches. Crowded subways and buses may bring strangers into what would ordinarily be classed as intimate spatial relations, but subway riders have defensive devices which take the real intimacy out of intimate space in public conveyances. The basic tactic is to be as immobile as possible and, when part of the trunk or extremities touches another person, withdraw if possible. If this is not possible, the muscles in the affected areas are kept tense. For members of the non-contact group, it is taboo to relax and enjoy bodily contact with strangers! In crowded elevators the hands are kept at the side or used to steady the body by grasping a railing. The eyes are fixed on infinity and are not brought to bear on anyone for more than a passing glance.

It should be noted once more that American proxemic patterns for intimate distance are by no means universal. Even the rules governing such intimacies as touching others cannot be counted on to remain constant. Americans who have had an opportunity for considerable social interaction with Russians report that many of the features characteristic of American intimate distance are present in Russian social distance. As we shall see in the following chapter, Middle Eastern subjects in public places do not express the outraged reaction to being touched by strangers which one encounters in American subjects.

Personal Distance

"Personal distance" is the term originally used by Hediger to designate the distance consistently separating the members of non-contact species.

It might be thought of as a small protective sphere or bubble that an organism maintains between itself and others.

Personal Distance—Close Phase

(Distance: one and a half to two and a half feet)

The kinesthetic sense of closeness derives in part from the possibilities present in regard to what each participant can do to the other with his extremities. At this distance, one can hold or grasp the other person. Visual distortion of the other's features is no longer apparent. However, there is noticeable feedback from the muscles that control the eyes. The reader can experience this himself if he will look at an object eighteen inches to three feet away, paying particular attention to the muscles around his eyeballs. He can feel the pull of these muscles as they hold the two eyes on a single point so that the image of each eye stays in register. Pushing gently with the tip of the finger on the surface of the lower eyelid so that the eyeball is displaced will illustrate clearly the work these muscles perform in maintaining a single coherent image. A visual angle of 15 degrees takes in another person's upper or lower face, which is seen with exceptional clarity. The planes and roundness of the face are accentuated; the nose projects and the ears recede; fine hair of the face, eyelashes, and pores is clearly visible. The three-dimensional quality of objects is particularly pronounced. Objects have roundness, substance, and form unlike that perceived at any other distance. Surface textures are also very prominent and are clearly differentiated from each other. Where people stand in relation to each other signals their relationship, or how they feel toward each other, or both. A wife can stay inside the circle of her husband's close personal zone with impunity. For another woman to do so is an entirely different story.

Personal Distance—Far Phase

(Distance: two and a half to four feet)

Keeping someone at "arm's length" is one way of expressing the far phase of personal distance. It extends from a point that is just outside easy touching distance by one person to a point where two people can touch fingers if they extend both arms. This is the limit of physical domination in the very real sense. Beyond it, a person cannot easily "get his hands on" someone else. Subjects of personal interest and involvement can be discussed at this distance. Head size is perceived as normal and details of the other person's features are clearly visible. Also easily seen are fine details of skin, gray hair, "sleep" in the eye, stains on teeth, spots, small wrinkles, or dirt on clothing. Foveal vision covers only an area the size of the tip of the nose or one eye, so that the gaze must wander around the face (*where the eye is directed* is strictly a matter of cultural conditioning). Fifteen-degree clear vision covers the upper or lower face, while 180-degree peripheral vision takes in the hands and the whole body of a seated person. Movement of the hands is detected, but fingers can't be counted. The voice level is moderate. No body heat is perceptible. While olfaction is not normally present for Americans, it is for a great many other people who use colognes to create an olfactory bubble. Breath odor can sometimes be detected at this distance, but Americans are generally trained to direct the breath away from others.

Social Distance

The boundary line between the far phase of personal distance and the close phase of social distance marks, in the words of one subject, the "limit of domination." Intimate visual detail in the face is not perceived, and nobody touches or expects to touch another person unless there is some special effort. Voice level is normal for Americans. There is little change between the far and close phases, and conversations can be overheard at a distance of up to twenty feet. I have observed that in overall loudness, the American voice at these distances is below that of the Arab, the Spaniard, the South Asian Indian, and the Russian, and somewhat above that of the English upper class, the Southeast Asian, and the Japanese.

Social Distance—Close Phase

(Distance: four to seven feet)

Head size is perceived as normal; as one moves away from the subject, the foveal area of the eye can take in an ever-increasing amount of the person. At four feet, a one-degree visual angle covers an area of a little more than one eye. At seven feet the area of sharp focus extends to the nose and parts of both eyes; or the whole mouth, one eye, and the nose are sharply seen. Many Americans shift their gaze back and forth from eye to eye or from eyes to mouth. Details of skin texture and hair are clearly perceived. At a 60-degree visual angle, the head, shoulders, and upper trunk are seen at a distance of four feet; while the same sweep includes the whole figure at seven feet.

Impersonal business occurs at this distance, and in the close phase there is more involvement than in the distant phase. People who work together tend to use close social distance. It is also a very common distance for people who are attending a casual social gathering. To stand and look down at a person at this distance has a domineering effect, as when a man talks to his secretary or receptionist.

Social Distance—Far Phase

(Distance: seven to twelve feet)

This is the distance to which people move when someone says, "Stand away so I can look at you." Business and social discourse conducted at the far end of social distance has a more formal character than if it occurs inside the close phase. Desks in the offices of important people are large enough to hold visitors at the far phase of social distance. Even in an office with standard-size desks, the chair opposite is eight or nine feet away from the man behind the desk. At the far phase of social distance, the finest details of the face, such as the capillaries in the eyes, are lost. Otherwise, skin texture, hair, condition of teeth, and condition of clothes are all readily visible. None of my subjects mentioned heat or odor from another person's body as detectable at this distance. The full figure—with a good deal of space around it—is encompassed in a 60-degree glance. Also, at around twelve feet, feedback from the eye muscles used to hold the eyes inward on a single spot falls off rapidly. The eyes and the mouth of the other person are seen in the area of sharpest vision. Hence, it is not necessary to shift the eyes to take in the whole face. During conversations of any significant length it is more important to maintain visual contact at this distance than it is at closer distance.

Proxemic behavior of this sort is culturally conditioned and entirely arbitrary. It is also binding on all concerned. To fail to hold the other person's eye is to shut him out and bring conversation to a halt, which is why people who are conversing at this distance can be observed craning their necks and leaning from side to side to avoid intervening obstacles. Similarly, when one person is seated and the other is standing, prolonged visual contact at less than ten or twelve feet tires the neck muscles and is generally avoided by subordinates who are sensitive to their employer's comfort. If, however, the status of the two parties is reversed so that the subordinate is seated, the other party may often come closer.

At this distant phase, the voice level is noticeably louder than for the close phase, and it can usually be heard easily in an adjoining room if the door is open. Raising the voice or shouting can have the effect of reducing social distance to personal distance.

A proxemic feature of social distance (far phase) is that it can be used to insulate or screen people from each other. This distance makes it possible for them to continue to work in the presence of another person without appearing to be rude. Receptionists in offices are particularly vulnerable as most employers expect double duty: answering questions, being polite to callers, as well as typing. If the receptionist is less than ten feet from another person, even a stranger, she will be sufficiently involved to be virtually compelled to converse. If she has more space, however, she can work quite freely without having to talk. Likewise, husbands returning from work often find themselves sitting and relaxing, reading the paper at ten or more feet from their wives, for at this distance a couple can engage each other briefly and disengage at will. Some men discover that their wives have arranged the furniture back-to-back — a favorite sociofugal device of the cartoonist Chick Young, creator of "Blondie." The back-to-back seating arrangement is an appropriate solution to minimum space because it is possible for two people to stay uninvolved if that is their desire.

Public Distance

Several important sensory shifts occur in the transition from the personal and social distances to public distance, which is well outside the circle of involvement.

Public Distance — Close Phase

(Distance: twelve to twenty-five feet)

At twelve feet an alert subject can take evasive or defensive action if threatened. The distance may even cue a vestigial but subliminal form of flight reaction. The voice is loud but not full-volume. Linguists have observed that a careful choice of words and phrasing of sentences as well as grammatical or syntactic shifts occur at this distance. Martin Joos's choice of the term "formal style" is appropriately descriptive: "Formal texts . . . demand advance planning . . . the speaker is correctly said to think on his feet." The angle of sharpest vision (one degree) covers the whole face. Fine details of the skin and eyes are no longer visible. At sixteen feet, the body begins to lose its roundness and to look flat. The color of the eyes begins to be imperceivable; only the white of the eye is visible. Head size is perceived as considerably under life-size. The 15-degree lozenge-shaped area of clear vision covers the faces of two people at twelve feet, while 60-degree scanning includes the whole body with a little space around it. Other persons present can be seen peripherally.

Public Distance—Far Phase

(Distance: twenty-five feet or more)

Thirty feet is the distance that is automatically set around important public figures. An excellent example occurs in Theodore H. White's *The Making of the President 1960* when John F. Kennedy's nomination became a certainty. White is describing the group at the "hideaway cottage" as Kennedy entered:

> Kennedy loped into the cottage with his light, dancing step, as young and lithe as springtime, and called a greeting to those who stood in his way. Then he seemed to slip from them as he descended the steps of the split-level cottage to a corner where his brother Bobby and brother-in-law Sargent Shriver were chatting, waiting for him. The others in the room surged forward on impulse to join him. Then they halted. A distance of perhaps 30 feet separated them from him, but it was impassable. They stood apart, these older men of long-established power, and watched him. He turned after a few minutes, saw them watching him, and whispered to his brother-in-law. Shriver now crossed the separating space to invite them over. First Averell Harriman; then Dick Daley; then Mike DiSalle, then, one by one, let them all congratulate him. Yet no one could pass the little open distance between him and them uninvited, because there was this thin separation about him, and the knowledge they were there not as his patrons but as his clients. They could come by invitation only, for this might be a President of the United States.

The usual public distance is not restricted to public figures but can be used by anyone on public occasions. There are certain adjustments that must be made, however. Most actors know that at thirty or more feet the subtle shades of meaning conveyed by the normal voice are lost as are the details of facial expression and movement. Not only the voice but everything else must be exaggerated or amplified. Much of the nonverbal part of the communication shifts to gestures and body stance. In addition, the tempo of the voice drops, words are enunciated more clearly, and there are stylistic changes as well. Martin Joos's *frozen style* is characteristic: "Frozen style is for people who are to remain strangers." The whole man may be seen as quite small and he is perceived in a setting. Foveal vision takes in more and more of the man until he is entirely within the small circle of sharpest vision. At which point— when people look like ants—contact with them as human beings fades rapidly. The 60-degree cone of vision takes in the setting while peripheral vision has as its principal function the altering of the individual to movement at the side.

24

*Lyman and Scott provide us with a category system for classi-
fying territories: public, home, interactional, and body territories. Each type of territory has its own rules guiding the type
of activity, degree of ownership, and response to territorial invasions. While many people now use the term **personal space**
instead of body territory, this system is frequently used to
describe spatial communication.*

Territoriality
A Neglected Sociological Dimension*

Stanford M. Lyman and Marvin B. Scott

All living organisms observe some sense of territoriality, that is, some
sense — whether learned or instinctive to their species — in which control
over space is deemed central for survival. Although man's domination
over space is potentially unlimited, in contemporary society it appears
that men acknowledge increasingly fewer *free* territories for themselves.

Free territory is carved out of space and affords opportunities for idiosyncrasy and identity. Central to the manifestation of these opportunities
are boundary creation and enclosure. This is so because activities that
run counter to expected norms need seclusion or invisibility to permit
unsanctioned performance, and because peculiar identities are sometimes
impossible to realize in the absence of an appropriate setting. Thus the
opportunities for freedom of action — with respect to normatively
discrepant behavior and maintenance of specific identities — are
intimately connected with the ability to attach boundaries to space and
command access to or exclusion from territories.

The Types of Territories

We can distinguish four kinds of territories, namely, *public territories,
home territories, interactional territories* and *body territories.*

© 1967 by the Society for the Study of Social Problems. Abridged with permission from
Social Problems, Vol. 15, No. 2, Fall 1967, pp. 236-249.

*We are grateful to Donald Ball and Edwin Lemert for their critical reading of the manuscript.

Public Territories

Public territories are those areas where the individual has freedom of access, but not necessarily of action, by virtue of his claim to citizenship. These territories are officially open to all, but certain images and expectations of appropriate behavior and of the categories of individuals who are normally perceived as using these territories modify freedom. It is commonly expected that illegal activities and impermissible behavior will not occur in public places. Since public territories are vulnerable to violation in both respects, however, policemen are charged with the task of removing lawbreakers from the scene of their activities and restricting behavior in public places.

Public territories are thus ambiguous with respect to accorded freedoms. First, the official rights of access may be regularly violated by local custom. Second, status discrepancy may modify activity and entrance rights. For example, the ambiguity in the distinction between minors and adults is a source of confusion and concern in the regulation of temporal and access rights to those whose status is unclear. Finally, activities once forbidden in public may be declared permissible, thus enlarging the freedom of the territory; or activities once licit may be proscribed, thus restricting it. Hence display of female breasts is now permitted in San Francisco nightclubs, but not on the streets or before children. Nude swimming enjoys police protection at certain designated beaches, but watching nude swimmers at these same beaches is forbidden to those who are attired.

Home Territories

Home territories are areas where the regular participants have a relative freedom of behavior and a sense of intimacy and control over the area. Examples include makeshift club houses of children, hobo jungles, and homosexual bars. Home and public territories may be easily confused. In fact "the areas of public places and the areas of home territories are not always clearly differentiated in the social world and what may be defined and used as a public place by some may be defined and used as a home territory by others." Thus, a home territory that also may be used as a public one is defined by its regular use by specific persons or categories of persons and by the particular "territorial stakes" or "identity pegs" that are found in such places.

Home territories may be established by "sponsorship" or "colonization." An example of the former is found in the merchant emigrants from China who established caravansaries in certain quarters of Occidental cities which served as public trading establishments but also as living quarters, employment agencies, meeting places, and courts for their Landsmänner. Colonization occurs when a person or group lays claim to a formally free territory by virtue of discovery, regular usage, or peculiar relationship. Thus certain restaurants become home territories to those who are impressed with their first meal there; to those who eat there on specific occasions, such as luncheons, birthdays, or after sporting events; and to those who are intimate with the waitress.

It is precisely because of their officially open condition that public areas are vulnerable to conversion into home territories. The rules of openness are sufficiently broad and ambiguous so that restrictions on time, place, and manner are difficult to promulgate and nearly impossible to enforce. Armed with a piece of chalk children can change the public sidewalk into a gameboard blocking pedestrian traffic. Despite building codes and parental admonitions youngsters convert abandoned buildings or newly begun sites into forts, clubs, and hideaways.

But children are not the only colonizers on the public lands. Beggars and hawkers will stake out a "territory" on the sidewalks or among the blocks and occupy it sometimes to the exclusion of all others similarly employed. The idle and unemployed will loiter on certain streetcorners, monopolizing the space, and frightening off certain respectable types with their loud, boisterous, or obscene language, cruel jests, and suggestive leers. Members of racial and ethnic groups colonize a portion of the city and adorn it with their peculiar institutions, language, and rules of conduct.

Among the most interesting examples of colonizing on the public lands are those attempts by youths to stake out streets as home territories open only to members of their own clique and defended against invasion by rival groups. Subject always to official harassment by police and interference by other adults who claim the streets as public territories, youths resolve the dilemma by redefining adults as non-persons whose seemingly violative presence on the youth's "turf" does not challenge the latter's proprietorship. Streets are most vulnerable to colonizing in this manner and indeed, as the early studies of the Chicago sociologists illustrated so well, streets and knots of juxtaposed streets become unofficial home areas to all those groups who require relatively secluded yet open space in which to pursue their interests or maintain their identities.

Interactional Territories

Interactional territories refer to any area where a social gathering may occur. Surrounding any interaction is an invisible boundary, a kind of social membrane. A party is an interactional territory, as are the several knots of people who form clusters at parties. Every interactional territory implicitly makes a claim of boundary maintenance for the duration of the interaction. Thus access and egress are governed by rules understood, though not officially promulgated, by the members.

Interactional territories are characteristically mobile and fragile. Participants in a conversation may remain in one place, stroll along, or move periodically or erratically. They may interrupt only to resume it at a later time without permanently breaking the boundary or disintegrating the group. Even where "settings" are required for the interaction, mobility need not be dysfunctional if the items appropriate to the setting are movable. Thus chemists may not be able to complete a discussion without the assistance of a laboratory, but chess players may assemble or disassemble the game quite readily and in the most cramped quarters.

Body Territories

Finally, there are body territories, which include the space encompassed by the human body and the anatomical space of the body. The latter is, at least theoretically, the most private and inviolate of territories belonging to an individual. The rights to view and touch the body are of a sacred nature, subject to great restriction. For instance, a person's rights to his own body space are restricted where norms govern masturbation, or the appearance and decoration of skin. Moreover, rights of others to touch one's body are everywhere regulated, though perhaps modern societies impose greater restrictions than others.

Body space is, however, subject to creative innovation, idiosyncrasy, and destruction. First, the body may be marked or marred by scars, cuts, burns, and tattoos. In addition, certain of its parts may be inhibited or removed without its complete loss of function. These markings have a meaning beyond the purely anatomical. They are among the indicators of status or stigma.

The human organism exercises extraterritorial rights over both internal and external space. In the latter instance the space immediately surrounding a person is also inviolate. Thus conversations among friends are ecologically distinguishable from those between acquaintances or strangers. A person who persists in violating the extraterritorial space of another of the same sex may be accused of tactlessness and suspected of homosexuality, while uninvited intersex invasion may indicate unwarranted familiarity. Moreover, eye contact and visual persistence can be a measure of external space. Thus two strangers may look one another over at the proper distance, but as they near one another, propriety requires that they treat one another as non-persons unless a direct contact is going to be made.

Control over "inner space" is the quintessence of individuality and freedom. Violations of "inner space" are carried out by domination, ranging in intensity from perception of more than is voluntarily revealed to persuasion and ultimately hypnosis. Demonstration of idiosyncrasy with respect to "inner space" is exemplified by the modifications possible in the presentation of self through the uses of the several stimulants and depressants.

Territorial Encroachment

We can distinguish three forms of territorial encroachment: violation, invasion, and contamination.

Violation of a territory is unwarranted use of it. Violators are those who have repulsed or circumvented those who would deny them access. Violators are also, by virtue of their acts, claimants in some sense to the territory they have violated. Their claim, however, may vary in scope, intensity, and objective. Children may violate the graves of the dead by digging "for treasure" in the cemetery, but unlike ghouls, they are not seeking to remove the bodies for illicit purposes. Some territories may be violated, however, merely by unwarranted entrance into them. Among these are all those territories commonly restricted to categorical groups such as toilets, harems, nunneries, and public baths — areas commonly restricted according to sex. Other territories may not be necessarily violated by presence but only by innovative or prohibited use. Thus some parents regard family-wide nudity as permissible, but hold that sexual interest or intercourse among any but the married pair is forbidden. Interactional territories are violated when one or more of the legitimate interactants behaves out of character.

Invasion of a territory occurs when those not entitled to entrance or use nevertheless cross the boundaries and interrupt, halt, take over, or change the social meaning of the territory. Such invasions, then, may be temporary or enduring.

Contamination of a territory requires that it be rendered impure with respect to its definition and usage. Cholera may require that a portion of the city be quarantined. In a racial caste society the sidewalks may be contaminated by low caste persons walking upon them. Home territories may be contaminated by pollution or destruction of the "home" symbols.

Contamination of bodily territories occurs whenever the immediate space of or around the body is polluted. The removal by bathing of material involuntarily attached to the skin constitutes a ritualized purification rite of considerable importance in industrial societies.

However, body space may be contaminated in many ways, by smell, look, touch, and by proximity to contaminated persons or things. The sensitivity with respect to touch illustrates the complex nature of this contamination and also its peculiarly social character. The rules regarding touch are highly developed in American society and are clear indicators of social distance between individuals and groups. Typically, older people can touch younger ones, but suspicions of sexual immorality modify such contacts. Women who are friends or relatives may greet one another with a light kiss (commonly called a "peck") on the cheek, but not on the lips. Men who are long absent may be greeted by male friends and relatives with a hearty embrace and a touching of the cheeks, but the embrace must not be overlong or tender. Indeed, "rough-housing," mock-fighting, and pseudo-hostility are commonly employed in masculine affective relationships. Touch which would otherwise be contaminating is exempt from such designation when it takes place in situations of intense social action, e.g., on a dance floor, or in situations when the actors are not privileged to interact, e.g., crowded buses. At other times bodies contaminated by impermissible contacts are restored to their pure state by apologies.

Body space may be contaminated by a kind of negative charismatic contact whereby objects which, though neutral in themselves, carry contaminating effect when transferred directly to the body. Thus a comb or toothbrush may not be lent or borrowed in certain circles since to use someone else's tools of personal hygiene is to contaminate oneself. Typically, when clothing, especially clothing that will directlly touch the skin, is lent, it is proper for the lender to assure the borrower that the apparel is clean, and that it has not been worn by anyone since its last cleaning.

Reaction to Encroachment

We have already suggested that something of a reciprocal relation exists between the territorial types. For example, a public swimming pool — while officially open to all persons — might be conceived by certain regular users as an exclusive area. Strangers seeking access by virtue of their diffuse civic rights might be challenged by those whose sense of peculiar propriety is thus violated. Such a confrontation (sometimes called "when push meets shove") could result in retreat on the part of the party seeking admittance, flight on the part of those favoring denial, or strategy and tactics on the part of the contending parties to expand the area of legitimate access on the one hand, and withhold entirely or restrict the meaning of entry on the other.

Of course, the occupants of a territory may extend its use to others whose presence is not regarded as a threat. The most common situation is that in which common usage will not destroy or alter the value of the territory. When public territories have been colonized by users who do not fully monopolize the space, who embroider it by their presence, or whose occupancy still allows for other public and colonizing usages, the colonists will not be seriously opposed. Delinquent gangs who often define the streets of a neighborhood as a home territory do not usually regard the presence of local adults and children as an encroachment on their own occupancy. Unwarranted intrusion on interactional territories may be countenanced if the unwelcome guest indicates his willingness to be present on this occasion alone with no future rights of reentry, or to listen only and not to interrupt the proceedings. Bodies usually invulnerable to feel and probe by strangers may be violated if circumstances render the act physically safe, socially irrelevant, or emotionally neutral. Thus female nurses may massage their male patients with mutual impunity, and striptease dancers may perform unclothed upon a raised stage out of reach of the audience. However, all such contacts will tend to be defined as territorial encroachment when the claimants threaten obliteration, monopoly, or fundamental alteration of a territory. Under these conditions, the holders of territory are likely to react to unwelcome claimants in terms of *turf, defense, insulation,* or *linguistic collusion.*

Turf Defense

Turf defense is a response necessitated when the intruder cannot be tolerated. The animal world provides a multitude of examples which are instructive with respect to the human situation. Here we may be content, however, to confine ourselves to the human scene. When Chinese merchants sought "colonizing" rights among the urban merchants of San Francisco, they were welcomed and honored. A few years later, however, the appearance of Chinese miners in the white Americans' cherished gold fields called forth violent altercations and forced removals. In contemporary American cities delinquent gangs arm themselves with rocks, knives, tire irons, and zip guns to repel invaders from other streets. Among the "primitive" Kagoro the choice of weapons is escalated in accordance with the social distance of the combatants; poison spears and stratagems are employed exclusively against hostile strangers and invaders.

Turf defense is an ultimate response, however. Other more subtle repulsions or restrictions are available to proprietors wishing to maintain territorial control.

Insulation

Insulation is the placement of some sort of barrier between the occupants of a territory and potential invaders. The narrow streets, steep staircases, and regularized use of Cantonese dialects in Chinatowns serve notice on tourists that they may look over the external trappings of Chinese life in the Occidental city but not easily penetrate its inner workings. Distinct uniforms distinguishing status, rights, and prerogatives serve to protect military officers from the importunities of enlisted men, professors from students, and doctors from patients. Bodily insulation characteristically takes the form of civil inattention and may be occasioned by a subordinate's inability to repel invasion directly. Another common form of insulation involves use of body and facial idiom to indicate impenetrability. It may be effected by the use of sunglasses, or attained accidentally, by dint of culturally distinct perceptions of facial gestures, as, for example, often happens to orientals in Western settings. It can also be attained by conscious efforts in the management and control of the mouth, nostrils, and especially the eyes.

Linguistic Collusion

Linguistic collusion involves a complex set of processes by which the territorial integrity of the group is reaffirmed and the intruder is labelled as an outsider. For example, the defending interactants may engage one another in conversation and gestures designed to so confuse the invader that he responds in a manner automatically labelling him eligible for either exclusion from the group or shameful status diminution. In one typical strategy the defending interactants will speak to one another in a language unfamiliar to the invader.

In another recognizable strategy, the participants continue to engage in the same behavior but in a more exaggerated and "staged" manner. Mood and tone of the voice are sometimes regulated to achieve this effect. Thus persons engaged in conversation may intensify their tone and include more intra-group gestures when an outsider enters the area. Professors may escalate the use of jargon and "academese" in conversations in the presence of uninvited students or other "inferiors."

Reaction to the Absence of Free Space

Exercising freedom over body territory provides a more fruitful approach to those for whom public territories are denied and home territories difficult or impossible to maintain. The body and its attendant inner and external space have an aura of ownership and control about them that is impressed upon the incumbent. The hypothesis we wish to suggest here is that as other forms of free territory are perceived to be foreclosed by certain segments of the society, these segments, or at least those elements of the segments not constrained by other compelling forces, will utilize more frequently and intensively the area of body space as a free territory. Three forms of such utilization are prominent: *manipulation, adornment,* and *penetration.*

Manipulation rests upon the fact that the body is adjustable in a greater number of ways than are positively sanctioned and that by modifying the appearance of the self one can establish identity, and flaunt convention with both ease and relative impunity. Thus children, separated from one another for being naughty and enjoined from conversation, may sit and ''make faces'' at one another, conforming to the letter of their punishment but violating its principle. Teenagers, denied approval for the very sexual activity for which they are biologically prepared, and also enclosed more and more from private usage of public territories for such purposes, have developed dance forms which involve little or no body contact but are nevertheless suggestive of the most intimate and forbidden forms of erotic interaction. Further, male youth — enjoined from verbal scatological forms by customs and by rules of propriety — have developed a gesture language by which they can communicate the desired obscenity without uttering it.

Adornment of the body is another response. By covering, uncovering, marking, and disfiguring the body individuals can at least partly overcome whatever loss of freedom they suffer from other encroachments. Body space may also be attended by filling in the apertures in nose, mouth and ears by rings, bones, and other emblematic artifacts; by marking upon the skin with inks and tatoos; and by disfigurements, scars, and severance of non-vital members. An alternative mode of adornment, that appears to be directed definitely against elements of the core culture, is the refusal to use instruments of personal hygiene. We have already noted how these instruments acquire a peculiar aspect of the personal charisma of the user so that people do not customarily borrow the comb, toothbrush, and razor of another unless the contamination that occurs thereby is neutralized. Here, however, adornment occurs by simply *not* washing, combing, shaving, cutting the hair, etc. Like public nudity this form of assertiveness and reaction to oppression has the advantage of inhibiting a like response among those who are offended by the appearance created thereby, but, unlike stripping in public, has the added advantage of being legal.

Penetration refers to the exploitation and modification of inner space in the search for free territory. One might hypothesize that the greater the sense of unfreedom, the greater the exercise of body liberty so that penetration is an escalated aspect of manipulation and adornment. There is, as it were, a series of increasing gradations of body space. The ultimate effort is to gain freedom by changing one's internal environment. The simplest form of this is cultivating a vicarious sense of being away, of transporting the self out of its existential environment by musing, daydreaming, or relapsing into a reverie. However, voluntary reorganization of the inner environment can be assisted by alcohol and drugs. Contemporary college youth sometimes partake of hallucinogenic and psychedelic drugs in order to make an inner migration (or "take a trip" as the popular idiom has it).

Conclusion

The concept of territoriality offers a fruitful approach for the analysis of freedom and situated action. Although the early school of ecology in American sociology provided a possible avenue for this kind of exploration, its practitioners appear to have eschewed the interactionist and phenomenological aspects of the subject in favor of the economic and the biotic. Nevertheless, much of their work needs to be examined afresh for the clues it provides for understanding the nature and function of space and the organization of territories. Similarly the work done by the students of non-human animal association provides clues to concept formation and suggestions for research.

25 *This chapter describes the design of homes. According to Mehrabian we must consider arousal, pleasure, and dominance when designing homes and the chapter demonstrates how this can be accomplished.*

Today's Homes

Albert Mehrabian

Not many of us can afford to hire an interior decorator, and even fewer can afford to have our homes designed and built for us. But the best decorators and architects intuitively create designs which successfully key into the three basic emotional dimensions of arousal, pleasure, and dominance.

The homes most of us are forced to buy or rent, however, are usually built and decorated in accordance with economic considerations and established traditions rather than with serious attention to the emotional impact of the various rooms. They are often rather poorly laid out, consisting basically of a series of rectangular boxes connected by doors of varying widths. If the house is a large two-story structure, the boxes on the first floor are the "socializing" areas like dining room, family room, kitchen, living room, and possibly a den or a library, with the second-floor boxes usually given over to bedrooms and large bathrooms. If the house is a ranch-type structure, all the boxes are of course on the same level. In any case, these boxes often are not situated properly to be used for what they were designed—some may be too far away and inaccessible. For instance, a spacious and attractive patio may be situated to the side of the house, away from the living room, so that the only access to it is via one of the bedrooms. It won't be used; instead, the favorite spot will be a smaller and less attractive patio adjacent to the living room.

A "family room" may be stuck off somewhere in a remote wing of the house; it may have a northerly exposure and hence not receive much sunlight; its windows may open onto the neighbor's garage. Also, it may have a long, narrowish shape which precludes informal or circular arrangements of furniture. This room will not be used as a family room; instead, the husband or wife will use it to take naps. On the other hand, the kitchen may be large and bright; it might face the backyard with its trees, grass, or flowers. It may contain a fairly large table with room for books, newspapers, or bills to be spread out upon it by several members of the family, yet not so large that conversation from one end to the other is forced. This will become the family room. Here the members of the family will tend to gather together or at least linger after eating. Friends who drop in during the day will often be received here rather than in other areas of the house. In a more extreme case, and simply due to its strategic location, an austere dining area adjoining the kitchen may serve as the gathering spot for the family and their close friends while a large and luxuriously furnished living room far off somewhere goes to waste.

What then are some of the considerations in deciding whether an area will be used at all or whether it will be used for its assigned purpose? Because a pleasant environment causes approach behavior—causes us to affiliate with other people or simply desire to stay in it—there is no reason why any room in one's house should be unpleasant. Because moderately high arousal levels are needed for people to socialize with one another, all rooms that will be used to entertain guests, or in which the family will gather for any purpose other than dining, should possess a moderately high load. Areas that will be used for tasks requiring relatively low levels of arousal—eating, sleeping, unwinding, or doing complex work requiring concentration—should be very pleasant but low-load. Since few of us will be entertaining heads of state, and since few of us can afford expensive furnishings in areas that rarely will be used, there is seldom need for extremely formal sitting or dining rooms done in classic, costly, dominant styles.

Before further discussion of interior decor and its relation to room choice for different activities, let us contemplate the effects of floor plans on room use. Consider a basic floor plan that would satisfy the needs of most families. Assuming, for the moment, that we are talking about a single-story structure up to $50,000 in price variations of this plan would differ primarily in terms of the size and, to a certain extent, the placement of the bedrooms.

What the plans would have in common is the socializing core, consisting of kitchen, family room, and living room in something like the following arrangement:

Figure 1

Even though most of the family eating would be done in the kitchen area, part of the living room adjacent to the kitchen might be given over to more elaborate dining occasions. This kitchen/family room/living room core could be placed in such a way as to provide maximum sunlight and the most pleasant and stimulating views available — of the grounds, of a garden, of the cityscape, or whatever. Preferably, the family room ought to face the backyard or patio area so that the family could make use of this outdoor space for recreation, games, or barbecues, and still have ready access to the kitchen facilities.

In a servantless household, whoever does the cooking is the crucial person and cannot be isolated, since his or her activities tend to form the center of gravity. In addition, the kitchen is the source of certain elemental blessings — food in the refrigerator, a glass of water, ice cubes, or an ice cold beer. In many households, the everyday liquor is kept in or very near the kitchen, unless there is a separate wet bar and refrigerator somewhere else. In other words, people have many reasons for gravitating toward the kitchen, which tends to form the home's natural heart.

It makes sense then that a kitchen should be livable and attractive. It should be well-ventilated and have good uniform lighting throughout.

Surfaces should be easy to clean. Highly textured floors or counters which trap particles are difficult to clean and should be avoided unless they considerably enhance the pleasantness of the facility. The stove, oven, sink, and refrigerator should be arranged so that there is an easy flow of movements without too many steps, with dishes, pots, and pans placed within fairly easy reach. Problems arise when, for instance, the sink and some counter space are along one wall and the remaining counter space is along the opposite wall. If the kitchen is large enough, it is possible to have a central island which includes a stove, grill, chopping-board area, and even an extra sink; located in the center of the kitchen, it minimizes unnecessary movement. Some pots and pans can be hung above so they are readily accessible to the person working at the stove. The logic of minimizing movement also applies to the storage of different items in the various cabinets and shelves. Items or ingredients that are frequently used should be placed in cabinets or shelves that are within easiest reach.

When the kitchen is surrounded by and not segregated from the main living areas in which many different activities can take place—eating, watching TV, entertaining, doing homework, playing games—the result is a functional but nonspecialized core that greatly enhances a family's cohesiveness. This arrangement also lends itself nicely to large-scale entertaining, since one can have a big party without boxing the guests in. They will have room to mingle and also will be able to feel the presence of others in different parts of the core area.

Families which consist predominantly of nonscreeners will require slightly different variations of the basic floor plan than families in which most members are screeners. Remember that nonscreeners, compared to screeners, are more likely to avoid arousing and unpleasant tasks and environments. Thus, areas of the home where demanding and somewhat unpleasant chores are performed must be especially private and free of distractions (low-load) for nonscreeners. They ought to be able to shield the areas they choose to work in—their bedrooms, studies, or even parts of the living room or den—from noise and interruptions by others. An alternative approach is to make special efforts to create pleasant work areas for nonscreeners who are bound to perform an occasional unpleasant task. A larger chunk of the total floor space of the house could be devoted to individual, pleasant, and more segregated bedrooms to accommodate nonscreeners, whereas parts of the core could just as easily serve as work areas for the screeners. Bedrooms which will be used by nonscreeners as work areas, places to unwind, or to perform complex and arousing mental tasks should not be too highly loaded in their decor. They should be quite flexible in terms of lighting and other forms of controllable environmental stimuli to make absolute silence or darkness readily attainable.

Generally, the design of a house can be improved by observing actual family activity patterns. One can discover how, and how frequently, the various spaces are used and whether the usage conforms to the anticipated functions. This kind of analysis will pinpoint spaces that are wasted and others which serve many more functions than they were designed for. It also will reveal the quality of family life, such as its cohesiveness and the home design features it requires.

The relationship of this core, or the entire home for that matter, to its surroundings can be considered using the idea that more loaded, pleasant environments are preferred to a greater extent, whereas more loaded, unpleasant environments are avoided more. A house that faces unpleasant, noisy, crowded, polluted streets with heavy traffic can be shielded by hedges, a garden, potted plants, or trees; here the challenge is even greater to try to create pleasant and stimulating interior areas. On the other hand, a house that faces a garden with trees in a noise- and pollution-free setting is usually designed with much exposure to the outside, providing stimulation from variations in sunlight, cloud patterns, and wind. This is especially the case when the vegetation, flowers, and trees attract birds, squirrels, and lizards, whose habits and activities can be a rich source of stimulation. Views from different vantage points within such a house enable the residents to have changing input from their pleasant surroundings as they socialize, do light reading, work, eat, or bathe.

When we design and decorate a core area intended to encourage people to interact enjoyably with one another, we must make this area both pleasant and stimulating. Our studies have shown that socializing not only involves conversation but includes the essential element of verbal and nonverbal exchanges of liking. Even though these subtle exchanges, which include eye contact, head nods, and gesturing, are seemingly not attended to, they have a powerful effect on whether people continue to converse and whether they enjoy doing it. Findings have also shown that such exchanges of liking increase in pleasant surroundings; that is, regardless of with whom we converse, we are more prone to be positive if we are in a more pleasant setting.

When people feel dominant, as when they are on their own home territory, environmental load also contributes to their gregariousness. You will recall that two factors, novelty and complexity, combine to give any environment its characteristic load. Even if we furnish a living area in novel, rare, unexpected, or surprising ways, it will sooner or later become familiar and thus less arousing to all but those who haven't been there before. Probably the only practical way to increase the novelty of such an environment is to redecorate from time to time, adding, subtracting, or shifting things around. For this reason, it is a good idea to select furnishings that are light, movable, and admit of several pleasant combinations. Large, bulky pieces that fit only a few corners or wall spaces, or a great many built-ins, will lock you into one static and potentially boring pattern. It is somewhat easier to make the socializing environment a complex one with lots of colors, textures, and other stimuli for the eye and ear. Aquariums, mobile sculptures, and fireplaces are good decorating items precisely because they are colorful and incorporate motion. Mirrors or milar surfaces which are situated so as to reflect the most colorful, warm, and complex areas of a room have the effect not only of increasing the perceived size of the room but also of increasing its complexity. Mirrors placed opposite blank walls or plain draperies should be avoided because of the resulting colder and more distant (low-arousal) feeling. Potted plants and flowers not only contribute heavily to the pleasure dimension but add complexity and novelty through their changing shapes. Also, the different green shades provided by plants contrast sharply, especially with the now fashionable white walls. Tapestries, textured wallpapers, and cork, brick, or wood paneling all contribute more pleasant textures and color combinations of higher load than smooth-plastered, uniformly painted walls.

Aside from all of these primarily static devices for increasing environmental load, there is the tremendous potential contribution of music for increasing pleasure as well as load. Even a single piece of music consists of changing patterns over time; furthermore, a most sophisticated technology allows us to increase the novelty of the pieces we listen to or avoid excessively high-load (overly complex, unfamiliar, or dissonant) selections. The simple act of adjusting the volume of music to the desired level readily alters its load and reminds us of the unusual flexibility of this aspect of our home environments. At a casual get-together, for instance, the complexity, novelty, and intensity of music can be made to compensate for the arousal level of guests. If the pace of social interaction is pretty high, then the volume can be turned down; however, if the activity and arousal levels of guests begin to falter, the volume can be raised to a moderate level with livelier selections.

Lighting is extremely important. Brightly lit rooms are more arousing than dimly lit ones, and so the social area must have a good overall lighting capability. If you do a lot of entertaining — everything from large cocktail parties to small sit-down dinners — you must be able to vary the intensity of the lighting. When large numbers of relative strangers gather, very bright lights might cause them to feel a bit self-conscious initially. Ideally, one should have dimmers so that the lights could be somewhat lower at the beginning of the party and then be turned up as the party progresses. Note that often people will tend to crowd into the kitchen after a party has gone on for some time; the kitchen is usually brightly lit, and the brightness, density, or even cooking odors serve to increase arousal levels. On the other hand, since the social area will also be used for dining where in most cases bright lights will be too arousing, your lighting system should be flexible enough for you to dim the lights somewhat during meals. Because people tend to avoid dark corners, you should have enough lamps and other independent light sources so that all parts of the social area can be lit and hence used. And of course the social area should be placed in such a way as to take fullest advantage of natural light; the changing patterns of sunlight over the course of the day can be both pleasant and stimulating. Particularly colorful areas, tapestries, or large paintings might be spotlighted—where there is no light, there is no color. If you wish, for one reason or another, to be able to make the social area extremely arousing, colored lights might also be used. According to research findings, red lights would be most arousing; hand tremor and fast muscular reaction time, both indicators of arousal, are increased under deep red light. Colored lights also have the effect of changing the hue of familiar objects, making them look incongruous or strange, thus increasing their novelty. But such effects should be used carefully, and only when very high levels of arousal are wanted. For most social situations—unless everybody is drunk or stoned and hence physiologically quite depressed—such lighting or strobe lights may be too novel and cause avoidance. If you do a good deal of entertaining, it will probably be worthwhile to make the guest bathroom a fairly colorful and arousing one; otherwise the contrast between the loaded party environment and a very low-load guest bathroom will be disagreeable.

To use color effectively, we need to know its emotional effects, and these are readily summarized. Color is characterized by hue, brightness, and saturation. Hue is related to wavelength and hence determines whether colors are perceived as red, blue, green, and so on. Brightness refers to the intensity of light that is reflected; saturation refers to the concentration of vividness of the hue. The brighter or more saturated the color, the more pleasant it is. The most pleasant hues are blue, green, purple, red, and yellow, in that order. In terms of arousal, less bright and more saturated colors are more arousing. The most arousing hue is red, followed by orange, yellow, violet, blue, and green, with green being the least arousing. Thus, if we wanted to maximize arousal in a given room, we would probably use flocked, velvety, or otherwise textured deep red wallpaper, carpets, and curtains. Color schemes selected for the social core, for instance, would emphasize the more arousing hues and the more saturated colors. It is probably no accident that extremes of such a decorative scheme often prevailed in the better nineteenth-century brothels.

Lighting and colors may also be used in therapeutic ways. For example, brighter lights and more arousing and pleasant colors may be especially recommended for someone living alone who is prone to depression. If the interior designer manages to achieve a happy feeling within the physical environment, this can help his client to overcome depressed feelings and might even compensate for the client's somewhat nonarousing manner when people are over to visit.

Many living rooms are failures for entertaining not only because they are not colorful and are poorly lit but also because room shapes or the type and arrangement of furniture seriously depress arousal levels. Some rooms feel too large and cold and can easily be made to seem smaller by colors and textures on the walls. Since a high-load surface — one that is heavily textured and contains sharp color contrasts involving arousing colors — appears closer than a low-load one, the perceived shape of a room can be altered dramatically by judicious application of this principle. For example, ceilings can be "lowered" or "raised" by using more or less arousing colors and textures, respectively. When a room feels overly confining, less arousing surfaces must be used. A trick decorators often use is to paint opposite walls darker and lighter shades of the same color, thus making a narrow room seem wider.

Large rooms with furniture, especially long couches, set along the walls at wide intervals prevent guests from facing each other at the proper angles and also introduce too much distance between them. In our experiments, we've manipulated the arousing quality of social settings by having people interact from a variety of distances and orientations. When pairs of strangers are asked to wait in a room together, those who are allowed to sit at greater distances from each other tend to be more relaxed but socialize less. When pairs are inconspicuously positioned to wait together at closer range, there is more tension (arousal) but also more conversation, especially among whose who might otherwise be subdued due to their sensitivity to rejection. Of course, too small a distance (less than four feet in a face-to-face position) is excessively arousing and results in avoidance behavior. About four and a half feet is the optimum distance. Many living rooms require guests to interact at distances of nine feet or more and hence create serious environmental difficulties. Shy or self-conscious persons are particularly reluctant to attempt conversation at such distances, and almost everyone tends to lapse into more aloof or formal modes.

The angle at which strangers are seated in relation to each other is another crucial factor in how much they interact. Strangers who are seated parallel to each other, as on a couch, simply will not talk to each other very much. A face-to-face orientation will increase their arousal and greatly enhance sociability. When the angle through which people are turned away from each other exceeds 90°, the positiveness of conversation is curtailed sharply. Since people seated together on a couch are in effect separated by a 180° angle, couches are quite detrimental to social interaction. Couches designed to seat three or more persons become more socially inefficient the larger they get. Two people can orient themselves on a couch so as to face each other, but it is virtually impossible for three or more to do so. As a result, a couch designed to hold four people will usually contain only two. If, in a crowded situation, four people are forced to sit together on a couch, the quality and quantity of conversation among these four will be nothing to write home about.*

It is difficult to understand how couches have become such a standard item of living room furniture. If you must have a couch, it is important that it be surrounded by other chairs, as in the following arrangement:

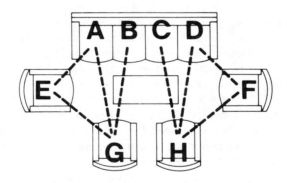

Figure 2

In this case, assuming that all seats are occupied, A and E will talk to each other, as will D and F. F and H, E and G, A-E-G, and D-F-H are also possible conversational groupings. But G will tend not to talk with H, nor will A, B, C, and D tend to talk amongst themselves. If you can't manage some such grouping, it would be far better for everyone to stand or sit on the floor or on packing crates than to stick four people alone somewhere on an isolated couch.

It is also better to have a number of smaller, more intimate conversational groupings within the social core rather than one large one. The quality of interaction within each of these groupings will most likely be pleasant and rewarding because people will not feel locked into one particular group. They will feel less self-conscious about approaching the group, as when they first enter, and will feel less uneasy about leaving it to get a drink, talk with someone in another group, go to the bathroom, or whatever. Some of the chairs could swivel so that members from different groups could casually adjust their orientation to interact with someone seated in another group. Furthermore, smaller groupings will in many cases present a more stimulating decor, especially if they give the impression of being randomly scattered throughout the floor space. This would also free areas for people to walk around in and form ad hoc standing clusters in which to seek their own optimum distances and orientations.

The load of the dining area or dining room ought to be lower than that in the living and family rooms. Otherwise the combined arousing effects of the setting, the act of eating, and the associated socializing would be far too high. So, given a choice between lowering the load of the physical setting or that of the food or the social interaction, people generally opt for the former. This helps explain many mealtime environmental preferences, such as a lower volume of music or no music, dimmer lights, special efforts to shut out noise or distractions from outside the home, and, in some homes, a taboo on arguments, discussions of money matters, or generally unpleasant and anxiety-provoking topics.

Bedrooms used primarily for sleeping do not have to be loaded, but they should be pleasant. Children who have difficulty going to sleep and make frequent trips back to the living room after they've been put to bed may be reacting to overly arousing cues in their bedrooms. These commonly include the presence of a sibling, conversation heard from the living room because of poor soundproofing, or noise and lights from outside the house.

A bedroom which will also be a prime sexual locus should probably contain more load. One of the reasons waterbeds are popular in motels which are known to be trysts is that the rocking and somewhat unpredictable motions of such beds serve to increase arousal. There should be a source of music in a bedroom; colored lights might also be considered. Certain motels now offer rooms containing closed circuit TVs or video cassettes featuring pornography; couples who opt for such rooms probably find that the pornographic element provides a desired increase in arousal level. It is likely that some such additional stimulus will gradually enter the private home market. However, among new or inexperienced sexual partners, a too highly loaded environment is unnecessary and most likely will be detrimental, especially to the male's performance.

The placement of bedrooms could involve a subtle design consideration with extremely beneficial effects for people who have problems with waking. Sunshine streaming through a large window in the morning is one of the most gentle and pleasant ways of being aroused from sleep since both the increased temperature and the intensity of light are arousing. When people live on a reasonably flexible schedule, bedrooms can be located with large windows facing southeast so that the early morning sunshine can conveniently and gradually arouse them. The flexibility of schedules is important in that the position of the sun changes during the different seasons and thus the waking time varies as much as an hour. However, it is possible to overcome this aspect by giving the bedroom an extremely large amount of exposure to sunlight, with windows along all walls facing southeast, or even by using skylights. In this case, the position of the curtains can be adjusted so that the desired sunlight reaches the bed at almost exactly the time it is wanted.

Note

*Immediacy — a closer and more face-to-face position — has a beneficial result on the relationships among people provided, of course, that the contact is within reasonable bounds and does not have excessive arousal due to total lack of privacy. Some of the commonly employed encounter group techniques — requiring strangers to hold hands and look into each other's eyes, to disrobe, or to massage one another — increase immediacy and exposure beyond levels of comfort. However, within the confines of the well-defined, socially artificial encounter group, excessively high levels of arousal are tolerated by participants because such interactions are carefully planned not to be threatening and to enhance positive feelings. Also, participants know these to be temporary and feel reassured by the fact that they can return to more normal and more private social conditions once they leave the group.

Key Terms and Concepts

Hall, *Distances in Man*

flight	space	personal distance
critical	loudness	social distance
personal and social	dynamism	public distance
distances	boundary	
territory	intimate distance	

Lyman and Scott, *Territoriality*

territoriality	sponsorship	contamination
free territory	colonization	turf defense
encroachment	mobile	insulation
public territory	fragile	linguistic collusion
home territory	inner space	manipulation
interactional territory	violation	adornment
body territory	invasion	penetration

Mehrabian, *Today's Homes*

arousal	family activity	mirrors
pleasure	patterns	lighting
dominance	novelty	color
screeners and	complexity	angles between
nonscreeners	load	people

Part Six

Tactile Communication
(Haptics)

Touch is one of the most basic human needs; yet, touch *deprivation* is a problem in our modern world. Research shows that people need touch for physical and psychological *health*. However, we touch and are touched less and less as we grow older. Except for "licensed touchers" such as a nurse or a masseuse, some people are rarely touched by their friends and intimates.

Touch *rules* are very strong and guide who is allowed to touch whom. In general, people with more power and status are free to touch those with less power and status. Some areas of the body such as the hands, arms, shoulders, and upper back may be touched by almost anyone. Other areas such as the head, neck, torso, buttocks, legs and feet may be touched by only a select few.

Touches may be *ritualized* or not. Ritual touches are those which occur as part of ceremonial practices and other rigid· behavior patterns. Handshakes are a part of the greeting ritual and patting someone on the back at an athletic contest is part of the congratulatory ritual. Other touches are not part of rituals and these may communicate many different meanings such as liking and control. There are, of course, many cultural differences in touch.

Touch is a powerful channel of communicating, in part because it is so commonly associated with two of the stronger messages we send; sex and dominance. In the United States, touch norms restrict touch. This is particularly true for men. Consider the people you touch and who touch you.

26

Thayer provides an overview of touch. In this chapter he discusses the rules and functions of touch and the role of culture and gender. Thayer also describes attitudes toward touch and its role in the creation of intimacy. Finally, the chapter discusses the relationship between touch and status.

Close Encounters

Stephen Thayer

In May 1985, Brigitte Gerney was trapped beneath a 35-ton collapsed construction crane in New York City for six hours. Throughout her ordeal, she held the hand of rescue officer Paul Ragonese, who stayed by her side as heavy machinery moved the tons of twisted steel from her crushed legs. A stranger's touch gave her hope and the will to live.

Other means of communication can take place at a distance, but touch is the language of physical intimacy. And because it is, touch is the most powerful of all the communication channels — and the most carefully guarded and regulated.

From a mother's cradling embrace to a friend's comforting hug, or a lover's caress, touch has the special power to send messages of union and communion. Among strangers, that power is ordinarily held in check. Whether offering a handshake or a guiding arm, the toucher is careful to stay within the culture's narrowly prescribed limits lest the touch be misinterpreted. Touching between people with more personal relationships is also governed by silent cultural rules and restraints.

The rules of touch may be unspoken, but they're visible to anyone who takes the trouble to watch. Psychologist Richard Heslin at Purdue University, for instance, has proposed five categories of touch based on people's roles and relationships. Each category includes a special range of touches, best described by the quality of touch, the body areas touched and whether the touch is reciprocated.

Functional-professional touches are performed while the toucher fulfills a special role, such as that of doctor, barber or tailor. For people in these occupations, touch must be devoid of personal messages.

Social-polite touches are formal, limited to greeting and separating and to expressing appreciation among business associates and among strangers and acquaintances. The typical handshake reflects cordiality more than intimacy.

Friendship-warmth touches occur in the context of personal concern and caring, such as the relationships between extended-family members, friendly neighbors and close work mates. This category straddles the line between warmth and deep affection, a line where friendly touches move over into love touches.

Love-intimacy touches occur between close family members and friends in relationships where there is affection and caring.

Sexual-arousal touches occur in erotic-sexual contexts.

These categories are not hard and fast, since in various cultures and subcultures the rules differ about who can touch whom, in what contexts and what forms the touch may take. In the Northern European ''noncontact cultures,'' overall touch rates are usually quite low. People from these cultures can seem very cold, especially to people from ''contact cultures'' such as those in the Mediterranean area, where there are much higher rates of touching, even between strangers.

In the United States, a particularly low-touch culture, we rarely see people touch one another in public. Other than in sports and children's play, the most we see of it is when people hold hands in the street, fondle babies or say hello and goodbye. Even on television shows, with the odd exceptions of hitting and kissing, there is little touching.

The cultural differences in contact can be quite dramatic, as researcher Sidney Jourard found in the 1960s when he studied touch between pairs of people in coffee shops around the world. There was more touch in certain cities (180 times an hour between couples in San Juan, Puerto Rico, and 110 times an hour in Paris, France) than in others (2 times an hour between couples in Gainesville, Florida, and 0 times an hour in London, England).

Those cultural contact patterns are embedded early, through child-rearing practices. Psychologist Janice Gibson and her colleagues at the University of Pittsburgh took to the playgrounds and beaches of Greece, the Soviet Union and the United States and compared the frequency and nature of touch between caregivers and children 2 to 5 years old. When it came to retrieving or punishing the children, touching rates were similar in all three countries. But on touches for soothing, holding and play, American children had significantly less contact than those from the other cultures. (Is that why we need bumper stickers to remind us: ''Have you hugged your child today?'')

Generalizations about different national or ethnic groups can be tricky, however. For example, despite widespread beliefs that Latin Americans are highly contact-oriented, when researcher Robert Shuter* at Marquette University compared public contact between couples in Costa Rica, Colombia and Panama, he found that the Costa Ricans both touched and held their partners noticeably more than the couples did in the other two countries.

Within most cultures the rules and meanings of touch are different for men and women, as one recent study in the United States illustrates. Imagine yourself in a hospital bed, about to have major surgery. The nurse comes in to tell you what your operation and after-care will be like. She touches you briefly twice, once on the hand for a few seconds after she introduces herself and again on the arm for a full minute during the instruction period. As she leaves she shakes your hand.

Does this kind of brief reassuring touch add anything to her talk? Does it have any kind of impact on your nervousness or how you respond to the operation? Your reaction is likely to depend upon your gender.

Psychologist Sheryle Whitcher, while working as a graduate student with psychologist Jeffrey Fisher of the University of Connecticut, arranged for a group of surgery patients to be touched in the way described above during their preoperative information session, while other patients got only the information. Women had strikingly positive reactions to being touched; it lowered their blood pressure and anxiety both before surgery and for more than an hour afterwards. But men found the experience upsetting; both their blood pressure and their anxiety rose and stayed elevated in response to being touched.

Why did touch produce such strikingly different responses? Part of the answer may lie in the fact that men in the United States often find it harder to acknowledge dependency and fear than women do; thus, for men, a well-intentioned touch may be a threatening reminder of their vulnerability.

These gender differences are fostered by early experiences, particularly in handling and caretaking. Differences in parents' use of touch with their infant children help to shape and model "male" and "female" touch patterns: Fathers use touch more for play, while mothers use it more for soothing and grooming. The children's gender also affects the kinds of touches they receive. In the United States, for example, girls receive more affectionate touches (kissing, cuddling, holding) than boys do.

By puberty, tactile experiences with parents and peers have already programmed differences in boys' and girls' touching behavior and their use of personal space (see "Body Mapping," this article). Some results of this training are evident when men and women greet people. In one study, psychologists Paul Greenbaum and Howard Rosenfeld of the

---

* Editor's note: Robert Shuter is a communication researcher.

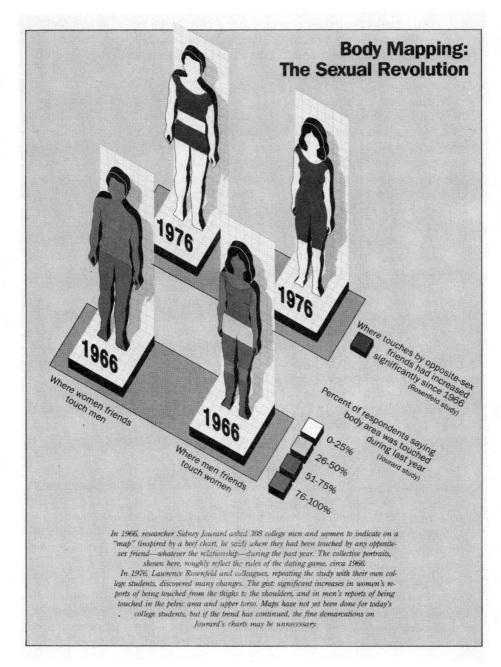

Body Mapping: The Sexual Revolution

Where touches by opposite-sex friends had increased significantly since 1966 (Rosenfeld study)

Percent of respondents saying body area was touched during last year (Jourard study)

0-25%

26-50%

51-75%

76-100%

Where women friends touch men

Where men friends touch women

In 1966, researcher Sidney Jourard asked 308 college men and women to indicate on a "map" (inspired by a beef chart, he said) where they had been touched by any opposite-sex friend—whatever the relationship—during the past year. The collective portraits, shown here, roughly reflect the rules of the dating game, circa 1966.

In 1976, Lawrence Rosenfeld and colleagues, repeating the study with their own college students, discovered many changes. The gist: significant increases in women's reports of being touched from the thighs to the shoulders, and in men's reports of being touched in the pelvic area and upper torso. Maps have not yet been done for today's college students, but if the trend has continued, the fine demarcations on Jourard's charts may be unnecessary.

University of Kansas watched how travelers at the Kansas City International Airport touched people who greeted them. Women greeted women and men more physically, with mutual lip kisses, embraces and more kinds of touch and holding for longer periods of time. In contrast, when men greeted men, most just shook hands and left it at that.

How do you feel about touching and being touched? Are you relaxed and comfortable, or does such contact make you feel awkward and tense? Your comfort with touch may be linked to your personality. Psychologist Knud Larsen and student Jeff LeRoux at Oregon State University looked at how people's personality traits are related to their attitudes toward touching between people of the same sex. The researchers measured touch attitudes through questions such as, "I enjoy persons of my sex who are comfortable with touching," "I sometimes enjoy hugging friends of the same sex" and "Physical expression of affection between persons of the same sex is healthy." Even though men were generally less comfortable about same-sex touching than women were, the more authoritarian and rigid people of both sexes were the least comfortable.

A related study by researchers John Deethardt and Debbie Hines at Texas Tech University in Lubbock, Texas, examined personality and attitudes toward being touched by opposite-sex friends and lovers and by same-sex friends. Touch attitudes were tapped with such questions as, "When I am with my girl/-boyfriend I really like to touch that person to show affection," "When I tell a same-sex intimate friend that I have just gotten a divorce, I want that person to touch me" and "I enjoy an opposite-sex acquaintance touching me when we greet each other." Regardless of gender, people who were comfortable with touching were also more talkative, cheerful, socially dominant and nonconforming; those discomforted by touch tended to be more emotionally unstable and socially withdrawn.

A recent survey of nearly 4,000 undergraduates by researchers Janis Andersen, Peter Andersen and Myron Lustig* of San Diego State University revealed that, regardless of gender, people who were less comfortable about touching were also more apprehensive about communicating and had lower self-esteem. Several other studies have shown that people who are more comfortable with touch are less afraid and suspicious of other people's motives and intentions and have less anxiety and tension in their everyday lives. Not surprisingly, another study showed they are also likely to be more satisfied with their bodies and physical appearance.

These different personality factors play themselves out most revealingly in the intimacy of love relationships. Couples stay together and break

* Editor's note: Andersen, Andersen, and Lustig are communication researchers.

apart for many reasons, including the way each partner expresses and reacts to affection and intimacy. For some, feelings and words are enough; for others, touch and physical intimacy are more critical.

In the film *Annie Hall,* Woody Allen and Diane Keaton are shown split-screen as each talks to an analyst about their sexual relationship. When the analyst asks how often they have sex, he answers, "Hardly ever, maybe three times a week," while she describes it as "constantly, three times a week."

How important is physical intimacy in close relationships? What role does touch play in marital satisfaction? Psychologists Betsy Tolstedt and Joseph Stokes of the University of Illinois at Chicago tried to find out by interviewing and observing couples. They used three measures of intimacy: emotional intimacy (feelings of closeness, support, tolerance); verbal intimacy (disclosure of emotions, feelings, opinions); and physical intimacy (satisfaction with "companionate" and sexual touch). The researchers also measured marital satisfaction and happiness, along with conflicts and actual separations and legal actions.

They found that each form of intimacy made its own contribution to marital satisfaction, but—perhaps surprisingly to some—physical intimacy mattered the least of the three. Conflict and divorce potential were most connected to dissatisfaction with emotional and verbal intimacy.

Touch intimacy may not usually have the power to make or break marriages, but it can sway strangers and even people close to you, often without their knowledge. The expressions "to put the touch on someone" and "that person is an easy touch" refer to the persuasive power of touch. Indeed, research shows that it is harder to say no to someone who makes a request when it is accompanied by a touch.

Politicians know this well. Ignoring security concerns, political candidates plunge into the crowd to kiss babies and "press the flesh." Even a quick handshake leaves a lasting impression—a personal touch—that can pay off later at election time.

A momentary and seemingly incidental touch can establish a positive, temporary bond between strangers, making them more helpful, compliant, generous and positive. In one experiment in a library, a slight hand brush in the course of returning library cards to patrons was enough to influence patrons' positive attitudes toward the library and its staff. In another study, conducted in restaurants, a fleeting touch paid off in hard cash. Waitresses who touched their customers on the hand or shoulder as they returned change received a larger percentage of the bill as their tip. Even though they risked crossing role boundaries by touching customers in such familiar ways, their ingratiating service demeanor offset any threat.

Touchy Issues

Touch is a gesture of warmth and concern, but it can also be seen as intrusive, demeaning or seductive. Because of these ambiguous meanings, touch can sometimes be problematic for therapists, who must be careful to monitor their touch behavior with clients. Because difficult legal and ethical issues surround possible misinterpretation of touch, many therapists avoid physical contact of any sort with their clients, except for a formal handshake at the first and last sessions. But in a number of body-oriented psychotherapies, such as Wilhelm Reich's character analysis and Alexander Lowen's bioenergetic therapy, touch is used deliberately as part of the treatment process; it is meant to stir emotions and memories through the body and not just the mind.

Imagine meeting your therapist for the first time. You are greeted in the waiting room and guided into the consultation room. You have the therapist's full attention as you speak about what brings you to therapy. Twice during the session the therapist briefly touches you on the arm. Before you leave, you make an appointment to meet again.

How are you likely to evaluate your first session? Do you think the therapist's touch might affect your reactions to therapy or to the therapist? Could it affect the process of therapy?

Sessions like the one just described have been studied by psychologist Mark A. Hubble of Harding Hospital in Worthington, Ohio, and colleagues, using therapists specially trained to touch their clients in consistent ways during their first counseling session. Results show that, compared with clients who were not touched, those who were touched judged the therapist as more expert. In an earlier, similar study by researcher Joyce Pattison, trained judges rated clients who had been touched as deeper in their self-exploration.

Although there are clearly some risks, perhaps more therapists should consider "getting in touch" with their clients by adding such small tactile gestures to their therapeutic repertoire.

In certain situations, touch can be discomforting because it signals power. Psychologist Nancy Henley of the University of California, Los Angeles, after observing the touch behavior of people as they went about their daily lives, has suggested that higher-status individuals enjoy more touch liberties with their lower-status associates. To Henly, who has noted how touch signals one's place in the status-dominance hierarchy, there is even a sexist "politics of touch." She has found that women generally rank lower than men in the touch hierarchy, very much like the secretary-boss, student-teacher and worker-foreman relationships. In all of these, it is considered unseemly for lower-status individuals to put their hands on superiors. Rank does have its touching privileges.

The rules of the status hierarchy are so powerful that people can infer status differences from watching other people's touch behavior. In one experiment by psychologists Brenda Major and Richard Heslin of Purdue University, observers could see only the silhouettes of pairs of people facing each other, with one touching the other on the shoulder. They judged the toucher to be more assertive and of a higher status than the person touched. Had the touch been reciprocal, status differences would have disappeared.

Psychologist Alvin G. Goldstein and student Judy Jeffords at the University of Missouri have sharpened our understanding of touch and status through their field study of touch among legislators during a Missouri state legislative session. Observers positioned themselves in the gallery and systematically recorded who initiated touch during the many floor conversations. Based on a status formula that included committee leadership and membership, they discovered that among these male peers, the lower-status men were the ones most likely to initiate touch.

When roles are clearly different, so that one individual has control or power over the other, such as a boss and a secretary, then touch usually reflects major dominance or status differences in the relationship. But when roles are more diffuse and overlapping, so that people are almost equal in power — as the legislators were — then lower-status people may try to establish more intimate connections with their more powerful and higher-status colleagues by making physical contact with them.

Touching has a subtle and often ambivalent role in most settings. But there is one special circumstance in which touch is permitted and universally positive: In sports, teammates encourage, applaud and console each other generously through touch. In Western cultures, for men especially, hugs and slaps on the behind are permitted among athletes, even though they are very rarely seen between heterosexual men outside the sports arena. The intense enthusiasm legitimizes tactile expressions of emotion that would otherwise be seen as homosexually threatening.

Graduate student Charles Anderton and psychologist Robert Heckel of the University of South Carolina studied touch in the competitive context of all-male or all-female championship swim meets by recording each instance of touch after success and failure. Regardless of sex, winners were touched similarly, on average six times more than losers, with most of the touches to the hand and some to the back or shoulders; only a small percent were to the head or buttocks.

This swimming study only looked at touch between same-sex team-mates, since swim meets have separate races for men and women. Would touch patterns be the same for mixed-gender teams, or would men and women be inhibited about initiating and receiving touches, as they are in settings outside of sports? Psychologists David Smith, Frank Willis and Joseph Gier at the University of Missouri studied touching behavior of men and women in bowling alleys in Kansas City, Missouri, during mixed-league competition. They found almost no differences between men and women in initiating or receiving touches.

Without the social vocabulary of touch, life would be cold, mechanical, distant, rational, verbal. We are created in the intimate union of two bodies and stay connected to the body of one until the cord is cut. Even after birth, we need touch for survival. Healthy human infants deprived of touch and handling for long periods develop a kind of infant depression that leads to withdrawal and apathy and, in extreme cases, wasting away to death.

As people develop, touch assumes symbolic meaning as the primary system for expressing and experiencing affection, inclusion and control. Deprived of those gestures and their meanings, the world might be more egalitarian, but it would also be far more frightening, hostile and chilly. And who would understand why a stranger's touch meant life to Brigitte Gerney?

Montagu explains the importance of touch for healthy human
development. The chapter also describes gender differences in
touch behavior.

27

Skin and Sex

Ashley Montagu

Early deprivations of tactile experience may lead to behavior calculated
to provide substitutes for such tactile deprivations in the form of self-
manipulation of various kinds, masturbation and toe, finger, or
thumbsucking, pulling or fingering the ears, nose, or hair. It is an
interesting fact that among nonliterate peoples who generally give their
children all the tactile stimulation they require, fingersucking or
thumbsucking seldom occurs. Moloney, for example, writes, "My
observations in Africa, Tahiti, and the islands around Tahiti, the Fiji
Islands, Islands in the Caribean, Japan, Mexico and Okinawa confirmed
for me the fact that most babies in these areas are breastfed and carried
on the person of the mother. In these areas I noted that thumbsucking
was practically non-existent."

Moloney believes that the thumb becomes a substitute for the mother,
just as the pellets of paper do, which schizoid or schizophrenic children
so often roll between their fingers. As Lowenfeld has put it, the fingers
act like antennae or feelers which probe the surroundings for ensuing
motor activities.

The oft-heard complaint directed by women at the clumsiness,
crassness, and incompetence of men in their sexual approaches and in
sexual intercourse itself, men's lack of skill in foreplay and their failure
to understand its meaning, almost certainly substantially reflects the lack
of tactile experience that many males have suffered in childhood. The
roughness with which many men will handle women and children
constitutes yet another evidence of their having been failed in early tactile

experience, for it is difficult to conceive of anyone who had been tenderly loved and caressed in infancy not learning to approach a woman or a child with especial tenderness. The very word "tenderness" implies softness, delicacy of touch, caring for. The gorilla, that gentle creature, is the most frequently slandered animal when women wish to describe the sexual approaches of the average male. Sex seems to be regarded as a tension releaser rather than as a profoundly meaningful act of communication in a deeply involved human relationship. In many of its elements the sexual relationship reproduces the loving-mother-child relationship. As Lawrence Frank has put it,

> Tactile communication in adult mating, both as foreplay and in intercourse, has been elaborated and refined by some cultures into the most amazing array of erotic patterns which through a variety of tactual stimulation of various parts of the body serve to arouse, prolong, intensify, and evoke communication. Here we see tactile communication, reinforced and elaborated by motor activities and language, by concomitant stimulation, visual, auditory, olfactory, gustatory, and the deeper muscle senses, combined to provide an organic-personality relationship which may be one of the most intense human experiences. It is, or can be, considered an esthetic experience in that there may be little or no instrumental, purposive, or cognitive elements, with greater or less loss of space-time orientation. But the elementary sexual processes of the human organism may be transformed and focused into an interpersonal love relationship with an identified person to whom each is seeking to communicate, using sex not for procreation, as in the mating of a female in heat ready to be fertilized, but as 'another language,' for interpersonal communication. Here we see how the primary tactile mode of communication, which has been largely overlaid and superseded by auditory and visual signs and symbols, is reinstated to function with elementary organic intensity, provided the individuals have not lost the capacity for communication with the self through tactile experiences.

It may well be asked, if men are affected in this manner by lack of early tactual experience, how are women affected? The answer to that question is: Much in the same manner as the women discussed earlier in this chapter, who longed to be held and cuddled. These women were affected by more or less frigidity, a condition which they could easily conceal by pretending to excitements they did not feel, or by a nymphomania which abnormally craves tactual satisfactions. Once again it must be emphasized that it is not being suggested that such conditions are entirely the results of tactual deprivations in early life, but only that they may, in part, be so.

Women have always in great numbers complained of the male's lack of tenderness sexually and in general. May not this deficiency have become rather more epidemic in the recent period as a consequence, again at least in part, of the abandonment of breastfeeding and the reduction in the tactual experiences of the child?

Many mothers early begin to reject demonstrations of love by their sons in the mistaken fear that unless they do so they will cause their sons to become too deeply attached to them. There are many fathers who reject their sons' embraces because, as one such father, a physician, remarked to me, "I don't want him to become a homosexual." The appalling ignorance revealed in such attitudes is very damaging, and would serve to reinforce the male's inability to relate himself tactually to another human being.

To be roughly handled has been considered by many women, especially women of the working classes, an indispensable evidence of love. There is, for example, the well-known feminine Cockney supplication to her man which illustrates this: "If ya loves us, chuck us abaht." The sexual element was very evident in the flagellation epidemics of medieval times, as a penance which the church at first approved and then forbade, when it realized the sensuality involved. That the participants in such flagellation episodes were more than anxious to receive the caresses of the whip suggests that a great many infants in medieval times received an inadequate amount and quality of tactile stimulation.

28 Crusco and Wetzel conducted a study to determine the effect of touching on restaurant tipping. Results indicate that touch increases tipping even if the customer is not aware of it.

The Midas Touch
The Effects of Interpersonal Touch on Restaurant Tipping

April H. Crusco and Christopher G. Wetzel

Interpersonal touch is a form of nonverbal behavior in which meaning is derived from a myriad of environmental and personal cues. Touch as a source of information feedback can be decoded as an expression of affiliation, love, or sexual interest; it can signal dominance or aggression; and it can guide the recipient's attention as part of a greeting/parting process (Knapp, 1978).

Touch research has frequently demonstrated positive effects from the innocuous touch of another. Tactile contact has increased positive affect or liking ratings of another (Alagna, Whitcher and Fisher, 1979; Fisher, Rytting and Heslin, 1976; Florez and Goldman, 1982; Hubble, Noble and Robinson, 1981; Jourard and Friedman, 1970; Silverthorne, Noreen, Hunt and Rota, 1972; Whitcher and Fisher, 1979); it has influenced the purchasing behavior of shoppers (Smith, Gier and Willis, 1982); and it has increased compliance to legitimate requests (Kleinke, 1977).

Adapted with permission from: Crusco, A.H., & C.G. Wetzel, The Midas Touch: The Effects of Interpersonal Touching on Restaurant Tipping. *Personality and Social Psychology Bulletin,* 10, (4), pp. 512-517. © 1984. Reprinted by permission of Sage Publications, Inc.

Authors' Note: We would like to thank Nancy Fleming and Jennifer Dunlap for serving as waitress/confederates and Mike Seligman and Allen LeBlanc for letting us conduct the research in their restaurants. Thanks are also due to Dave Hansen, Bill Kulick, and Marsha Walton for their advice and assistance in data and manuscript preparation. Manuscript preparation was partially supported by an Andrew W. Mellon Faculty Development grant to the second author. Reprint requests should be addressed to Chris Wetzel, Rhodes College, 2000 N. Parkway, Memphis, TN, 38112.

Research has also revealed sex differences in touch interactions and reactions to touch. Females are touched more than males; males touch females twice as much as females touch males; and males generally respond less positively to being touched than do females (Fisher, et al., 1976; Goldberg and Lewis, 1969; Henley, 1973; Sussman and Rosenfeld, 1978; Cowen, Weissberg and Lotyczewski, 1983; Whitcher and Fisher, 1979). Touching generally flows from a high status toucher to a lower status touchee, and being touched can signify inferiority or dependency. Sex effects have thus been interpreted as males' expression of dominance over females (Henley, 1973). For example, Whitcher and Fisher (1979) examined whether therapeutic touch could reduce patient anxiety. Nurses, during the course of a routine preoperative instruction, touched some of their patients on the arm for one minute while they examined a pamphlet with them. Females who were touched reacted more favorably than did control patients on affective, behavioral, and physiological (blood pressure) measures, whereas touched males reacted more negatively than controls. Whitcher and Fisher hypothesized that the nurse-patient relationship led males to interpret the touch as conveying a message of relative inferiority and dependency.

The purpose of this study was to determine the effects of touch in a previously unexamined, nonreactive, natural setting where experimental control could be exercised. Diners in a restaurant were administered one of two types of touch by a waitress just before the diners left their tips. A brief touch on the hand was expected to produce positive affect towards the waitress for both male and female customers and hence increase the amount of tip. However, a touch on the shoulder, often used as sign of dominance by high status individuals, might not be viewed as positively, especially by males. Servants, after all, are not expected to dominate their employers. Hence, the shoulder touch condition may reduce tipping compared to the hand touch condition, and more so for male than for female customers.

Method

Subject Selection

Subjects were 114 diners, 79 males and 35 females, from two restaurants. Any customer who was a friend of the waitress/confederate was eliminated. Teen-aged males and college-aged females dining in groups greater than two were not selected as subjects because they generally do not tip. Approximately 25% of the participants were excluded because they either tipped before the touch manipulation was executed, or because the tip left on the table could not be definitely linked to them.

Procedure and Setting

A majority of the data (79 subjects) was collected in one restaurant by one waitress who was blind to the experimental hypotheses. A second waitress collected data on an addition 17 diners. A third waitress collected 18 observations in a second restaurant. All three waitresses were in their early to mid-twenties. Both restaurants were located in a small college community; they served lunch, dinner and cocktails; and they were frequented by business people, college students, and permanent residents of Oxford, Mississippi. A large majority of the participants were college students.

In both restaurants, the waitress was responsible for collecting the bill, and she randomly assigned diners to the experimental condition after she had collected the customer's money but before she returned with change. The touch manipulation was carried out during the change-returning transaction. Thus the waitress was blind to the touch manipulation when she was serving her customer. After returning change, the waitress asked the subjects to fill out a restaurant survey, seal it in an envelope, and leave it on the table.

Touch Manipulation

Participants were randomly assigned to one of three levels of touch. In the Fleeting Touch condition, the waitress twice touched the diner's palm with her fingers for one-half second as she returned the diner's change. In the Shoulder Touch condition, she placed her hand on the diner's shoulder for one to one and one-half seconds. In the No Touch condition, there was no physical contact with the customer. The waitresses were carefully trained to behave consistently during the change-returning transaction. The waitress approached the customers from their sides or from slightly behind them, made contact but did not smile as they spoke "Here's your change" in a friendly but firm tone, bent their bodies at an approximately 10 degree angle as they returned the change, and did not make eye contact during the touch manipulation.

Dependent Variables

The percentage of bill gratuity (tip%) left for the waitress served as a behavioral measure of the diners' reactions to being touched; a restaurant attitude survey assessed the diner's affective reactions. The survey consisted of nine, seven-point semantic differentials that assessed the goodness, pleasantness and comfortableness of the dining experience, the helpfulness, friendliness, and quality of the waitressing, and the positivity, attractiveness, and comfortableness of the restaurant's atmosphere. Because all nine items intercorrelated .50 or higher (with many in the .90's), they were summed to form a single attitudinal measure.

Results

Statistical analyses indicated that:

1. Tipping was higher if the weather was sunny, it was later in the week, and there were more people in the party.
2. The Shoulder Touch and the Fleeting Touch increased tipping an equal amount. This finding is not influenced by gender, weather, day of the week, number in party, or the individual waitress.
3. Touch did not influence perceptions of the pleasantness of the restaurant.
4. Males tipped more than females, and also rated the restaurant as more positive.
5. There was no relationship between tipping and perceptions of the restaurant.

Discussion

This study employed a novel behavioral measure (tip%) to assess the effects of two types of touch in a field setting, something not previously done in the literature. We found that males did not significantly differ from females in their reactions to both types of touches, and in fact showed a tendency to be less negatively influenced by the shoulder touch than did females. (As all the touchers were female, any sex differences would have been difficult to interpret). Our failure to find males reacting more negatively to being touched than did the females may have occurred because male diners felt secure enough about their role and status that they benevolently viewed the waitress' innocuous touch as playful endearment or affiliation. Males' status may have been secure because (1) in a restaurant there are few contextual cues present that signal lowered status or dependency, or (2) the waitress-diner relationship may have the status lines clearly drawn. Whether similar results would occur with male waiters needs to be addressed by future research.

Although there was a trend in that direction, the shoulder touch did not significantly decrease tipping compared to the hand touch. It may be that the shoulder touch, preceded as it was in this experiment by a notification that change was coming, was justified and unambiguous; both factors have been shown to facilitate positive reactions to touch (Kleinke, 1977; Sussman and Rosenfeld, 1978).

Our failure to find touch effects on the restaurant attitude survey is not terribly disturbing given that other researchers have frequently obtained significant behavioral effects without obtaining significant effects on cognitive, evaluative, or self-report ratings (Pattison, 1973; Smith, et al., 1982; Whitcher and Fisher, 1979). Pattison's hypothesis, that survey and self-report data are unreliable, seems unlikely because we obtained a much larger sex main effect on our survey than on the tip%. Thus the survey was sensitive enough to detect sex differences and apparently was more sensitive than our behavioral measure. A second explanation, that innocuous touches like ours have short-term effects, seems unlikely given the contiguity of the tipping and the survey. Most customers filled out the survey immediately after leaving the tip, and a few may have completed the survey before placing their tip. A third possibility is that the customers were unaware of the touch or, even if aware, it did not affect their conscious, verbal explanatory system (Nisbett and Wilson, 1977; Wilson, 1983). Although the unobtrusive nature of our experiment precluded our asking our subjects if they were aware of being touched by the waitress, Fisher, et al. (1976) and Silverthorne, et al. (1972) have found that many of their subjects were unaware that they had been touched. Thus brief, fleeting, unobtrusive touches like ours may have subliminal effects.

References

Alagna, F.J., S.J. Whitcher, & J.D. Fisher. (1979). Evaluative reaction to interpersonal touch in a counseling interview. *Journal of Counseling Psychology, 26,* 465-472.

Cowen, E.L., R.P. Weissberg, & B.S. Lotyczewski. (1983). Physical contacts in interactions between clinicians and young children. *Journal of Consulting and Clinical Psychology, 51,* 132-138.

Cunningham, M.R. (1979). Weather, mood, and helping behavior: Quasiexperiments with the Sunshine Samaritan. *Journal of Personality and Social Psychology, 37,* 1947-1956.

Fisher, J.D., M. Rytting, & R. Heslin. (1976). Hands touching hands: Affective and evaluative effects of an interpersonal touch. *Sociometry, 39,* 416-421.

Florez, C.A., & M. Goldman. (1982). Evaluation of interpersonal touch by the sighted and blind. *Journal of Social Psychology, 116,* 229-234.

Freeman, S., M.R. Walker, R. Borden, & B. Latane. (1975). Diffusion of responsibility and restaurant tipping: Cheaper by the bunch. *Personality and Social Psychology Bulletin, I,* 584-587.

Goldberg, S., & M. Lewis. (1969). Play behavior in the year-old infant: Early sex differences. *Child Development, 40,* 21-31.

Henley, N.M. (1973). The politics of touch. In P. Brown (Ed.), *Radical Psychology.* New York: Harper & Row.

Hubble, M.A., F.C. Noble, & E.F. Robinson. (1981). The effect of counselor touch in an initial counseling session. *Journal of Counseling Psychology, 28,* 533-535.

Jourard, S.M., & R. Friedman. (1970). Experimenter-subject distance and self-disclosure. *Journal of Personality and Social Psychology 15(3),* 278-282.

Kleinke, C.L. (1977). Compliance to requests made by gazing and touching experimenters in field settings. *Journal of Experimental Social Psychology, 13,* 218-223.

Knapp, M.L. (1978). *Nonverbal communication in human interaction* (2nd ed.). New York: Holt, Rinehart & Winston.

Nisbett, R.E., & T.D. Wilson. (1977). Telling more than we can know: Verbal reports on mental processes. *Psychological Review, 84,* 231-259.

Pattison, J.E. (1973). Effects of touch on self-exploration and the therapeutic relationship. *Journal of Consulting and Clinical Psychology; 40(2),* 170-175.

Silverthorne, C., C. Noreen, T. Hunt, & L. Rota. (1972). The effects of tactile stimulation on visual experience. *Journal of Social Psychology, 88,* 153-154.

Smith, D.E., J.A. Gier, & F.N. Willis. (1982). Interpersonal touch and compliance with a marketing request. *Basic and Applied Social Psychology, 3(1),* 35-38.

Sussman, N.M., & H.M. Rosenfeld. (1978). Touch, justification and sex: Influences on the aversiveness of spatial violations. *Journal of Social Psychology, 106,* 215-225.

Whitcher, S.J., & J.D. Fisher. (1979). Multidimensional reaction to therapeutic touch in a hospital setting. *Journal of Personality and Social Psychology, 37,* 87-96.

Wilson, T.D. (1983). Strangers to ourselves: The origins and accuracy of beliefs about one's own mental states. Unpublished manuscript, University of Virginia.

29 *This chapter discusses meanings of touch. Jones found that touch is used to communicate positive affect, playfulness, and control, and is part of rituals and tasks.*

Communicating With Touch

Stanley E. Jones

Touch is our most intimate and involving form of communication and helps us to keep good relationships with others. That is why we use expressions like "Let's stay in touch," "I'll contact you when I get back," and "I was touched" (by what another person said or did). Most people say touching makes them feel good about themselves and that they would like to touch more than they do. It is important, however, to know how to touch appropriately, and this involves knowing how to communicate each of the many meanings of touch.

My colleague Elaine Yarbrough and I asked college students to act as "participant observers" by recording all of their touches with others over several days. A participant observer is a person who participates in the communication being studied but also observes and records the events. In this study, participant observers used the Touch Observation Form provided in Figure 1.

Data were collected from nearly 1,500 touches. Two kinds of events were separately analyzed: (1) touch sequences, consisting of a series of touches (139 cases), and (2) individual touches, consisting of single instances of contact (1,069 cases).

Touch Sequences

Touch sequences are two or more touches communicatively related to one another within the same interaction. A touch sequence occurs when

This chapter was written specifically for this book and is based in part on the following article: Jones, Stanley E., and Yarbrough, A. E. (1985). A naturalistic study of the meanings of touch. *Communication Monographs, 52,* 19-56.

FIGURE 1.
TOUCH OBSERVATION FORM

Name _____ Date _____

Use arrows to link entries which are part
of the same interaction. Ex.   1.
                                 ↓
                               2.

Indicate where applicable: BM—Best Male Friend;
BF—Best Female Friend; MO—Mother; FA—Father

1.
Initiator of touch
A. Me
B. Other
C. Mutual
D. Unclear
(1 letter)

2a.
Parts of body when ini-tiated
(1 or more letters @ blank: note 2-handed touches)
Initiator   Receiver
touched   touched
with: on:

2b.
Parts of body when mu-tual or unclear
(1 or more letters per blank)
Me: Other:

3.
Place
A. Mine
B. Other's
C. Neutral
(Specify bldg. and room)

4.
Time of day
(Include a.m. or p.m.)

1. _____
2. _____
3. _____

5.
Accompanying verbal statement
(Paraphrase if necessary)
When:
A. Immediately prior to touch
B. Immediately after touch
C. During
By: (M) Me; (O) Other

6.
Touch translated into verbal state-ment
(Make into short sentence if possible; note voice tone or facial expression if critical to meaning)

7.
(Mark "Psych" for touches you reject internally only)
Acceptance/Rejection
A. Touch accepted by me
B. Touch rejected by me
C. Touch accepted by other
D. Touch rejected by other
(Spec. with letter; explain how & why t. is rejected)

1. _____
2. _____
3. _____

8.
Type of touch
A. Caressing/holding
B. Feeling/Caressing
C. Prolonged holding
D. Holding/pressing ag.
E. Spot touching
F. Accidental brushing
G. Handshake
H. Pat I. Squeeze J. Punch
K. Pinch L. Other
(1 or more letters)

9.
Purpose of participants
A. Give/get info (spec.)
B. Ask/give favor
C. Persuading
D. Persuaded
E. Casual talk
F. Deeptalk
G. Greeting
H. Departing
I. Any other (specify)
Me   *Other*

10.
Others present
(Male &/or female)
(Specify relation to you us-ing letters from Category 11)

11.
Relationship to other
A. Relative (spec.)
B1. Close Friend
B2. Not close friend
C. Acquaintance
D. Co-worker
E. Superior
F. Subordinate
G. Stranger
H. Other (spec.)
Spec. if intimate

1. _____
2. _____
3. _____

12.
Nature of social occa-sion
A. Work
B. Class
C. Party
D. Informal meeting
E. Other (spec.)
For public places, spec-ify function (bar, etc.)

13.
Status of other
A. Higher 1. Formal
B. Lower 2. Informal
C. Equal
(1 letter and 1 no.)

14.
Age of other
(Approximate)

15.
Sex of other
(M/F)

16.
Race of other
A. Anglo
B. Black
C. Chicano
D. Asian
E. Other (spec)

1. _____
2. _____
3. _____

17.
Standing or sitting
Me: Other:

1. _____
2. _____
3. _____

18.
Any other contextual factors you think influenced your touches:

_____
_____
_____

one person touches another and the second person touches back, or when one person touches another more than once. Two basic types of sequences were found: repetitive and strategic.

Sometimes one touch is not enough, and repetition intensifies the meaning. In repetitive sequences, each of the touches has the same meaning. In the overwhelming majority of cases, the touches are all strictly positive (not playful or controlling). For example, in the "support" sequence, one person comforts and reassures another. If you are tucking someone in bed when they are sick, just pulling the covers up to the chin is not sufficient. You also need to fluff up the pillow, gently brush the forehead, pat the shoulder or chest, and so forth. As another example of a type of repetitive sequence, opposite-sex "best friends" who are not romantic partners tend to use a version of "repetitive affection" by exchanging pats, caresses, or spot touches back-and-forth. This "ping-pong" trading of touches seems to symbolize the equality of this kind of relationship.

Strategic sequences are touches which move from one meaning to another, usually with a "surprise" at the end. For example, in the affection-to-control sequence, one person "softens up" the other with one or more affection touches, and then touches while asking the other person to do something (a control touch, even though it resembles earlier touches). In one case when a couple was watching television together on a couch, the female first cuddled against the male; a minute later, the male kissed the female; several minutes later, the male put his arm around the female and said, "Will you get me some water?" There is a "gamey" quality about strategic sequences because they imply an ulterior or hidden motive. If overused in a relationship, they might undermine the impact of other, more straightforward touch messages.

Individual Touches

Individual, single touches are more common than sequences. If done at the right time to convey an accurate meaning, they can have considerable effect. Touches are oftentimes subtle and hard to interpret unless you understand the language of touch. The same touch can have different meanings. For example, a simple contact of a hand to a shoulder or elbow can convey "Hi, how are you?" "I want to comfort you," "Do this for me," or a variety of other meanings. Also, different touches can have the same meaning (a kiss, a hug, or just a pat can communicate affection). The secret to understanding touches is to read them in the total context, including such things as what is said, the nature of the relationship, and the social situation.

A blueprint for touching. The research revealed 18 different meanings of touch which can be grouped into 7 overall types: Positive affect (emotion), playfulness, control, ritual, hybrid (mixed), task-related, and accidental touches. These are summarized in Table 1, which can be read as a blueprint for how to touch. On the left-hand column of the table are the names of each type with a definition of the meaning. In the next column, on the right, is a description of the "key features" of the meaning, the way the touch is done or elements of the context which must ordinarily be present for the meaning to come across clearly. In the far right column are examples of each kind of touch. Sometimes "enactment types" are described, distinctively different ways the same meaning can be conveyed. If you imagine what the touch would look (and feel) like, or act out the touches with someone else, the way each meaning is communicated becomes clearer.

In the table, the abbreviation "NVBP" means "non-vulnerable body parts" (hand, arm, shoulder, and upper back). "VBP" means "vulnerable body parts" (all other body regions). "Close relationships" refers to romantic intimates, close friends, and immediate family members.

Exercises for Understanding Touch

1. Keep a record of your own touches for one or more complete days using photocopies of the Touch Recording Form and writing down the specifics immediately after each touch. (Tell other people it's a class assignment if they ask, but don't go into detail.) There will be space to record three touch events on each copy (lines 1, 2, and 3 throughout the form). Record every contact; indicate if it was initiated by you or someone else, mutually initiated (like a hug or handshake), or whether the initiator was unclear (accidental touches). When you're done, analyze the results by counting up the touches:

   a. Were you more of a toucher or a "touchee?" How many touches did you experience per day? (Average is about twelve for females, eight for males.)

   b. With whom did you have touches most (kinds of relationships, category eleven on the form)?

   c. What meanings did you communicate? Were there some rejected touches and why? Are there other meanings you would like to communicate?

TABLE 1 Characteristics of Meaning Categories for Individual Touches

Category (definition, # of cases)	Key Features	Typical Examples and Enactment Types
A. Positive Affect Touches		
1. Support—serves to nurture, reassure or promise protection (39 cases)	(1) Situation calls for comfort or reassurance (100%) (2) Hand (100%), and sometimes an arm, directed to 1-2 body parts (89.7%) (3) Initiated by person who gives support (84.6%)	(1) Knowing from a conversation the night before that a roommate is worried about a test, the toucher pats him on the shoulder when he sees him in the morning and says, "You'll do O.K." (2) After a friend expresses sadness about an event, the toucher silently reaches out and squeezes her arm. (3) Cuddling a crying child who is injured. (Hugs are rare events, reserved for a person who expresses strong distress.)
2. Appreciation—expresses gratitude (16 cases)	(1) Situation: receiver has performed service for toucher (100%) (2) Touch initiator verbalizes appreciation, usually some version of "thanks" (87.5%)	(1) A boss touches a subordinate on the shoulder at the end of a day's work and says, "Thanks for the way you handled things." (2) A woman kisses a close male friend on the cheek after a meal he prepared and says "Thanks a lot."
3. Inclusion—draws attention to act of being together; suggests psychological closeness (32 cases)	(1) Sustained touch (100%) (2) Close relationship (90.6%), mainly sexual intimates and close friends; only 2 cases involve immediate family members other than spouses	(1) A couple walks down the street holding hands or with arms around one another. (2) A couple sits on a couch watching television with one person leaning against the other. (3) A male and a female who are close friends talk in a restaurant with knees touching.

4. *Affection* — expresses generalized positive regard beyond mere acknowledgement (56 cases)	(1) Close relationships (85.7%) (2) A residual category; absence of a more specific positive affect meaning suggests affection	(1) (Highly intense form) Spontaneously hugging a romantic partner or close friend and saying words of endearment ("Hi, sweetheart," "I love you," etc.). (2) (Less intense, but more common type) Patting or caressing a close person when passing by in the room. (3) (Examples are varied and include hugs, kisses, and less involving, simple contacts.) The lack of a specific situation calling for touch — such as a sad event or a greeting — defines pure affection. (Rare between men.)
5. *Sexual* — expresses physical attraction or sexual interest (21 cases)	(1) Sexually intimate relationships (100%) (2) Holding and/or caressing (100%) (3) VBP (95.2%), including or restricted to "sexual" body parts — chest (women), pelvis, and/or buttocks (85.7%)	(1) Movement from one to another type of holding and/or caressing (e.g., lovers embracing and caressing; multiple kinds of touching distinguish it from affection). (2) A simple hand touch to a sexual body part (e.g., reaching over and touching an intimate on the buttock).

B. Playful Touches

1. *Playful Affection* — serves to lighten interaction; seriousness of affection qualified (26 cases)	(1) Affectionate or sexual messages with play signal (100%)	(1) A male saying "How's about a kiss?" (I'm just kidding around) to a close female friend or romantic partner, followed by a quick kiss. (2) With others present, a male puts his arm around his male roommate, who is doing the dishes, and says, "You'd make a good wife" (I'm teasing about being affectionate).
2. *Playful Aggression* — serves to lighten interaction; seriousness of aggression qualified (26 cases)	(1) Aggressive message with play signal (100%) 2) Initiated, not mutual (100%)	(1) Aggressive touch with a comment which clarifies the intent as play (e.g., saying "Let's wrestle," and then performing a mock half-nelson to the other person — notice the importance of the early verbal warning). (2) Aggressive comment with a touch play signal (e.g., a customer says to a waitress, "No, we don't want the check and tear it up," with a smile and light touch to her arm).

C. Control Touches

Category	Characteristics	Examples
1. *Compliance* — attempts to direct behavior and oftentimes also attitudes or feelings of another (75 cases)	(1) Initiated by person attempting influence (92%) (2) Verbalization occurs (states or implies requested action) (90.7%)	(1) A boss touches an employee on the shoulder and says, "Could you get this done by 5 o'clock?" (Touch translation: "I really want you to do it.") (2) Grabbing a companion by the upper arm and saying, "Let's hurry across the street."
2. *Attention-getting* — serves to direct the recipient's perceptual focus (66 cases)	(1) Initiated by person requesting attention (100%) (2) Initiator verbalizes (clarifies purpose) (100%) (3) Brief touches (spot, pat, brush) directed to 1-2 body parts (84.8%)	(1) Patting a companion on the shoulder and saying, "Look at this!" (2) Spot touching a stranger on the arm to say, "Excuse me, do you have the time?"
3. *Announcing a Response* — calls attention to and emphasizes a feeling state of initiator; implicitly requests affect response from another (46 cases)	(1) Initiated by person announcing response (91.3%) (2) Verbalization by toucher(s) announces feeling directly or indirectly (97.8%)	(1) A woman touches her female friend and says, "Can you believe he did that?"(Translation: "I hope you feel the same way about him.") (2) A woman touches her male companion and says, "I'm so excited about today!" (Translation: "Get psyched!") (3) A man slaps another man on the shoulder and says "Congratulations!" (I'm happy for you). (Or, an exchange of hand-to-hand slaps— mutual congratulations.)

D. Ritualistic Touches

1. *Greeting* — serves as part of the act of acknowledging another at the opening of an encounter (43 cases)	(1) Situation is beginning of interaction (100%) (2) Verbalization of standard greeting phrase (93%), before or during touch, not after (88.4%) (3) Hand to one body part (90.6%) (4) (Near to key feature) Minimal form of contact (handshake, spot touch, pat or squeeze) (83.7%)	(1) (Formal) handshake greeting (mainly used between males). (2) (Slightly more informal) Hand to body part greeting, usually to shoulder or arm (mainly female-male or female-female touches).
2. *Departure* — serves as part of the act of closing an encounter (20 cases)	(1) Situation is end of an encounter (100%) (2) Verbalization of standard departure phrase (90%), before or during touch, not after (85%) (3) Hand to one body part (85%)	(1) Male pats male friend on shoulder when leaving. (2) Female touches lower back of female friend when leaving.

E. Hybrid Touches

1. *Greeting/Affection* — expresses affection and acknowledgement at the initiation of an encounter (79 cases)	(1) Situation is beginning of interaction (100%) (2) Verbalization occurs (88.6%) (3) Close relationships (86.1%) (4) VBP touches (86.1%)	(1) Hug and/or brief kiss between male and female (usually close friends, romantic partners, or parent and son or daughter). (2) Hug between female friends. (3) (Most common after a period of absence — most of a day or longer; rare between men.)
2. *Departure/Affection* — expresses affection and serves to close an encounter (72 cases)	(1) Situation is end of interaction (100%) (2) Verbalization occurs (94.4%) (3) Close relationships (94.4%) (4) VBP touches (91.6%), principally hugs and/or kisses (84.7%)	(1) Opposite-sex prolonged hug with a kiss (at the airport, for instance; same relationships as greeting/affection). (2) Hug between female friends when one is leaving. (3) (More common and more extensive the longer the expected separation; rare between men.)

F. Task-Related Touches

1. *Reference to appearance* — a touch which points out or inspects a body part or artifact referred to in a verbal comment about appearance (11 cases)	(1) Words accompany and justify the touch (100%) (2) Spot touch by a hand to a VBP (100%) (3) Close relationships (90.1%)	(1) A woman inspects a female friend's necklace and says, "This is pretty." (2) A woman brushes a male friend's hair with her hand and says, "I like your haircut." (3) (Males rarely use this touch, although they could, saying "Nice suit," while feeling the material at the lapel.)
2. *Instrumental Ancillary* — a touch which occurs as an unnecessary part of the accomplishment of a task (56 cases)	(1) Hand-to-hand contacts (91.1%) (2) Instrumental act is clear in itself, but task doesn't require touch (100%)	(1) Most common is handing an object to someone and allowing hand-to-hand contact (e.g., a clerk returning change to a customer).
3. *Instrumental Intrinsic* — touch which accomplishes a task in and of itself (54 cases)	(1) Instrumental meaning is clear from the touch itself — a helping touch (100%)	(1) Assisting a person in putting on a coat. (2) Placing a hand on a person's forehead to check for a temperature (implies support, but mainly accomplishes a task). (3) Putting suntan lotion on a person's back (may imply flirtation or affection).

G. Accidental Touches

1. *Accidental* — touches which are perceived as unintentional (86 cases)	(1) Touches consist of single, momentary contacts, principally brushes (89.5%), with a few spot touches (9.3%) (2) Touches seem to be mistakes (100%), although a secondary message (like flirtation or attention-getting) might be implied.	(1) Brushing a person when passing by, getting up to go, etc. (2) (Bumps or brushes between strangers are usually rejected, unless an apology is given.)

2. Observe and record touches of others in some likely location. Airports, railway stations, or bus terminals are good places for observation, especially at departures. (Or, for observing touches between parents and children, preschools at the beginning or end of the day are good locations.) The same categories as in Exercise 1 may be used (although you may have to guess about relationships between adults). Analyze the results:

   a. What differences in touching did you observe for men with men, women with women, and men with women? (Or, what were the differences in the way mothers or fathers touched daughters or sons?)

   b. Did you notice any other nonverbal behaviors which preceded goodbyes (or hellos) like waving, extending arms for a touch, etc.?

Suggestions for Further Reading

1. For more details on touch meanings and sequences, see:

   Jones, Stanley E., and Yarbrough, A. Elaine (1985). A naturalistic study of the meanings of touch. *Communication Monographs, 52,* 19-56.

2. For information on male and female differences in touching, see:

   Greenbaum, Paul E., and Rosenfeld, Howard M. (1980). Varieties of touching in Greetings: Sequential structure and sex-related differences. *Journal of Nonverbal Behavior, 5,* 13-25.

   Jones, Stanley E. (1986). Sex differences in touch communication. *The Western Journal of Speech Communication, 50,* 227-241.

3. For a discussion of the importance of touch, especially with infants and young children, see:

   Montagu, Ashley (1971). *Touching: The Human Significance of the Skin.* New York: Harper & Row.

30
Touch avoidance is the nonverbal tendency to avoid the touch of people of the same and/or opposite sex. Andersen and Leibowitz developed and tested a measure of touch avoidance. People who are touch avoidant were found to be less confident and open about themselves.

The Development and Nature of the Construct of Touch Avoidance

Peter A. Andersen
and Kenneth Leibowitz

Based on a review of the literature, it was hypothesized that:

1. Touch avoidance is positively related to communication apprehension. *Communication apprehension* is the anxiety or nervousness you feel about communication (McCroskey, 1970). Since people who are apprehensive about communicating avoid communication and closeness, it is likely that they will also avoid touch.
2. Touch avoidance is negatively related to self-disclosure. *Self-disclosure* is a message about the self that we communicate to others (Wheeless and Grotz, 1975). People who are willing to disclose accept closeness and intimacy and should not avoid touch.
3. Touch avoidance is negatively related to self-esteem. *Self-esteem* consists of the positive or negative feelings we have about ourselves (Deustch, 1961). Studies show that people who feel good about themselves are willing to touch more (Silverman, Pressman, & Bartel, 1973; Watson, 1975). Therefore, people with high self-esteem should not be touch avoidant.
4. Touch avoidance is positively related to age. Since age is related to the amount of touch (Scheflen, 1972), it should also be related to touch avoidance.
5. Males will be more touch avoidant of same-sex persons than will females.

Edited with permission from: Andersen, P.A., and Leibowitz, K. (1978). The development and nature of the construct of touch avoidance. *Environmental Psychology and Nonverbal Behavior*, 3, 89-106.

6. Females will be more touch avoidant of opposite-sex persons than will males. Many studies show touch and sex are related. In general, females are more touch oriented than males (Jourard and Rubin, 1968). However, because of sex roles there may be differences in touch depending on whether the other person is of the same or opposite sex.
7. Marital status will have a significant effect on touch avoidance of opposite-sex persons.
8. Marital status will have a significant effect on touch avoidance of same-sex persons. Though marriage is an important cultural role in American society, little research has examined touch or touch avoidance. As a result, these two hypotheses were explored.
9. Protestants will experience higher levels of touch avoidance than non-Protestants. An important part of cultural influences on touch is a person' religious training. Previous research has found that Christian religions, particularly fundamentalist Protestant religions, discourage touch (Montagu, 1971).

Methods and Results

Three studies were conducted in order to construct a *Touch Avoidance Measure* (TAM) and to test the nine hypotheses. In the first study, subjects were 204 undergraduate students enrolled in a basic communication course at West Virginia University. Items were created to measure Touch Avoidance (see Figure 1) and were found to reliably (effectively) measure avoiding touch with persons of the same sex (TAM 1) and avoiding touch with persons of the opposite sex (TAM 2).

In the second study, subjects were 351 primary and secondary school teachers from throughout the state of West Virginia. Subjects completed the Touch Avoidance Measure as well as measures of self-disclosure (Wheeless and Grotz, 1975, in press), self-esteem (Berger, 1952; McCroskey and Richmond, 1975), age, sex, and marital status.

The measures were tested and found to be effective. Other statistical tests indicated that:

1. People who are touch avoidant also tend to be apprehensive about communication, disclose less about themselves, and disclose more negative information.
2. Touch avoidance did not differ between people of high and low self-esteem.
3. Older people avoid touching people of the opposite sex more than do younger people.
4. Males avoid touching people of the opposite sex more than do females.
5. Females avoid touching people of the opposite sex more than do males.

6. Martial status is not related to touch avoidance.
7. Protestants avoid touching people of the opposite sex more than do non-Protestants.

Figure 1 Touch Avoidance Instrument

Directions: This instrument is composed of 18 statements concerning feelings about touching other people and being touched. Please indicate the degree to which each statement applies to you by circling whether you (1) Strongly Agree, (2) Agree, (3) Are Undecided, (4) Disagree, or (5) Strongly Disagree with each statement. While some of these statements may seem repetitious, take your time and try to be as honest as possible.

*1. A hug from a same-sex friend is a true sign of friendship. 1 2 3 4 5
 2. Opposite sex friends enjoy it when I touch them. 1 2 3 4 5
*3. I often put my arm around friends of the same sex. 1 2 3 4 5
*4. When I see two people of the same sex hugging, it revolts me. 1 2 3 4 5
 5. I like it when members of the opposite sex touch me. 1 2 3 4 5
*6. People shouldn't be so uptight about touching persons of the same sex. 1 2 3 4 5
 7. I think it is vulgar when members of the opposite sex touch me. 1 2 3 4 5
 8. When a member of the opposite sex touches me, I find it unpleasant. 1 2 3 4 5
*9. I wish I were free to show emotions by touching members of the same sex. 1 2 3 4 5
 10. I'd enjoy giving a massage to an opposite sex friend. 1 2 3 4 5
*11. I enjoy kissing persons of the same sex. 1 2 3 4 5
*12. I like to touch friends that are the same sex as I am. 1 2 3 4 5
*13. Touching a friend of the same sex does not make me uncomfortable. 1 2 3 4 5
 14. I find it enjoyable when my date and I embrace. 1 2 3 4 5
 15. I enjoy getting a back rub from a member of the opposite sex. 1 2 3 4 5
*16. I dislike kissing relatives of the same sex. 1 2 3 4 5
 17. Intimate touching with members of the opposite sex is pleasurable. 1 2 3 4 5
*18. I find it difficult to be touched by a member of my own sex. 1 2 3 4 5

SEX: Male _____   STUDENT ID NUMBER: _____
 Female _____

RELIGION: Protestant _____   AGE: _____
 Catholic _____
 Jewish _____   CURRENTLY MARRIED: _____
 Other _____   CURRENTLY UNMARRIED:_____
 None_____

* Indicated TAM 1 (same sex touch-avoidance) items.
 Other items are TAM 2 (opposite sex touch—avoidance) items.

In the third study, the Touch Avoidance Measure was tested to see if scores were stable (did not change) over time. Subjects were 163 primary and secondary school teachers from throughout the state of West Virginia who filled out the Touch-Avoidance Measure on the first and third class meetings of the semester. The scores of the Touch Avoidance scale are fairly stable over time. Participants reported basically the same amount of avoidance in the first and third class periods.

References

Berger, E.M. The relations between expressed acceptance of self and expressed acceptance of others. *Journal of Abnormal and Social Psychology, 47,* 1952, 778-782.

Deutsch, M. In the interpretation of praise and criticism as a function of their social contract. *Journal of Abnormal and Social Psychology, 62,* 1961, 391-400.

Jourard, S.M., and Rubin, J.E. Self-disclosure and touching: A study of two modes of interpersonal encounter and their interpretation. *Journal of Humanistic Psychology, 8,* 1968, 39-48.

McCroskey, J.C. Measures of communication bound anxiety. *Speech Monographs, 37,* 1970, 269-277.

McCroskey, J.C. *The validity of the PRCA as an index of oral communication apprehension.* Paper presented at the annual convention of the Speech Communication Association, Houston, 1975.

McCroskey, J.C., and Richmond, V.P. *Self-credibility as an index of self-esteem.* Paper presented at the annual convention of the Speech Communication Association, Houston, 1975.

Montagu, A. *Touching: The human significance of the skin.* New York: Columbia University Press, 1971.

Scheflen, A. *Body language and social order.* Englewood Cliffs, NJ: Prentice-Hall, 1972.

Silverman, A.F., Pressman, H.E., and Bartel, H.W. Self-esteem and tactile communication. *Journal of Humanistic Psychology, 13,* 1973, 73-77.

Watson, W.H. The meaning of touch: Geriatric nursing. *Journal of Communication, 25,* 1975, 104-112.

Wheeless, L.R., and Grotz, J. The conceptualization and measurement of self-disclosure. *Human Communication Research,* in press.

Wheeless, L.R. & Grotz, J. *Self-disclosure and trust: Conceptualization, measurement, and interrelationships.* Paper presented at the annual convention of the International Communication Association, Chicago, 1975.

Key Terms and Concepts

Thayer, *Close Encounters*

rules
5 types of touch
culture
contact and noncontact cultures
communication development
gender differences

greetings
personality traits
intimacy and marital satisfaction
power
status
sports

Montagu, *Skin and Sex*

communication development

gender differences

Crusco and Wetzel, *The Midas Touch*

effects of touch
status

gender differences

Jones, *Communicating with Touch*

repetitive sequences
strategic sequences

touch meanings
enactments

Andersen and Leibowitz, *The Development and Nature of the Construct of Touch Avoidance*

touch avoidance
immediacy
gender
contextual factors
communication apprehension

self-disclosure
self-esteem
age
marital status
religion

Part Seven

Paralanguage and Silence Communication

The voice carries many messages other than words. Paralinguistic cues such as voice pitch, speaking rate, pausing, and loudness are all important for understanding nonverbal messages. For example, lower pitched voices are often seen as more credible and powerful. Listen to radio announcers and see how both men and women have lower pitched voices than most of us. Interestingly, male voices in the United States are among the lowest pitched in the world, and the pitch differences between men and women cannot be explained by physiology alone. In addition, voices that don't vary much are seen as more powerful. As a result, people with low pitched, unchanging voices are seen as very powerful.

We must also consider two other aspects of paralanguage: *voice qualities* and *vocalizations*. Voice quality is the characteristic way a person's voice sounds. Some people have very "flat" sounding voices. These people do not have much vocal or pitch variety and draw out the sound of the letter "a." Flat sounding voices are perceived as more masculine.

Vocalizations are specific sounds we make that are not words. Examples include "uh huh," "um," and "ugh." These sounds have meaning even though they are not words. For example, we say "uh huh" when we agree and use "ugh" when exerting a lot of effort.

Silence is a particularly important paralinguistic cue. Think of the times you have been silent with people. You were probably feeling one of three emotions: comfort/security, anxiety, or boredom. Silence is a very significant message, and its meaning varies with the situation and the relationship.

Paralanguage plays an important role in detecting deception. People control facial cues better than their voice and, therefore, lie more effectively with their faces. As a result, you will be a more accurate lie detector if you pay more attention to the voice than the face. In fact, many people are better lie detectors over the phone than they are face-to-face. Lie detection is discussed in greater detail in Appendix A.

The voice also plays a major role in the communication of emotion. People recognize emotion from vocal cues about as well as from facial cues. In general, negative emotions are more accurately recognized. However, there is a great deal of difference among individuals. Some people express their emotions more clearly than others.

The voice also provides messages about personality and attitudes. There are regional and international differences in accent that are important for our relationships. There are also gender differences. The voice provides a powerful tool for expression that goes far beyond the words that it forms. Skilled communicators use this tool to full advantage.

31   In this chapter Michael Argyle provides an overview of paralanguage. Argyle describes the characteristics of the voice and its functions in communication. In addition, regional and gender differences are discussed.

Nonverbal Vocalizations

Michael Argyle

Vocalizations consist of sounds, of different frequencies and intensities, put together in different sequences. Some of these are encoded and decoded as meaningful speech, while others express emotions or interpersonal attitudes, or convey information about the sender.

The most objective way of describing sounds is in terms of their acoustic properties, which are:

1. Duration, rate of speech.
2. Amplitude (perceived as loudness)
3. F_0, fundamental frequency (perceived as pitch) and pitch range.
4. Spectrum of frequency $\times$ amplitude (perceived as voice quality, e.g., robust, hollow, shrill).
5. Pitch contour, i.e., change of frequency with time (Scherer 1982).

Another way of describing sounds is by verbal labels which can be used by listeners, such as breathy, nasal, throaty, resonant, clipped, harsh, warm, etc.

It is useful to distinguish between the sounds which are part of language and those which are independent of it.

Emotional Cries

These include moans and groans, shrieks and screams, crying and laughing, oohs and ahs, even roaring and grunting, and are of interest since they are the most similar to animal vocalizations. They have nothing to do with language.

Adapted with permission from: Argyle, M. (1988). *Bodily Communication*. Reprinted by permission of the Peters Fraser & Dunlop Group Ltd.

Language

In terms of evolution, language is a later system which has been incorporated in the vocal channel, superimposed on more primitive vocal messages.

Vocalizations Linked to Speech

Prosodic signals are really part of language—e.g., rising pitch to ask a question, pauses and other aspects of timing to show syntax, loudness to give emphasis. Although prosodic signals appear to be part of language, they also convey emotional information.

Synchronizing signals. The synchronizing of utterances is partly achieved by vocal signals, such as a falling pitch at the end of an utterance.

Filled pauses, ers and ahs, are not emotional sounds, but one of a number of kinds of speech disturbance; others are repetitions, stutters, incoherent sounds, omissions, sentence changes, and incompleteness.

Paralinguistic Aspects of Vocalization

These express emotions and attitudes to other people by the way in which words are spoken; the non-verbal message is given simultaneously with the verbal one. This information is conveyed by speech qualities like pitch, loudness, and speed. Other aspects of paralinguistics overlap with prosodic signals. "Pitch contour" can be a prosodic signal indicating end of utterance; it can also be a paralinguistic cue for emotion.

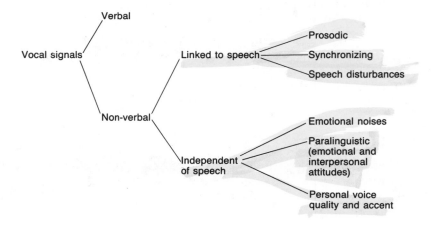

Figure 1   Nonverbal Vocalizations

Information About the Speaker

The way a person speaks can convey information about his or her personality, age, sex, social class, regional origins and, above all, who they are. We can classify these different signals as shown in Figure 1.

The Communication of Emotion

Much research has used posed vocal expressions, where performers have been asked to read something as if they were in some emotional state. Other studies have used role-played scenarios, while some have used mood-induction procedures to produce the required emotions. Here, as elsewhere in bodily communication, posed expressions are not quite the same as the real thing. Posed fearful voices increase raised maximum pitch correctly, for example, but do not raise the minimum pitch (Williams and Stevens 1972).

Several different methods have been employed to remove the effects of the verbal contents of speech — reading neutral passages or counting, using a band-pass filter which cuts out sounds over 400 or 500 Hz, random splicing of tapes in 2-in. segments, and playing tapes backwards.

Davitz and his colleagues (1964) carried out an important series of studies in which senders posed up to fourteen expressions while reading neutral passages, like "I'm going out now, if anyone calls say I'll be back shortly." They found the range of accuracy of senders and receivers, and which emotions were communicated most accurately.

In these and similar studies, with between four and ten emotions, the average accuracy level is 56 per cent versus about 12 per cent by chance, which is about the same as the recognition of facial expressions. Some emotions are more easily recognized: negative ones are decoded more easily than positive ones — anger, followed by sadness, indifference, and unhappiness (Scherer 1981). Joy and hate have been found easier to recognize than shame or love. Some emotions are often confused with each other, because their acoustic properties are similar. Emotions with a high level of activation are confused, e.g., anger, elation, and fear, as are those with a low level, e.g., sadness and indifference.

One problem is that some senders are easier to decode than others; Davitz (1964) found a range of 23-50 per cent for different senders. They are easier to decode if they exaggerate, followed by posed performances, with natural ones the most difficult. Receivers also vary in sensitivity — from 20 to 50 per cent in the Davitz studies.

In order to separate encoding from decoding, acoustic measurements are needed. An example of encoding research is an experiment by Williams and Stevens (1972) using three male actors as senders, and two acoustic measures of voice quality. In a rare study of real and intense fear, it was found that the pitch range of the pilot of a crashing plane shifted from 168-272 Hz to 288-492; both upper and lower limits of pitch were raised (Williams and Stevens 1972).

An example of decoding research is a study by Scherer and Oshinsky (1977) who incorporated a wide range of acoustic variables in sounds from a Moog synthesizer, and asked judges to rate the emotions.

Many such studies have now been done on how emotions are encoded. Scherer (1986) reviewed thirty-nine of them. Some of the main findings are as follows:

Joy, elation: raised pitch, pitch range in an utterance, pitch variability, intensity, speech rate, gentle contours.

Depression: lowered pitch, pitch range, intonation, intensity, speech rate, less energy at high pitches.

Anxiety: raised pitch, faster speech, more speech disturbances (except for ah-errors), silent pauses, breathy voice quality, but there is wide individual variation, e.g., some people speak slower when anxious. Nervous public speakers have more and longer silent pauses. Raised pitch speed, and hesitations in speech indicate deception.

Fear: raised pitch, pitch range, variability, high energy at higher pitches, speech rate, special voice quality as in crying.

Anger: raised pitch in rage, lowered in cold anger, raised intensity, harsh voice quality, higher speech rate, sudden increases of pitch and loudness on single syllables (Scherer 1986).

To what extent are these cues used to encode emotions? The main dimension for both senders and receivers is clearly arousal — communicated by loudness, pitch, and speed, which correlate together. Joy, confidence, anger, and fear all score high. To discriminate between these emotions we have to look at more subtle acoustic parameters. In fact, variables which communicate each emotion are quite similar to those shown above.

The importance of sequential information was shown in an experiment in which tapes were played backwards; this reduced decoding accuracy from 89 per cent to 43 per cent (Knower 1941), showing that contour is important. Synthesizing sounds with all components except spectral structure reduced accuracy from 85 per cent to 47 per cent (Lieberman and Michaels 1962), so the frequency distribution is important too.

Pitch contour produces some finer differences (Frick 1985).

happy: gentle contours
angry: sudden increases
surprise: rising pitch
sarcasm: fall on stressed syllable

contempt: fall at end of phrase
coquetry: upward glide on last syllable
question: rise at end of non-ah utterance

The voice is a "leakier" channel than the face, i.e., it is not so well controlled and is more likely to reveal true feelings. Men attend more than women to this leaky channel.

Interpersonal Attitudes

There is some overlap here with emotion, since no distinction is made in the voice between anger as an emotional state, and as an attitude directed towards particular individuals. The Davitz studies, for example, did not distinguish between the two and included admiration, affection, amusement, anger, boredom, despair, disgust, dislike, fear, and impatience—all of which can be directed towards others. In a series of studies by the author and colleagues (1970) a number of interpersonal styles were created, using tones of voice (while counting numbers), facial expressions, and head orientations. We had no difficulty in creating tones of voice, corresponding to friendliness, hostility, superiority, and inferiority. Mehrabian (1972) found that tone of voice contributed slightly less than facial expression but much more than the contents of speech to impressions of interpersonal attitudes.

Everyone knows what friendly voices are like: they are like happy ones which, as we have seen, are high pitched, with a lot of gentle upward pitch variation, pure tones, and regular rhythm. Infants produce such sounds very early in life—cooing while smiling. Hostile voices are like the angry ones described before—loud, fast, harsh, sharply rising pitch contours, often lowered pitch—babies make these sounds too (Scherer and Oshinsky 1977).

Dominant and submissive are communicated a little differently. Dominant is expressed by a loud voice, low pitch, broad spectrum, often slow. Submissive, like animal appeasement, is higher pitched, sometimes very high, with less resonance, final rising pitch contours, similar to friendly but more tense, anxious, and higher (Frick 1985).

As with the expression of emotion, the voice is often more truthful, more "leaky" than words. Weitz (1972) rated the voices of eighty supposedly "liberal" white students as they rehearsed the instructions they were to give to another subject, known to be black or white. It was found that tone of voice (rated for *friendly* and *admiring*) predicted friendly behaviour towards black subjects, e.g., physical proximity and choice of intimate task. On the other hand verbally expressed attitudes to blacks were *negatively* correlated both with tone of voice and friendly behaviour. Those expressing very positive attitudes in fact showed covert rejection of blacks. Tone of voice is leakier than the face, as was shown in connection with the expression of emotion.

Tone of voice is important in social skills and in maintaining relationships. Noller (1984) found that one nonverbal variable which discriminated between happily and unhappily married couples was that the happy couples made more use of the vocal channel for wife-husband communication.

Vocal style has been found to affect persuasiveness. Mehrabian and Williams (1969) found that speakers who spoke faster, louder, and with more intonation were perceived as more persuasive. Later experiments studied the amount of persuasion achieved, and found that the above style is indeed more successful (e.g., Miller, et. al., 1976). In one experiment tapes were speeded up, slowed down, or altered in pitch. Slower tapes were judged to be less truthful and persuasive, more passive; higher pitched tapes were judged similarly (Apple, Streeter, and Krauss 1979).

The credibility of a speaker depends on other aspects of vocal style. Pearce and Conklin (1971) found that an actor was judged as more credible when using a serious, scholarly voice (low pitch and volume, small variation in both) than when using a more emotional delivery. Addington (1968) found that throaty, nasal, breathy, or tense deliveries were found low in credibility and competence.

Other research on social skills has found that social influence needs a combination of assertiveness and rewardingness (Argyle 1983). It is interesting that it is impossible to achieve this combination with the face, since they require opposed expressions. It is possible to signal this combination with the voice, however.

Accent affects persuasiveness and credibility. In Britain an educated "r.p." (received pronunciation) accent is regarded as more expert and trustworthy, produces more co-operation, and is more likely to be given a job (Giles and Powesland 1975).

Voice and Personality

If judges are asked to rate the personalities associated with different voices, there is quite a high level of agreement between them. However, there is much less agreement between these judgements and objective measures of personality. We should expect some connection between voice and personality, since people do have some consistency in the emotions and attitudes which they express.

Extroversion is one of the best-established dimensions of personality, and it does correlate with voice—higher pitch (for males), greater vocal affect, faster speech, and fewer pauses (for females). Scherer (1978) produced a "lens" model showing how extroversion, for American males, is encoded as pitch and vocal affect, which are perceived as loudness and (lack of) gloom, and interpreted as extroversion (Figure 2).

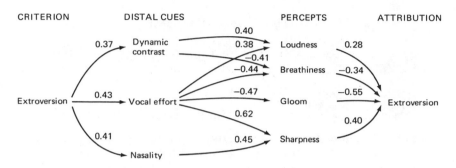

Figure 2 The "lens" model for extroversion.

A number of experiments have varied the speech style of the same speaker to see how judgements of personality are affected. Rate of speech is one of the most influential variables; faster speech is perceived as potency, extroversion, and competence. Pitch has two effects: raised pitch is judged as extroversion, assertiveness, confidence, and competence, but also as tense and nervous, perhaps because raised pitch is a cue for emotional arousal, which is generalized by perceivers to be a personality trait (Scherer 1979a).

Anxious people do not have quite the same speech qualities as those produced by anxious situations. They speak fast, but with silent pauses, especially long pauses (over 1½ seconds); perhaps they need more planning time, and succeed in controlling other kinds of speech disfluency (Siegman 1985).

Another group who have been found to have a particular kind of voice are "type A" personalities—those who are competitive, aggressive, impatient, and with a strong drive to succeed. They may succeed, but they are also susceptible to coronary heart disease. Their voices are loud, fast, with explosive emphasis, a lot of variation in speed, and little pause before speaking (Jacobs and Schucker 1981).

Research on judgements of voices have found three main dimensions—socioeconomic status, pleasing v. displeasing, and active-passive (Mulac 1976). There is extensive evidence on the stereotypes associated with different voices. Addington (1968) asked male and female performers to speak in nine different ways, and these were then rated by judges on forty scales. There was most agreement on the scales for old-young, masculine-feminine, enthusiastic-apathetic, energetic-lazy, and good-looking-ugly, with interjudge reliabilities of 0.80 or more. Some of the main perceived links with personality were as follows:

> breathy: younger, more artistic
> flat: more masculine, sluggish, colder, withdrawn
> nasal: socially undesirable in various ways
> tense: older, unyielding, cantankerous
> throaty: older, realistic, mature, sophisticated, well-adjusted
> orotund: energetic, healthy, artistic, sophisticated, proud,
>   interesting, enthusiastic
> fast: animated, extroverted
> varied in pitch: dynamic, feminine, aesthetically inclined.

It is not fully understood what the origins of these stereotypes are. They may be based partly on true associations with personality, partly on the voices of those for different ages, sexes, and cultural groups, partly on analogy—loud, pleasant, shaky, for example.

However, accuracy of judging personality from voice alone is not very great. Judgements from voice have been found to correlate with overall judgements based on voice, face, and contents of speech less well than judgements based on face or verbal contents (O'Sullivan, et al., 1985).

Voice and Social Class

Voice is one of the basic cues to social class. This is because in Britain and many other countries there are class differences in accent as a result of historical processes such as the Victorian public schools' propagation of a particular accent and the BBC's of another. A number of experiments in England and the USA have shown that class can be inferred from accent alone. Sissons (1971), at Oxford, found that accent and clothes were the two best single cues to class. Many people try to modify their accent towards that of a higher class, but this is difficult to do. Ellis (1967) found that speakers' real class could still be judged, with a correlation of 0.65, when they were imitating upper-class accents. Harms (1961) found that American students could judge class after the first 10-15 seconds of taped conversation.

Accent varies greatly between situations. Labov (1966) found that with increasingly careful speech, for example when reading lists of words, lower-class Americans shifted not only towards upper-middle-class speech, but on some indices they "hyper-corrected," i.e., they went beyond upper-class speech. In England it has been found that there is a hierarchy of accents of different status. There is some evidence about the vocal characteristics of these accents. Middle-class and educated accents are more clearly articulated, use more intonation, and are less blurred. Consonants are sounded more clearly and there is less stumbling over words. This is not the whole story, though, since there are additional features of accents which are quite arbitrary, and serve solely as indicators of social class.

Regional Accents

Having categorized the speaker by social class, listeners then apply whatever stereotyped beliefs they have about different social classes to the owner of a voice. Giles and Powesland (1975) used the "matched guise" method to study this process. Speakers were used who could simulate the accents of different social groups in Britain, and tape-recordings were then assessed by judges. The most prestigeful voices in Britain, with "received pronunciation" (r.p.), were judged to be most ambitious, self-confident, intelligent, determined, and industrious. In a study which used thirteen different accents, a single dimension of prestige was obtained: r.p., American and French, north of England, Cockney, and Birmingham. Furthermore, people with less prestigeful accents and from the regions where these are spoken, to a large extent shared these stereotypes. However, Scots judging Scottish accents and Yorkshiremen judging Yorkshire accents judged the speakers to have greater personal integrity and to be more good-natured and good-humoured than r.p. speakers.

Lambert, et al., (1961), working in Montreal with English- and French-speaking Canadians, found evidence for similar shared ethnic stereotypes. Anisfield and colleagues (1962) in America found that a speaker using a Jewish accent was rated as shorter, less good-looking, and lower in leadership—by Jews as well as by Gentiles. They were also rated as higher in humour, entertainingness, and kindness by Jews but not by Gentiles.

Gender

This can be recognized with almost complete success from voice alone. The main difference between males and females is that women's voices are higher pitched, though there is some overlap in the distributions. Women's voices also have greater variation in pitch, especially upward contours (surprise, appeasement), while men use more falling pitch contours. Men talk louder. In addition they try to control conversations and interrupt more. The overall conversational style of men has been characterized as more assertive and less polite (Lakoff 1973). However, both men and women use more assertive voices when talking to men, despite a common belief that women are more submissive with men than with women (Hall and Braunwald 1981).

Use is made of gender stereotypes in deciding whether a voice is male or female, and the stereotypes do not entirely correspond to the actual differences between the sexes. For example, the use of tag-questions is regarded as female, whereas in fact there is no difference. But it is widely believed that male speech is loud and aggressive, women's speech friendly, gentle, and trivial (Smith 1979).

On the decoding side, women attend less than men to the vocal channel, and more to facial expression (p.286f.). This may be because the vocal channel is leakier, revealing what people want to conceal, or because the vocal channel is more concerned with power and dominance, the face with friendship and attraction.

Vocalizations Related to Speech

The ''prosodic'' signals of pitch, stress, and timing are able to convey information about emotions and other aspects of the speaker. They are also able to modify the meaning of the message. This is shown by the method used by Noller (1984) in which spouses were asked to send verbally ambiguous messages to give different meanings. Similar effects can be produced by words or NV vocalizations, for example emotions can be aroused by emotive words or emotive expressions, tension can be created by leaving crucial words to the end, or by the manner of delivery. Extra messages can be added by using accents or special intonations, using question intonation for statements, and in other ways.

Pitch

We have discussed pitch changes as a cue for emotions and attitudes. Perhaps the most basic meaning of a raised pitch is emphasis, interest, and excitement, and it is often accompanied by upward movements of mouth, eyebrows, hands, and shoulders. In addition there are standard pitch patterns in every language for different kinds of sentences. In English, for example, questions beginning with ''How,'' ''What,'' etc., are spoken with a falling pitch; but questions with an inversion of subject and verb are spoken with a rising tone. Pitch patterns can be varied to ''frame'' or provide further meaning for an utterance. ''Where are you going?'' with a rising pitch on the last word is a friendly enquiry, whereas with a falling pitch it is suspicious and hostile. This expresses more than a paralinguistic attitude to the recipient of the question; it indicates additional thoughts on the part of the speaker, and indicates what sort of answer is needed. Pitch pattern can negate the words spoken, sarcastically, or when the word "yes" is spoken to indicate such unwillingness that it really means "no." Changes of pitch can also be used to accent particular words, though this is usually done by loudness.

Stress

The prosodic system of any language includes rules about the patterns of loudness of words in different kinds of sentences. In English the main nouns and verbs are usually stressed. The same sentence may be given different meanings by stressing different words, as in "they are hunting *dogs*," and "they are *hunting* dogs"; or a sentence may retain the same basic meaning but attention can be directed to quite different parts of the message, as in "*Professor Brown's daughter* is *fond* of *modern music*" — each of the italicized words could be stressed, and this could change the significance of the utterance. In stresing *daughter* there is some implicit reference to a *son* — a case where a NV signal refers or helps refer to an absent object. Speakers can also make soft contrast by speaking some words very quietly.

Duncan and Rosenthal (1968) found that the amount of stress placed on words in the instructions given to experimental subjects had a marked effect on their responses. Subjects were asked to rate the "success" or "failure" of people shown in photographs. There was a correlation of 0.74 between their ratings and the amount of emphasis placed by the experimenter on the words *success* and *failure* when describing the scale to be used.

Pauses

Utterances vary in speed, for example a subordinate clause is spoken faster, and a slower speed is used to give emphasis. Pauses are frequent in speech. Pauses of under 1/5 second are used to give emphasis. Longer ones are used to signal grammatical junctures, for example the ends of sentences and clauses. Other pauses occur in the middle of clauses and may coincide with disfluencies, such as repetitions and changes of sentence. About half of speech is taken up by pauses. Unfilled pauses are longer if a speaker has a more difficult task. Most unfilled pauses come at grammatical breaks, before phonemic clauses, often before fluent or complex strings of words, suggesting that the pauses are providing time for planning. However, not all pauses are like this and some may be due to anxiety (Siegman and Feldstein 1979).

References

Addington, D.W. (1968). The relationship of selected vocal characteristics to personality perception. *Speech Monographs, 35,* 492-503.

Annisfeld, M., N. Bogo, & W. Lambert. (1962). Evaluative reactions to accented English speech. *Journal of Abnormal and Social Psychology, 65,* 223-231.

Apple, W., L.A. Streeter, & R.M. Krauss. (1979). Effects of pitch and speech rate on personal attributes. *Journal of Personality and Social Psychology, 37,* 715-727.

Argyle, M. (1983). *The Psychology of Interpersonal Behavior* (4 ed.). Harmondsworth: Penguin.

Argyle, M., V. Salter, H. Nicholson, M. Williams, & P. Burgess. (1970). The communication of inferior and superior attitudes by verbal and non-verbal signals. *British Journal of Social and Clinical Psychology, 9,* 221-231.

Davitz, J.R. (1964). *The Communication of Emotional Meaning.* NY: McGraw Hill.

Duncan, S.D., & R. Rosenthal. (1968). Vocal emphasis in experimenter's instruction reading as unintended determinant of subjects' responses. *Language and Speech, 11,* 20-26.

Ellis, D.K. (1967). Speech and social status in America. *Social Forces, 45,* 431-451.

Frick, R.W. (1985). Communicating emotion: The role of prosodic features. *Psychological Bulletin, 97,* 412-429.

Giles, H., & P.F. Powesland. (1975). *Speech Style and Social Evaluation.* London: Academic Press.

Hall, J.A., & K.G. Braunwald. (1981). Gender cues in conversations. *Journal of Personality and Social Psychology, 40,* 99-110.

Harms, L.S. (1961). Listener judgments of status cues in speech. *Quarterly Journal of Speech, 47,* 164-168.

Jacobs, D.R., & B. Schuker. (1981). Type A behavior pattern, speech, and coronary heart disease. In J.K. Darby (ed.), *Speech Evaluation in Medicine.* NY: Grune and Stratton.

Knower, F.H. (1941). Analysis of some experimental variations of simulated vocal expressions of the emotions. *Journal of Social Psychology, 14,* 369-372.

Labov, W. (1966). *The Social Stratification of Speech in New York City.* Washington, D.C.: Center for Applied Linguistics.

Lakoff, R. (1973). Language and woman's place. *Language in Society, 2,* 45-80.

Lambert, W.E., R.C. Hodgson, R.C. Gardner, & S. Fillenbaum. (1960). Evaluational reactions to spoken languages. *Journal of Abnormal and Social Psychology, 60,* 44-57.

Lieberman, P., & S.B. Michaels. (1962). Some aspects of fundamental frequency and envelope amplitudes as related to the emotional content of speech. *Journal of the Acoustical Society of America, 34,* 922-927.

Mehrabian, A. (1972). *Nonverbal Communication.* Chicago and New York: Aldine-Atherton.

Mehrabian, A. & M. Williams. (1969). Nonverbal concomitants of perceived and intended persuasiveness. *Journal of Personality and Social Psychology, 13,* 37-58.

Mulac, A. (1976). Assessment and application of the revised speech dialect attitudinal scale. *Communication Monographs, 43,* 238-245.

Noller, P. (1984). *Nonverbal Communication and Marital Interaction.* Oxford: Pergamon.

O'Sullivan, M., P. Ekman, W. Friesen, & K.R. Scherer. (1985). What you say and how you say it: The contribution of speech content and voice quality to judgments of others. *Journal of Personality and Social Psychology, 48,* 54-62.

Pearce, W.B., & F. Conklin. (1971). Nonverbal vocalic communication and perceptions of a speaker. *Speech Monographs, 38,* 235-241.

Scherer, K.R. (1978). Inference rules in personality attribution from voice quality: The loud voice of extraversion. *European Journal of Social Psychology, 8,* 467-487.

Scherer, K.R. (1979). Personality markers in speech. In K.R. Scherer and H. Giles (eds.), *Social Markers in Speech.* Cambridge: Cambridge University Press.

Scherer, K.R. (1981). Speech and emotional states. In J.K. Darby (ed.), *Speech Evaluation in Psychiatry.* NY: Grune & Stratton.

Scherer, K.R. (1986). Vocal affect expression: A review and model for further research. *Psychological Bulletin, 99,* 143-165.

Scherer, K.R., & J.S. Oshinsky. (1977). Cue utilization in emotion attribution from auditory stimuli. *Motivation and Emotion, 1,* 331-346.

Siegman, A.W. (1985). Anxiety and speech disfluencies. In A.W. Siegman & S. Feldstein (eds.), *Multichannel Integrations of Nonverbal Behavior.* NY: Erlbaum.

Siegman, A.W., & S. Feldstein. (1979). *Of Speech and Time.* NY: Erlbaum.

Sissons, M. (1971). The psychology of social class. In M. Keynes, *Money, Wealth and Class.* Open University Press.

Smith, P.M. (1979). Sex markers in speech. In K.R. Scherer and H. Giles (eds.), *Social Markers in Speech.* Cambridge: Cambridge University Press.

Weitz, S. (1972). Attitude, voice and behavior. *Journal of Personality and Social Psychology, 24,* 14-21.

Williams, C.E., & K.N. Stevens. (1972). Emotions and speech: Some acoustical correlates. *Journal of the Acoustical Society of America, 52,* 1238-1250.

Newman describes the role of silence in interpersonal
communication. Two experiments were conducted in order to
examine how people perceive silence. The findings indicate
that when silence occurs appropriately during an activity it
is perceived positively. If there is no appropriate activity and
the silence is merely part of a conversation, people see silence
as anxiety producing.

32

The Sounds of Silence in Communicative Encounters

Helen M. Newman

Much of social conversation consists of an intertwining of periods of active verbal communicative exchange and (often shorter) periods of interactive, mutual silence. The fact that people perceive and respond to interactive silences — periods during which no verbal communication is occurring — is quite apparent. People even report feelings of discomfort associated with silence, as well as customary attempts to "cover up awkward silences" in conversations. There often appears to be a "demand to interact" which characterizes much of dyadic and small group communication — a built-in assumption that when people are engaged in focused conversation it is their responsiblility to keep verbal communication active. Silence might, at times, represent a threat to this responsibility.

Little research has been conducted to explore the more subjective aspects of the interactive silence, as experienced in ordinary social activity. Much of the silence literature concerns itself with silence as a feature of conversation structure or of speech production (Jaffee & Feldstein, 1970; Howell & Vetter, 1969; Goldman-Eisler, 1967; Martin, 1970). Other analyses have centered on forms and functions of silence (see Bruneau, 1973, for a review), as well as the relationships between silence and personality variables (Chapple, 1942; Hayes & Meltzer, 1972). While

Adapted with permission from: Newman, H.M. (1982). The Sounds of Silence in Communicative Encounters. *Communication Quarterly, 30,* 142-149.

the clinical literature addresses the phenomenology of the two-person silence, conclusions are drawn mainly from therapist-patient communication (Weisman, 1955; Slavson, 1966). Seigman & Feldstein (1979) consider more directly how durations of silence might correlate with affective states, interpersonal attraction, and cognitive processes. However, for the most part, their focus centers upon those pauses occurring within one individual's speaking turn. Their focus also centers upon the more objectively defined properties of conversation as identified in temporal speech patterns which characterize various kinds of interaction.

The present investigation was a preliminary attempt to explore some possible effects of silence within dyadic conversations, and to illuminate conditions under which silence may promote feelings of discomfort and reduced interpersonal involvement. It was reasoned that the overall experience of the "two-person silence" would depend mainly upon the following factors: 1) the nature of the implicit demands for verbal communication as imposed by the situation and/or the relationship between the two people; 2) the nature of each individual's interpretation and evaluation of the silences.

The notion that messages of silence might be evaluated differently within different relationship contexts receives support from research on relational rules and definitions (Morton, Alexander, & Altman, 1976; Watzlawick, Beavin & Jackson, 1967). Negative evaluations of silence might be more likely to occur in interactions where the threat of disapproval or negative evaluation from others exists to begin with. Thus, in interactions between acquaintances, silence might disrupt the orderly, structured, and predictable flow of conversation (Kendon, Harris, & Key, 1975; Scheflen, 1968) which enables interactions to proceed with little difficulty. This disruption might, in turn, arouse discomfort, "mindfulness," or self-conscious awareness (Langer, 1978; Duval & Wicklund, 1972). On the other hand, relationships with intimates, as well as particular social activities, might induce a climate of interpersonal acceptance, making it less likely that silence will be interpreted as a failure to meet social norms or personal expectations. In such contexts, silence would not be perceived as incompatible with interpersonal rapport.

It is not only the presence of silence, per se, but also the interpretations, attributions, and evaluations triggered off during period of silence which directly mediate feelings of comfort vs. discomfort within a conversation (Ellis, 1977; Meichenbaum, 1977). These interpretations and evaluations might influence individuals' responses to silences within their conversations (e.g., silence-breaking, discomfort) as well as influence general patterns of interpersonal perception, self-perception, and interpersonal relatedness (Newman, 1981a; Harris, 1980). Thus, the cumulative intrapersonal awareness which accompanies communicative silences would, immediately and retrospectively, constitute important dimensions of interpersonal relating and communication satisfaction (see Newman, 1981).

Study #1: How Observers Perceive and Evaluate Conversations With and Without Silence

Chapple (1971) stated that synchrony in conversational rhythms occurs when small amounts of mutual pause are present, and that synchronous conversations may promote more interpersonal attraction. This line of thought was carried further in study #1. Outside observers were asked to record their perceptions of a tape-recorded telephone conversation. The conversation either did or did not contain silences and either was a real dialogue (reflected meaningful verbal exchange) or a "dual monologue" (reflected poor quality of verbal communication). Because silences are generally not sanctioned in conversations between acquaintances, the following hypotheses were made:

H_1: observers would attribute more negative features to the conversation containing periods of interactive silence than to the conversation without periods of silence.

H_2: observers would perceive a "true dialogue" containing periods of silence to be a less positive interaction than a "dual monologue" without silence.

Method

Conversations: Two scripts were constructed for use in this experiment. One conversation was a dialogue between two people named Jack and Shirley. The other conversation was actually two monologues interwoven so as to *appear* as a real dialogue between two persons named Chris and Rita. Each of the scripts was enacted and tape recorded by confederates. The confederates were instructed to keep a fairly constant tone, pace and rhythm for the two conversations and to enact them with normal pauses. The resulting tapes were then re-recorded with the systematic addition of blank tape spliced into six sections of the conversation. This created the effect of having expanded interactive silences, of about 4- to 7-second duration, included within two otherwise intact conversations.

Procedure: Eighty male and female college students, drawn from four equivalent classes, were employed as subjects for the study. Each of the four subject groups heard one of the following conversations: the dialogue with silence, the dialogue without silence, the dual-monologue with silence, or the dual-monologue without silence. The following directions were given: "You are about to hear a short telephone conversation between two people named Shirley and Jack (Rita and Chris); Listen carefully to the tape—afterwards I will be asking you some questions about the conversation." After listening to the tape-recordings, subjects were presented with a set of nine-point bipolar scales for use in responding to questions about the conversations. These included questions about the participants themselves (e.g., levels of involvement, discomfort, intimacy, enjoyment) and measures of the quality of the conversation (e.g., liveliness, emotionality, awkwardness, speed). Subjects were also asked to indicate what features of the conversation prompted their evaluations.

Results and Discussion

Statistical analyses indicated that conversations containing silences are perceived as less successful, slower, more awkward, less emotional, and generally less positive that conversations without silences. In addition, communicators are seen as less comfortable when silence is present even if the quality of the conversation (as reflected in the content) is minimal.

Study #2 How Observers Perceive and Evaluate Conversations When Silence is Legitimized

The results obtained from study #1 indicated that conversations containing silences are evaluated more negatively, along a number of dimensions, than conversations without silences. In study #2, a related issue was addressed: Would these differences in subjects' rating still obtain if the silences occurring in a conversation between two acquaintances were "legitimized" in some way (i.e., if the "demand to communicate" was removed)? Accordingly, subjects were asked to evaluate conversations with and without silences when the interactants were ostensibly either working on a sculpting assignment or not working on a sculpting assignment. These two conversations are referred to as "conversation-with-activity" and "conversation-without-activity." The following predictions were made:

H_1: For conversations-without-activity, the interaction containing silence would evoke more negative evaluations than the interaction without silence.

H_2: For conversations-with-activity, the interaction containing silence would not be evaluated less favorably than its counterpart interaction without silence.

Study #2 was also designed to address a related question: what inferences would subjects make regarding the thoughts and feelings the communicators were experiencing during their interactive silences? The following was predicted:

H_3: More overall thinking, a greater amount of negative thoughts about self, conversation, and other, and a greater degree of discomfort would be attributed to participants in the conversation-without-activity, as opposed to participants in the conversation-with-activity.

Method

Subjects: Sixty-four male and female college students, drawn from two equivalent classes, were employed as subjects in the study. Each set of subjects listened to part of a tape-recorded conversation. Within each class, however, two different sets of written instructions were provided. Thus, each class made up two of the four treatment groups required for the study.

Conversations: The conversation was a short, friendly interaction between a college-aged man and woman, role-played by confederate actors. A second version of the conversation was constructed (using methods described in study #1) so as to include several segments of interactive silence.

Procedure: Subjects heard one of the two recorded conversations (with vs. without silences) with either the addition or absence of information designed to legitmize the occurence of silence. The resulting four experimental conditions were: conversation-without-activity, silence; conversation-with-activity, silence; conversation-without-activity, no silence; conversation-with-activity, no silence.

Subjects in the ''without-activity'' conditions were led to envision a conversation between two classmates (Shirley and Jack) which was occurring while they sat together at a table waiting for their art class to begin. Subjects in the ''with-activity'' conditions were led to envision a conversation between two classmates (Shirley and Jack) who were sitting at the same table in an art class and each working on clay sculptures. After listening to the tape recordings, subjects evaluated the conversations by answering the same questionnaire employed in study #1. This concluded participation in the study of half of the subjects. Those subjects who heard the conversation-with-activity with silence and the conversation-without-activity with silence were given additional instructions. They were asked to listen again to two short segments taken from the conversation they had just heard. Each of these segments consisted of a 5-6 second interactive silence, preceded and followed by a line or so of dialogue. Subjects were then asked to describe what they thought Jack (or Shirley) was feeling and thinking during each silence.

Results and Discussion

Statistical analyses indicated that:

1. Conversations occurring during an activity are evalauted as less awkward, more successful and less slow than conversations without accompanying activity.

2. Silence leads to less favorable impressions of conversations when interactants are not participating in an activity while conversing. Outside observers believe that the interactants feel badly when silence occurs when there is no other activity going on.

3. Conversations in which there is both participation in an activity and silence promote the most favorable impressions of the four types of conversations in the study. These conversations are seen as friendlier and smoother, and participants are seen as enjoying each other and the conversation to a greater extent.

4. When asked what they thought the interactants were thinking during silences, outside observers list more negative feelings and thoughts about conversations when an activity does *not* accompany the conversation and list more neutral and positive thoughts about conversations accompanied by an activity.

Conclusions

One of the conclusions to be drawn from this research is that silence takes its meaning partly from the larger context in which it is embedded. Comfort vs. discomfort with interactive silence will greatly depend upon whether or not people view the presence of silence as compatible with or in violation of the implicit relational or situational norms which govern that particular interaction. A context designed to legitimize periods of silence can induce a more positive feeling for an entire interaction, in much the same way that a conversation without many periods of silence can induce more positive evaluations.

Another conclusion suggested by this research is that people assess their enjoyment of a conversation on the basis of how successfully and comfortably they have kept themselves and/or the other person actively involved (i.e., by sustaining a synchronous rhythm which leaves little opportunity for self-consciousness). If this is so, it would follow that conversations in which many silences occur might not only reduce a sense of interpersonal involvement, but also promote negative feelings about self, other, and the entire interaction. This is primarily the case if the intrapersonal activity stimulated during silence takes the form of discomforting thoughts concerned with "what the silence implies about oneself and one's relationship to another person."

In this research, observers' thoughts and attributions came very close to matching reported experiences of actual encounters with silence, as gathered thorough subsequent questionnaire interviews. Respondents, in over 86% of these cases, reported feeling uncomfortable when silences occurred in their day-to-day interactions; they reported feeling a "pressure to talk" coupled with "fear of disapproval from others." Apparently a concern of many people, during silences, is that their conversation partner will "think that they are stupid," (or lacking in certain communication skills). Such findings point the way toward more general consideration for future research. For example, what are the implicit rules which influence people in their choice of verbal and nonverbal behaviors and in their styles of responding to various communicative messages? What are the internalized social and cultural expectations or standards against which people measure their own (and others') communicative performances? When do these expectations stimulate the particular forms of "rule-following behavior" and "scripting" which researchers have already identified (Schegloff, 1968; Cushman & Pearce, 1977; Schank & Abelson, 1977)? And what affective consequences follow from failure to meet these expectations?

Investigation of the intrapersonal awarenesses which accompany periods of silence, as well as other interpersonal messages, might help to reveal some of these "rules" which indivduals are adhering to within their interactions. For example, silences are apparently regarded as something to avoid in conversations between acquaintances. Therefore, in particular interactions, silences can be a sign of personal inadequacy, as well as a potential sign of interpersonal incompatibility and awkwardness. It is no wonder, then, that people might adhere to a standard of "protecting themselves and others from the threat of silence." This responsibility is particularly necessary if one's conversation is to be viewed as an involving, comfortable, and/or enjoyable one.

This research was intended to contribute to a growing body of literature illuminating the reciprocal influence of intrapersonal and interpersonal communication systems (Newman, 1981-b). It was also an attempt to inquire into the ways in which individuals evaluate, experience, and generally construct their interactions (Stryker, 1977; House, 1977; Berger & Luckman, 1976). As the findings demonstrate, the content and objective properties of two conversations may be almost identical, and yet the interactions will still be perceived and experienced in distinctly different ways. The mere presence of silence alone, for example, can apparently change the entire texture of an interaction for the people experiencing it. Without considering the unobservable awareness and evaluations which accompany various kinds of conversations, feelings of involvement, intimacy, compatibility, and satisfaction cannot effectively be predicted (Golding, 1978; Swensen, 1973; Newman, 1981a). Varying degrees of discrepancy between interpersonal message responses and intrapersonal awareness might provide the basis for various dimensions of interpersonal distancing, deception (Knapp & Comadena, 1979), and communication apprehension (McCroskey & Richmond, 1980), as well as the experience of communication quality and communication satisfaction.

References

Berger, P.L. and Luckmann. T. *The social construction of reality; A treatise in the sociology of knowledge.* New York: Doubleday, 1966.

Bruneau, T. Communicative silences: forms and functions. *Journal of communication.* 1973, *23*, 17-46.

Chapple, E.D. The measurement of interpersonal behavior. *Transactions of the New York Academy of Science*, 1942, 4, 222-233.

Chapple, E.D. Towards a mathematical model of interaction: some preliminary considerations. In P. Kay (Ed.) *Explorations in mathematical anthropology.* Cambridge: MIT Press. 1971.

Cushman, D.P. and Pearce. W. B. Generality and necessity in three types of theory about human communication with special reference to rules theory. *Human Communication Research*, 1977, 3, 344-353.

Duval, S. and Wicklund, R.A. *A theory of objective self awareness.* New York: Academic Press, 1972.

Ellis, A. Rational-emotive therapy: reasearch data that suggests the clinical and personality hypotheses of RET and other modes of cognitive-behavior therapy. *The Counseling Psychologist*, 1977, 7, 2-42.

Golding, S.L. Towards a more adequate theory of personality: psychological organizing principals. In H. London (Eds.) *Personality: A new look at metatheories.* New York: Halsted. 1978.

Goldman-Eisler, F. Sequential temporal patterns and cognitive processes in speech. *Acta Neurologica Psychiatrica Belgica.* 1967.67. 841-51.

Harris, L. Analysis of a paradoxical logic: a case study. *Family Process.* 1980, *19*, 19-33.

Hayes, D.P. and Meltzer, L. Interpersonal judgements based on talkativeness: fact or artifact? *Sociometry*, 1972, 35, 538-561.

House, J.S. The three faces of social psychology. *Sociometry*, 1977, 40(2), 161-77.

Howell, R.W. and Vetter, H.J. Hesitation in the production of speech, *Journal of General Psychology*, 1969, *81*, 261-276.

Jaffe, J. and Feldstein S. *Rhythms of dialog.* New York: Academic Press, 1970.

Kendon, A., Harris R.M., and Key, M.R. (Eds.) *Organization of behavior in face-to-face interaction.* The Hague: Mouton, 1975.

Knapp, M.L. and Comadena, M.E. Telling it like it isn't: A review of theory and research on deceptive communications. *Human Communication Research*, 1979, 5(3). 270-285.

Langer, E.J. Rethinking the role of thought in social interaction. In J.H. Harvey, W.J. Ickes & R.F. Kidd (Eds.) *New direction in attribution research* (Vol. 2) Hillsdale, New Jersey: Lawrence Erlbaum Associates, 1978.

Martin, J.G. On judging pauses in spontaneous speech. *Journal of Verbal Learning and Verbal Ability*. 1970, 9, 75-78

McCroskey, J.C. and Richmond, V.P. *The quiet ones: Communication aprehension and shyness*. Dubuque, Iowa: Gorsuch-Scarisbrick, 1980.

Meichenbaum, D. *Cognitive behavior modification*. New York, Plenum, 1977.

Morton, T.L., Alexander, J.F., and Altman, I. Communication and relationship definition, In G.R. Miller (Ed.) *Explorations in interpersonal communication*, Beverly Hills, California: Sage Publications, 1976.

Newman, H. Communication within ongoing relationships: An attributional perspective. *Personality & Social Psychology Bulletin*, 1981a, 7(1), 59-70.

Newman, H.M. Interpretation and explanation: Influences on communicative exchanges within intimate relationships. *Communication Quarterly*, 1981b, 29(2), 123-131.

Schank, R. and Abelson, R. *Scripts, plans, goals and understanding: An inquiry into human knowledge structures*. Hillsdale, New Jersey: Erlbaum, 1977.

Scheflen, A. Human communication: behavioral programs and their integration. *Behavioral Science*, 1968, 7, 29-37.

Schegloff, E. Sequencing in conversation openings. *American Anthropologist*, 1968, 7, 1075-95.

Siegman, A. and Feldstein. S. (Eds.) *Of speech and time: Temporal speech patterns in interpersonal contexts*. Hillsdale, New Jersey: Lawrence Erlbaum Associates, 1979.

Slavson, S.R. The phenomenolgy and dynamics of silence in psychotherapy groups. *International journal of group psychotherapy*, 1966, 16, 395-404.

Stryker, S. Developments in two social psychologies: Toward an appreciation of mutal relevance, *Sociometry*, 1977, 40(2), 145-160.

Swensen, C.H. *Introduction to interpersonal relations*. Glenview, Illinois: Scott, Foresman, 1973.

Watzlawick, P., Beavin, J., and Jackson, D. *Pragmatics of human communication: a study of interactional patterns, pathologies, and paradoxes*. New York: W.W. Norton & Co., 1967.

Weisman, A.D. Silence and psychotherapy, *Psychiatry*, 1955. 18. 241-260.

Key Terms and Concepts

Argyle, *Nonverbal Vocalizations*

vocalizations
prosodic signals
synchronizing signals
filled pauses
56% accuracy

expression of emotion and
  personality
pitch
stress
pauses

Newman, *The Sounds of Silence in Communication Encounters*

silence
mindfulness
attributions
comfort versus discomfort

evaluation
meanings
rules

Part Eight

Smell
(Olfactics)

People in the United States spend more on smell than any other group in the world. Sales of perfumes, colognes, and deodorants are at all time highs in this country. This emphasis on smell is almost an "obsession!"

In many ways our sense of smell is not highly developed. Most people are not very accurate in *naming* various common smells. However, people are generally quite good at recognizing the smell of their own body.

Individuals have a unique, individual scent. Some have labeled this an *olfactory signature*. This is probably more obvious among animals who mark their territory with their scent. Have you ever wondered why cats rub their faces against your pants leg? Cats' scent glands are located near their whiskers and they are marking you with their scent when they rub up against you in this manner!

Scent seems to play a role in *attraction* and *sexuality*. The popular press has probably over-emphasized this relationship. However, research does suggest that people who have lost their sense of smell often lose interest in sex. Others have suggested that humans secrete *pheromones*, chemicals used to attract sexual partners.

Regardless of the scientific basis, it is clear that millions of people in the United States believe that perfumes and colognes are useful in attracting sexual partners and the advertising industry has taken advantage of this belief. Interestingly, most perfumes and colognes block natural scents. This makes us less unique.

Scent is also highly related to *taste*. If you can't smell something, you will have a difficult time identifying its taste.

Finally, smells are all around us as part of our *environment*. Cities have different odors from the countryside. People's homes have characteristic odors. The recent conflict between smokers and nonsmokers is at least partly over questions of odor. Allergies are at least somewhat scent-related.

Despite the popularity of perfumes and colognes, and the popular press' ideas about the importance of smell, little research has been conducted in this area. As a result, we do not know as much about the role of smell in communication as we do about some of the other codes.

33 *In this chapter William Cain discusses the identification of odors. In general, people are not very effective at identifying common odors. Cain writes about what can be done to improve this ability. The chapter also describes how companies try to use smell in their marketing.*

Educating Your Nose

William S. Cain

If you want to frustrate your friends, give them 10 common substances to smell. They will most likely "block" on the names of at least a few. They may be able to describe the odor in general terms — sweet, woody, fruity, solventlike. Their descriptions may show that they know something about the smell — whether an odor comes from an edible or inedible source, for example. But the exact identity of the origin of the smell will probably elude them.

When it comes to identifying odors, people are strangely inconsistent and often imprecise. When exposed to a smell whose origins are not obvious, they may feel on the verge of identifying it — "it's on the tip on my tongue." — but they often cannot come up with the name without prompting.

Among those most frustrated by the hit-or-miss nature of odor identification are neurologists, who frequently use tests of olfaction in diagnosing patients with head injuries, chronic allergies, certain viral illnesses and other disturbances. On the other hand, manufacturers of synthetic flavorings take advantage of our general inability to distinguish between odors and their labels, knowing that consumers will often accept even a copy of a natural flavor if the label on the container causes them to "find" the intended odor in the product.

For more than a decade, experimental psychologists believed that the typical person, when tested, could identify no more than about 16 substances by their odors. More recent experiments at the John B. Pierce Foundation Laboratory at Yale challenge this belief. We have now

The Grand Classifiers of Smell

Over the centuries a few scientists have felt a strong compulsion to bring order to the world of smell sensation through elaborate classification schemes. Although most of these pioneers were intimately familiar with a range of odoriferous materials, the schemes they came up with were based largely on their own perception and intuition, rarely on any experimental evidence. While their schemes were innocuous, the early classifiers led future researchers on some wild-goose chases.

The great 18th-century botanical and medical taxonomist Linnaeus, history's most compulsive classifier, decided that the odor world comprised seven categories: (1) aromatic, (2) ambrosial (musky), (4) alliaceous (garlicky), (5) hircine (goaty), (6) repulsive, and (7) nauseous. His successors in the 19th and 20th centuries kept the Linnaean tradition strongly alive by refining his system, devising new ones, and arguing about which was best. The Dutch physiologist Hendrik Zwaardemaker's adoption of the Linnaean class of aromatic odors at the turn of the 20th century provides a good illlustration of how these categories were refined by various theorists, most of whom were headed for obscurity: "This group comprises the aromatic odors of Linnaeus, the series 3 and 4 of Fourcroy, the camphors and the volatile acids of Lorry, the first, fourth, and fifth groups of Froehlich, and finally the spicy, caryophyllaceous, camphorous, santalaceous, citronous, herbaceous, methaceous, anis and almond-like series of Rimmel." Zwaardemaker settled on five subclasses of aromatic odors. He went on to refine other Linnaean classes as well.

There is nothing wrong with erecting odor classification systems. They can be particularly useful for perfumers, chemists, and others who need to describe the odors of newly synthesized chemicals and product ingredients. In fact, when applied to a specific substance like beer, they can be quite important for quality control.

A problem arises, however, when the classifiers believe that a given scheme embodies reality, and that they have in one respect or another uncovered sensory building blocks. For Zwaardemaker, the classification system lay at the heart of olfactory physiology. Such mistaken beliefs have given rise to entire theories of olfaction. These included such passing fiction as distinct sites for classes of "minty" and floral" odors.

The theories generated some research, but virtually no understanding of olfactory functioning. Why? Because the analysis of odor quality into fundamentals reflects the cognitive structure of the analyzer more accurately than it does any basic element of olfaction. Unlike taste research, which has shown that sensations such as sweet and sour function independently to some extent, olfaction researchers have yet to demonstrate that smells in different "categories" are functionally distinct.

For lack of a better insight, some experts have wasted years in pursuit of the Holy Grail of a perfect olfactory classification scheme. And they still failed to recognize that the experience of smell itself depends on the words available to describe it.

—W. S. C.

demonstrated that people can improve their ability to identify odors through practice. More specifically, they can improve it through various cognitive interventions in which words are used to endow odors with perceptual or olfactory identify.

The role of cognition in virtually all aspects of chemosensory experience has long been neglected. The sensation of smell is not simply a physiological response to a stimulus. The labels we give to odors not only help us to remember them, but as perfume manufacturers have discovered, they may even influence how we perceive them.

When cognitive limitations are circumvented, we have found, most people can identify a large number of objects by smell. The crucial importance of cognitive processes for smell may help explain why some elderly people are not as good at identifying odors as the young and why women can generally name more odors than men. (For this reason, we usually use women as subjects in our research.)

Learning the Language of Smell

Although the connection between odor and cognition has largely escaped notice until recently, a few scientists did develop ambitious schemes in the past for classifying smells. But the language of their classification schemes is incompatible with the way ordinary people identify smells. Rather than describe an odor with a series of adjectives — say, fruity, fishy, or musky — most people automatically describe it in terms of the object from which it arises. That seems entirely reasonable, since outside the laboratory odors are identified initially through a congruity of sight and smell. Objects that look different tend to smell different. Objects that look the same tend to smell the same. The same motive that drives people to apply different terms to the objects apple, banana, and lemon, drives them similarly to apply different names to odors. Once attached to odors, the names form the only acceptable categorization: names define odors, and even give them an internal "address" for retrieval from memory storage.

If the words that people attach to odors reflect both how and how well an odor is encoded, then perhaps an externally endowed name can manipulate both the odor experience and its subsequent identifiability. Such manipulations cannot be entirely arbitrary if they are to work. They must make sense in terms of whatever partial knowledge the participants already possess. The simplest example of modifiability seems to lie in the ability of a name to transform a smell from the vague to the clear. When presented with an object to smell, people may fail to identify it exactly but may decide that it smells somewhat fishy, somewhat goaty, and

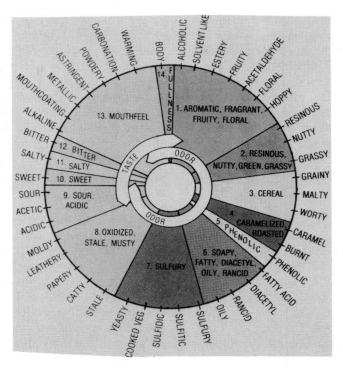

Figure 1
The Beer Flavor Wheel

An example of a sophisticated smell vocabulary used in industry. Developed by the American Society of Brewing Chemists, the wheel enables people involved in various stages of beer production to make qualitative judgements based on standardized terms. Both tastes and odors are included on the wheel. The inner ring depicts general categories, the outer ring more specific qualities in each category.

somewhat oily. If asked to remember this personally generated label— *fishy-goaty-oily*—for subsequent use, most people have difficulty. If, however, people are told the true name, or realize it spontaneously, the sensation takes on a new clarity. Knowledge that the fishy-goaty-oily smell actually comes from leather typically transforms the odor impression into that of leather.

Just how many odor categories can a person keep straight? The answer has ranged from just a few to many, depending upon experimental circumstances that in retrospect have less to do with olfaction than with cognition.

The experiment that led to the rather low estimate of 16 identifiable smells asked subjects to identify many unfamiliar odors. After seeing how many odors the subjects could name initially, the researchers then attempted to improve that ability through repeated tests. The participants were allowed to choose labels that were meaningful to them (like *fishy-goaty-oily*) rather than the chemical names for some of the obscure odors used in the experiment.

After considerable practice, subjects reached their peak performance, called the "channel capacity" for odor quality, or the maximum number of odors they could identify. Though not apparent at the time, the personally chosen labels probably offered them little advantage. Experiments in our lab show that the formation of new associations between words and odors proceeds at a painfully slow pace. Thus the low figure of 16 identifiable odors probably has more to do with the difficulty of learning names for unfamiliar odors than it does with the subjects' actual channel capacity.

In our studies at the Pierce Foundation Laboratory, we decided to use only everyday objects that would have strong associations with sights, smells, and names learned over a period of years. We chose 80 substances that we felt virtually every American adult could identify. The substances included meat (liverwurst), fish (sardines), fruits (orange), spices (ginger), snacks (potato chips), condiments (barbecue sauce), beverages (beer), confections (carmel), household products (shoe polish), medical products (Band-Aids). raw materials (clay), personal products (baby powder), and other common items (leather, pencil shavings, crayons). When asked to smell them one at a time, participants (young women wearing blindfolds) could, on the average, accurately identify 36 of them.

But on the average, they could *not* correctly name the remaining 44 odors, although they seemed to "know" many of them (or, at least, they often indicated as much). They came close to a correct identification of 18 of the 44, but they were further off the mark for the other 26. Failure to identify, then looked in part like failure to retrieve the correct label, even though an association between odor and label already existed in memory. The probability that an odor would precipitate a tip-of-the-tongue experience varied from substance to substance even for substances of equal familiarity. For instance, most participants found the odors from burnt paper, prune juice and vinegar all highly familiar, but they gave more incorrect responses for prune juice.

This initial test of identification was only the beginning of our experiment. Next, we wanted to find out whether people could improve their ability to identify odors with the help of corrective feedback on labels.

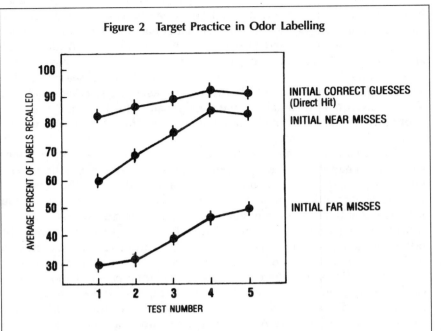

Figure 2   Target Practice in Odor Labelling

INITIAL CORRECT GUESSES
(Direct Hit)

INITIAL NEAR MISSES

INITIAL FAR MISSES

An experiment showing that the more accurate people are in labeling an odor, the easier it is for them to remember the original label in connection with that odor. After a trial run, the preliminary guesses of 12 subjects on each of 80 odors were divided into direct hits (correct names, say lemon*), near misses (*lime*), and far misses (a generic term—*fruit*, or a vague association— "the hall closet"). In five later tests, subjects who scored direct hits were able to use those labels with 90 percent accuracy. The near misses were remembered with 80 percent accuracy. The far misses improved over time, but were still much harder to remember than the more accurate labels.*

After the initial inspection of the 80 substances, we asked participants to apply their own labels, right or wrong, on five subsequent occasions two to three days apart. On each of those occasions, participants received corrective feedback with their original label. If a person first called beer by the name *wine*, then any subsequent response other than *wine* would lead to the feedback "You called that wine." This exercise allowed us to see whether an objectively poor label that came spontaneously from a participant's repertoire served as well as or worse than an objectively good label. The self-generated labels were usually worse. If, for instance, a person had first called a lemon by the name *lemon* (a direct hit), she stood about an 85 percent chance of using *lemon* correctly on the next round of testing. If she had first called lemon by the name *lime* (a near miss), then she stood about a 60 percent chance of calling it *lime* on the next round. If she had first called it *fruit* (a far miss), then she later stood only about a 30 percent chance of calling it *fruit* (see graph).

This outcome made us wonder if the original label reflected how well a participant had initially encoded the odor in memory. Saying the word *fruit* for the highly familiar substance lemon implies vague encoding of the odor during the inspection period, that is , failure to register the odor as itself. Even with corrective feedback, the probability that the same vaguely encoded stimulus would evoke the same response, fruit, was quite low. Nevertheless, corrective feedback did appear to help to some degree. Participants made steady, session-by-session progress with all types of labels, even poor ones.

We discovered that progress in spite of poor associations could be explained by something else. In another experiment, we allowed participants to change a label whenever it seemed desirable. The experiment revealed that in our previous studies, participants had apparently not improved the association between an odor and poor label, but had sometimes realized that other labels were better and from then on had used them as mental reminders. Later interviews revealed the strategy again and again: ''I eventually realized that what I had called 'wood' was actually maple syrup. After that, it was easy to remember to say 'wood' whenever I smelled maple syrup.'' Thus, only better labels led to better performance, including many cases in which a participant switched from a far miss to a near miss. Each improvement of label brought with it a sharp increase in the probability of success on that substance in the next test session two to three days later. A switch from a far miss to a direct hit carried a larger chance of success than a switch to a near miss.

Psychophysical experiments on quality discrimination and on odor thresholds have failed to support the assertion that women have a keener sense of smell than men. But our own studies have demonstrated that women actually make better use of their sense smell.

We asked 102 men and 103 women how well they thought the typical person could identify each of the 80 items in our substance set. The respondents rated identifiability on a 4-point scale ranging from excellent to poor. Men and women agreed in their evaluations to a remarkable degree. We also asked them to guess whether each item could be identified better by men or by women. Again, the two groups agreed. With the exception of about 16 stereotypically ''male'' substances, such as beer, cigar butts, machine oil, and pine shavings, the two groups felt that women would do better. In addition to the ''female'' analogues of the stereotypically ''male'' items (Ivory soap, nail-polish remover, bleach, and baby powder),

The Smell of Success in Marketing

Does a distinctive odor help to establish a product's identifiability among consumers? Experts in marketing have gradually come to believe that it does. In one of our experiments we uncovered some evidence that, in fact, it does — and dramatically so.

We wanted to compare people's impression of how easy it is to identify the common products on our list with how easy it actually is. A group of 103 women were given the names of 80 products and asked to rate them on a 4-point scale according to how easy they thought it would be to identify them. Then we asked a different group (a dozen women) to actually identify each of the items on the list; they were tested five times each and the results were averaged.

The top 10 in expected and actual identifiablity are shown below. Five of the top 10 in the right column have odors unique to a particular brand. Invariably, when identifying these substances, the participants mentioned the brand name. Thus, they did not say just baby powder, but Johnson's baby powder — and the same for Crayola crayons, Ivory soap, Vicks VapoRub, and Bazooka bubble gum. We included the specific products in the test because we suspected they were brand-leaders in their respective categories; but we hardly expected that they would be more easily identified than such generic terms as orange, vinegar, lemon, ammonia, and peanut butter.

Expected Identifiability	Actual Identifiability
1. Ammonia	1. Johnson's baby powder
2. Coffee	2. Chocolate
3. Mothballs	3. Coconut
4. Perfume (brand not specified)	4. Crayola crayons
5. Orange	5. Mothballs
6. Lemon	6. Ivory soap (bar)
7. Bleach	7. Vicks VapoRub
8. Vinegar	8. Bazooka bubble gum
9. Nail-polish remover	9. Coffee
10. Peanut butter	10. Caramel

—W. S. C.

there was agreement that women would more accurately identify most foods. About 85 percent of the respondents felt that women would be better at naming a group of spices, including vanilla extract, oregano, nutmeg, ginger, garlic powder.

Clearly those substances will have a more distinct identity to someone who prepares food than to someone who only eats it. Yet about 80 percent of our respondents also predicted that women would be better than men at identifying common fruits and confections, and about 65 percent predicted women would be better at identifying odors of snack foods, luncheon meats, fish, and condiments.

Their intuitions turned out to be correct. In actual experiment women indeed outperformed men, even on most of the stereotypically male items. Men managed to avoid a shutout by exhibiting marginal superiority on seven items: bourbon, Brut aftershave, Crayola crayons, horseradish, rubbing alcohol, soap, and Vicks VapoRub (see graph). It appears that women can retrieve the names of odors more readily at the outset, can employ their own labels better and can even use true (correct) labels supplied by the experimenter to better advantage.

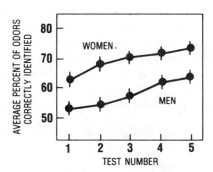

Figure 3
Women's Keener Sense of Smell

Outcome of an experiment that tested 22 men and 24 women on learning 80 odors, over a period of 10 days. After a trial run, subjects were told the names of some of the odors. The ability of both men and women to come up with the correct names improved over time. But on the average, women correctly identified more items on the initial test and maintained their advantage in four later trials.

It seems unlikely that women's superiority in odor identification is primarily an expression of a biological advantage, we think it reflects different experience. Rather than learn about odors incidentally, as men do, women usually learn about them more directly and deliberately. Some people are better at olfactory information processing than others, and a person's ability probably depends on biological factors that have less to do with gender than with intelligence and a variety of other factors, such as age, occupation hobbies, and cultural priorities. Still, a combination of those factors, in America at least, somehow leads to female superiority.

But it seems that with appropriate training men can eventually manage to catch up with women. If the true label contributes to odor encoding and can be more easily recalled subsequently, can performance in the identification experiment be enhanced by merely reminding participants of the label? We thought it might. Replacing a personally generated but perhaps inadequate name with the true name, we reasoned, should impart definition to the stimulus, allowing the best possible encoding and permitting excellent retrieval.

That is exactly what happened in a later experiment. We first reminded participants of the labels for the 80 common substances during an initial phase. After that, our subjects had an average of 78 percent correct on their first test, and by the fifth test their accuracy had climbed to 94 percent. By that time, they could identify odors up to the limit of their discriminative capacity. This outcome implies that with appropriate help in encoding and retrieval, people can identify as many substances as they can discriminate and for which they possess well-learned names — presumably hundreds and perhaps even thousands.

Susan Schiffman, a psychologist at Duke University, and Clair Murphy, a psychologist at Monell Chemical Senses Center in Philadelphia, have discovered that older people are often unable to identify the flavors of foods accurately. Their inability hinges on smell rather than taste and perhaps more on impaired cognitive processing than on sensory disability. Older people commonly suffer from an inability to encode stimuli, remember names or use verbal mediation. And all three abilities play a role in successful odor identification.

We asked young women (average age, 18) and healthy, active older women (average age, 76) to identify odors in a set of 40 substances. Before participating, all candidates passed a test designed to eliminate those with sensory impairment. Half of the older people failed, showing that sensory deficits are quite common. In addition, older people who had passed the screening test still showed marked deficits in odor identification, whether they used their own or experimenter-supplied labels.

The older women have poorer labels than the young women, an outcome that in itself would lead us to anticipate poorer performance in subsequent testing. The disparity between the two age groups on the basis of label quality alone actually exceeded our expectation and seemed due, in large measure, to the older women's inability to benefit from corrective feedback given for their own labels. That led us to wonder whether the older people would profit at all from prompting with the true names. When told the true names during the inspection period, the younger women performed much like the young women in the previous study, eventually getting more than 90 percent right. The older women were less successful, but improved somewhat over time, finally getting about 50 percent correct.

Odor Testing and Disabilities

Our research on the importance of cognition for odor identification has already had important practical benefits. We have, for example, designed a new neurological test for smell that is more accurate than older versions in assessing sensory functioning.

In the past, neurological tests for smell were so poorly designed that physicians were instructed to accept as normal those who could recognize and name about five odors quickly, those who could recognize odors but not name them, and even those who could detect odors and distinguish among them but could neither recognize nor name them. The tests had less to do with sensory ability than with cognitive ability, but only the former is really important for early detection of frontal brain tumors and some hormonal disorders.

Our experiments suggested that, in neurological tests, the use of highly familiar substances and clues to their names would help patients retrieve odor names and eliminate the confusion between cognition and sensory ability. We gave patients a list containing the names of 11 test substances: Johnson's baby powder, Juicy Fruit gum, chocolate, cinnamon, coffee, leather, mothballs, peanut butter, potato chips, Ivory soap, and wintergreen. Those substances had in the past proven to be highly identifiable. The list also contained the names of "distractor" items: burnt paper, garlic, ketchup, orange, black pepper, rubber, sardines, spoiled meat, tobacco, turpentine, and wood shavings. Some of the distractors were included to detect people who have a smell disorder called parosmia, which distorts their sense of smell.

The procedure has worked extremely well in testing patients ranging from under 10 to over 65 years of age. In comparison with other criteria—a somewhat cumbersome clinical judgment derived from a lengthy questionnaire—our odor-identification test has so far not misclassified a single patient. Patients deemed by our criteria to have normal olfaction have scored, on the average, well above 90 percent on our identification task. Patients deemed hyposmic (having a weak sense of smell) or anosmic (with virtually no sense of smell) have performed very poorly.

Our experiments have taught us that the sense of smell can seem either deficient or surprisingly proficient, depending on how we ask the simple question "Do you know what this smell is?" It can appear deficient when we are groping for names of new smells or sometimes even when we seek to retrieve the names of old smells. It can appear remarkably proficient when, with a little prompting if necessary, we manage to enlarge the number of smells people can identify.

That makes us optimistic about the latent talent we all have for odor identification and gives researchers the incentive to look at the talent of special groups, such as young children, people with appetite disorders (anorexia or obesity), and people with loss of sight or hearing. With some idea of the odor-identification talent that normal people possess, we can feel more kinship with the blind deaf-mute Julia Brace who, according to William James, was "employed in the Hartford Asylum to sort the linen of its multitudinous inmates, after it came from the wash, by her wonderfully educated sense of smell."

34 *Kalich discusses the perfume industry in the United States. He explains how advertising is used to build an image for products, focusing on some of the most popular brands.*

What's in a Smell?

Timothy Kalich

Elizabeth Taylor has drawn headlines in recent months for becoming two thirds of her former self, but the attention will soon shift from Taylor's midriff to Taylor's nose, which has been professionally employed in the creation of Elizabeth Taylor's Passion, one of a dozen new women's fragrances being launched in the United States this fall. Late this month Taylor will wind up a nine-city U.S. tour of high-class department stores and specialty shops where Passion—a blend of gardenia, jasmine, rose, ylang-ylang, patchouli, and a number of other scents—can be bought for about $200 an ounce, in a limited-edition signature package. Taylor, who is fifty-five, considered putting her name on lines of furs and lingerie, and even on a line of caftans like those she once wore, but decided to produce perfume instead, because fragrance had always been a particular interest of hers. Indeed, she has for years been wont to mix and match retail fragrances, to piquant effect, in her dressing room. Parfums International, which markets Passion for Chesebrough-Pond's is expected to spend $10 million in the next three months alone to advertise and promote Elizabeth Taylor's perfume. By year's end, the company predicts, some 30 million American women will have been exposed to Passion. A significant fraction of them, the company hopes, will also have succumbed to it.

More fragrance is bought in the United States than in any other country—not surprisingly, perhaps. But also more and more "straight juice," as it is called, is manufactured here, and it seems clear that the locus of the perfume industry has at last crossed the Atlantic. In the period from 1984 to 1986 some seventy new fragrances were launched in the United States, as opposed to only forty in France. While much of the best perfume is still very French, just as much of the best wine is, there is a new pluralism in perfume which parallels that in wine. There is also a

Reprinted with permission: Kalich, Timothy, "What's In a Smell?" as originally published in the October 1987 issue of *The Atlantic Monthly*.

good bit of successful fakery, because scientists now know how to break down scents and then reconstitute them, and because American courts have ruled that no one can patent the way something smells.

The perfume industry does have its troubles these days. On paper it may seem to be in fine shape, because the dollar volume of sales of fragrance, which totaled $2.5 billion in the United States in 1986, has been increasing during the 1980s at about seven percent a year. But this statistic hides the fact that the amount of perfume sold is actually declining; the price of fragrance is simply rising faster. It is a hoary rule of marketing that a rise in price that puts a commodity out of reach of the many may increase its attractiveness to the few. Unfortunately, the few are becoming somewhat fewer. The market for prestige perfumes is pretty much restricted to what industry economists call "gotrocks ladies"—women in households with annual incomes over $40,000 and who are over forty but still young enough to have a sense of smell (Elizabeth Taylor, for instance). But many affluent Baby Boom women, who are about to meet these demographic criteria, do not fit the classic gotrocks-lady mold. They prefer to spend their money on things other than fragrance. William Fitzgerald, an economist and marketing consultant in Maryland who specializes in the fragrance industry, says that a glut of new fragrances in the 1980s—there are some 800 fragrances currently on the market—has led to a sense of boredom among consumers. "The cachet, the romance, of fragrance has been crimped in this decade," he says. Meanwhile the current group of gotrocks ladies is not getting any younger. All told, the number of American women who use fragrance at least occasionally has declined from 60 million in 1980 to 55 million today.

The perfume market has always been a two-tiered one, with a relatively small number of buyers of small bottles of real perfume and eau de parfum that cost large amounts of money, and a larger number of buyers of somewhat larger bottles of cologne and eau de toilette that are considerably more affordable but not always cheap. The two tiers have been moving apart, and in the process each has also become unstable. At the top of the line the rapid introduction of new perfumes, such as Giorgio, Obsession, and Passion, has created enormous turbulence and, from a businessman's perspective, enormous risk. At the bottom of the line copycat versions of top-of-the-line fragrances have undercut, by underpricing, the old mainstays of the discount-house and drugstore trade. All of this has occurred even as Americans, who now bathe with some frequency, have grown increasingly fond of smelling like themselves.

I owe my introduction to the world of perfume—my experience of it had consisted mainly of a trip just before Mother's Day each year to the cosmetics counter at Rexall Drug—to a recent conversation with Deborah Sampson Shinn, who is a guest curator at the Museum of the City of New

York and the person chiefly responsible for gathering the objects for the exhibit "Scents of Time: Reflection of Fragrance and Society," which opens in New York this month and which will travel next year to Washington, Chicago, and Los Angeles. I learned a lot of things from Shinn: for example, that the making of perfume was primarily an Italian industry until Catherine de Médicis, of Florence, moved to France in 1533, and brought a perfumer with her; that Louis XIV· was partial to potent animal scents, which he apparently deemed less noisome than the odors he was trying to conceal; and that men wore as much fragrance as women until the 1890s, when Oscar Wilde, an ardent proponent of lavender water, was put on trial for the crime (as it then was in Britain) of homosexuality. Today, sales of women's fragrances are double those of men's, and 80 percent of all men's after-shaves and colognes are in fact bought by women, as gifts. A quarter of all women's fragrances are bought by men, also as gifts, and most such purchases by men occur during the annual perfume "season," which begins in October and ends, like many another season, on the last shopping day before Christmas. When a man buys a woman perfume, three times out of ten it's the only one that most men can readily think of: Chanel No. 5.

Perfume is made out of natural oils, scented chemicals, various fixatives, alcohol, and sometimes distilled water. The person who creates a scent is known in the trade as *le nez* — "the nose" — but these days the nose is as likely to be a fragrance house (which "ghostwrites" a scent for its client) as it is an individual perfumer on the payroll of Calvin Klein or Charles of the Ritz. The perfumer works with a palette of about 5,400 raw materials — 400 natural oils, extracted from flowers, roots and grasses, and 5,000 aroma-chemicals, which are either reconstitutions of natural scents or scents, such as hawthanol and hexalon, that do not occur in nature. Aroma-chemicals were invented not only because they expand a perfumer's resources but also because natural oils are expensive. A pound of rose absolute, for example, costs $1,300, and must be extracted from no fewer than six million handpicked rosebuds. A pound of synthetic rose costs only about $500. What binds together a perfume's numerous raw materials, of which there may be as many as 1,200, is the fixative. There are a number of synthetic ones, but civet, a secretion of Ethiopia's civet cat, is the natural fixative of choice. Others include castoreum (a secretion of the Canadian beaver), musk (a secretion of the Himalayan musk deer), and ambergris (which is found in the digestive tract of the sperm whale).

The finest perfumes are still made the old-fashioned way, more or less, but however strange and exquisite the process of manufacturing, the process of packaging and marketing has always been just as exquisite and strange (and has accounted for most of the price of the best fragrances). In today's perfume market, which industry analysts describe as mature, newcomers have only two to three years to make a dent with their marketing strategies.

In the past few years Obsession, by Calvin Klein, and Giorgio, by Giorgio of Beverly Hills, have taken very different routes to success in the prestige-perfume market.

Calvin Klein hewed hard to a well-established principle in fragrance marketing and spent a great deal of money on advertising. The company launched Obsession in 1985 with a $17 million promotional campaign featuring sexually provocative photographs of nude men and women. The advertisements generated lots of free publicity and $30 million in sales in Obsession's first year. In a 1986 independent survey 33 percent of all department and specialty stores reported that Obsession was their best seller. Many other fragrance houses, including older, established ones like Nina Ricci, which makes L'Air du Temps, have employed marketing strategies similar to that for Obsession. The hottest new perfume in 1986 was, of course, Poison, which Christian Dior launched with an $11 million advertising and promotional budget; Dior will have spent $13 million more to promote Poison by the end of this year. Glorious, the new entry from Gloria Vanderbilt, was launched last April with a $14 million advertising and promotion campaign.

Giorgio of Beverly Hills, in contrast, adopted a strategy that had never been tried successfully before. Giorgio was launched in 1981, during an economic recession and amid a lull in new fragrance introductions, as a mail-order perfume. Operating on a relatively bare-bones budget, Giorgio of Beverly Hills placed scent-strips of its brash new fragrance in upscale women's magazines like *Vogue* and *Harper's Bazaar*, and included a bind-in card. Orders came swiftly and in volume, kicking off the era of aromatic magazines. The popularity of its fragrance established, Giorgio followed up with a splashy exclusive retail launching at Bloomingdale's in New York. What made Giorgio such a phenomenon in the industry, according to Allan G. Mottus, a marketing consultant in New York, was that it "created consumer demand first and then got the stores to follow."

Whatever the marketing strategy, the stakes tend to be very high and the cash-in period increasingly short. Camille Duhe, the editor of the health and beauty trade journal *Product Marketing*, says "The hot new fragrance seems to be the only thing the consumer wants at the moment. Then there's another hot new product six months later and *that's* all the consumer wants." A lot of the newer fragrances have shown little staying power. Also, it seems that new fragrances don't expand the market for perfume. They just (perhaps temporarily) eat into everyone else's market share.

Some perfume companies have decided that trying to compete dollar for dollar with their rivals could prove suicidal. They have revived "limited distribution" as a way of fostering an aura of exclusivity as well as of holding down costs. Many manufacturers of prestige perfumes have found that launching a new frangrance in a big way nationwide doesn't make sense anymore, because retailers demand considerable concessions in the form of free samples, live models to walk the floor, and newspaper advertising. Knowing that the market for perfumes that cost at least $150 an ounce is restricted to perhaps a few thousand people each in communities like Greenwich, Grosse Pointe, and Palm Springs, they have elected to tout the relative unavailability — and thus the utter desirability — of their products. By the end of this year, for example Christian Dior plans to decrease by one half the number of outlets where its fragrances can be bought. *Women's Wear Daily* made *exclusivity*—"one of the most important words in the fragrance industry"—the theme of its semi-annual fragrance review last spring.

Marketing strategies alone cannot, however, create a loyal base of repeat customers. "There are so many fragrances in the market," says Steve Raphel, the director of fragrance development for J. Manheimer, Inc., a fragrance and natural-oils house in New York City. "To get the consumer to try your perfume, the packaging has to be brillant, the name has to be brilliant, the advertising has to be brilliant. But what will bring the customer back to buy it again is not the packaging, bottle, or the advertising. It's the scent."

If what consumers really want is the scent, Mark Laracy believes, then they should buy fragrances from him. Laracy is the father of "knockoff" perfumes — imposters that smell almost exactly like one or another of the prestige brands but sell for less than half the price. Knockoff perfumes have been enormously successful. As Laracy points out, prestige brands "have created mass awareness and demand for a product that very few women can either find or afford." In 1981, after being fired as a group vice-president in the fragrance division of Charles of the Ritz, Laracy established his own company, Parfums de Coeur, and began to market Ninja, a low-priced version of Opium, a popular Yves Saint Laurent fragrance. Laracy has since introduced six other women's fragrances, with Primo, his knockoff of Giogio, the most successful to date. Parfums de Coeur had retail sales of $100 million last year and an approximately 65 percent share of the rapidly growing knockoff market. Most of its fragrances are sold at drugstores, discount stores, and department stores of the second rank.

Comparative advertising is Laracy's trademark. The copy on the Primo package reads, "If you like Giorgio, you'll *love* Primo," and the advertising emphasizes the difference in price between the Laracy fragrance and the prestige brand. While Giorgio cologne spray sell for about $45 an ounce, a one-ounce bottle of Primo cologne can be had for $7.50. Laracy says that he spends as much per ounce on raw materials as do the manufacturers of the prestige brands he is copying. "The juice in the bottle is an extremely low percentage of their overall cost," he explained to me recently. "We can charge so much less because we have simple packaging. We're not spending twenty million dollars in advertising and promotion. We deal with chain drugstores, who are less costly to do business with. And we take lower profit margins than (the prestige manufacturers) do."

Needless to say, the perfume establishment has not embraced Laracy and his kind, and some perfume manufacturers have gone to court to defend their products. Last year Calvin Klein sued Parfums de Coeur for trademark infringement in marketing Confess, a knockoff of Obsession, In a preliminary ruling a federal judge in Minneapolis has said that Parfums de Coeur's comparative slogans are not illegal but that the company has not gone far enough in letting customers know that its product is not the original Obsession. Laracy has responded with an antitrust suit charging that Calvin Klein persuaded a scent-strip supplier to stop doing business with Parfums de Coeur. Laracy says of Obsession that the fragrance is itself an imitation—"nothing more than (Guerlain's) Shalimar with a twist."

Despite the court battles and the war of words, Laracy and almost everyone else in the industry agree that knockoffs are a competitive threat not so much at the prestige department store, where half of all fragrance business is done and where designer perfumes have their base, as at the drugstore. The consumer who buys a knockoff scent generally does not have the money or the desire to spend $150 for an ounce of perfume anyway. Knockoffs are attractive to the person who would otherwise buy the relatively moderately priced products of, say, Coty and Revlon. Because these are more expensive than the knockoff scents that are beginning to supplant them, drugstores saw their income from sales of fragrance actually decline in 1986.

William Fitzgerald, the economist, forecasts only nominal growth for the fragrance industry over the next decade. He predicts that poor showing will winnow out some of the minor players and discourage new entrants, thereby concentrating market share among a smaller number of companies. He is not very complimentary about a lot of the prestige perfumes that have been created in recent years—"With the exception of Giorgio, Obsession, and Poison, they have been dogs in terms of smell"—and he is not very optimistic that, in the eyes of most consumers, fragrance can retain a glamorous image for very much longer. In this regard the availability of knockoffs is clearly taking a toll. "The public," Fitzgerald says, "is being told more and more that you might as well go into your kitchen and mix up a batch."

That, of course, is just what Elizabeth Taylor did, sort of, and now she wants to sell the result for $200 an ounce. The way things are going, industry analysts say, Passion will have considerable difficulty making a splash. But if it does, and you like it, you'll probably love All the Way, or whatever the Passion knockoff scent is called. It can't be far behind.

Key Terms and Concepts

Cain, *Educating Your Nose*

odor recognition	channel capacity	age
cognition	marketing	abilities
categories of smell	tip-of-the-tongue	disabilities
memory	gender differences	

Kalich, *What's In a Smell?*

perfume industry	cologne	le nez
perfume	eau de toilette	knockoffs

Part Nine

Temporal Communication
(Chronemics)

How long have you set aside to complete this reading assignment? In planning our day, we rely on time to *organize* our activities. Some events don't typically occur in the morning (for example, happy hour or a formal dance). Some activities are useful because they take up very little time (listening to a song on the radio) or can be stopped and started as needed (crossword puzzles or VCR tapes).

Chronemics, the study of time, is in its infancy. It is obvious that time plays a major role in our everyday lives. This role is reflected in watches, calendars, appointment books, and schedules.

We each have our *individual* sense of time and our own personal rhythm and sense of pacing. Some of us are morning people, while others perform better in the evening. Some people are quick-paced, while others move along slowly, but surely.

When two or more people are together their senses of time must be similar. This is called *interactional* time. Will they get together in the morning or afternoon? Will it be a short conversation or a long one, and how will each person know when the conversation is over? Will it be a fast-paced interaction? These are all questions of interactional time. Successful relationships are often built on partners guarding their interaction time together. The relationship may be threatened if one person allows other activities such as work or external relationships to interfere with interaction time.

Institutions and *cultures* have their own ideas of time. Some jobs require the employee to be in the office from 9 to 5, while others have more flexible hours. The 9 to 5 timing of traditional jobs has caused major problems in large cities where rush-hour crowding has reached crisis proportions. Cultures also are said to have different time systems. Latin American countries operate at a much slower pace than the United States.

So time plays a role in many areas of your life. It may be useful to figure out your own personal timing system by keeping track of when you feel the most energetic, how you schedule your activities, and on what days of the week you are most successful.

35

In this chapter Bruneau provides a useful overview of time. He talks about different ways that time has been seen throughout history, and presents eight ways of defining time. This is one of the most difficult chapters in the book because it deals with abstract concepts.

Chronemics
The Study of Time in Human Interaction
Tom Bruneau

It is time, not space, which is the truly "hidden dimension" or variable in the study of human communication. While most communication researchers and theorists would perhaps agree that "time talks" or that temporal behavior is often communicative, there has been a reluctance to discuss in an elaborate fashion how time is related to people communicating.[1] There seem to be a number of major reasons for the neglect of the study of time as a primary communication variable.

The Neglect of Time as a Communication Variable

One of the reasons for a lack of focus on time as a major variable in communication study is related to assumptions about clock-time. Clocks and time-keeping devices have been viewed *as time* rather than being viewed as *the measure of time.* In other words, we have often assumed a *representation* of constant motion as linear progression to be time itself. However, clocks merely convert an assumed constancy of motion into units or intervals which are assumed to be equal—a mechanical ideal which has almost been realized with atomic clocks. Clocks, in short, measure space and not time. Even if we accept what clocks appear to measure as time itself, it is only one view of the meaning of time—and a limiting view at that. Cultures with a heavy reliance on clock-time tend to view time in spatial terms, as in most industrial-technological societies.

Adapted with permission: Bruneau, T. (1977). The Study of Time in Human Interaction. *Communication, 6,* 1-30.

People who view time in a constant and spatial manner, consequently, become blind to a view of time as variable and relative. As the British psychologist, John Cohen, would say, "it is conceivable that our reliance on watches and other artificial aids has led to an atrophy of our 'sense of time'. . . ." [2]

Euclidian space and Newtonian time are one and the same—both being extended from an Aristotelian concept of time as uniform motion through linear space. Euclidian space and Newtonian time have been uncritically accepted and perpetuated by communication researchers and theorists even four decades after the relativity revolution. Newtonian time is reflected in the construction and use of present-day communication research tools, in present-day conceptualizations of communication process, and in present-day communication research designs and communication models. While some researchers and theorists studying human communication infrequently point to temporal relativity as important and not to be ignored—they go on to ignore this communication variable in their own work. Most basic behavioristic concepts, strategies, and models, for instance, are hopelessly Newtonian extensions. The use of statistics and the use of numbers in the structuring of data are further examples—both unitize and treat data in linear space-time. Even those communication researchers dealing with multivariant statistical procedures talk of "change over time"—not understanding that one credible definition of the nature of time is that change is time or time dynamically varies with degrees and rhythms of perceived change. "Change over time," in this view, then, would appear to be an absurd statement. John Cohen expressed the problem of the lack of focus on time well: "A scientific world picture which claims to be all embracing cannot turn a blind eye to the experience of time which gives form and structure to our lives." [3]

Token and apologetic mention of the "dynamics" of human communication seems to be the extent of present concern for temporal relativity in the study of human communication. However, such token focus breeds neglect of time as a major communication variable of the first importance. A truly dynamic view of communication will require a reconceptualization of time as variable. A dynamic view will have to concern people as the significant and authentic clocks of the world. We are time and time is us. As the American educator, John Dewey, once said, "Temporal seriality is the very essence . . . of the human individual." [4]

Another reason for the neglect of time as a communication variable is language habituation. Most languages contain large numbers of conceptions and usages which perpetuate particular views of human temporality. I share with others the belief that languages help to define physical, social, and cultural realities. More importantly and seldom recognized is the notion that the conceptions of space-time within particular languages appear to be interdependently associated with particular views of reality held in social and cultural orders — as well as *most influential in the construction and maintenance of these particular realities.* This seems obvious if we adopt a view that any reality is constructed, makes itself manifest, and is maintained because of the manner in which time and space are conjugated. For example, in the English language, according to word frequency study, the words "is" and "it" are among the most frequently used words.[5] The frequent usage of "is" and "it" are indicative of a cultural stress on states of existence (to be), being as opposed to becoming, and a tendency toward or a need for *stasis.* All of these states are spatial views of reality — as they perpetuate the belief that reality can be or is constant, that process can be clearly objectified, and that stopping and stillness are real states of living organisms.

Notions of time and space are intricately bound to the languages of cultural groups. One of the reasons why new views concerning human temporality are not accepted, then, is because to accept new views of time would require an entire change of the language of a culture as well as a change of the particular realities of a cultural group. Radical change can follow new beliefs about space-time — such radical change is resisted.

Another major reason for the lack of focus on temporality as a communication variable is the difficulty, abstractness, and elusiveness of the meaning of time. Many have attested to the study of time as a complex and intellectual challenge. For example, Alfred North Whitehead, the American philosopher and mathematician, once said: "It is impossible to meditate on time and the creative passage of nature without an overwhelming emotion at the limitation of human intelligence."[6] J.T. Fraser, Founder and Secretary of the International Society for the Study of Time, has remarked that, ". . . the search for the nature and meaning of time is a challenge second to none."[7] Further, the philosopher of time, Alexander, has asserted that, "To realize the importance of time as such is the gate of wisdom."[8] Such statements appear to be hyperbolisms — until one actually begins to study time with a deep, personal commitment and until one departs from any particular habitual view of time-experiencing.

Compounding any resistance to the study of time resulting from its complexity is the multidisciplinary nature of time study. The student of time must approach time from a wide variety of disciplines — in an age when keeping pace with a particular area of inquiry or a specialty is demanding enough. Also, the time literature is not only wide in scope, it is enormous in volume.

The elusive and abstract nature of time is another barrier to the study of time in human communication. Even at the definitional level, time can be viewed from many biases. At the semantic level of inquiry, the concept of time has many denotations and many more connotations. For example, *The Oxford English Dictionary* lists about sixty major denotations for the word "time."

Chronemics: A Definitional Focus

The word, *chronemics*, has yet to be adequately defined.[9] The area of chronemics has yet to be born as an area of inquiry as important as "proxemics" (the study of the meaning of human spatiality) and "kinesics" (the study of the meaning of human motion). Presently, however, there appear to be signs of an increased mention of time in the communication literature in the area of nonverbal inquiry. While chronemics has not yet been born, there are signs of pregnancy, of early formulations based in traditional assumptions about time and space.

Briefly and generally defined, *chronemics* is the study of human temporality as it relates to human communication. Human communication in the context of this definition should be taken to imply all human behavior, in all contexts and situations, in all social and cultural orders, and involving the nature and use of all known and unknown channels of communication. I believe it is necessary to include "unknown" channels of communication here, because some views of time seem to hint at the possibility of new channels of communication. Also, time as a relative variable, itself, can be considered as a channel of communication channels. It should be understood, too, that human communication implies all forms of intra-personal and brain-mind communication *as* a form of behavior. Certain views of psychological or mental time, for instance, seem to hold powerful implications for the manner in which "physical" or "external" realities obtain and are transformed.

Let us also define *chronemics* as the study of human temporality as it is *interdependent with and influences* human behavior, particularly behavior in the context of human relations. Further, chronemics should be understood to involve the study of human communication as it relates to interdependent and integrated levels of time-experiencing. These interdependent levels of time-experiencing should be understood to be *necessarily* involved to some degree in any sophisticated study of the chronemics of human behavior—any potential study involving the chronemics of human behavior would have to at least recognize these various levels of time-experiencing. The interdependent levels of time-experiencing subsumed under a *chronemics* of human behavior are briefly outlined below.

Biological Time

Briefly, biological time in the human animal concerns biochemical codings as they relate to internal clocks, biological rhythms, and the influence and regulation of internal clocks and rhythms on the induction of periodicity and the nature of the periodic behavior of human beings. Biological time should be also understood to involve the variable rates of human metabolism, the functioning and effects of endocrinic and exocrinic systems, as well as the neurochemical activities of the cortical and subcortical systems and their effects. Biological time should be also understood to include the effects of the ingestion of a wide variety of chemical agents. A wide variety of psychogenic stimulants and depressants are in current and widespread use throughout the world, and many of these drugs affect human temporality on several levels of time-experiencing. Further, biological time should be viewed as affecting human behavior throughout the entire life-span. The processes of growth and aging seem to be highly involved in changes in biological time and timing.

Physiological Time

In brief, physiological time is an extension of biological time-experiencing. Physiological time involves the physics of human behavior, especially in terms of human sensory experience at the level of reflexive, impulsive, instinctive, or automatic response. At the level of information processing set, physiological time involves states of sensory orientation, vigilance, and levels of arousal, awareness, and attentiveness. It should be understood that physiological time also involves not only the state of physiological mechanisms, but the state of such mechanisms in interaction with the nature of a wide variety of external or environmental stimuli with particular characteristics. These environmental stimuli, of course, would include one's orientation and awareness toward one's own sensory activities as well as those of other human beings.

Perceptual Time

Perceptual time is an extension of physiological time-experiencing. Perceptual time involves the manner in which information is accommodated, assimilated, organized, and processed. This includes the perceptual processing of languages regardless of medium. Perceptual time is especially involved in the manner in which seriality, succession, and duration are imposed on continuous data or stimuli. Perceptual time, in other words, involves the imposition of discrete, but variable, unitization on the flow of continuous stimuli. At this level, chunking of human experience occurs and basic, space-time configurations are created and previously acquired space-time configurations are processed. At another level of analysis, perceptual time has been viewed as the manner in which people estimate or judge durations of intervals. Large numbers of "time estimation" studies exist in the literature of time. It should be understood that our variable sense of time passing is not only related to biological time and physiological time, but this time sense is highly related to the manner in which particular individuals impose discontinuity on continuous stimuli as well as how individuals regulate the processing of space-time configurations. The manner in which humans process information at the level of perceptual time is highly related to the sense of time passing slowly or quickly in relation to the events of most human activities. In short, novel or unusual space-time configurations which have acquired habituation produce a sense of time passing slowly or even dragging. This phenomenon corresponds to the feeling of time seeming to pass like magic while moving through space in an exploratory fashion as opposed to time seeming to pass at a constant rate or slowly when moving through space habitually.

Objective Time

Objective time can be defined as time which has been objectified, unitized into consenual units, regularized, and is used as a referent for the pacing of human activity. Clocks are measures of one form of objective time. However, a large number of regular occurrences which act as temporal signals take place throughout the waking day. These temporal signals help people to keep time or help people to regularize their behavior—with or without protest. Some of these temporal signals induce repetitive behaviors or pace repetitive behaviors. Collectively, these temporal signals become regularized and objectified and act very much like clocks. Pacers are temporal signals people use to pace their activities in a regular fashion. These pacers, unlike clocks and watches of high quality, run both fast and slow depending on the associated and interdependent behaviors which are paced or which have come to be paced by those controlling human behavior and clock-time. Objective time in another sense refers to the timing of events and the participation of people in timed events. Objective time can also refer to people's resistance or acceptance toward being timed and serving time. Objective time, in other words, deals also with the interplay of objective and "free time" or "time outs" from regularized and objective behavior.

Conceptual Time

Conceptual time is an extension of objective time and refers to how people systematize notions of time and space in a consensual manner. Conceptual time also refers to habitual syntactical and lexical treatment of temporal experience — that is, the language referring to or associated with temporal experience. In any language, there exist ranges and clusters of semantic terms and syntactical usages related to temporal experience. Many cliches, for example, are temporal referents, e.g.: "better late than never," "at this point in time," "last but not least," "slow but sure," "busy as a bee," "this day and age," "it was a momentous decision," etc. Of particular interest are those clusters of temporal symbols which are associated with the jargon of specific professions, work situations, and particular social groups and social activities and events. Very little attention has been given to the study of conceptual time as it is expressed and is inherent in various social, scientific, or technical languages. While focus on tense systems in languages is considered basic to linguistic study, little attention has been given to how such tense systems influence the cultural or social rigidity of time conceptions specific to various social or cultural groups or how such tense systems relate to the manner in which time-experiencing is objectified. What is more, the tenses of language have been viewed in a categorical manner, rather than in a manner which would include degrees of tenseness or tensed temporal direction.

Psychological Time

Psychological time is defined here as human time-experiencing at the level of higher cortical functioning, e.g., memory, anticipation, modes of thinking, levels of consciousness, etc. At one level of psychological time, of course, conceptual time is dynamically involved as a psycholinguistic variable. However, psychological time also concerns our temporal perspective, (referred to as "time perspective" in the time literature). Our psychological orientations to the past, present, and future are not simply related to thinking styles, these orientations also involve certain modes and levels of consciousness. Psychological time refers to the manner in which we are often unconscious during a wide variety of mental functions: sleep, day-dreaming, mind-wandering, reverie, deep thinking in any time perspective, etc. Some have viewed psychological time as equivalent to "subjective" or "personal" time. It does seem to be the case that one's characteristic levels of consciousness-unconsciousness interact in a unique way with one's other levels of time-experiencing in either congruent or incongruent ways to yield particular personalities.

A psychology of time also concerns pathological temporal rigidity in time perspective or in terms of the lack of flexibility in the personal coordinating of the various levels of time-experiencing (those mentioned above and those yet to be mentioned). It would be a mistake to consider these problems to be the problems of the "psychologically disturbed" or "psychiatrically impaired" alone. These problems seem to exist periodically at different levels of severity in the lives of most people in complex societies. On the other hand, rigidity in temporal perspective is often condoned, required, and rewarded. For instance, thinking in a futuristic manner which results in needed innovations can be met with reward. A present orientation can be enjoyable and relaxing or rewarding during critical observation. An orientation toward memories and nostalgia near the edge of the final abyss might be expected or encouraged by others. Some people, for instance, value a person who appreciates the past or future, but may not value a person lost in personal memories or who is "chronically" reliving his personal past or traveling in his speculative future — especially while the soup boils over, evaporates, or burns on the kitchen range.

A number of schools of psychology concern themselves with different definitions of time as well as different orientations to the nature of psychological functioning. Therefore, a unified definition of psychological time is not possible. For example, a psychoanalytic view of psychological time includes the relative timelessness of unconscious functioning, while a behavioral view often neglects mental relativity altogether.

Social Time

Briefly, social time can be defined as the utilization and *integration of levels of time-experiencing* (those outlined above) by human individuals as they interact with other individuals. Social time should also be understood to involve not only interpersonal communication, but the characteristic manner in which various human groups integrate various levels of time-experiencing among their members in the socializing process. Just as individuals are unique in their integration of various levels of time-experiencing, so too are human groups. Just as an individual person can be viewed as a complex space-time configuration comprising levels of time-experiencing, a group can be considered as a very complex space-time configuration which undergoes complex temporal integrations and reintegrations among group members as well as in terms of the group's total space-time configuration characteristics. In that space-time configurations are different from group to group, it follows that intergroup communication will be involved in temporal adjustments and also concern intergroup temporal congruence or incongruence.

The manner in which individuals share time-experiencing together and how individuals in a group integrate their divergent personal-time configurations may profoundly affect whether groups are created, how groups are maintained, or whether or not groups will dissolve. Social time also concerns the notion of social event and the temporal characteristics of short-term groups during events. Each event is unique as a social time configuration and deserving of study of its temporal uniqueness or in terms of the manner in which levels of time-experiencing between individuals are shared.

Cultural Time

Cultural time is defined as the utilization and integration of levels of time-experiencing (those levels outlined above) of individuals or groups in the context of intracultural situations. In the intracultural situation, cultural time is equivalent to social-time configurations which are characteristic of social groups belonging to a particular culture. However, many social groups within a particular culture meet regularly for the purpose of perpetuating particular cultural time-experiencing. For example, many cultural rites, ceremonies, and ritualistic events have unique temporal characteristics which are unique to particular cultural groups and their very identities. Many of these cultural events are special because they are intended to reaffirm in an active manner special kinds of time-experiencing. Trances during religious ceremonies or festivals are examples.

In intercultural or cross-cultural situations, cultural time refers to the manner in which individuals or groups of different cultures utilize and integrate their particular levels of time-experiencing configurations for the purpose of communicating with each other.

Chronemics and the Interdependence of Levels of Time-Experiencing

The manner in which various levels of time-experiencing are interdependent with other levels of time-experiencing is a complex matter deserving years of further study, volumes of print, and countless hours of discussion. Suffice it to say, in this brief attempt to outline a new area of inquiry in the study of communication, that there are no clear boundaries between the levels of time-experiencing outlined here. Not only are there no clear boundaries between levels, all levels can influence all other levels. In fact, all levels can be and often are involved in any communication event. I believe each level of time-experiencing can influence each other level in a systematic manner. But, to explicate my belief in a systemic manner will require more space and time than is allowed here and now — it will also require years of psychological time on my part.

It should be noted that basic to time-experiencing at all levels is the experience of conflict, of the tensive motion between equilibrium and disequilibrium. One of the basic meanings of time can be found in the word, "tension." A tensive state model of the various levels of time-experiencing might be feasible as an approach to explaining the levels of time-experiencing and their integration in the analysis of chronemic behavior. Such a model and one claiming a high degree of practicality, however, will have to await much more focus on human temporality by communication researchers and theorists. It is not likely that a handful of students of time, each with their particular biases and unique temporalities, can alone outline and develop a chronemics of human behavior. A chronemics of human behavior as a viable area of inquiry in the study of human interaction will require dedicated efforts by many persons who are generalists and who are interdisciplinarians with serious intent and high, multitensive energy.

The development of chronemics as an area of inquiry will also require large numbers of studies which focus on particular levels of time-experiencing and, especially, on how certain levels interact. The study of levels of time-experiencing in a multitude of communication situations and circumstances should be viewed as a very plausible opportunity presently. It is toward this opportunity that I have attempted to briefly outline and sketch-out a new area of the study of human communication.

Summary

Reasons for the lack of focus on human temporal experiencing in a variable and relative manner were briefly outlined. A new area of study, *chronemics*, was defined and then outlined in terms of levels of human time-experiencing. Such levels were said to be highly interdependent and dynamically related to all of human behavior and especially important in the understanding and further investigation of the nature of human communication at many levels of analysis.

References

1 Indicative of the lack of focus is the fact that this article is one of the first articles to focus directly on the relationship between time and communication. I also believe it is the first article to include the word, "chronemics" in its title and the first attempt to outline "chronemics" as a major area of communication study.

2 Cohen, John. "Subjective Time," in *The Voices of Time*, ed. J.T. Fraser (New York: George Braziller, 1966) p. 257.

3 Cohen, John. *Homo Psychologicus* (London: George Allen and Unwin, 1970) p. 106.

4 Dewey, John. "Time and Individuality," in *Time and Its Mysteries*, Series II, ed. D.W. Hering, et al. (New York: New York University Press, 1940) p. 92.

5 I believe the equivalents for "is" and "it" will be found to be among the most frequently used words in most European languages and, perhaps, the most frequently used concepts in a number of Non-European languages.

6 Whitehead, Alfred N. *Concept of Nature* (Cambridge: Cambridge University Press, 1920) p. 73.

7 Fraser, J.T. *The Voices of Time: A Cooperative Survey of Man's View of Time as Expressed by the Sciences and the Humanities* (New York: George Braziller, 1966) p. xxiv.

8 Alexander, S. *Space, Time and Deity*, Vol. 1 (New York: Macmillan, 1927) p. 36.

9 This term was first proposed by Fernando Poyatos. I believe the Poyatos definition of the term, "chronemics," is not adequate for the following reasons: this definition views time as space-something which can be "handled" and as an atomistic concept, as an "element"; this definition assumes time to be a thing to be used rather than a relative experience; the definition does not distinguish between various kinds of time-experiencing; and the definition assumes time to be *a priori* to human interaction or events rather than experience which is *created* and altered by people eventually and interactively. Other than these objections, the Poyatos definition is an excellent first attempt to define a complex area of communication study.

Gonzalez and Zimbardo explain the role of time in people's lives. They surveyed over 11,000 people in the United States and around the world and identified 7 different ways of experiencing time. They call these time perspectives.

36

Time in Perspective
Alexander Gonzalez
and Philip G. Zimbardo

There is no more powerful, pervasive influence on how individuals think and cultures interact than our different perspectives on time — the way we mentally partition time into past, present and future. Every child learns a time perspective appropriate to the values and needs of his society. Where religion stresses ancestor worship, for example, the past is sacred and of primary significance. Nomads and others who live on a subsistence level develop a keen sense of the present and a limited sense of the future.

As industrialization, capitalism and technology flourished in Western society, thinking became dominated by a preoccupation with the future. Savings banks and insurance agencies, important institutions in our society, became viable only after people had developed a sense of an extended future.

Our temporal perspective influences a wide range of psychological processes, from motivation, emotion and spontaneity to risktaking, creativity and problem-solving. Individual behavior is regulated by subjugating the urgencies of the present to the learned demands of past and future. Without an articulate sense of the future, the force of obligations, liabilities, expectations and goal-setting is diminished.

Without a time perspective in which the past blends into the present, how could we establish a sense of personality — a sense of self that is stable through time — or extract causality and consistency from possibly coincidental, random events in our lives? George Orwell recognized the importance of time perspective when in *1984* he created a Ministry of

Truth to destroy it. By deliberately rewriting the past to "say of this or that event, *it never happened,*" governments can reconstruct what was to fit more acceptably into what ought to have been, given what is.

But we do not need a Ministry of Truth to bias our time perspective. Many people today have abandoned the past as irrelevant to achieving future objectives. Some have gone a step further, giving up the present time as an equal waste of time — a concern that interferes with the delay of gratification and task perseverance necessary to "make it" in their jobs. Others have never developed a meaningful sense of the future; they cannot shift focus away from the concrete reality and sensory temptations of the present to consider abstract future goals. Their temporal bias gives precedence to events that can be directly experienced here and now.

To see how these different time perspectives relate to characteristics such as age, sex, income and occupation, we asked *Psychology Today* readers in February last year to complete a two-page questionnaire called "The Times of Your Life," a version of the Stanford Time Perspective Inventory. Respondents provided demographic information and indicated, on a 5-point scale from "very characteristic" to "very uncharacteristic," how well each of 31 statements described them. They also selected from among six time perspectives the one that best matched their own.

The box below summarized the demographic data. Most of the 11,892 people who returned the survey came from the United States — all 50 states. Five percent came from Canada, Mexico, Puerto Rico, the Virgin Islands, four European countries and as far away as Saudi Arabia. Many teachers sent in batches of surveys filled out by their students in junior and senior high schools, colleges and adult-education classes.

The diverse sample included an 8-year-old boy and a 93-year-old great-grandmother, many ministers and prisoners (one on death row), a self-reported millionaire, others living at the poverty level, professional athletes and retired military officers. A surprising 72 percent of the sample consisted of those who were firstborn (46 percent) and secondborn (26 percent). Three out of four indicated a willingness to discuss their answers in a follow-up and provided their phone numbers.

The most statistically "typical" respondent was a 34-year-old white woman, firstborn, a college graduate in a skilled occupation, earning more than $25,000, living in California or New York. Because respondents are self-selected, findings from this *Psychology Today* reader survey cannot be generalized beyond this sample. Nevertheless, the size and variability of the sample are desirable qualities in exploratory stages of research such as ours.

Profile of Respondents

Sex

Men	33%
Women	67%

Age

8-19	12%
20-29	27%
30-39	26%
40-49	19%
50-59	11%
60 and over	5%

Education

High school graduate or less	21%
Some college	27%
College graduate	24%
Some graduate school	3%
Master's degree	18%
Professional degree (doctor, lawyer, engineer)	2%
Ph.D.	5%

Income

Less than $10,000	28%
$10,000 to $15,999	14%
$16,000 to $25,999	23%
$26,000 to $35,999	17%
$36,000 to $45,999	8%
$46,000 to $60,999	5%
$61,000 to $99,999	3%
$100,000 or above	2%

Occupation

Artist, writer, designer, craftsperson	5%*
Homeworker	5%
Manager, administrator, businessperson	17%
Professional with advanced degree	9%
Teacher, counselor, social worker, nurse	17%
Technician, skilled worker	4%
Semiskilled or unskilled worker	2%
White-collar worker	10%
Student	20%
Retired	3%
Unemployed	1%
Others (farmer, military, prisoner)	6%

*Percentages add up to less than 100 because they were rounded off.

Ethnic Background

Caucasian/white	89%
Black	3%
Hispanic	3%
Asian American	1%
Native American, Pacific Islander and other	4%

Self-Rated Perspectives

Asked to select one phrase from among six that best characterized their personal time perspectives, 57 percent of our respondents choose a "balanced orientation of present and future," and another 33 percent feel they are primarily "future oriented." Only 9 percent are "present oriented," and a mere 1 percent report that they focus mainly on the past. Among those who are future oriented, more focus on short-term rather than long-term goals (20 percent versus 13 percent). And twice as many of those with a present orientation describe themselves as "enjoying the moment" rather than "avoiding planning or thinking ahead" (6 percent versus 3 percent).

Perhaps a balanced orientation is the most popular choice because it seems more socially desirable than the other options. In any case, the percentage of respondents who rate themselves as balanced increases steadily with age, from 50 percent of the teenagers to 63 percent of those 40 or older. More women than men feel they have a balance orientation; this is especially true among homemakers and teachers.

Men are more likely than women to report a future focus, a tendency that increases as income goes up. The focus on short-term goals is most apparent among those in professional occupations, and least for the retired, homemakers and semiskilled or unskilled workers. Students are the most preoccupied with long-term future orientation; retired people are the least.

Professionals, managers and teachers are least likely to enjoy living for the moment. Unskilled and semiskilled workers, younger people and the less affluent are most likely to focus on the present.

A past orientation, rare for all groups, is found mostly among the retired, homemakers and blue-collar workers. Because we knew from previous research with our survey that few people in our society have a past orientation, we excluded items that explored this perspective from the questionnaire that ran in *Psychology Today*. Instead, we focused on items that would reflect different aspects of present and future orientations.

Seven Time Perspectives

We began our current research by analyzing the psychological aspects of what it meant to be future or present oriented. For each of these perspectives, we prepared a specific statement that seemed to capture its essence. Thus "delaying gratification," an aspect of a future time sense, was represented by the statement "I am able to resist temptations when I know there is work to be done." Similarly, the "action-without-reflection" feature of a present orientation was represented by "I do things impulsively, making decisions on the spur of the moment."

We reduced an initial pool of about 70 such items to the 31 used in this survey through a statistical technique called factor analysis. This method enables one to identify a set of underlying factors that contribute to a complex ability or trait and to measure the relative importance of each factor. We then factor-analyzed data from the *Psychology Today* survey to assess how the 31 items were perceived by the sample as a whole, and by various subgroups selected by age, sex, income and occupation.

By analyzing the statistical correlations among the items, we found that 25 of them clustered together in different combinations to form seven distinctively different factors: four future-oriented, two present-oriented and one that is a measure of time sensitivity or emotional reaction to the pressure of time. We gave each of the factors a name (see the "Seven Time Zones" table) based on what we felt were the distinctive characteristics of its cluster.

As part of our analysis, we established four age categories — 19 years old and younger; young adults, 20 to 39; middle-aged, 40 to 59; and elders, 60 years and older. When we compared the scores for each of the seven time factors on the basis of age, gender, income level and occupation, we uncovered a number of consistent patterns among them.

Seven Time Zones

(All items are listed in order of their significance within each factor.)

Factor 1: Future, work motivation—perseverance

A. Meeting tomorrow's deadlines and doing other necessary work comes before tonight's partying.

B. I meet my obligations to friends and authorities on time.

C. I complete projects on time by making steady progress.

D. I am able to resist temptations when I know there is work to be done.

E. I keep working at a difficult, uninteresting task if it will help me get ahead.

The items that make up this factor were the ones noted highest as a group by the Psychology Today *sample. The factor embodies a positive work motivation and a sterotypically Protestant work ethic of finishing a task despite difficulties and temptations.*

Factor 2: Present, fatalistic, worry-free, avoid planning

A. If things don't get done on time, I don't worry about it.

B. I think that it's useless to plan too far ahead because things hardly ever come out the way you planned anyway.

C. I try to live one day at a time.

People with this orientation live one day at a time, not to enjoy it fully but to avoid planning for the next day and to minimize anxiety about a future they perceive as being determined by fate rather than by their efforts.

Factor 3: Present, hedonistic

A. I believe that getting together with friends to party is one of life's important pleasures.

B. I do things impulsively, making decisions on the spur of the moment.

C. I take risks to put excitiment in my life.

D. I get drunk at parties.

E. It's fun to gamble.

In contrast with the present-oriented people described by Factor 2, hedonists fill their days with pleasure-seeking, partying, taking risks, drinking and impulsive action of all kinds. Many teenagers fall into this category. Among older hedonists, gambling is often an important element.

Factor 4: Future, goal seeking and planning

A. Thinking about the future is pleasant to me.

B. When I want to achieve something, I set subgoals and consider specific means for reaching those goals.

C. It seems to me that my career path is pretty well laid out.

Compared to future Factor 1, the items here center less on work per se and more on the pleasure that comes from planning and achieving goals.

Factor 5: Time press

A. It upsets me to be late for appointments.

B. I meet my obligations to friends and authorities on time.

C. I get irritated at people who keep me waiting when we've agreed to meet at a given time.

This factor doesn't fall neatly into a present or future orientation (although it does correlate positively with the future factors). It centers on a person's sensitivity to the role time plays in social obligations and how it can be used as a weapon in struggles for status.

Factor 6: Future, pragmatic action for later gain

A. It makes sense to invest a substantial part of my income in insurance premiums.

B. I believe that "A stitch in time saves nine."

C. I believe that "A bird in the hand is worth two in the bush."

D. I believe it is important to save for a rainy day.

These people act now to achieve desirable future consequences. We had thought that the item "A bird in the hand is worth two in the bush" would be characteristic of present orientation. Instead, our respondents saw it as advice to do or have something concrete now rather than gambling on an uncertain outcome. Thus it is a conservative strategy to safeguard future options.

Factor 7: Future, specific, daily planning

A. I believe a person's day should be planned each morning.

B. I make lists of things I must do.

C. When I want to achieve something, I set subgoals and consider specific means for reaching those goals.

D. I believe that "A stitch in time saves nine."

Factor 7 describes individuals obsessed with the nitty-gritty of getting ahead. They adopt a somewhat compulsive attitude toward daily planning, make lists of things to do, set subgoals and pay attention to details.

Age and Gender

Both men and women become more future oriented as they age — with one exception, goal seeking and planning. Women 20 to 39 years old are the least preoccupied with goal seeking. Sensitivity to time pressures is also age-related, with older people people indicating more emotional reactions to lateness and time pressure.

Those 19 and younger are significantly lower than any of the other age groups in their work motivation, daily planning and time sensitivity. We would expect them to be the most present oriented of any group, and they are, if you combine both present Factors 2 and 3, fatalism and hedonism. However, people 60 and older are as fatalistic as those 19 and younger, with older women being the most fatalistic of all. The dubious honor of being most hedonistic goes not to teenagers, who come in second, but to young male adults. Among women, young adults are the most hedonistic.

Income and Gender

How much money one makes relates closely to temporal perspective. Annual income goes up as future orientation increases, and down as present orientation becomes more dominant. Those with incomes of less than $16,000 differ from wealthier people in a variety of ways. They report less motivation to work, goal seeking, pragmatic action and daily planning, and they are much more fatalistic as well as hedonistic. This present-oriented bias is at its strongest among the men with the lowest incomes.

The mixture of factors that best predicts high income is future-oriented work motivation, goal seeking and daily planning, coupled with low scores on fatalism. Pragmatism does not vary among women with different incomes, and very little among men, although men with low incomes focus least on pragmatic action. Women become less hedonistic as income goes up. Among men, those with the lowest incomes are the most hedonistic, followed by those with the highest incomes. Men of every income level are considerably more hedonistic than are women.

Women score significantly higher than men across all income levels on three of the four future factors: work motivation, pragmatic action and daily planning. On goal seeking, the top-income men score higher than the top-income women. The generally stronger future orientation of women on these survey items contrasts with what the respondents said when we asked them directly to choose their personal time perspective from among six options. In answer to that question, as mentioned earlier, more men than women rated themselves as being future oriented.

Occupations

As the ''Time-Bound Occupations'' table shows, different kind of jobs best represent each of the future and present factors. It seems likely that two processes are at work here. Individuals select certain occupations because they already have the time orientation called for. Once in the job, success and satisfaction depend on intensifying the orientation further.

The time orientation that individuals develop early in life depends chiefly on their socioeconomic class and their personal experiences with its values, influences and institutions. A child with parents in unskilled and semi-skilled occupations is usually socialized in a way that promotes a present-oriented fatalism and hedonism. A child of parents who are managers, teachers or other professionals learns future-oriented values and strategies designed to promote achievement.

We have found in other studies that present-oriented people, especially fatalists, tend to see their world as one in which rewards are controlled by others. Men and women who are future oriented, especially those high in work motivation and goal seeking, see themselves as in charge of their own destinies. In an industrial, technologically based society such as ours, a present-oriented time sense dooms most people to life at the bottom of the heap. There is no place for fatalism, impulsivity or spontaneity when the marketplace is run on objectives, deadlines, budgets and quotas.

We believe that many of the explanations that have emphasized motivation or ability in accounting for differences among individuals, groups or cultures can be more accurately understood in terms of differing time perspectives. If so, what we need is remedial time-perspective

Time-Bound Occupations		
	Most*	**Least***
F₁-Future **Work Motivation**	Manager White collar	Student Semiskilled/ unskilled
F₂-Present **Fatalism**	Semiskilled/ unskilled Homemaker	Professional Manager
F₃-Present **Hedonism**	Student Semiskilled/ unskilled	Homeworker Retired
F₄-Future **Goal Seeking**	Professional Teacher	Semiskilled/ unskilled White collar
F₅-**Time Sensitivity**	Retired Manager	Student Farmer/Military/ Prisoner
F₆-Future **Pragmatic Action**	Retired Homemaker	Artist Student
F₇-Future **Daily Planning**	Teacher Professional	Semiskilled/ unskilled Student

training rather than another round of programs based on incentives and education concerned only with the acquisition of knowledge. Chronic problems, such as delinquency and the high incidence of unwanted pregnancies among teenagers, historically have resisted change through these latter approaches, but might be vulnerable to time-perspective modification.

Learning to Shift Gears

As Robert Levine and Ellen Wolff mention elsewhere in this issue [see pages 322-327 in this reader] in ''Social Time,'' the clash of time perspectives also accounts for some of the misunderstandings between us and people from Latin American and Mediterranean countries. From their strong present and past perspectives, they see us as obsessed with working, efficiency, rationality, delaying gratification and planning for what will be. To us, they are inefficient, lazy, imprudent, backward and immature in their obsession with making the most of the moment.

It is probably unrealistic to expect either type of culture to accept, or even fully understand, the other's time perspective. but by acknowledging how our temporal perspectives direct our thinking, feeling and behavior into narrow channels, we can choose a more balanced, situationally appropriate orientation. When it is time to work, a future orientation is needed to determine the best means to the ends you have chosen. But when it is time to play, to consume food, to enjoy social relationships and other pleasures, it makes sense to suspend work motivation, daily planning, pragmatic action and goal seeking. Then is the time to adopt a measure of hedonism. To live a life in but one time zone diminishes the richness of human experience and limits our options.

*This chapter explains the relationship between time and
culture. Levine and Wolff explain how time is treated in places
such as Brazil, California, New York, Japan and other places
around the world, describing the accuracy of clocks and the
pace at which people move and work.*

37

Social Time:
The Heartbeat of Culture

Robert Levine with Ellen Wolff

> If a man does not keep pace with his companions,
> perhaps it is because he hears a different drummer.

This thought by Thoreau strikes a chord in so many people that it has
become part of our language. We use the phrase "the beat of a different
drummer" to explain any pace of life unlike our own. Such colorful
vagueness reveals how informal our rules of time really are. The world
over, children simply "pick up" their society's time concepts as they
mature. No dictionary clearly defines the meaning of "early" or "late"
for them or for strangers who stumble over the maddening incongruities
between the time sense they bring with them and the one they face in
a new land.

I learned this firsthand, a few years ago, and the resulting culture shock
led me halfway around the world to find answers. It seemed clear that
time "talks." But what is it telling us?

My journey started shortly after I accepted an appointment as visiting
professor of psychology at the federal university in Niteroi, Brazil, a
midsized city across the bay from Rio de Janeiro. As I left home for my
first day of class, I asked someone the time. It was 9:05 a.m., which
allowed me time to relax and look around the campus before my 10 o'clock
lecture. After what I judged to be half an hour, I glanced at a clock I was
passing. It said 10:20! In panic, I broke for the classroom, followed by
gentle calls of "Hola, professor" and "Tudo bem, professor?" from

unhurried students, many of whom, I later realized, were my own. I arrived breathless to find an empty room.

Frantically, I asked a passerby the time. "Nine forty-five" was the answer. No, that couldn't be. I asked someone else. "Nine fifty-five." Another said: "Exactly 9:43." The clock in a nearby office read 3:15. I had learned my first lesson about Brazilians: Their timepieces are consistently inaccurate. And nobody minds.

My class was scheduled from 10 until noon. Many students came late, some very late. Several arrived after 10:30. A few showed up closer to 11. Two came after that. All of the latecomers wore the relaxed smiles that I came, later, to enjoy. Each one said hello, and although a few apologized briefly, none seemed terribly concerned about lateness. They assumed that I understood.

The idea of Brazilians arriving late was not a great shock. I had heard about *mānha* the Portuguese equivalent of *mañana*, in Spanish. This term, meaning *tomorrow* or *the morning*, stereotypes the Brazilian who puts off the business of today until tomorrow. The real surprise came at noon that first day, when the end of class arrived.

Back home in California, I never need to look at a clock to know when the class hour is ending. The shuffling of books is accompanied by strained expressions that say plaintively, "I'm starving. . . . I've got to go to the bathroom. . . . I'm going to suffocate if you keep us one more second." (The pain usually becomes unbearable at two minutes to the hour in undergraduate classes and five minutes before the close of graduate classes.)

When noon arrived in my first Brazilian class, only a few students left immediately. Others slowly drifted out during the next 15 minutes, and some continued asking me questions long after that. When several remaining students kicked off their shoes at 12:30, I went into my "starving/bathroom/suffocation" routine.

I could not, in all honesty, attribute their lingering to my superb teaching style. I had just spent two hours lecturing on statistics in halting Portuguese. Apparently, for many of my students, staying late was simply of no more importance than arriving late in the first place. As I observed this casual approach in infinite variations during the year, I learned that the *mānha* stereotype oversimplified the Anglo/Brazilian differences in conceptions of time. Research revealed a more complex picture.

With the assistance of colleagues Laurie West and Harry Reis, I compared the time sense of 91 male and female students in Niteroi with that of 107 similar students at California State University in Fresno. The universities are similar in academic quality and size, and the cities are both secondary metropolitan centers with populations of about 350,000.

We asked students about their perceptions of time in several situations, such as what they would consider late or early for a hypothetical lunch appointment with a friend. The average Brazilian student defined lateness for lunch as 33½ minutes after the scheduled time, compared to only 19 minutes for the Fresno students. But Brazilians also allowed an average of about 54 minutes before they'd consider someone early, while the Fresno students drew the line at 24.

Are Brazilians simply more flexible in their concepts of time and punctuality? And how does this relate to the stereotype of the apathetic, fatalistic and irresponsible Latin temperament? When we asked students to give typical reasons for lateness, the Brazilians were less likely to attribute it to a lack of caring than the North Americans were. Instead, they pointed to unforeseen circumstances that the person couldn't control. Because they seemed less inclined to feel personally responsible for being late, they also expressed less regret for their own lateness and blamed others less when they were late.

We found similar differences in how students from the two countries characterized people who were late for appointments. Unlike their North American counterparts, the Brazilian students believed that a person who is consistently late is probably more successful than one who is consistently on time. They seemed to accept the idea that someone of status is expected to arrive late. Lack of punctuality is a badge of success.

Even within our own country, of course, ideas of time and punctuality vary considerably from place to place. Different regions and even cities have their own distinct rhythms and rules. Seemingly simple words like "now" snapped out by an impatient New Yorker, and "later," said by a relaxed Californian, suggest a world of difference. Despite our familiarity with these homegrown differences in tempo, problems with time present a major stumbling block to Americans abroad. Peace Corps volunteers told researchers James Spradley of Macalester College and Mark Phillips of the University of Washington that their greatest difficulties with other people, after language problems, were the general pace of life and the punctuality of others. Formal "clock time" may be a standard on which the world agrees, but "social time," the heartbeat of society, is something else again.

How a country paces its social life is a mystery to most outsiders, one that we're just begining to unravel. Twenty-six years ago, anthropologist Edward Hall noted in *The Silent Language* that informal patterns of time "are seldom, if ever, made explicit. They exist in the air around us. They are either familiar and comfortable, or unfamiliar and wrong." When we realize we are out of step, we often blame the people around us to make ourselves feel better.

Appreciating cultural differences in time sense becomes increasingly important as modern communications put more and more people in daily contact. If we are to avoid misreading issues that involve time perceptions, we need to understand better our own cultural biases and those of others.

When people of different cultures interact, the potential for misunderstanding exists on many levels. For example, members of Arab and Latin cultures usually stand much closer when they are speaking to people than we usually do in the United States, a fact we frequently misinterpret as aggression or disrespect. Similarly, we assign personality traits to groups with a pace of life that is markedly faster or slower than our own. We build ideas of national character, for example, around the traditional Swiss and German ability to "make the trains run on time." Westerners like ourselves define punctuality using precise measures of time: 5 minutes, 15 minutes, an hour. But according to Hall, in many Mediterranean Arab cultures there are only three sets of time: no time at all, now (which is of varying duration) and forever (too long). Because of this, Americans often find difficulty in getting Arabs to distinguish between waiting a long time and a very long time.

According to historian Will Durant, "No man in a hurry is quite civilized." What do our time judgments say about our attitude toward life? How can a North American, coming from a land of digital precision, relate to a North African who may consider a clock "the devil's mill"?

Each language has a vocabulary of time that does not always survive translation. When we translated our questionnaires into Portuguese for my Brazilian students, we found that English distinctions of time were not readily articulated in their language. Several of our questions concerned how long the respondent would wait for someone to arrive, as compared with when they hoped for arrival or actually expected the person would come. In Portuguese, the verbs "to wait for," "to hope for" and "to expect" are all translated as "esperar." We had to add further words of explanation to make the distinction clear to the Brazilian students.

To avoid these language problems, my Fresno colleague Kathy Bartlett and I decided to clock the pace of life in other countries by using as little language as possible. We looked directly at three basic indicators of time: the accuracy of a country's bank clocks, the speed at which pedestrians walked and the average time it took a postal clerk to sell us a single stamp. In six countries on three continents, we made observations in both the nation's largest urban area and a medium-sized city: Japan (Tokyo and Sendai), Taiwan (Taipei and Tainan), Indonesia (Jarkarta and Solo), Italy (Rome and Florence), England (London and Bristol) and the United States (New York and Rochester).

What we wanted to know was: Can we speak of a unitary concept called "pace of life"? What we've learned suggests that we can. There appears to be a very strong relationship (see chart on the next page) between the accuracy of clock time, walking speed and postal efficiency across the countries we studied.

We checked 15 clocks in each city, selecting them at random in downtown banks and comparing the time they showed with that reported by the local telephone company. In Japan, which leads the way in accuracy, the clocks averaged just over half a minute early or late. Indonesian clocks, the least accurate, were more than three minutes off the mark.

I will be interested to see how the digital-information age will affect our perceptions of time. In the United States today, we are reminded of the exact hour of the day more than ever, through little symphonies of beeps emanating from people's digital watches. As they become the norm, I fear our sense of precision may take an absurd twist. The other day, when I asked for the time, a student looked at his watch and replied, "Three twelve and eighteen seconds."

" 'Will you walk a little faster?' said a whiting to a snail. 'There's a porpoise close behind us, and he's treading on my tail.' "

So goes the rhyme from *Alice in Wonderland*, which also gave us that famous symbol of haste, the White Rabbit. He came to mind often as we measured the walking speeds in our experimental cities. We clocked how long it took pedestrians to walk 100 feet along a main downtown street during business hours on clear days. To eliminate the effects of socializing, we observed only people walking alone, timing at least 100 in each city. We found, once again, that the Japanese led the way, averaging just 20.7 seconds to cover the distance. The English nosed out the Americans for second place—21.6 to 22.5 seconds—and the Indonesians again trailed the pack, sauntering along at 27.2 seconds. As you might guess, speed was greater in the larger city of each nation than in its smaller one.

Our final measurement, the average time it took postal clerks to sell one stamp, turned out to be less straightforward than we expected. In each city, including those in the United States, we presented clerks with a note in the native language requesting a common-priced stamp—a 20-center in the United States, for example. They were also handed paper money, the equivalent of a $5 bill. In Indonesia, this procedure led to more than we bargained for.

At the large central post office in Jakarta, I asked for the line to buy stamps and was directed to a group of private vendors sitting outside. Each of them hustled for my business: "Hey, good stamps, mister!" "Best stamps here!" In the smaller city of Solo, I found a volleyball game in progress when I arrived at the main post office on Friday afternoon. Business hours, I was told, were over. When I finally did get there during business hours, the clerk was more interested in discussing relatives in

The Pace of Life in Six Countries

	Accuracy of Bank Clocks	Walking Speed	Post Office Speed
Japan	1	1	1
United States	2	3	2
England	4	2	3
Italy	5	4	6
Taiwan	3	5	4
Indonesia	6	6	5

Numbers (1 is the top value) indicate the comparative rankings of
each country for each indicator of time sense.

America. Would I like to meet his uncle in Cincinnati? Which did I like better: California or the United States? Five people behind me in line waited patiently. Instead of complaining, they began paying attention to our conversation.

When it came to efficiency of service, however, the Indonesians were not the slowest, although they did place far behind the Japanese postal clerks, who averaged 25 seconds. That distinction went to the Italians, whose infamous postal service took 47 seconds on the average.

"A man who wastes one hour of time has not discovered the meaning of life. . ."

That was Charles Darwin's belief, and many share it, perhaps at the cost of their health. My colleagues and I have recently begun studying the relationship between pace of life and well-being. Other researchers have demonstrated that a chronic sense of urgency is a basic component of the Type A, coronary-prone personality. We expect that future research will demonstrate that pace of life is related to rate of heart disease, hypertension, ulcers, suicide, alcoholism, divorce and other indicators of general psychological and physical well-being.

As you envision tomorrow's international society, do you wonder who will set pace? Americans eye Japan carefully, because the Japanese are obviously "ahead of us" in measurable ways. In both countries, speed is frequently confused with progress. Perhaps looking carefully at the different paces of life around the world will help us distinguish more accurately between the two qualities. Clues are everywhere but sometimes hard to distinguish. You have to listen carefully to hear the beat of even your own drummer.

Key Terms and Concepts

Bruneau, *Chronemics*

measures of time	meaning	objective time
time and space	chronemics	conceptual time
change	biological time	psychological time
stasis	physiological time	social time
culture	perceptual time	cultural time

Gonzalez and Zimbardo, *Time in Perspective*

time perspective	future orientation	socio-economic
industrialization	seven time	differences
balance	perspectives	seven time zones
past orientation	age	occupations
present orientation	gender	culture

Levine and Wolff, *Social Time*

rules	social time	accuracy of clocks
early or late	regional differences	walking speed
mãnha	pace	postal clerks' speed
clocks	vocabulary of time	health
punctuality		

Appendix A

Deception and Deception Detection

Research shows that deception is more common in our lives than most of us would like to believe. In one study, college students reported that only slightly more than one-third of all their statements were completely honest during a typical day. Americans are convinced that their political leaders lie to them consistently, and consumers have learned to be suspicious of sales claims. Given this picture, deception and deception detection are crucial topics.

Deception involves deliberately modifying our behavior to create a false impression. People have argued for years whether certain lies, often called "white lies" are unethical. Regardless of the ethical judgment, it is important to understand how lies are communicated.

Research shows that people are not very effective lie detectors. Most of us are mislead by cues that have nothing to do with successful detection. We all have *stereotypes* of liars: shifty eyes, fast talking, etc. Conversely, we have different stereotypes of truthful people: looking us straight in the eye, forceful delivery, adequate detail, etc. Good liars use these stereotypes against us to create a false impression.

One of the best ways to detect deception is to look for *deviations* or irregularities. These deviations occur in a number of ways. First, if you know the person well you can judge if their presentation differs from their normal style. Such deviations are often signs of deception. For example, if a friend looks at your eyes more frequently than normal, they may be lying. In general, our chances of detection increase the more familiar we are with the person. However, sometimes we can be too close to the person, and then they can lie to us because we trust them and assume they are telling the truth.

Second, you can see if the behavior pattern differs from the way most people typically behave. For example, deception may be occurring if a sales person talks in a higher pitched voice at a faster rate than normal.

Third, you can see if two or more channels of nonverbal communication differ from each other. For example, deception is indicated if facial cues are relaxed but the person's posture is constantly shifting.

Certain nonverbal channels are better for detecting deception than others. In general, the more *aware* we are of a channel and the better able we are to consciously control the channel, the *worse* the channel is for detecting deception. For example, most of us can control our facial expressions while talking. As a result, good detectors learn to place less emphasis on facial cues. On the other hand, our voice and body tend to provide more deception cues. In addition, very quick, small movements tend to be beyond conscious control and these are also good cues for detection.

You can see that deception is a common occurrence and detection is no easy task. Research does show that practice and reading articles such as those contained in this Appendix will help you become a better detector.

38

Goleman explains how to tell when someone is lying to you. The chapter describes the most common clues to lying and then describes the best lie detectors. Finally, Goleman discusses gender differences in lie detection.

Can You Tell When Someone is Lying to You?

Daniel Goleman

"I liked her. . .because of the way she immediately put everyone at their rest," a high-pitched almost whiny male voice says on the tape I'm listening to. His words are pressured, slurred. He pauses for an instant, then continues, "Umm. . .there was little tension between people. . .between everybody in the house. Uh. . .she, um, she has a lot of good. . ."

I don't trust this guy; I don't believe him. He's lying about this woman. I'm sure of it. Something in the way he insists that she put people at their ease, that there was no tension. Why bring it up, then? Then there's the way he pauses before each rush of words. He's tense. I can hear it in his voice. He's *pretending* to like her.

I check the words "pretending to like" on my scoring sheet just as another man's voice—this one speaking in neutral tones announces "Number 20" in a series of statements about people. Then, after a few seconds' pause, the previous voice speaks again, now describing someone else: "In many ways she remains, she remains very much like, you know, very much like a child, and uh. . .in a nice way, though, not um. . .and yet in some way somehow has matured emotionally so that you. . . ."

He's more relaxed this time. His voice is pitched lower, and the pace of his words is slower. I think he's telling the truth this time, I mark "Likes."

"Number 21," the announcer says.

I am taking a tape-recorded test of the ability to detect lies, in which people describe someone they know, but in some instances purposely misrepresent their feelings about that person. In the last five years, a group of researchers under the tutelage of social psychologist Robert Rosenthal at Harvard University has given hundreds of subjects tests of this sort in an effort to determine how people maneuver on the morass of distortions and lies that can be glimpsed beneath the surface of our social lives.

The Rosenthal group's professional interest in lying stems less from concern about moral issues than from a longstanding fascination with nonverbal messages and the otherwise hidden realities that they convey. Unlike philosphers and theologians, the researchers are not particularly interested in making ethical distinctions, in sorting out great from small lies. They are more interested in studying the little lies and insincerities that are often necessary to smooth interactions in our everyday lives.

Rosenthal and his colleagues have looked long and without flinching at what makes people good liars and good lie detectors. More precisely, their research has suggested answers to a number of intriguing questions that nobody has investigated very thoroughly in the past: How do children learn to tell and detect lies? Are there any reliable signs that a person is lying? What kinds of people are best at detecting lies? Are there sex differences in the ability to spot lies? Is skill in lie detection a social advantage or a liability? One further question has been largely ignored by researchers: What are the ethics of studying the process of deception?

Much of the research on these issues has been done by two Rosenthal protégés. Miron Zuckerman, now an associate professor of psychology at the University of Rochester, and Bella DePaulo, currently assistant professor of psychology at the University of Virginia. Both had participated in Rosenthal's earlier studies of empathy, which they investigated chiefly by using the so-called PONS test (Profile of Nonverbal Sensitivity). That test assesses how well a person can interpret nonverbal messages. It consists of a series of videotapes of a young woman expressing feelings ranging from motherly love to hatred. The direct message is muffled, so the viewers have to detect it from nonverbal cues.

The PONS gets at empathy because the young woman tries to portray the emotion as best she can. From this test it was fairly easy for the Rosenthal group to derive methods of studying sensitivity to attempted deception.

The search for clues to lies is ancient. A papyrus dating back to 900 B.C. bears this description of a liar: "He does not answer questions, or gives evasive answers; he speaks nonsense, rubs the great toe along the ground, and shivers; he rubs the roots of the hair with his fingers."

Contemporary research shows that people have not changed much in their perception of liars and lying. Certain kinds of behavior, much like that described almost 3,000 years ago, regularly make human beings suspect that others are lying to them. Among the responses often taken to be signs of dishonesty are smiling, stammering, fidgeting, vagueness, long pauses in speaking, and answers that seem too quick, too short, too long, or too elaborate. According to DePaulo and her colleagues, "Any deviation from a humdrum response, whether in the direction of overplay or an underplay, can serve to signal fraudulence."

Unfortunately, the signal is very likely to be misleading. When Robert Krauss, a social psychologist at Columbia University, and his co-researchers compared the signs that observers used to detect lies with the behavior that actually accompanied lies, they found that most of the presumed clues did not correlate with deception. In a study by Robert Kraut at Cornell, subjects interpreted the same behavior as a sign of truth or falsehood, depending on how suspicious the observer was to begin with. If a subject was primed to expect a lie, he would take a long pause as confirmation that the speaker was lying. An observer who was led to trust the speaker took the identical hesitation as evidence of truth.

It is no wonder, therefore, that when DePaulo, Zuckerman, and Rosenthal reviewed nearly 50 studies of people as lie detectors, they concluded that detecting a lie is not as easy as we might think. As a matter of fact, there are no foolproof signs of lying.

Clues to Lying

But some signs are at least more reliable than others. Research shows that voice pitch is a more dependable indicator than facial expression — thus confirming the wisdom of the artist who depicted justice as wearing a blindfold.

Oddly enough, however, not many people seem to recognize that the ears are better than the eyes at distinguishing truth from falsehood. When Krauss asked subjects to name the signs they relied on to uncover lies, not one person mentioned the human voice. DePaulo's subjects revealed a similar ignorance. She asked 251 college students, "If you wanted to know whether someone was lying to you, do you think you could tell better by telephone or in person, or could you tell about as well either way?" Of the 251, the vast majority — 220 — said that a face-to-face meeting would be best. Only seven made the correct choice, the telephone. The conclusion is that if you're going to tell a lie, you're better off face-to-face. If you suspect one, you'll do better over the telephone. (See "Getting the Phone's Number," *Psychology Today,* April 1982).

In all, the results of more than 20 studies point to the value of words — particularly the tone in which they are spoken — as clues to lie detection. On the basis of these findings, DePaulo speculated that "people might be helped in their lie-detection attempt by a little hint," the hint being,

"Pay particular attention to the tone of voice." To test her speculation, she and her colleagues asked college students to watch a videotape of people describing acquaintances and to figure out which ones were lying about liking or disliking them.

A quarter of the students were told to pay particular attention to what the speakers said, another quarter to how they said it, and another to how the speakers looked. The rest were left to their own devices. Those told to note with special care *how* the words were said did the best at detecting lies.

The result may surprise some readers, since it is reasonable to presume that people can readily control their tone of voice and use it to mislead. The available evidence though, suggests otherwise. For one thing, because of the acoustics of the skull, the voice we hear as we speak does not sound the same to us as to our listeners. This may explain the almost universal reaction of dismay when people first hear their recorded voices. On tape, people hear inflections and tonal qualities that leak their feelings but are unnoticed by them as they speak. As a matter of fact, clinicians have long recognized the leaky nature of tone of voice, and often rely on it for clues to a patient's true feelings.

None of this means that nonverbal cues are useless for unmasking liars; quite the contrary. It is a commonplace that the body yields clues to a person's true feelings. Deception research shows that different kinds of body language provide better clues to deception than others. Constructing a speculative hierachy of "leaky channels," the Rosenthal group put discrepancies between two channels of communication (a smiling face with an angry voice, perhaps) at the top of the list as the leakiest. Next came fleeting body movements or facial expressions, tone of voice, the body in general, and lastly, the face. Initially, the ordering of the leakage hierachy was an educated guess, since no one had ever compared more than two of the channels for leakage at any one time. Later, the researchers demonstrated that their speculations were consistent with their results.

A discrepancy, the Rosenthal group proposed, is the leakiest of channels because it involves two modes of communication that are hard to control simultaneously. A liar might be very careful in how he phrased his lie, might even remember, say, to smile in its support, but might not be skillful enough to control the anger in his voice. That discrepancy could tip off an alert observer. Discrepancies, of course, are typical of irony, sarcasm, and humor—but those are intended. Discrepancies during the telling of a lie are unintentional leaks.

A bit less revealing, or leaky, are micro-lapses that take the form of brief, unintended changes, such as a muted hand movement or a fleeting smile.

It was face expert Paul Ekman (see "The 7,000 Faces of Dr. Ekman, *Psychology today*, February 1981) and his colleague Wallace Friesen who first suggested why the face should be the least leaky nonverbal channel — and thus the best liar. A person's ability to deceive, they proposed, varies with the "sending capacity" of the channel that is used. The greater that channel's sending capacity — that is, the more messages it can send, the more quickly it can send them, and the more visible they are — then the more deceptive the channel can be. The face, Ekman and Friesen argue, has maximal sending capacity. Therefore, it is especially well equipped to tell lies, and provides the least reliable cues for someone trying to detect lies. By contrast, the body is less controllable, slower, and less obvious. Its reduced sending capacity makes lying with the body difficult, but it also makes the body a leaky channel: Gestures and other body movements (for example, fidgeting or other signs of nervousness) often betray deceit.

On the whole, unpremeditated lies probably are more easily detected than planned lies, DePaulo suggests, because of the advantage rehearsal gives. Planning a lie ahead of time makes the liar less likely to have to pause for words and more free to control tone of voice and other potential leaks. Suspicions may make a person more easily misled — particularly if he relies on looking the liar in the eye and focuses on the liar's demeanor. Such overattentiveness to the face (which leaks less) could interfere with noting leaky cues, such as tone of voice.

Good Lie Detectors

Dozens of studies suggest that most people just aren't very good at detecting deception. Another conclusion that emerges from this research is that the ability to recognize a lie does not necessarily carry with it the ability to say what the liar's true feelings may be.

Yet another basic fact is that some people are skilled at identifying certain kinds of deception but are easily fooled by other kinds. The Rosenthal group distinguishes between "sugar-coated" lies, in which positive feelings mask negative ones, and "vinegar-coated" lies, in which feigned negative feelings hide true positive ones. Their research method is by now familiar. They had volunteers tell sugar-coated lies by describing people they disliked as though they like them; vinegar-coated lies were descriptions of people whom the volunteers liked, rendered as though they disliked them. The volunteers watched videotapes of one another and tried to guess whether or not a given description was a lie. Those who proved to be clever at detecting sugar-coated lies were not particularly good at recognizing vinegar-coated ones, and vice versa.

One characteristic often found in good lie detectors has been labeled "social participation," a more or less self-explanatory term referring to people who are outgoing, friendly, and active in many social groups. In general, these people are "interaction specialists" — good communicators who seem to follow the credo that interactions go most smoothly when people are straightforward in what they say and do. Perhaps for that very reason, they are particularly sensitive to lies. Not surprisingly, such people often tend to be poor liars themselves.

Another characteristic of good lie detectors is social anxiety, as measured by a questionnaire devised by David Lykken at the University of Minnesota that requires respondents to choose between pairs of unpleasant alternatives. In each pair, one choice is social, involving other people, and one is not. An example: hearing someone comment on how strangely you are dressed, versus cleaning out a cesspool. The socially anxious more often choose to endure the nonsocial pain. The uneasiness and sensitivity these people experience in social situations seems to alert them to signs that they are being lied to. They are good at sending their own true feelings, but poor at telling lies, possibly because of timidity at the prospect of being caught in a lie.

One much-studied trait that might well seem related to lie detection turns out not to be: Machiavellianism. People high in this trait (as measured on a scale designed by Richard Christie of Columbia University) are not particularly adept at detecting other people's falsehoods. However, their belief that others are manipulatable, and their willingness to take advantage of this vulnerability, help make Machiavellians devious enough to lie with great success and little regret.

Are Women Too Polite?

When the Rosenthal group began to study deception, they were in for a surprise. Earlier research had shown overwhelmingly that women are far superior to men at reading nonverbal messages. When asked to say what feeling a tone of voice or a gesture reflected, women were right much more often than men were. But Rosenthal and his collegues discovered that women's empathy seemed to fail them when they were asked to decode leaks. The more leaky a tone of voice, the more discrepant a message; the more furtive a look, the less well women did in interpreting it. Men showed just the opposite pattern: As comunications became more leaky and deception more blatant, the men's accuracy in detecting lies improved relative to the women's. The sex difference showed up when Rosenthal and DePaulo studied 242 high-school and college students. The method the researchers used was to administer a whole battery of tests designed to assess the leakage hierarchy, the rank-ordering of clues to deception described above. The pattern was clear. Women were far better than men at reading the face. But their advantage decreased steadily as they confronted more leaky channels, including hand gestures and the tone of voice.

"Women," say Rosenthal and DePaulo, "may be more polite than men in their decoding of nonverbal cues." In the researchers' view, noticing leaks is a form of "eavesdropping," and paying attention to a person's slips and leaks is therefore tantamount to rudeness.

To Rosenthal and DePaulo, it seemed possible that women might be penalized more than men for being too perceptive at reading leaks, and so might learn to ignore them. The first step the researchers took to test this idea was to devise a study that would show whether either sex pays a social penalty for detecting deception.

At the high school where the researchers had given the leakage hierarchy test, they asked teachers to rate the students who had taken it on popularity with their own and with the opposite sex, and on their degree of "social understanding." When the ratings were compared with leakage detection, there was a strong (though not statistically significant) trend for social effectiveness to go along with insensitivity to the leakier channels. "There are indications," DePaulo and Rosenthal conclude, "that eavesdropping skill may not be as socially beneficial as skill decoding less 'leaky' channels." That is, social life may run more smoothly for those who politely ignore other people's obvious leaks. Rosenthal and DePaulo assume that this is especially true for women, in keeping with the "standards of politeness and social smoothing-over" that are part of the traditonal woman's role.

Oddly, the high-school students themselves did not seem to find eavesdropping damaging to their social lives. When asked to rate the quality of their relations with both sexes, the students' evaluations did not correlate at all with sensitivity to leaks. Indeed, there was a tendency for those good at detecting leaks to be more pleased with their social life. "For our younger students," Rosenthal and DePaulo observe, "skill at eavesdropping on increasingly leaky channels was associated with increasingly better social relationships, as they perceived these relationships."

But the high-school students may have been deluding themselves. When the same survey was done with college students, the pattern was reversed: Skill at eavesdropping on leaks was associated with increasingly poor social relationships, as the students perceived them. "Perhaps," Rosenthal and DePaulo comment, "those students have learned, as have the younger students' teachers, that it may not be beneficial to social relationships to be an effective eavesdropper on leaked nonverbal cues." With maturity, it would seem, comes discretion.

Rosenthal and DePaulo soon found some support for their idea that society rewards women more than men for this kind of discretion. They had already observed that their female subjects gave more credence to the face, the least leaky channel, than male subjects did. When the researchers compared the women's ratings of their social life with the degree to which they gave primacy to the face, a telling piece of evidence emerged. The more attention women paid to the face, the better they considered their relationships, particularly with men. Rosenthal and DePaulo think it may be that "women are reinforced with better opposite-sex relationships when they attend to the better-controlled channels and learn to avoid eavesdropping on the more poorly controlled, more leaky channels.

While the facts are clear, there are differences in what they seem to say about women's social motives. One reading of women's greater "politeness" could be that it signifies a submissive role vis-à-vis men. This interpretation irks some researchers on nonverbal messages. One of these is Judith Hall, who was once a graduate student of Rosenthal's and collaborator on much of his empathy research, and is now a lecturer in the Harvard Psychology Department.

"The theory," says Hall, "is that the woman confronts the leaky cues and says to herself, maybe unconsciously, 'Oh my God, I'm in deep trouble if I respond to this accurately.' Whereas it may have nothing to do with their response to leakiness per se, or with being accommodating. It's just that this skill has little importance in social intelligence, it's not that crucial in daily life. Social life works by ignoring little social lies. Women seem wiser to this than men. It seems to me that the profile of women as a group of interpreters of social cues is one of 'savvyness' — being good at what's useful and not so good at something that isn't so useful."

In an article in the *Annals of the New York Academy of Sciences*, DePaulo makes a similar point with the question, "Are we better off seeing right through a person's true underlying feelings or might we sometimes do better not to see what another person does not want us to know?" In the case of deception that might do us harm, she notes, the ability to detect lies is obviously an asset. And in professions such as psychiatry or police work, such sensitivity is particularly useful. In everyday life, this is not necessarily so.

"It seems," writes DePaulo, "that what children are learning as they grow older, probably through socialization, is politely to read what other people want them to read, and not what they really felt. The polite mode of decoding is probably an easier way of dealing with interpersonal information than a more probing and skeptical style would be. . . People who begin to doubt external appearances are first of·all going to experience more uncertainty; they may also feel guilt about their

suspiciousness and lack of trust; and finally they might find out
something about the other person's feelings toward them that they might
be much happier not to know. The person who knows when deception
is occurring and who knows what other people are feeling has a more
accurate grasp of what the interpersonal world is really like. But in some
ways, under some circumstances, maybe being good at understanding
social and interpersonal cues is just no good at all.''

What DePaulo writes echoes what Erving Goffman pointed out 25 years
ago: Most situations call for overlooking social lies; it is tactless and
ungraceful to call our family, friends, and associates on them. Or as Judith
Hall paraphrases Goffman, ''You can be too smart socially. Smooth
interaction requires that people not notice or comment on every little
lapse in decorum, or every little bit of insincerity. Social life works by
ignoring little social lies.''

In this chapter Miller and Burgoon provide a detailed list of the nonverbal cues associated with credibility and deception and summarize these cues in a useful table.

39

Factors Affecting Assessments of Witness Credibility

Gerald R. Miller and Judee K. Burgoon

Judgements of the demeanor of witnesses are central to the trial process. Since trial outcomes usually hinge on assessing the relative likelihood and/or veracity of conflicting information claims, legal decision makers — whether they be the judges and jury members of the traditional trial or the hearing officers and mediators of some of the newer, less formal modes of dispute resolution — cannot escape the responsibility of evaluating witness credibility. Miller and Boster (1977) mention the notion of the trial as a test of credibility as one of three important ways of conceptualizing the trial process, characterizing this perspective as demanding attention "not only to the factual information presented, but also to the way in which it is presented, the apparent qualifications of witnesses, and numerous other relevant factors (pp. 28-29)."

In the assessment of witness demeanor, the issue of intent to deceive, or deliberate falsehood, may or may not enter into the judgment. For instance, assume a judge or a juror is skeptical about testimony because a witness seems confused and hesitant when responding to questions. Under such circumstances, the judge or juror may absolve the witness of any duplicity: for example, "I feel this witness is trying to testify accurately but seems uncertain of what happened." Or the judge or juror may mentally indict the witness for lying: for example, "I feel this witness is a perjurer."

This distinction between honest error and outright deception fits nicely with the results of several studies investigating the major dimensions of communicator credibility (Berlo, Lemert, & Mertz, 1969-1970; Cronkhite & Liska, 1976; McCroskey, 1966; Whitehead, 1968). Despite some minor variations in these factor analytic studies, two major dimensions of credibility that emerge consistently are *competence* and *trustworthiness*. The former is most germane to assessments of witness credibility when intent to deceive seems unlikely, whereas the latter relates primarily to situations where the judge or juror believes the witness may be offering untruthful testimony.[1] Other frequently identified dimensions such as *dynamism, composure,* and *sociability,* while emerging as orthogonal components in some of the investigations, probably act as antecedents that influence perceptions of competence and trustworthiness. For example, if a witness lacks dynamism and composure, as reflected by a barely audible voice, high incidence of vocal disruptions such as nonfluency, and numerous nonverbal adaptors such as self-touching and fidgeting with clothing (Ekman & Friesen, 1969); he or she is likely to be perceived as relatively incompetent and/or untrustworthy.

The preceding example anticipates one of our two major objectives in this chapter: identifying variables that should and do influence judges' and jurors' assessments of witness credibilty. Our second major objective is to examine the findings of studies concerned with the ability of observers to detect deception perpetrated by relative strangers, both to ascertain how skillful persons are at this task and to isolate variables that facilitate or inhibit accurate detection of deception.[2]

Actually our efforts regarding the first objective are more modest than initially implied, since our discussion focuses on nonverbal and verbal characteristics associated with the actual presentation of testimony — characteristics that can be considered *intrinsic determinants* of credibility (Miller, Bauchner, Hocking, Fontes, Kaminski, & Brandt, 1981). Obviously, there are also numerous *extrinsic determinants* of credibility — attributes and characteristics witnesses bring with them to the courtroom setting. Some of the more obvious include education, occupational status, socio-economic status, general reputation, race, sex, and physical appearance. Futhermore, extrinsic and intrinsic determinants often interact to shape overall perceptions of credibility. Thus, a hesitant, nonfluent witness of acknowledged impeccable character is likely to be perceived as nervous or uncertain, but a witness of shady reputation who manifests the same behaviors probably will be viewed as an unconvincing liar.

Unfortunately, space limitations prevent us from surveying all of these areas thoroughly. In the following sections, we first examine nonverbal communication behaviors associated with judgments of credibility; we next consider some verbal characteristics of testimony proper that relate to credibility assessments; and finally, we examine the question of observers' accuracy in detecting deception. Although the final product falls short of a comprehensive, holistic picture of the perceptual process of evaluating witnesses, it does provide useful clues regarding some of the important presentational variables impinging on this process and also supplies a tentative answer to the question of how well courtroom decision makers can identify deceptive testimony.

Nonverbal Cues Associated With Credibility

Nonverbal cues that may be used by witnesses to establish their credibility or by jurors to evaluate credibility are of utmost importance. Hocking, Miller, and Fontes (1978) report that observers, asked to make judgments of the truthfulness of strangers, indicated a subjective estimate of about 58% confidence in their judgments when they viewed the strangers responding with no accompanying audio — that is, when their judgments were based entirely on the strangers' nonverbal behaviors. Adding the audio portion yielded only a modest increase in subjective judgments of confidence to about 64%. This result is consistent with much other research showing that people rely more heavily on nonverbal than verbal cues in interpreting social meaning, especially when the cues are spontaneously presented or inconsistent (Argyle, Alkema, & Gilmour, 1971; Bugental, 1974; Mehrabian & Wiener, 1967).

Diverse bodies of literature offer insights into the nonverbal cues associated with witness credibility and truthfulness, though little of the research has been conducted in the courtroom. In general, the research can be divided into that which takes the perspective of an *encoder* and that which takes the perspective of a *decoder*. In the former category are studies exploring nonverbal behaviors manifested by persons attempting to present themselves favorably, to be persuasive, or to deceive others; in the latter are studies centering on the cues perceived by observers as credible, persuasive, or deceptive.

Credible and Deceptive Encoding Behaviors

Several studies have examined the behaviors exhibited by individuals intent on enhancing their credibility and persuasiveness. For example, Timney and London (1973) had people roleplay jurors whose task was to convince another juror of the correctness of their own decision. In their study as well as others (Maslow, Yoselson, & London, 1971; Mehrabian & Williams, 1969), cues that correlated with intention to persuade and appearance of confidence included those indiciating more *extroversion and involvement,* such as forceful, rhythmic gestures, more eye contact, higher vocal volume, and faster speaking rate; moderate *relaxation,* such as a somewhat relaxed posture, fewer anxiety revealing behaviors, and fluent speech; and more *positivity,* such as more affirmative head nods, more facial activity, and greater intonation. These cues are summarized by nonverbal code in Table 1.

Other studies focusing on the negative end of the credibility continuum have examined the behaviors manifested by communicators engaged in lying to or misleading others. Ekman and Friesen (1969, 1975) identify four general strategies for managing emotional expressions, all of which are relevant to courtroom deceit by witnesses. First, a witness may *qualify* a given expression by adding another expression that comments about the first, as when a person smiles at his or her own foolish statement. Though the qualifying expression is typically not used to distort the meaning of the original one, it can be used effectively to introduce ambiguity, and hence, deception. Second, a witness may *curtail* a response, providing an abbreviated version of a normal performance, in the hope that less opportunity will be provided for deception detection. A third strategy involves *modulation* — the over-or under-intensification of emotions — as when a witness chooses to exaggerate or minimize the emotions expressed. Finally, a witness may *falsify* an emotional expression by simulating a feeling not actually experienced, neutralizing the expression to show nothing of what is felt, or masking the true feeling through substitution of another expression.

As another general guide to deceptive practices, Ekman and Friesen (1969) contend that the body regions providing the best deception clues are the hands and the feet because they are less carefully monitored by persons engaged in deception. The trunk may also reveal intensity, though not evaluative valence. By contrast, the face is most carefully controlled and therefore may present less valid information, the exception being micromomentary facial cues (fleeting facial expressions such as a grimace), which are not easily detected by the naked eye. Translated to the courtroom, this means that the most valuable cues are typically not available, while those that are most easily misinterpreted constitute the primary fund of available visual information. In a later section of this chapter, we discuss the accuracy of observers in detecting deception when viewing each of the body regions.

While the physical arrangement of many courtrooms poses some practical problems for jurors in discerning witness deception, many cues are still available to the skilled observer. It must be stressed, however, that these behaviors do not stem exclusively from deception. Similar communication patterns may appear under conditions of stress, negative

Table 1
Nonverbal Correlates of Credibility and Deception

Nonverbal code	Cues encoded as		Cues decoded as	
	Persuasive/credible	Deceptive	Persuasive/credible	Deceptive
Kinesics	More or continous eye contact	Reduced eye contact (fewer, briefer glances)	More eye contact	Less eye contact
	More affirmative head nods	Fewer head nods		
	More facial activity	Less smiling; less happiness; displeased mouth movements; micromomentary expressions; but more pleasant faces by highly anxious	More facial activity; more involvement	Less seriousness; less empathy; more smiling
	More gestures by women; more rhythmic, forceful gestures	Fewer gestures; fewer illustrators; more hand shrugs	More gestures; more illustrators	Excessive gestures
	Moderate levels of postural relaxation; less trunk swivel by women	Frequent shifts in leg/body positon; tense leg and foot positions; less leg and foot movement; leg crossing by males; body blocks; abortive, restless flight movements	Moderate relaxation	More tension and anxiety; more postural shifts
		Physiological indicators: blushing, blinking, shaking, perspiring, dilated or instable pupils		
Proxemics	Smaller reclining angle	Body less directly facing audience	Body less directly facing audience for males	
		Less forward lean	Closer distances	
		Greater distances		

Haptics	Fewer adaptor behaviors and self-manipulations; but more self-manipulations with receptive audience	More self, face-play and object adaptors; longer adaptors	Less self-manipulations and adaptors	Less self-grooming
Vocalics	Higher volume Faster speaking rate More fluency More intonation	Slower or faster speaking rate than normal More nonfluencies Higher pitch More pause or probe openings More response latency Shorter work duration; shorter speaking time	Higher volume Moderate to slightly faster speaking rate More fluency More intonation and pitch variety Lower pitch More vocal involvement Conversational delivery style	More nonfluencies More response latency
Overall		Contradictions or inconsistencies among non-verbal cues More information from hands and feet than face	Use of General American Dialect Positive violations of expectations (e.g., dressing unappealingly but conveying effective verbal message)	Greater reliance on voice than face and on face than body

affect, or disinterest. Consequently, accurate determination of when such cues signal dissembling is difficult and interpretations must be made cautiously. Single cues may be particularly misleading; reasonable judgments are possible only when a consistent pattern of cues presents itself.

In a review of early deception research, Knapp, Hart, and Dennis (1974) proposed a number of functions of deception cues that provide a useful classification scheme. Six of these functions are relevant to nonverbal cues. The first, most obvious configuration of cues shows *underlying anxiety or nervousness.* A host of physiological indicators—blushing, perspiring, increased blood pressure, altered breathing cycle, shaking, altered latency, rate of blinking, and increased Galvanic Skin Response— may be present when a person is lying (Cutrow, Parks, Lucas, & Thomas, 1972). Unfortunately, many of these signs are detectable only with the aid of sophisticated equipment. One autonomic response available to the unaided observer is pupil size: prevaricators typically show pupil dilation (often a slow dilation followed by rapid constriction) or pupil instability (Berrien & Huntington, 1943; Clark, 1975; Heilveil, 1976). Other bodily activity indicative of anxiety and tension includes random body and limb movements, such as abortive, restless flight movements; frequent shifts of leg or body positions; frequent leg crossing by males (Ekman & Friesen, 1969, 1972, 1974; Feldman, Devin-Sheehan, & Allen, 1978; Knapp et al., 1974; McClintock & Hunt, 1975) and excessive use of adaptor behaviors (behaviors that relieve physiological or psychological needs), particularly self-adaptors such as tearing at fingernails, holding knees, digging into palms; face-play adaptors such as scratching the nose or chin; and object adaptors such as playing with a pencil or smoking a cigarette (Knapp et al., McClintock & Hunt). These latter behaviors, however, do not appear consistently, as evidenced by their failure to arise in some investigations (Ekman & Friesen, 1974). It is likely that well-rehearsed witnesses would display few self-adaptors, although inadvertent touching of face and hair might still be observed. Finally, at the vocal level, lying has commonly been accompanied by a higher fundamental frequency, or pitch (Ekman & Friesen, 1974; Ekman, Friesen, & Scherer, 1976; Streeter, Krauss, Geller, Olson, & Apple, 1977) and occasionally, though not consistently, by increased nonfluencies (supported by Mehrabian, 1971; not supported by Knapp et al., 1974).

A second configuration of cues shows *underlying reticence or withdrawal.* Such behaviors as fewer illustrative gestures, postural body blocks, orienting the body to face others less directly, less forward body lean, and increased interpersonal distance may be exhibited (Ekman & Friesen, 1972; Ekman et al., 1976; Knapp et al., 1974; Mehrabian, 1971). These cues all translate into reduced *immediacy,* a global term for the degree of closeness and desire for approach that exists between people.

Eye contact may also be reduced (Knapp et al., 1974; Mehrabian, 1971), although some studies have shown that people who greatly value manipulative skills (high Machiavellians) and people with time to plan their performances may carefully control their eye contact to keep it as normal as possible (Exline, Thibaut, Hickey, & Gumpert, 1970; McClintock & Hunt, 1975, Matarazzo, Wiens, Jackson, & Manaugh, 1970). In terms of vocal cues, research results have been mixed. Although a majority of studies have found more pauses and openings for questioner probes when communicators are lying (Feldman et al., 1978, Knapp et al., 1974), longer delays in responding (response latencies) (Baskett & Freedle, 1974, Cutrow et al., 1972; Goldstein, 1923; Krauss, Geller & Olson, 1976; Kraut, 1978; Matarazzo et al., 1970), shorter word duration and a trend toward shorter speaking time (Knapp et al., 1974; Mehrabian, 1971; Motley, 1974); other studies have either found shorter response latencies for some communicators who are lying (English, 1926; Marston, 1920) or have not supported differences in speaking duration (Matarazzo et al., 1970). Even though Goldstein (1923) found support for a methodological explanation of latency differences, the conflicting results still point to variability in the conditions under which certain vocal cues will be exhibited.

A third category of cues involves *excessive behaviors that deviate from a communicator's normal response patterns.* These behaviors generally express more extreme feelings than are actually felt, such as more outward composure than is experienced inwardly or feigned favorable reactions. In addition to the reduction in immediacy behaviors mentioned earlier, these cues include fewer head nods, fewer gestures, less leg and foot movement, more pleasant facial expressions, and either a faster or slower speaking rate (Mehrabian, 1971, 1972). Increases in pleasant facial expressions seem attributable to the deceiver trying to placate the observer and are likely to occur only among highly anxious communicators. More skillful communicators experience less anxiety and consequently display less of the negative affect that characterizes this type of "pleasant" expression. As for speaking rate changes, it appears that they are also mediated by stress level: Under conditions of minimal discomfort (presumably when telling the truth) or extreme discomfort (induced by certain deception circumstances), speaking rate is usually faster; under moderate discomfort (that may accompany other deceptive circumstances), the rate of speech is usually slower than normal. In generalizing to the courtroom, then it would be necessary to estimate the level of stress involved before predicting the speaking rate that would signal deception.

While superficially the face may reveal some pleasantness, a fourth category of behaviors generally shows *underlying negative affect* (Mehrabian, 1971; Zuckerman, DeFrank, Hall, Larrance, & Rosenthal, 1979). Specific cues that have often been observed include reduced glances, a trend toward fewer mutual glances, less frequent smiling, and displeased mouth movements (Feldman et al., 1978; Knapp et al., 1974; McClintock & Hunt, 1975). Feldman et al., as well as Zuckerman et al., also found that persons engaged in deception showed less general happiness and facial pleasantness, as judged by observers.

The fifth configuration of cues originally classified by Knapp et al. (1974) as indirect responses, shows underlying vagueness or uncertainty. Many vagueness and uncertainty cues are linguistic and will be discussed later, but a few nonverbal cues are relevant. One such cue, the hand shrug, a show of helplessness involving turning out of the palms, is an unmonitored behavior that frequently accompanies deceit (Eckman & Friesen, 1972, 1974). Other nonverbal correlates include a less direct body orientation (Exline et al., 1970; Mehrabian, 1971) and the previously mentioned increases in silence and hesitations before speaking. Tangentially related is the Zuckerman et al. (1979) finding that observers rate deceptive voices less dominant and assertive than honest voices.

The final category involves incongruous responses, or cues that show external behavior to be in contradiction with actual feelings. The few empirically validated cues in this category include momentary facial expressions of negative emotions that may occur with generally pleasant faces (Haggard & Isaacs, 1966) and other simultaneously occurring, contradictory nonverbal cues, such as greater eye contact coupled with increased self-touching or pleasant faces coupled with reticence and anxiety cues (Knapp et al., 1974; McClintock & Hunt, 1975). Cues that have been the subject of conjecture include failure to emphasize remarks with naturally occurring gestures, nonverbal behaviors that are not synchronized with vocal rhythm, and nonverbal messages that are inconsistent with verbal ones.

All of the correlates of deception discussed above are summarized in Table 1, where they can be compared to those cues accompanying encoding that are intended to be persuasive and credible.

General Degree of Accuracy in Detecting Deception

Two points about accuracy deserve mention. First, in those studies where accuracy in judging truthful versus untruthful responses has been compared (Ekman & Friesen, 1974; Littlepage & Pineault, 1979; Maier & Janzen, 1967), observers identify lies somewhat better than truthful behavior. While this may suggest that nonverbal "clues" are more readily spotted when deceptive messages are being sent, the possibility of lying bias cannot be dismissed; that is since observers are cued to expect deception, they may lean toward overestimating the number of lies communicated. Such a bias would, of course, inflate the accuracy scores for untruthful messages and suppress the scores for truthful ones.

Second, as would be expected, there are marked individual differences in ability to deceive (Hocking *et al.*, 1979; Kraut, 1978). Some communicators are good liars—almost all their messages, both truthful statements and lies, are judged as truthful. Others are poor liars—almost all their messages, regardless of veracity, are judged as untruthful. These differences underscore the need for careful control of the samples of statements presented to observers in deception studies. At least two approaches to this problem are possible: Researchers can use equal numbers of truthful and untruthful statements for each communicator/deceiver (Hocking, et al., 1979), on the assumption that the number of good and poor liars will balance out, or researchers can use previously tested samples for communicator/deceivers that fall near the midpoint of the accuracy range (Brandt, Miller, & Hocking, 1980a).

Notwithstanding possible procedural problems, one particularly crucial conclusion emerges from the studies thus far conducted: *Observers are not very successful in detecting deception perpetrated by relative strangers.* It is not wholly justified to treat dichotomous judgments of truth or falsity as if they conform to a binomial probability distribution, for it is unlikely that persons approach their daily communicative transactions with the assumption that lying and telling the truth are equally probable events. Nevertheless, the fact remains that observers in most prior studies would probably have done as well had they flipped a coin to determine if the communicator/deceivers were lying, particularly since lying and telling the truth occurred with equal frequency in a majority of the studies. To the extent that these findings are generalizable to situations involving assessment of witness veracity, they paint a discouraging picture concerning jurors' ability to make accurate assessments.

Moreover, this picture is further clouded by the propensity of observers to express considerable confidence in their judgment even when they are wrong. Hocking (1976) and Littlepage and Pineault (1979) report that observers were quite confident of most of their veracity judgments even though many were erroneous. Translated to the courtroom environment, this finding raises the specter of jurors evaluating a witness's veracity inaccurately while remaining very certain of the correctness of their evaluations.

Given the substantial body of folklore and conventional wisdom regarding the ways liars reveal themselves by their nonverbal behaviors, what accounts for the apparent lack of observer success in detecting deceptive messages? One possible explanation lies in the view of motivation, or drive, expressed in drive-reduction learning theories

(Brown, 1961). This view holds that drive is a generalized energizer which increases the vigor of all competing response tendencies. For complex activities, such as communicating, high drive inhibits task performance; more specifically, it produces the kinds of verbal and nonverbal disruptions stereotypically associated with lying. Increased drive can be triggered by various antecedents, only one of which is knowledge of intent to deceive another. Thus, as mentioned earlier, many behavioral displays that are taken as evidence of lying may actually result from drive-producing factors associated with the person (e.g., communication apprehension or manifest anxiety) or with the situation (e.g., publicly testifying in court about an extremely stressful experience such as a rape). Stated differently, many behaviors thought to signal deceit are precisely those expected of an anxious or strongly motivated witness, and this behavioral correspondence probably results in numerous faulty inferences, or misattributions, of lying.

Effects of Available Facial and Body Cues on Detecting Deception

Ekman and Friesen's (1969, 1974) *leakage hypothesis* posits that the body provides a richer source of useful nonverbal cues for detecting deception than does the face. These theorists reason that people are aware of the necessity to control nonverbal behavior to deceive successfully, but that in seeking to exert such control, they are more conscious of the face than the body. Consequently, in deceptive transactions, the body "leaks" more valuable nonverbal information than the face.

To test this hypothesis Ekman and Friesen (1974) had student nurses either lie or tell the truth about their self-feelings while viewing a segmentalized film stimulus. This stimulus contained pictures of pleasant landscapes and badly disfigured burn victims. Since the nurses always said they were feeling pleasant and relaxed, they consistently told the truth when viewing the landscapes and consistently lied when viewing the burn victims.

Results indicated that observers who saw the nurses' bodies only were more accurate in detecting deception than their counterparts who saw the faces only, but only when observers had first viewed a sample of the deceivers' truthful communication (familiarization manipulation). While differing significantly, the degree of successful detection was not particularly high for observers in either condition: observers in the face/familiar condition had a mean accuracy of .45 as compared with a mean of .56 for those subjected to the body/familiar treatment.

Several limitations of this study prevent generalizing of its findings confidently to the courtroom setting. We have already mentioned that procedures such as eliminating the verbal behavior of communicator/deceivers and showing observers shots of only the body depart markedly from the realm of everyday social transactions. Even more troublesome is the fact that nurses consistently told the truth while viewing pleasant landscapes and lied consistently while viewing burn victims. In terms of the drive-reduction interpretation previously outlined, stressful pictures of burn victims would be likely to trigger anxiety and to culminate in behaviors stereotypically associated with lying. Consequently, the cards seem to be stacked in favor of lying judgments, but it is hard to ascertain whether the nonverbal cues used by observers were occasioned by the communicator/deceivers' knowledge of intent to deceive or by the anxiety they experienced when viewing the unpleasant pictures of burn victims. This interpretative ambiguity is further illustrated by the fact that, when compared to honest conditions, mean accuracy is consistently higher in all the deception conditions employed in the study.

In a study designed to investigate the effects of several variables on detecting deception, Hocking, et al., (1979) replicated Ekman and Friesen's (1974) findings for self-feeling deception: Observers who viewed only the body of communicator/deceivers were significantly more accurate in detecting deception than observers who viewed the head only or the head and body. For factual lying, however, the outcome was reversed: observers who viewed the head only and the head and body were more accurate than observers who saw the body only. In addition, the analyses for factual lying revealed that observers who also heard the communicator/deceivers' verbal responses were more accurate than those who did not, a finding that bodes well for the actual trial setting. Interestingly, this difference in accuracy ratings for audio and visual as opposed to video only was not observed for self-feeling deception.

To further confuse matters, Littlepage and Pineault (1979) have reported an extended replication of Ekman and Friesen's (1974) results using factual deception and permitting observers to hear the accompanying verbal behavior. Their results showed that the superiority of body cues held only for untruthful statements: Facial cues yielded an accuracy mean of only .35 as compared to a mean of .85 for body shots; for honest statements, the mean was .70 for facial shots and .66 for shots of the body. Littlepage and Pineault also interpret their results to show that prior exposure to the deceivers' truthful behavior is unnecessary for confirmation of the leakage hypothesis, because their observers were not provided with an extensive sample of truthful responses. It should be noted, however, that all communicator/deceivers were first required to state their names truthfully, and while admittedly limited, this procedure ensured observers of an initial sample of truthful behavior.

What conclusions germane to juror assessment of witness veracity can be drawn from these conflicting findings? Encouragingly, the results of both the Hocking, et al. (1979) and Littlepage and Pineault (1979) studies regarding factual lying suggest that accuracy of detection is not adversely affected, and may in fact be enhanced, by including the verbal response of witnesses. Concerning the possible superiority of nonverbal body cues as helpful indicators of deception, the findings, though mixed, lend some credence to the leakage hypothesis. If this hypothesis is tenable, it underscores two pragmatic issues associated with the trial setting: First, it may be difficult for jurors to focus on the body at the expense of the face, even if instructed to do so; second, the design and construction of many witness stands prevents jurors from observing those body cues considered essential for accurate assessment of witness veracity.

Summary

The research reviewed in this chapter has suggested several potentially useful generalizations about factors influencing perceptions of witness credibility:

1. *Certain patterns of nonverbal and vocal cues are somewhat systematically associated with deceptive communication.* Included among these cues are behaviors symptomatic of underlying anxiety and of reticence or withdrawal, excessive behaviors that deviate from a communicator's normal response patterns, behaviors signaling negative affect, behaviors indicative of vagueness or uncertainty, and incongruous responses suggesting that external behavior contradicts actual feelings.

2. *When asked to report those nonverbal cues that signal deceptive messages, observers mention many of the actual behaviors associated with deceptive encoding.* This finding suggests that observer difficulty in detecting deception stems primarily from inability to detect or to interpret nonverbal cues, rather than from ignorance of or misinformation about the cues themselves.

3. *Despite knowledge of relevant cues, observers are not notably successful in detecting deception perpetrated by relative strangers.* In attempting to determine whether a communicator was lying or telling the truth, observers in most studies were right about half the time. Furthermore, when messages were presented via different modes that transmit varying amounts of nonverbal and vocalic behavior, there was

no evidence to indicate that success in detecting deception was positively related to the amount of available nonverbal information. Indeed, there was some indication that observers were most successful when nonverbal information was minimal, as when they were asked to base veracity judgments on examination of a written transcript.

We offer these generalizations cautiously for two reasons: First, because little extant research has occurred in the confines of actual courtrooms; second, because most available research focuses on one or two strands of the complex fabric of social perceptions that constitute jurors' and judges' evaluations of witnesses. To tread cautiously is not to negate the value of present findings; some empirical evidence is certainly better than none. Still, many unanswered questions remain; indeed, the scientific jury will be required to remain out for some time to come if it hopes to return a confident verdict on the issue of factors affecting the assessment of witness credibility.

Notes

[1]Competence and trustworthiness also correspond to the most common legal reasons for seeking to impeach witnesses. In most cases, impeachment can be based on the witness's incompetence to testify about issues (competence) or possible self-interest and bias on the part of the witness (trustworthiness).

[2]Several recent studies have examined the influence of degree of familiarity on the ability of observers to detect deception (Bauchner, n.d.; Brandt, Miller, & Hocking, 1980 a,b). As would be expected, these studies indicate that if observers know something about a communicator/deceiver's truthful communication style, they are more accurate in detecting deception. Since jurors who were familiar with witnesses would normally be excused from jury duty, studies dealing with attempts to detect deception on the part of relative strangers are most relevant to the trial setting.

References

Addington, D.W. The effect of vocal variations on ratings of source credibility. *Speech Monographs*, 1971, *38*, 242-247.

Apple, W., Streeter, L.A., & Krauss, R.M. Effects of pitch and speech rate on personal attributions. *Journal of Personality and Social Psychology*, 1979, *37*, 715-727.

Argyle, M., Alkema, F., & Gilmour, R. The communication of friendly and hostile attitudes by verbal and non-verbal signals. *European Journal of Social Psychology*, 1971, *1*, 385-402.

Baskett, F., & Freedle, R.O. Aspects of language pragmatics and the social perception of lying. *Journal of Psycholinguistic Research*, 1974, *3*, 112-131.

Bauchner, J.E. *The effects of familiarity on observers' abilities to detect deception.* Unpublished doctoral dissertation in progress, Michigan State University, (n.d.).

Bauchner, J.E., Brandt, D.R., & Miller, G.R. The truth-deception attribution: Effects of varying levels of information availability. In B.D. Ruben (Ed.), *Communication yearbook I.* New Brunswick, NJ: Transaction Books, 1977.

Bauchner, J.E., Kaplan, E.P., & Miller, G.R. Detecting deception: The relationship of available information to judgmental accuracy in initial encounters. *Human Communication Research,* 1980, *6,* 251-264.

Berlo, K.D., Lemert, J.B., & Mertz, R.J. Dimensions for evaluating the acceptability of message sources. *Public Opinion Quarterly,* 1969-1970, *33,* 563-576.

Berrien, F., & Huntington, G. An exploratory study of pupillary responses during deception. *Journal of Experimental Psychology,* 1943, *32,* 443-449.

Bradac, J.J., Bowers, J.W., & Courtright, J.A. Three language variables in communication research: Intensity, immediacy, and diversity. *Human Communication Research,* 1979, *5,* 257-269.

Brandt, D.R., Miller, G.R., & Hocking, J.E. Effects of self-monitoring and familiarity on deception detection. *Communication Quarterly,* 1980, *28,* 3-10. (a).

_____. The truth-deception attribution: Effects of familiarity on the ability of observers to detect deception. *Human Communication Research,* 1980, *6,* 99-110. (b)

Brown, B.L., Strong, W.J., & Rencher, A. C. Perceptions of personality from speech: Effects of manipulations of acoustical parameters. *Journal of the Acoustical Society of America,* 1973, *54,* 29-33.

Brown, B.L., Strong, W.J., & Rencher, A. C. Fifty-four voices from two: The effects of simultaneous manipulations of rate, mean fundamental frequency and variance of fundamental frequency on ratings of personality from speech. *Journal of the Acoustical Society of America,* 1974, *55,* 313-318.

Brown, J.S. *The motivation of behavior.* New York: McGraw-Hill, 1961.

Buck, J.F. The effects of negro and white dialectical variations upon attitudes of college students. *Speech Monographs,* 1968, *35,* 181-186.

Bugental, D.E. Interpretations of naturally occurring discrepancies between words and intonation: Modes of inconsistency resolution. *Journal of Personality and Social Psychology,* 1974, *30,* 125-133.

Bugental, D.E., Kaswan, J.W., & Love, L.R. Perception of contradictory meanings conveyed by verbal and nonverbal channels. *Journal of Personality and Social Psychology,* 1970, *16,* 647-655.

Burgoon, J.K. A communication model of personal space violations: Explication and an initial test. *Human Communication Research,* 1978, *4,* 129-142.

Burgoon, J.K., Stacks, D.W., & Woodall, W.G. A communicative model of violations of distancing expectations. *Western Journal of Speech Communication,* 1979, *43,* 153-167.

Clark, W.R. *A comparison of pupillary response, heart rate, and GSR during deception.* Paper presented at the meeting of the Midwestern Psychological Association, Chicago, April 1975.

Cooper, J., Darley, J.M., & Henderson, J.E. On the effectiveness of deviant- and conventional-appearing communicators. *Journal of Personality and Social Psychology,* 1974, *29,* 752-757.

Cronkhite, G., & Liska, J. A critique of factor analytic approaches to the study of credibility. *Communication Monographs,* 1976, *43,* 91-107.

Cutrow, R.J., Parks, A., Lucas, N., & Thomas, K. The objective use of multiple physiological indices in the detection of deception. *Psychophysiology*, 1972, *9*, 578-588.

Delia, J.G. Dialects and the effects of stereotypes on impression formation. *Quarterly Journal of Speech*, 1972, *58*, 285-297.

DePaulo, B.M., Rosenthal, R., Eisenstat, R.A., Rogers, P.L., & Finkelstein, S. Decoding discrepant nonverbal cues. *Journal of Personality and Social Psychology*, 1978, *36*, 313-323.

Ekman, P., & Friesen, W.V. Nonverbal leakage and clues to deception. *Psychiatry*, 1969, *32*, 88-106.

_____. Hand movements and deception. *Journal of Communication*, 1972, *22*, 353-374.

_____. Detecting deception from the body or face. *Journal of Personality and Social Psychology*, 1974, *29*, 288-298.

_____. Unmasking the face. Englewood Cliffs, NJ: Prentice-Hall, 1975.

Ekman, P., Friesen, W.V., & Scherer, K.R. Body movement and voice pitch in deceptive interaction. *Semiotica*, 1976, *16*, 23-27.

English, H. Reaction-time symptoms of deception. *American Journal of Psychology*, 1926, *37*, 428-429.

Exline, R., Thibaut, J., Hickey, C., & Gumpert, P. Visual interaction in relation to Machiavellianism and an unethical act. In R. Christie and F.L. Geis (Eds.), *Studies in Machiavellianism*. New York: Academic Press, 1970.

Fay, P.J., & Middleton, W.C. The ability to judge truthtelling or lying from the voice as transmitted over a public address system. *Journal of General Psychology*, 1941, *24*, 211-215.

Feldman, R.S., Devin-Sheehan, L., & Allen, V.L. Nonverbal cues as indicators of verbal dissembling. *American Educational Research Journal*, 1978, *15*, 217-231.

Giles, H. Communication effectiveness as a function of accented speech. *Speech Monographs*, 1973, *40*, 330-331.

Giles, H., & Powesland, P.F. *Speech style and social evaluation*. New York: Academic Press, 1975.

Goldstein, E. Reaction times and the consciousness of deception. *American Journal of Psychology*, 1923, *34*, 562-581.

Haggard, E., & Isaacs, K. Micromomentary facial expressions as indicators of ego mechanisms in psychotherapy. In L. Gottschalk and A. Auerbach (Eds.), *Methods of research in psychotherapy*. New York: Appleton, 1966.

Heilveil, I. Deception and pupil size. *Journal of Clinical Psychology*, 1976, *32*, 675-676.

Hocking, J.E. *Detecting deceptive communication from verbal, visual, and paralinguistic cues: An exploratory experiment*. Unpublished doctoral dissertation, Michigan State University, 1976.

Hocking, J.E., Bauchner, J.E., Kaminski, E.P., & Miller, G.R. Detecting deceptive communication from verbal, visual, and paralinguistic cues. *Human Communication Research*, 1979, *6*, 33-46.

Hocking, J.E., Miller, G.R., & Fontes, N.E. Videotape in the courtroom: Witness deception. *Trial*, 1978, *14*, 52-55.

Knapp, M.L., Hart, R.P., & Dennis, H.S. An exploration of deception as a communication construct. *Human Communication Research*, 1974, *1*, 15-29.

Krauss, R.M., Geller, V., & Olson, C. *Modalities and cues in the detection of deception.* Paper presented at the meeting of the American Psychological Association, Washington, D.C., August 1976.

Kraut, R.E. Verbal and nonverbal cues in the perception of lying. *Journal of Personality and Social Psychology*, 1978, *36*, 380-391.

Lay, C.H., & Burron, B.F. Perception of the personality of the distant speaker. *Perceptual and Motor Skills*, 1968, *26*, 951-956.

Littlepage, G.E., & Pineault, M.A. Detection of deceptive factual statements from the body and the face. *Personality and Social Psychology Bulletin*, 1979, *5*, 325-328.

McClintock, C., & Hunt, R. Nonverbal indicators of affect and deception in an interview setting. *Journal of Applied Social Psychology*, 1975, *5*, 54-67.

McCroskey, J.C. Scales for the measurement of *ethos. Speech Monographs*, 1966, *33*, 65-72.

McPeek, R.W., & Edwards, J.D. Expectancy disconfirmation and attitude change. *Journal of Social Psychology*, 1975, *96*, 193-208.

Maier, N.R.F. Sensitivity to attempts at deception in an interview situation. *Personnel Psychology*, 1966, *19*, 55-65.

Maier, N.R.F., & Janzen, J. The reliability of persons making judgments of honesty and dishonesty. *Perceptual and Motor Skills*, 1967, *25*, 141-151.

Maier, N.R.F., & Thurber, J.A. Accuracy of judgments of deception when an interview is watched, heard, and read. *Personnel Psychology*, 1968, *21*, 23-30.

Maier, R.A., & Lavrakas, P.J. Lying behavior and evaluation of lies. *Perceptual and Motor Skills*, 1976, *42*, 575-581.

Marston, W.M. Reaction-time symptoms of deception. *Journal of Experimental Psychology*, 1920, *3*, 72-87.

Maslow, C., Yoselson, K., & London, H. Persuasiveness of confidence expressed via language and body language. *British Journal of Social and Clinical Psychology*, 1971, *10*, 234-240.

Matarazzo, J., Wiens, A., Jackson, R., & Manaugh, R. Interviewer speech behavior under conditions of endogenously present and exogenously-induced motivational states. *Journal of Clinical Psychology*, 1970, *26*, 141-148.

Meerloo, J.A. Camouflage versus communication: In the beginning was the lie. *Communication*, 1978, *3*, 45.

Mehrabian, A. Nonverbal betrayal of feeling, *Journal of Experimental Research in Personality*, 1971, *5*, 64-73.

_____. *Nonverbal communication.* Chicago, Aldine-Atherton, 1972.

Mehrabian, A., & Ferris, S.L. Inference of attitudes from nonverbal communication in two channels. *Journal of Consulting Psychology*, 1967, *31*, 248-252.

Mehrabian, A., & Wiener, M. Decoding of inconsistent communications. *Journal of Personality and Social Psychology*, 1967, *6*, 108-114.

Mehrabian, A., & Williams, M. Nonverbal concomitants of perceived and intended persuasiveness. *Journal of Personality and Social Psychology*, 1969, *13*, 37-58.

Miller, G.R., Bauchner, J.E., Hocking, J.E., Fontes, N.E., Kaminski, E.P., & Brandt, D.R. ". . .And nothing but the truth": How well can observers detect deceptive testimony? In B.D. Sales (Ed.), *The trial process*. New York: Plenum, 1981.

Miller, G.R., & Boster, F.J. Three images of the trial: Their implications for psychological research. In B.D. Sales (Ed.), *Psychology in the legal process*. New York: Spectrum, 1977.

Miller, G.R., & Fontes, N.E. *Videotape on trial: A view from the jury box*. Beverly Hills, CA: Sage Publications, 1979.

Miller, G.R., & Hewgill, M.A. The effect of variations in nonfluency on audience ratings of source credibility. *Quarterly Journal of Speech*, 1964, *50*, 36-44.

Motley, M. Acoustic correlates of lies. *Western Speech*, 1974, *38*, 81-87.

Mulac, A., Hanley, T.D., & Prigge, D.Y. Effects of phonological speech foreignness upon three dimensions of attitude of selected American speakers. *Quarterly Journal of Speech*, 1974, *60*, 411-420.

Pearce, W.B., & Brommel, B.J. The effect of vocal variations on ratings of source credibility. *Quarterly Journal of Speech*, 1972, *58*, 298-306.

Pearce, W.B., & Conklin, F. Nonverbal vocalic communication and the perception of a speaker. *Speech Monographs*, 1971, *38*, 235-241.

Rosenthal, R., & DePaulo, B.M. Expectancies, discrepancies, and courtesies in nonverbal communication. *Western Journal of Speech Communication*, 1979, *43*, 76-95.

Sereno, K.K., & Hawkins, G.J. The effects of variations in speakers' nonfluency upon audience ratings of attitude change toward the speech topic and speakers' credibility. *Speech Monographs*, 1967, *34*, 58-64.

Shulman, G. *An experimental study of the effects of receiver sex, communicator sex, and warning on the ability of receivers to detect deception*. Unpublished masters thesis, Purdue University, Indiana, 1973.

Streeter, L.A., Krauss, R.M., Geller, V., Olson, C., & Apple, W. Pitch changes during attempted deception. *Journal of Personality and Social Psychology*, 1977, *35*, 345-350.

Timney, B., & London, H. Body language concomitants of persuasiveness and persuasibility in dyadic interaction. *International Journal of Group Tensions*, 1973, *3-4*, 48-67.

Todd, W.B. *Linguistic indices of deception as manifested by women: A content analytic study*. Unpublished doctoral dissertation, Florida State University, 1976.

Toomb, J.K., Quiggins, J.G., Moore, D.L., MacNeil, L.B., & Liddell, C.M. *The effects of regional dialects on initial source credibility*. Paper presented at the meeting of the International Communication Association, Atlanta, April 1972.

Whitehead, J.L. Factors of source credibility. *Quarterly Journal of Speech*, 1968, *54*, 59-63.

Zuckerman, M., DeFrank, R.S., Hall, J.A., Larrance, D.T., & Rosenthal, R. Facial and vocal cues of deception and honesty. *Journal of Experimental Social Psychology*, 1979, *15*, 378-396.

In this section Ekman cautions the reader regarding deception detection. Nine cautions are provided in order to minimize the risk of making errors in detection.

40

Precautions in Interpreting Behavior Clues to Deceit

Paul Ekman

Evaluating behavioral clues to deceit is hazardous. The list below summarizes all the precautions for reducing those hazards. The lie catcher must always estimate the *likelihood* that a gesture or expression indicates lying or truthfulness; rarely is it absolutely certain. In those instances when it is — an emotion contradicting the lie leaking in a full, macro facial expression, or some part of the concealed information blurted out in words during a tirade — the suspect will realize that too and will confess.

1. Try to make explicit the basis of any hunches and intuitions about whether or not someone is lying. By becoming more aware of how *you* interpret behavioral clues to deceit, you will learn to spot your mistakes and recognize when you don't have much chance to make a correct judgment.

2. Remember that there are two dangers in detecting deceit: disbelieving-the-truth (judging a truthful person to be lying) and believing-a-lie (judging a liar to be truthful). There is no way to completely avoid both mistakes. Consider the consequences of risking either mistake.

3. The absence of a sign of deceit is not evidence of truth; some people don't leak. The presence of a sign of deceit is not always evidence of lying; some people appear ill-at-ease or guilty even when they are truthful. You can decrease the Brokaw hazard, which is due to individual differences in expressive behavior, by basing your judgments on a *change* in the suspect's behavior.

4. Search your mind for any preconceptions you may have about the suspect. Consider whether your preconceptions will bias your chance of making a correct judgment. Don't try to judge whether or not someone is lying if you feel overcome by jealousy or in an emotional wildfire. Avoid the temptation to suspect lying because it explains otherwise inexplicable events.

5. Always consider the possibility that a sign of emotion is not a clue to deceit but a clue to how a truthful person feels about being suspected of lying. Discount the sign of an emotion as a clue to deceit if a truthful suspect might feel that emotion because of: the suspect's personality; the nature of your past relationship with the suspect; or the suspect's expectations.

6. Bear in mind that many clues to deceit are signs of more than one emotion, and that those that are must be discounted if one of those emotions could be felt if the suspect is truthful while another could be felt if the suspect is lying.

7. Consider whether or not the suspect knows he is under suspicion, and what the gains or losses in detecting deceit would be either way.

8. If you have knowledge that the suspect would also have only if he is lying, and you can afford to interrogate the suspect, construct a Guilty Knowledge Test.

9. Never reach a final conclusion about whether a suspect is lying or not based solely on your interpretation of behavioral clues to deceit. Behavioral clues to deceit should only serve to alert you to the need for further information and investigation. Behavioral clues, like the polygraph, can never provide absolute evidence.

Key Terms and Concepts

Goleman, *Can You Tell When Someone is Lying to You?*

deception	telephone	sending capacity
PONS test	leak	planned lies
deviations	body cues	social participation
actual vs. perceived	discrepancies	social anxiety
signs of deception	between channels	gender and leakage
voice pitch	face	politeness

Miller and Burgoon, *Factors Affecting Assessments of Witness Credibility*

demeanor	involvement	vagueness
credibility	relaxation	contradictions
competence	positivity	expectations
trustworthiness	qualify	attributions
dynamism	curtail	saliency
composure	modulation	roles
sociability	falsify	antagonism
intrinsic and extrinsic	monitoring	degree of accuracy
determinants	anxiety	leakage hypothesis
encoder	reticence	presentational
decoder	deviations	modes
extroversion	underlying negative	
	affect	

Ekman, *Precautions in Interpreting Behavioral Clues to Deceit*

self awareness	preconceptions	suspicion
two types of mistakes	signs of emotion	previous knowledge
changes in behavior	mixed emotions	other cues

Appendix B

Applications to Interpersonal Relationships

Nonverbal communication plays an important role in initiating, maintaining, and ending interpersonal relationships. Our most important messages about relationships — signs of interest, attraction, power, liking, etc. — are sent nonverbally. These are called *metacommunication*, messages about messages. Metacommunication tells us how to interpret our verbal messages; whether to see the verbal message as caring or self-serving, persuasive or suggestive, sexual or friendly. In fact, research shows that often we prefer nonverbal metacommunication to verbal metacommunication because we do not like to talk about our relationships too explicitly or directly.

Nonverbal signs of interest are used to *establish interpersonal relationships*. Think about the last time you met someone new at a party. Nonverbal cues such as eye contact and smiling might have told you that the other person was interested in meeting you. Often distance cues are important too. When people want to meet each other they get closer. Nonverbal flirting and courtship behaviors may also be considered. People who do not know when other people like them are at a tremendous disadvantage in meeting people and are often quite lonely.

Nonverbal cues are also used to *develop and maintain relationships*. On dates, sexual intimacy is regulated by nonverbal cues and increasing intimacy is marked or indicated through more intimate physical contact. Two lovers express their feelings through eye contact, touch, and special gifts. In business, cues of status and power play a role in professional advancement.

Date rape, currently a major problem on college campuses, often involves interpretation of verbal and nonverbal cues. Date rape occurs when one person forces another to engage in sexual intercourse on a date. Conflicting messages are sometimes involved in this process. For example, if a woman is attracted to a man, but does not want sexual intimacy, she may verbally say no while nonverbally communicating sexual interest. Some men believe they have the right to listen to the nonverbal cues and force intimacy. This may result in date rape.

Finally, nonverbal cues are involved in *relationship termination*. There are many nonverbal signs that a relationship is ending, including decreased time together, less touching and mutual eye contact, and fewer smiles. At the very end, some people just walk away without saying anything at all. Others will provide a verbal message to clarify the nonverbal signs that the relationship is over.

The nonverbal signs of relationships are quite powerful. A friendship is reinforced through joint activities—the weekly card game, the annual trip to the river. The most intimate friendships are often marked by hugging, close distance, and presents. Similarly, romantic relationships are expressed nonverbally. Think of the most common symbols of romance—flowers, rings, and loving glances. The nonverbal side of our relationships cannot be ignored.

41

*Successful daters know whom to ask out. They learn the signs
of interest and pursue people who display these signs.
Muehlenhard, Koralewski, Andrews, and Burdick's research
shows that most college students prefer women to hint about
their interest and men to follow-up with a dating request. This
chapter describes the most common cues that women display
to indicate to a man an interest in dating.*

Cues That Convey
Interest in Dating

Charlene L. Muehlenhard, Mary A. Koralewski,
Sandra L. Andrews and Cynthia A. Burdick

Muehlenhard and colleagues were interested in learning how people
initiate dating. Over two-thirds of the males surveyed said they prefer
women to hint about their interest in dating. Less than one-third said
they prefer women who ask directly for a date. It is important, therefore,
to understand how women communicate to men an interest in dating.

The study identified 15 nonverbal cues that express a woman's interest
in dating. Their research shows that men and women agree that a woman
who displays these cues to a man is probably interested in dating him.
Many of the cues are nonverbal behaviors and are listed below. High and
moderate amounts of these cues are seen as expressing interest in dating,
while low amounts communicate disinterest. In addition, women who
use high amounts of the cues are seen as more attractive by men.

Adapted with permission from: Muehlenhard, C.L., Koralewski, M.A., Andrews, S.L.,
& Burdick, C.A. (1986). Cues that convey interest in dating. *Behavior Therapy, 17*, 404-419.

Cue	High Amount	Moderate Amount	Low Amount
Eye Contact	looks at him constantly	looks at him half the time	looks at him very little
Smiling	smiles almost constantly	smiles half the time	does not smile
Lean	leans toward	sits straight up	leans backward
Shoulder Orientation	faces directly (shoulders parallel)	partially faces (shoulders at 45 degree angle)	faces away (shoulders at 90 degree angle)
Distance	18 inches	4 feet	7 feet
Touching	brief touch above knee	brief touch on forearm	no touch
Catches His Eye (while hearing joke	laughs and catches eye	laughs, does not catch eye	does not laugh or catch eye
Attentiveness	stops what she is doing and looks at him	looks away while listening, toward while talking	glances at beginning, but then looks away
Attentiveness (looking at other people)	does not look at other people	looks at other women	looks at other men
Avoids Public Grooming	does not groom	mild grooming	excessive grooming
Animated speech	speaks quickly, accentuates, varied facial expressions	average tone & movement	slow monotone with little movement

42 *Flirting is an ancient practice that has been present throughout history. In this chapter, Moore reports the results of a flirting study conducted in singles bars. Researchers observed women in this setting to see how they selected male partners.*

Nonverbal Courtship Patterns in Women
Context and Consequences

Monica M. Moore

Introduction

Biologically, one of the most important choices made by an organism is the selection of a mate. The evolution of traits that would assist in the identification of "superior mates" prior to the onset of mating is clearly advantageous. One legacy of anisogamy is that errors in mate selection are generally more expensive to females than to males (Trivers 1972). Hence, the females of a wide variety of species may be expected to exhibit traits that would facilitate the assessment of the quality of potential suitors in respect to their inherited attributes and acquired resources. There are many examples of female selectivity in a variety of species, including elephant seals (LeBoeuf and Peterson 1969; Bertram 1975), mice (McClearn and Defries 1973), fish (Weber and Weber 1975), rats (Doty 1974), gorillas (Nadler 1975), monkeys (Beach 1976), birds (Selander 1972; Wiley 1973; Williams 1975), and a few ungulates (Beuchner and Schloeth 1965; Leuthold 1966).

Reprinted by permission of the publisher from "Nonverbal courtship patterns in women: Context and consequences." by Monica M. Moore. *Ethology and Sociobiology, 6*, pp. 237-247. Copyright 1983 by Elsevier Science Publishing Co., Inc.

Very few studies in the area of human mate selection and attraction have focused on the issue of female choice. Fowler (1978) interviewed women to identify the parameters of male sexual attractiveness. The results showed that the male's value as a sexual partner correlated with the magnitude of emotional and material security he provided. Baber (1939) found that women emphasize qualities such as economic status, disposition, family religion, morals, health, and education in a prospective marriage partner, whereas men most frequently chose good looks, morals, and health as important qualities. More recent studies (Coombs and Kenkel 1966; Tavris 1977) also found women rating attributes such as physical attractiveness as less important than did men. Reiss (1960) believes that many more women than men choose "someone to look up to" and Hatkoff and Luswell (1977) presented data that indicated that women want the men with whom they fall in love to be persons whom they can respect and depend on. Daly and Wilson (1978) conclude from cross-cultural data that a male's financial status is an important determinant of his mating success.

Although these reports are valuable, it is clear that the mechanisms and expression of male assessment and female choice in humans have received little attention. In addition, much of the information available regarding human female choice is derived from interviews or questionnaires. Few studies have focused on initial choice situations in field observations. There are several difficulties with a field approach. A major problem surrounds the determination that a choice situation is being observed when verbal information is unavailable. I suggest that this problem may be solved through observations of nonverbal behavior. Indeed, there appears to be a repertoire of gestures and facial expressions that are used by humans as courtship signals (Birdwhistell 1970), much as there is signaling between members of the opposite sex in other species. Even in humans courtship and the choice of a mate have been characterized as largely nonverbal, with the cues being so persuasive that they can, as one observer put it, "turn a comment about the weather into a seductive invitation" (Davis 1971, p. 97).

The focus of much study in the area of nonverbal communication has been description (Scheflen 1965; Birdwhistell 1970; Mehrabian 1972). The primary aim of this research has been the categorization and analysis of nonverbal behaviors. By employing frame-by-frame analysis of films, Birdwhistell and his associates have been able to provide detailed descriptions of the facial expressions and movements or gestures of subjects in a variety of contexts. Observations conducted in this fashion as well as field studies have resulted in the labeling of many nonverbal behaviors as courtship signals. For example, Givens (1978) has described five phases of courtship between unacquainted adults. Scheflen (1965) investigated flirting gestures in the context of psychotherapy, noting that both courtship behaviors and qualifiers of the courtship message were exhibited by therapists and clients. Eibl-Eibesfeldt (1971) used two approaches to describe flirting behavior in people from diverse cultural backgrounds. Employing a camera fitted with right angle lenses to film people without their knowledge, he found that an eyebrow flash combined with a smile was a common courtship behavior. Through comments made to women, Eibl-Eibesfeldt has been able to elicit the "coy glance," an expression combining a half-smile and lowered eyes. Kendon (1975) filmed a couple seated on a park bench in order to document the role of facial expression during a kissing round. He discovered that it was the female's behavior, particularly her facial expressions that functioned as a regulator in modulating the behavior of the male. Cary (1976) has shown that the female's behavior is important in initiating conversation between strangers. Both in laboratory settings and singles' bars conversation was initiated only after the female glanced at the male. These results are valuable in documenting the importance of nonverbal behavior in human courtship. But what is lacking is an ethogram of female solicitation behavior.

The purpose of this study was to describe an ensemble of visual and tactile displays emitted by women during initial meetings with men. I shall argue here that these nonverbal displays are courtship signals; they serve as attractants and elicit the approach of males or ensure the continued attention of males. In order to establish the immediate function of the described behaviors as courtship displays, I employed two classes of evidence described by Hinde (1975) for use in the establishment of the immediate function of a behavior: contextual evidence and consequential evidence. The rationale behind the use of consequential data was that behavior has certain consequences and that if the consequence appears to be a "good thing" it should have relevance for the immediate function of the behavior in question. It should be noted, however, that Eibl-Eibesfeldt (1970) has pointed out the danger in this approach because of interpretations of value on the part of the observer. Therefore, contextual information was provided as further documentation that the nonverbal behaviors in question were courtship signals. Hinde has noted that if certain behaviors are seen in some contexts but are absent in others their function must relate to those contexts in which they were observed. Together these two classes of information provide an indication of the immediate function of the behavior, in this case nonverbal behavior in women interacting with men. Thus, this study consisted of two parts: catalog compilation based on consequential information and validation of the catalog obtained through contextual data.

Development of the Catalog

Method

Subjects. For the initial study, more than 200 subjects were observed in order to obtain data to be used in the development of the catalog of nonverbal solicitation signals. Subjects were judged to be between the ages of 18 and 35 years. No systematic examination was made of background variables due to restrictions imposed by anonymity. All subjects were white and most were probably college students.

Procedure. Subjects were covertly observed in one social context where opportunities for male-female interaction were available, a singles' bar. Subjects were observed for 30 minutes by two trained observers. Focal subjects were randomly selected from the pool of possible subjects at the start of the observation period. We observed a woman only if she was surrounded by at least 25 other people (generally there were more than 50 others present) and if she was not accompanied by a male. In order to record all instances of the relevant behaviors, observers kept a continuous narrative account of all behaviors exhibited by a single subject and the observable consequences of those actions (Altmann 1974). The following criteria were used for identifying behaviors: a nonverbal solicitation behavior was defined as a movement of body part(s) or whole body that resulted in male attention, operationally defined, within 15 seconds following the behavior. Male attention consisted of the male performing one of the following behaviors: approaching the subject, talking to her, leaning toward her or moving closer to her, asking the subject to dance, touching her, or kissing her. Field notes were transcribed from concealed audio tape recorders. Estimates of interobserver reliability were calculated for 35 hours of observation using the formula:

$$\frac{\text{No. of agreements } (A + B)}{\text{No. of agreements } (A + B) + \text{No. seen by B only} + \text{No. seen by A only}}$$

(McGrew 1972). The range of interobserver reliability scores was 0.72-0.98, with the average score equaling .88. Low reliability scores were obtained only for behaviors difficult for an observer to catch in a darkened room, such as glancing behaviors.

Subsequently, five randomly selected subjects were observed for a period of at least one hour. Again observers kept a continuous narrative account of all nonverbal behavior exhibited by the woman.

The behaviors observed in courting women can be conceptualized in various ways: distance categories (Crook 1972), directional versus nondirectional, or on the basis of body part and movement employed in the exhibition of the nonverbal pattern (McGrew 1972). The third framework was chosen because the displays were most discretely partitioned along these dimensions.

Results

Fifty-two different behaviors were exhibited by the subjects in the present study. Nonverbal solicitation behaviors and their frequencies are summarized in Table 1 according to category. These behaviors were highly visible and most appeared very similar in form in each subject. In other words, each behavior was discrete, or distinct from all other solicitation behaviors.

Descriptions of nonverbal solicitation behaviors

Facial and Head Patterns.. A number of different facial and head patterns were seen in the women we observed. All women performed glancing behaviors, although the particular pattern varied among the individual subjects in the duration or length of time involved in eye to eye contact.

Type I glance (the room encompassing glance) was not restricted to an identifiable recipient. It was usually exhibited early in the evening and often was not seen later in the evening, particularly if the woman made contact with a man. The woman moved her head rapidly, orienting her face around the room. This movement was followed by another head movement that reoriented the woman's face to its original position. The total duration of the glance was brief, 5-10 seconds, with the woman not making eye contact with any specific individual. In some women this pattern of behavior was exaggerated: the woman stood up as her glance swept about the room.

The glancing behavior called the *type II glance (the short darting glance)* was a solicitation behavior that appeared directed at a particular man. The woman directed her gaze at the man, then quickly away (within three seconds). The target axis of the horizontal rotation of the head was approximately 25-45 degrees. This behavior was usually repeated in bouts, with three glances the average number per bout.

In contrast, *type III glance (gaze fixate)* consisted of prolonged (more than three seconds) eye contact. The subject looked directly at the man; sometimes her glance was returned. Again, this behavior was seen several times in a period of minutes in some subjects.

Another movement involving the eye area was an *eyebrow flash*, which consisted of an exaggerated raising of the eyebrows of both eyes, followed by a rapid lowering to the normal position. The duration of the raised eyebrow portion of the movement was approximately two seconds. This

Table 1. Catalog of Nonverbal Solicitation Behaviors

Facial and Head Patterns	Frequency	Gestures	Frequency	Posture Patterns	Frequency
Type I glance (room-encompassing glance)	253	Arm flexion	10	Lean	121
		Tap	8	Brush	28
		Palm	18	Breast touch	6
Type II glance (short darting glance)	222				
Type III glance (glaze fixate)	117				
Eyebrow flash	4	Gesticulation	62	Knee touch	25
Head toss	102	Hand hold	20	Thigh touch	23
Neck presentation	58	Primp	46	Foot to foot	14
Hair flip	139	Hike skirt	4	Placement	19
Head nod	66	Object caress	56	Shoulder hug	25
Lip lick	48	Caress (face/hair)	5	Hug	11
Lipstick application	1	Caress (leg)	32	Lateral body contact	1
Pout	27	Caress (arm)	23	Frontal body contact	7
Smile	511	Caress (torso)	8	Hang	2
Coy smile	20	Caress (back)	17	Parade	41
Laugh	249	Buttock tap	8	Approach	18
Giggle	61			Request dance	12
Kiss	6			Dance (acceptance)	59
Whisper	60			Solitary dance	253
Face to face	9			Point/permission grant	62
				Aid solicitation	34
				Play	31

behavior was often combined with a smile and eye contact.

Several behaviors involved the head and neck region. In *head tossing*, the head was flipped backwards so that the face was tilted upwards briefly (less than five seconds). The head was then lowered to its original position. The head toss was often combined with or seen before the *hair flip*. The hair flip consisted of the woman raising one hand and pushing her fingers through her hair or running her palm along the surface of her hair. Some women made only one hand movement, while in others there were bouts of hair stroking; the woman put her hand to her hair several times within a 30-second interval. The *head nod* was seen when the woman was only a short distance from the man. Usually exhibited during conversation, the head was moved forward and backward on the neck, which resulted in the face of the subject moving up and down. Another head pattern was called *face to face*. In this behavior pattern the head and face of the woman were brought directly opposite another person's face so that the noses almost touched, a distance of approximately five cm. A final behavior involving the head and neck was the *neck presentation*. The woman tilted her head sideways to an angle of approximately 45 degrees. This resulted in the ear almost touching the ipsilateral shoulder, thereby exposing the opposite side of the neck. Occasionally the woman stroked the exposed neck area with her fingers.

There were a number of signals that involved the lips and mouth of the observed subjects. *Lipstick application* was a rare behavior. The woman directed her gaze so that she made eye contact with a particular man. She then slowly applied lipstick to her lips. She engaged in this behavior for some time (15 seconds), repeatedly circling her lips. In contrast, the *lip lick* was seen quite often, particularly in certain subjects. The woman opened her mouth slightly and drew her tongue over her lips. Some women used a single lip lick, wetting only the upper or the lower lip, while others ran the tongue around the entire lip area. The *lip pout* was another behavior involving the mouth. The lips were placed together and protruded. Generally, the lower lip was extended somewhat farther than the upper lip, so that it was fuller in appearance.

Smiling was among the most prevalent behaviors observed in the sampled women. The smile consisted of the corners of the mouth being turned upward. This resulted in partial or sometimes full exposure of the teeth. In some women the smile appeared fixed and was maintained for long periods of time. The *coy smile* differed from the smile in that the woman displaying a coy smile combined a half-smile (the teeth were often not displayed or only partially shown) with a downward gaze or eye contact which was very brief (less than three seconds). In the latter case the woman's glance slid quickly away from an onlooker who had become aware that he was being looked at.

Laughing and giggling were generally responses to another person's comments or behavior and were very common. In some women the *laugh* was preceded by a head toss. *Giggling* was less intense laughter. The mouth of the woman was often closed and generally the sounds were softer.

Kissing was rather unusual in the bar context. The slightly protruded lips were brought into contact with another person's body by a forward head movement. Variations consisted of the area touched by the woman's lips. The most common targets were the lips, face, and neck of the man. The woman, however, sometimes puckered her lips and waited, as if "offering" them to the male.

Finally, the *whisper* was used by most of the subjects in the sample. The woman moved her mouth near another person's ear and soft vocalizations presumedly were produced. Sometimes body contact was made.

Gestures. There were several nonverbal patterns that involved movements of the hands and arms. Most were directed at a particular person. Some involved touching another individual. Others functioned at a distance.

Arm flexion occurred when the arm was flexed at wrist and elbow and was moved toward the body. It was often repeated two or three times in a bout. This behavior was often followed by the approach of another individual toward whom the subject gazed. If the male was in close physical proximity, the female sometimes used *tapping* instead to get his attention. The elbow or wrist was flexed repeatedly so that the woman's finger was moved vertically on an object (usually another person's arm).

Women occasionally *palmed*. Palming occurred when the hand was extended or turned so that the palm faced another person for a brief period of time, less than five seconds. In this study, palming was also recorded when the woman coughed or touched herself with the palm up.

In several women rapid movements of the hands and arms were seen accompanying speech. This behavior was labeled *gesticulation*. Arms and hands, while held in front of the woman's torso, were waved or extended upwards in an exaggerated, conspicuous manner. This behavior was often followed by a lean forward on the part of the man.

A hand gesture sometimes initiated by a woman was the *hand hold*. The woman grasped the man's hand so that her palm was next to the man's palm. This occurred on the dance floor as well as when the man was seated at the table with the woman. Generally, this behavior had a long duration, more than one minute.

There were several behaviors that appeared related to each other because they involved inanimate objects. The first of these was the *primp*. In this gesture the clothing was patted or smoothed, although to the observer it appeared in no need of adjustment. A shirt was tucked in or a skirt was pulled down. On the other hand, the *skirt hike* was performed by raising the hem of the skirt with a movement of the hand or arm so that more leg was exposed. This behavior was only performed by two women and was directed at a particular man. When another man looked the skirt was pushed rapidly into place. Instead of patting or smoothing clothing, subjects sometimes ''played with'' an object, called *object caress*. For example, keys or rings were often fondled. Glasses were caressed with the woman sliding her palm up and down the surface of the glass. A cigarette pack was another item frequently toyed with in an object caress.

Finally, many women touched other people in a caressing fashion. Each incidence of caressing was considered separately in terms of the part of the body that was touched, because the message, in each case, may have been quite different. In *caress (face/hair)* the woman moved her hand slowly up and down the man's face and neck area or tangled her hands in his hair. While the couple was seated, women have been observed stroking the man's thigh and inner leg, *caress (leg)*. The *buttock pat*, however, occurred while the couple was standing, often while dancing.

In this gesture the woman moved her hand, palm side down, up and down the man's buttocks. Other items in this group included *caress (arm)*, *caress (torso)*, and *caress (back)*.

Posture patterns. Compared to the two categories just presented, there were some behaviors which involved more of the body in movement. These I called posture patterns. Many of these behaviors could only a be accomplished while the woman was standing or moving about the room.

Lean was a common solicitation pattern. Generally while seated, the woman moved her torso and upper body forward, which resulted in closer proximity to the man. This movement was sometimes followed by a *brush* or a *breast touch*. The brush occurred when brief body contact (less than five seconds) was initiated by the woman against another individual. This occurred when a woman was walking across the room; she bumped into a man. The result was often conversation between the man and the woman. The breast touch also appeared accidental; and it was difficult to tell, except by length of time of contact, whether or not the movement was purposeful. The upper torso was moved so the breast made contact with the man's body (usually his arm). Most often the contact was brief (less than five seconds), but sometimes women maintained this position for several minutes.

There were four other actions that were similar to the brush and breast touch in that the woman made bodily contact with the man. In the *knee touch* the legs were brought into contact with the man's legs so that the knees touched. Interactants were always facing one another while seated. If the man and woman were sitting side by side, the woman may have initiated a *thigh touch*. The leg was brought into contact with the man's upper leg. *Foot to foot* resulted in the woman moving her foot so that it rested on top of the man's foot. Finally, rather than make contact with some part of her own body, an observed woman sometimes took the man's hand and placed it on her body. I called this behavior *placement*. For example, on two occasions, a woman put a man's hand in her lap. Other targets were the thigh or arm.

There was another constellation of behaviors that appeared related to each other. All of these behaviors were variations of some contact made between the woman's upper body and her partner's upper body. These were generally behaviors of long duration, more than one minute. The most common of these behaviors was the *shoulder hug*. In this signal, the partially flexed arm was draped on and around another person's shoulder. In contrast, the *hug* occurred when both arms were moved forward from a widespread position and around the man, thereby encircling him. The duration of his behavior, however, was brief (less than ten seconds). *Lateral body contact* was similar to shoulder hug except that the woman moved under the man's arm so that his arm was draped around her shoulders rather than vice versa. Similarly, *frontal body contact* occurred when the chest and thighs of the woman rested against the chest and thighs of the man. This behavior was like the hug except that there was no squeeze pressure and the arms did not necessarily encircle the other person. This posture pattern was often seen on the dance floor or when a couple was standing at the bar. *Hanging* was similar to frontal body contact except that the man was supporting the woman's weight. This behavior was initiated by the woman who placed her arms around the man's neck. She was then lifted off her feet while her torso and hips rested against the man's chest and hip. This was a behavior low in frequency and brief in duration, less than five seconds.

There were two behaviors that involved whole body movement. These were called *parade* and *approach*. Parade consisted of the woman walking across the room, perhaps on her way to the bar or the restroom. Yet rather than maintaining a relaxed attitude, the woman exaggerated the swaying motion of her hips. Her stomach was held in and her back was arched so that her breasts were pushed out; her head was held high. In general she was able to make herself "look good." The other behavior that involved walking was approach. The woman went up to the man and stood very close to him, within two feet. Usually verbal interaction ensued.

Some women followed an approach with a *request dance*. This was demonstrated nonverbally by the woman pointing and/or nodding in the direction of the dance floor. Two other categories involving dancing behavior were included in the catalog. *Dance (female acceptance)* was included because by accepting a dance with the man the woman maintained his attention. Another dancing behavior was one of the most frequently seen signals. It was called the *solitary dance* because, while seated or standing, the woman moved her body in time to the music. A typical male response was to request a dance.

Just as a woman, in agreeing to dance with a man, was telling him, nonverbally, that he was acceptable for the moment she also told him so when she allowed him to sit at her table with her. Thus, *point/permission grant* was given a place in the catalog. The woman pulled out the chair for the man or pointed or nodded in the direction of the chair. There was generally a verbal component to the signal which could not be overheard.

Aid solicitation consisted of several behaviors that involved the request of help by the subject. For example, the woman handed her jacket to the man and allowed him to help her put it on. Other patterns in this category included indicating that a drink be refilled, waiting to be seated, or holding a cigarette for lighting.

The final category of solicitation behavior was also a variety of posture patterns. Called *play*, these behaviors consisted of the woman pinching the man, tickling him, sticking out her tongue at him, or approaching him from behind covering his eyes. Some women sat on the man's lap, and several women in the sample came up behind men and stole their hats. All of these behaviors were simply recorded as play behavior.

Validation of the Catalog

Method

Subjects. Forty women were covertly observed for the second portion of the study, validation of the catalog. Subjects were judged between the ages of 18 and 35. All subjects were white. Again no systematic examination of background variables was possible.

Procedure. To justify the claim that the nonverbal behaviors described above were courtship signals, that is, carried a message of interest to the observing man, women were covertly observed in different social contexts. The four contexts selected for study were a singles' bar, a university snack bar, a university library, and university Women's Center meetings. These contexts were chosen in order to sample a variety of situations in which nonverbal solicitation might be expected to occur as well as situations in which it was unlikely to be exhibited. The selection of contexts was based on information collected through interviews and pilot observations. If nonverbal solicitation was found in situations where male-female interaction was likely but either was not found or occurred in lower frequencies where male-female interactions were impossible, then the immediate function of nonverbal solicitation can be said to be the enhancement of male-female relationships.

The methodology employed in this section was similar to that used in the development of the catalog. Focal individual sampling was the method of choice for the 40 subjects, ten in each of the four contexts. Each subject was randomly selected from those individuals present at the beginning of the observation period. Sessions were scheduled to begin at 9:00 P.M. and end at 11:00 P.M. in the bar context. This time was optimal because crowd density was at its peak. Sessions in the Women's Center context always began at noon or at 7:00 P.M. because that was the time at which programs were scheduled. Observations were randomly made in both the library and the snack bar contexts; for each context, four sessions were conducted at 11:00 A.M., three at 2:00 P.M., and three at 7:00 P.M. Subjects were observed for a period of one hour. (Any subject who did not remain for one hour of observation was excluded from the analyses.) Observations were conducted using either a concealed audio recorder or, when appropriate, paper and pen. No subject evidenced awareness of being observed. Again, we observed a woman only if she was surrounded by at least 25 other people and if she was not accompanied by a male.

Data for each woman consisted of a frequency measure, the number of nonverbal solicitation behaviors, described above, that she exhibited during the hour of observation. Observers counted not only the total number of nonverbal solicitation behaviors, but also kept a tally of the specific behaviors that were used by each woman.

Results

Frequency and Categorization of Nonverbal Solicitation Behaviors. Data collected on 40 subjects and the respective frequencies of their solicitation displays are given in Table 2. The results show that the emission of the catalogued behaviors was context specific in respect to both the frequency of displays and the number of different categories of the repertoire. The subjects observed in the singles' bar emitted an average of 70.6 displays in the sampled interval, encompassing a mean number of 12.8 different categories of the catalog. In contrast, the corresponding data from the snack bar, library, and women's meetings were 18.6 and 7.5, 9.6 and 4.0, and 4.7 and 2.1, respectively. The asymmetry in display frequency was highly significant. In addition, the asymmetry in the number of categories utilized was also significant.

Rate of display. The quartile display frequencies for the four contexts are given in Figure 1. As can be seen, the display frequency accelerated over time in the singles' bar context but was relatively invariant in the other three contexts.

Frequency of approach. If subjects are pooled across contexts in which males are present and partitioned into high- and low-display categories, where the high display category is defined as more than 35 displays per hour, the data show that the high-display subjects elicited greater than four approaches per hour, whereas low display subjects elicited less than 0.48 approaches per hour. The number of approaches to subjects by a male in each context is presented in Table 2. Approaches were most frequent in the singles' bar where displays were also most frequent.

For the three contexts in which males were present (the singles' bar, the snack bar, and the library), the number of approaches to the subject was compared to the number of categories employed in solicitation displays. Subjects were pooled across these contexts and divided into two groups — those who utilized less than ten categories and those who employed ten or more categories. The results were highly significant; regardless of when the woman utilized a high number of categories she was more likely to be approached by a male.

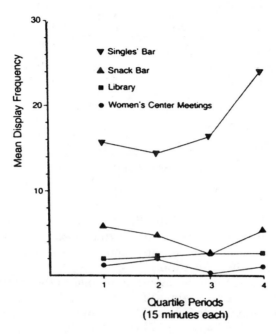

Figure 1

Frequency of occurrence for all solicitation behaviors for each quartile of the observation interval for each of the four social contexts.

Also given in Table 2 are the figures for female-to-male approaches. In both cases (female to male, and male to female), approaches were much higher in the bar context. To show that the number of male approaches correlated with frequency of female solicitation, Spearman rank correlations were determined for these measures. The correlation between number of male approaches and total number of solicitations, across all three contexts, equaled 0.89. Clearly, those women who signaled often were also those who were most often approached by a man; and this relationship was not context specific.

Discussion

The results of this study are in no way discoveries of "new" behaviors. The behaviors catalogued here have been described as courtship behaviors

Table 2. Social Context Display Frequency and Number of Approaches[a]

	Singles' Bar	Snack Bar	Library	Women's Meetings
Number of subjects	10	10	10	10
Total number of displays	706	186	96	47
Mean number of displays	70.6	18.6	9.6	4.7
Mean number of categories utilized	12.8	7.5	4.0	2.1
Number of approaches to the subject by a male	38	4	4	0
Number of approaches to a male by the subject	11	4	1	0

[a]The tabulated data are for a 60-minute observation interval. Assymetry in display frequency: X^2 = 25.079, df = 3, $p < 0.001$; assymetry in number of categories utilized: x^2 = 23.099, df = 3, $p < 0.001$.

by others. But there has been little firm evidence to support this claim of their function, aside from references to context. This study was the first attempt to bring all the behaviors together in catalog form and provide documentation of their function.

When we compare those behaviors contained in the catalog compiled in this study to other descriptions of courtship in humans, we find many areas of congruence. Scheflen (1965) has outlined four categories of heterosexual courtship behavior: courtship readiness, preening behavior, positional cues, and actions of appeal or invitation. Many of the behaviors observed in courting women are similar to those seen by Scheflen during psychotherapy sessions. For example, Scheflen's category of courtship readiness bears resemblance to parade behavior. Preening behaviors, as described by Scheflen, are similar to the hair flip, primp, skirt hike, and object caress catalogued here. Positional cues are found in the catalog under leaning, brushing, and caressing or touching signals. Finally, Scheflen's actions of appeal or invitation are included as aid solicitation, point/permission grant, request dance, palm and solitary dance. What appears to be absent in courting women are the qualifiers of the courtship message observed by Scheflen during psychotherapy.

There is significant continuity between the expressions and gestures described in this study and those Givens (1978) believed to be important during the first four phases of courtship. According to Givens, the essence of the first stage, the attention phase, is ambivalence. Behaviors seen by Givens during this stage and observed in this study include primping, object caressing, and glancing at and then away from the male. During the recognition phase Givens has observed head cocking, pouting, primping, eyebrow flashing and smiling, all of which were seen by me.

During the interaction stage, conversation is initiated and the participants appear highly animated. Indeed, women in this study, while talking to men, appeared excited, laughing, smiling, and gesticulating frequently. Givens has indicated that in the fourth stage, the sexual arousal phase, touching gestures are exchanged. Similarly, it was not unusual to see couples hold hands, caress, hug, or kiss after some period of interaction.

Givens' work has indicated that it is often the female who controls interaction in these early phases. The observations of Cary (1976) seem to bear this out and glancing behavior appears to be a significant part of the female role. In this study glancing often took place over a period of time prior to a male approach. As Crook (1972) has stated, males are generally hesitant to approach without some indication of interest from the partner, and repeated eye contact seems to demonstrate that interest. Rejection behaviors were not catalogued here, but it is entirely possible that one way women reject suitors is by failing to recognize their presence through eye contact.

Eibl-Eibesfeldt has also stressed importance of the eye area in two flirting gestures he has observed in several cultures. The first, a rapid raising and lowering of the eyebrows, accompanied by a smile and a nod, was seen rarely in this study. Raised eyebrows were sometimes seen in the bar context and when directed at a man with a quick glance to the dance floor were often followed by a request to dance. Raised eyebrows also sometimes followed comments by a man when he had joined a woman at her table. Eibl-Eibesfeldt (1970) has also presented pictures of women exhibiting what he calls the coy glance. Although the coy glance was sometimes seen in this study (here called the coy smile), it was more usual for a young American woman to use direct eye contact and a full smile. Yet the fact that these behaviors were observed is significant, and later cross-cultural studies may demonstrate that there are more behaviors that share the courtship message.

It appears then that although glancing behaviors were important in signaling interest, initially, other behaviors seemed to reaffirm the woman's interest later in the observation period. Behaviors such as nodding, leaning close to the man, smiling and laughing were seen in higher frequencies after the man had made contact with the woman and was dancing with her or was seated at her table. This accounts for the rise in frequency of solicitation near the end of the observation period in the bar context. Yet it is difficult to make any firm statements about a sequential pattern in the exhibition of solicitation behavior. Although these behaviors are distinct in form, variability among subjects with regard to timing was great. Neither was it possible to determine the potency of particular behaviors. Indeed, it often appeared as though behaviors had a cumulative effect; that is, the man waited to respond to the woman until after he had observed several solicitations.

However, it is clear that there is a constellation of nonverbal behaviors associated with female solicitation that has been recognized by many investigators in several contexts and with similar results (Morris 1971; Kerdon and Ferber 1973; Nieremberg and Calero 1973; Clore et al. 1975; Key 1975; Knapp 1978; Lockard and Adams 1980). This is strong circumstantial evidence supporting the current results that these are "real" contextually valid movements, not random behaviors. Furthermore, these expressions and gestures appear to function as attractants and advertisers of female interest.

Traditionally, women have had more control in choosing men for relationships, being able to pace the course of sexual advances and having the prerogative to accept or decline proposals (Hatkoff and Luswell 1977). Nonverbal solicitation is only one of the first steps in the sequence of behaviors beginning with mate attraction and culminating with mate selection. However, these courtship gestures and expressions appear to aid the woman in her role as discriminating chooser. Females are able to determine when and where they wish to survey mate potential by exhibiting or withholding displays. They can elicit a high number of male approaches, allowing them to choose from a number of available men. Or they may direct solicitations at a particular male.

What happens after the approach of a man then becomes increasingly important. Much of the basis of actual choice must rest on what the man says to the woman in addition to his behavior toward her and others. It seems reasonable that females would enhance their fitness by making the most informed judgment possible. Yet before interaction is initiated some initial choice is made. These initial impressions and the selection of those men deemed interesting enough to warrant further attention by a woman have been virtually ignored. If, indeed, the woman is exercising her right to choose, what sort of filter system is she using? Which men are chosen for further interaction and which are rejected? Literature cited earlier indicates that behaviors that indicate status, wealth, and dependability are attributes that women may access in initial encounters. At present data are not available to address these issues. But I believe that hypotheses regarding the particulars of human female choice can be tested through covert observation of female invitational behavior. Information obtained through observations in field settings can be added to verbal reports. The results of such a venture may present us with a more complete picture of the levels of selection involved in human female choice.

This research was done in partial fulfillment of the requirements for the doctoral degree in Experimental Psychology at the University of Missouri-Columbia. I wish to thank Esther Thelen and Charles H. Brown for their guidance and Denise Frank, Lynn Ricci, and Jonalee Slaughter for their assistance. Portions of this article were reported at the Meeting of the Animal Behavior Society in Knoxville, Tennessee in 1980.

References

Altmann, J. Observational study of behavior: sampling methods. *Behavior* 49: 227-267 (1974).

Baber, R.E. *Marriage and Family*. New York: McGraw-Hill, 1939.

Beach, R.A. Sexual attractivity, proceptivity and receptivity in female mammals. *Hormones and Behavior* 7: 105-138 (1976).

Bertram, B.C. Social factors influencing reproduction in wild lions. *Journal of Zoology* 177: 463-482 (1975).

Beuchner, J.K., and Schloeth, R. Ceremonial mating system in Uganda kob (*Adenota kob thomase* Neuman). *Zeitschrift fur Tierpsychologie* 22: 209-225 (1965).

Birdwhistell, R.L. *Kinesics and Context*. Philadelphia: University of Pennsylvania Press, 1970.

Cary, M.S. Talk? Do you want to talk? Negotiation for the initiation of conversation between the unacquainted. Ph.D. dissertation, University of Pennsylvania, 1976.

Clore, G.L., Wiggins, N.H., and Itkin, I. Judging attraction from nonverbal behavior: the gain phenomenon. *Journal of Consulting and Clinical Psychology* 43: 491-497 (1975).

Coombs, R.H., and Kenkel, W.F. Sex differences in dating aspirations and satisfaction with computer selected partners. *Journal of Marriage and the Family* 28: 62-66 (1966).

Crook, J.H. Sexual selection, dimorphism, and social organization in primates. In *Sexual Selection and the Descent of Man 1871-1971*, B. Campbell (Ed.). Chicago: Aldine, 1972.

—— The socio-ecology of primates. In *Social Behavior in Birds and Mammals: Essays on the Social Ethology of Animals and Man*, J.H. Crook (Ed.). London: Academic, 1972.

Daly, M., Wilson, M. *Sex, Evolution, and Behavior*. North Scituate, MA: Duxbury, 1978.

Davis, F. *Inside Intuition*. New York: McGraw-Hill, 1971.

Doty, R.L. A cry for the liberation of the female rodent: Courtship and copulation in Rodentia. *Psychological Bulletin* 81: 159-172 (1974).

Eibl-Eibesfeldt, I. *Ethology: The Biology of Behavior*. New York: Holt, Rinehart, and Winston, 1970.

——. *Love and Hate*. New York: Holt, Rinehart and Winston, 1971.

Fowler, H.F. Female choice: An investigation into human breeding system strategy. Paper presented to Animal Behavior Society, Seattle, June 1978.

Givens, D. The nonverbal basis of attraction: Flirtation, courtship, and seduction. *Psychiatry* 41: 346-359 (1978).

Hatkoff, T.S., Luswell, T.E. Male-female similarities and differences in conceptualizing love. In *Love and Attraction*, M. Cook, G. Wilson (Eds.). Oxford: Pergamon, 1977.

Hinde, R.A. The concept of function. In *Function and Evolution in Behavior*, S. Bariends, C. Beer, and A. Manning (Eds.). Oxford: Clarendon, 1975.

Kendon, A. Some functions of the face in a kissing round. *Semiotica* 15: 299-334 (1975).

Kendon, A., and Ferber, A. A description of some human greetings. In *Comparative Ecology and Behavior of Primates*, R.P. Michael and J.H. Crook (Eds.). London: Academic, 1973.

Key, M.R. *Male/Female Language*. Metuchen, NJ: Scarecrow, 1975.

Knapp, M.L. *Nonverbal Communication in Human Interaction*. New York: Holt, Rinehart, and Winston, 1978.

LeBoeuf, B.J., and Peterson, R.S. Social status and mating activity in elephant seals. *Science* 163: 91-93 (1969).

Leuthold, W. Variations in territorial behavior of Uganda kob *Adenota kob thomasi* (Neumann 1896). *Behaviour* 27: 215-258 (1966).

Lockard, J.S., and Adams, R.M. Courtship behaviors in public: Different age/sex roles. *Ethology and Sociobiology* 1(3): 245-253 (1980).

McClearn, G.E., and Defries, J.C. *Introduction to Behavioral Genetics*. San Francisco: Freeman, 1973.

McGrew, W.C. *An Ethological Study of Children's Behavior*. New York: Academic, 1972.

Mehrabian, A. *Nonverbal Communication*. Chicago: Aldine, 1972.

Morris, D. *Intimate Behavior*. New York: Random House, 1971.

Nadler, R.D. Sexual cyclicity in captive lowland gorillas, *Science* 189: 813-814 (1975).

Nieremberg, G.I., and Calero, H.H. *How to Read a Person Like a Book*. New York: Hawthorne, 1973.

Reiss, I.L. Toward a sociology of the heterosexual love relationship. *Marriage and Family Living* 22: 139-145 (1960).

Scheflen, A.E. Quasi-courtship behavior in psychotherapy. *Psychiatry* 28: 245-257 (1965).

Selander, R.K. Sexual selection and dimorphism in birds. In *Sexual Selection and the Descent of Man 1871-1971*, B. Campbell (Ed.). Chicago: Aldine, 1972.

Tavris, C. Men and women report their views on masculinity. *Psychology Today* 10: 34-42 (1977).

Trivers, R.L. Parental investment and sexual selection. In *Sexual Selection and the Descent of Man 1871-1971*, B. Campbell (Ed.). Chicago: Aldine, 1972

Weber, P.G., and Weber, S.P. The effect of female color, size, dominance and early experience upon mate selection in male convict cichlids, *cichlosoma nigrofasciatum Gunther* (pisces, cichlidae). *Behaviour* 56: 116-135 (1975).

Wiley, R.H. Territoriality and nonrandom mating in sage grouse. *Centrocercus urophasiamis. Animal Behavior Monographs* 6: 85-169 (1973).
Williams, G.C. *Sex and Evolution.* Princeton, NJ: Princeton University Press, 1975.

We have all heard of the look of love. In this chapter, the non-verbal elements of this look are described by Douglas and Atwell, concentrating on the voice and the eyes in expressing love.

43

Learning to Love

Jack D. Douglas
and Freda Cruse Atwell

Soft, gentle, and rhythmical sounds of peacefulness, reassurance, and love. When the human infant is born (and probably while in utero), the infant is genetically primed to respond with reassurance to the soft, gentle beat of the human heart. If a metronome is set to beat softly at the same rate as the human heart at rest, the baby is calmed by it, though not nearly as much as by the sound of a restful heartbeat. It seems that the baby when cuddled and suckled can respond emotionally to the reassuring heartbeat of the mother and others at the same time he or she responds to the soft, tender caressing.

Human vision is not clearly focused in the first several weeks and the infant learns to focus visual attention and distinguish visual patterns only slowly. First the child focuses attention on light and colors. Because pattern recognition involves immensely more complex neural processing of information, it is not surprising that this develops more slowly. But, from what we have already seen about the vital importance of the development of attachment, it is not too surprising to find that among the first visual patterns that a baby learns to recognize and respond to are those of the human face. First the baby recognizes the eyes and focuses attention on them, especially when they are brought near his or her own. Then the baby recognizes the rest of the face and begins to explore it with his or her own eyes. The child begins to show flickering patterns of smiling on his or her own face. Sometime between two and four months old, the child is able to recognize the complex pattern of facial expression we call a smile. Then the child begins to respond to the smile by smiling. Then the child smiles independently and elicits a smile in response. Smiling is one of the best-studied infant expressions (see Spitz and Wolf, 1946; Bowlby, 1979, pp. 37-40). For cross-cultural evidence of the strong genetic priming, see Landau (1977) and Super and Harkness (1982). Blind babies initially smile like seeing babies but, of course, do not develop the smiling response to adoration. Smiling is the beginning of the look of love. And it is the look of love that is the most convincing communication of love for human beings.

Any human experience that is vital to our survival and development normally makes use of several channels of perception and communication. This high "redundancy," or repetition, of love messages makes it far more likely they will be received and understood. Lower animals, as we are all aware from our close experience with dogs and cats, make far more use of taste and smell than we do. These remain important in our lives. It is even possible that they are far more important in building our early love partnerships than developmental psychologists have yet found. We are all aware from everyday experience that they are important to us adults sexually. But hearing and vision are far more important in human life than taste or smell. They are certainly the dominant senses in perceiving and communicating love. We have already seen how important the sound of love, especially the tone of love, is in human life. The looks of love, as perceived through vision, are even more important. The looks of love speak far louder to us than words, even louder than the very meaningful tone of love.

Feelings are the soul, the heart, the inner core of the human being. Feelings are of vital importance to us in themselves, but feelings also tell us most reliably what others will think about us and do toward us. If they love us, they will do all they can to help us. If they hate us, they will do all they can to hurt us. (Of course, situational perceptions and estimates of "interests" also affect our actions, until our emotions reach "passionate" levels and sweep away reason and self-control.) We need desperately to know how they feel about us. Our eyes are our most dependable means of determining what they feel toward us and all other signs of their feelings, such as their tones of voice, are generally interpreted in the context of what we see their feelings to be, at least once vision is fully developed (during the first year; see Plutchik and Kellerman, 1980; Ekman, 1972; Ekman et al., 1972; Izard, 1971, 1980).

Just as our eyes are the primary means by which we see their feelings, so their eyes are a primary means by which we perceive their feelings. Their eyes are the first important portal into their own souls. This is why writers have always seen the eyes as "soulful." Think how common it is to hear statements such as, "I could see from his eyes that he didn't mean it." Authors often talk about eyes "clouding over" when the person is angry, or "brightening" when they are joyful or loving. Regardless of whether there is a general darkening or brightening of eyes, the black pupil of the eye expands and contracts in response to our emotions. We subconsciously respond to those pupil contractions and expansions. When we are joyful or positively excited in any way by a person we are looking at, our pupils expand; when we are angry at them, our pupils contract. While we are not normally consciously aware of these pupil movements, our own feelings respond to them. When we see pupils looking at us expand, we respond more positively toward that person than we would otherwise have done; and when we see pupils contract, we feel less positive toward that person (Morris, 1977.) The baby's eyes, like his or her entire body and his or her basic patterns of action, are different from those of adults in ways that will elicit love from adults. The baby's pupils are larger in proportion to the eyes' total size than they will be when he or she grows up, thus eliciting more favorable emotional response. It may also be significant that babies often have lighter-colored eyes than when they grow up, because the lighter color sets off the black of the pupils.

Most of the information given off by the eyes about the feelings of the person do not come from the eyes themselves. Rather, the information comes from the gaze behavior of the eyes and, above all, from the facial expressions around the eyes, especially from the movements of the eyelids, the corners of the eyelids, and the eyebrows. Gaze behavior tells us when someone is paying attention to us and a great deal about the nature of this attention. The eyeballs of other primates are dark. The human eyeball is white. This, of course, sets off the pupils, allowing us to determine better whether they like or dislike us. But it also allows us to tell far better what the exact directions of their gazes are. We can track the movement of a viewer's eyes extremely rapidly and accurately. By doing so, we can tell just how long they look at us, whether they look us in the eye or look at some other part of our body (some being quite revealing, as when someone stares at your breasts or pubic region), whether they "stare" or look "shifty-eyed" (and all variations in between), whether they look intimate (close) or distant, and so on. An immense amount of information is conveyed about a person's feelings, thoughts, and intentions by gaze behavior. Consider, for example, Desmond Morris's example about a man looking at a beautiful woman and her looking back in return:

> In ordinary conversation, it is the moments where the eyes make brief contact, at the point of handing over the speaking role, that the variations in attention make themselves felt. It is there that the amorous male holds on a little too long. As he answers the beautiful girl's last statement he begins talking and reaches the point where normally he would turn away, but instead he is still staring at her. This makes her uncomfortable, because she is forced either to lock eyes with him, or to look away from him while is talking. If he continues to talk and stare while she deflects her eyes, it puts her into the "shy" category, which she resents. If she boldly locks eyes with him, then he has forced her into a "lover's gaze," which she also resents. But the chances are that he will not go this far. He will only increase his gaze-time by a tiny amount, just long enough for the message to get across without creating any embarrassment [Morris, 1977, pp. 75-76].

Gaze behavior is very important in communicating love. Someone who looks "shifty-eyed," looks "off into the distance," or "averts" the eyes from you entirely is not communicating a sincere love. (A shy lover may stare downward, probably at his or her feet, and dart a quick glance up at your eyes every now and then to see what you're feeling; but even that is not really being "shifty-eyed." It's honest enough; it's simply an insecure love.) The mother who loves her baby securely shows the full-faced, steady-eyed look of love, often "gazing" for 20 seconds or more (Stern, 1977, p. 18). As we described it above in our depiction of the primal scene of love, the mother often holds the baby's face directly in front of hers at just the right distance (approximately a foot away) so that she can focus her eyes completely on the baby's eyes and she looks fully into the baby's eyes with complete intimacy, that is, for the longest period of unblinking eye-fixation on the other's eyes found in human experience. She and her baby are looking into each other's souls. They are *communing* with each other, expressing and receiving adoration love and the sense of self. But, as important as gaze behavior is, it is not as important as the full facial expression. The look that the mother and child use to communicate their feelings of adoration love to each other involves this full gaze into each other's eyes, the eyelids, the corner of the eyelids, and the corner of the mouth. All the rest of the face (the eyebrows, forehead, the corners of the nostrils, and the cheeks) is loose, largely expressionless.

Consider the general expression of happiness or joyfulness, such as you might show a friend or even a new acquaintance of whom you think well. The *look of friendly greeting* is a full smile, a "happy face." The full smile is a very distinctive human facial expression. Other primates obviously feel and express good feelings to their fellows, but the human being does so far more and does so in this very distinctive way, which indicates that expressing joy toward and with other human beings is far more important for us than for other primates. Our guess is that all primates that have very extensive patterns of friendly and cooperative behavior will be found to have some similar means of expressing their joy-in-the-presence-of-others.

The joyful smile involves pulling the lips back wide (with lips either parted or closed) and the eyelids wide. As the intensity of the joy increases, the lips are pulled back so far the mouth opens, and the corners of the eyelids are pulled back so far that the eyebrows and forehead begin to crease. At the extreme, the whole face may "light up" and the joy be vented by laughter. This happy face is the one we see most of the time when mothers are playing with their babies. It expresses their common joy in each other, but it is not the look of adoration love.

The look of adoration love is rarely seen in photographs because it is *inherently linked* (as an undertone — see below) to the feeling and state of intimacy, and thus is inherently so private that it is nearly impossible to show it in full public view to strangers. It occurs very rarely by itself in movies and then almost always fleetingly. When it does occur in movies, it is almost always combined with sexual excitement in the look of Erotic love, which we shall come to next.

The look of adoration love relaxes the happy smile. The muscles that pulled back the lips and eyes in the look of joy are relaxed so completely that the eyes become languorous, possibly even sleepy, and the lips show only a faint smile or, at the extreme, may even turn down slightly. This is a look of adoration-love. We can see this look of love most clearly in Western paintings of the Mother of God or others adoring Christ or other children, as, for example, in Leonardo's "Virgin of the Rocks." (The smile of the Mona Lisa is enigmatic because the eyes show moderate adoration, but the mouth is smiling too much, and with a hint of coy flirtation, to communicate adoration-love.)

The look of sexual excitement involves a parting of the lips but still with relaxed muscles at the corner of the mouth, and an uplifting of the eyelids (and dilated pupils) at the far corners. This look can be made a sexual stare, or even an aggressive male look of sexual attack; by pulling the mouth down at the corners, jutting the jaw, knitting the brow, and tensing the muscles under the eyes. But it can also be made a look of adoration-love-and-sexual-excitement (that is, Erotic love) by showing the look of adoration love and adding the open mouth and a slightly tensed stare. This is the look that Marilyn Monroe and her Hollywood managers exaggerated slightly in the sexual direction (suggesting a somewhat more aroused sexual state and less adoration feeling, as happens during intercourse). When combined, it is a look of *Erotic love*. Sexual (lustful) arousal without adoration love looks aggressive, not adoring and intimate.

The look of sexual orgasm or ecstasy involves an even more open mouth (even of the tongue jutting out), the eyelids pulled down but the eyebrows up, and the eyeballs rolling toward the forehead (giving the appearance of sinking into oneself). This is a look of total joy, plus adoration love, plus sexual excitement with the glazed, rolling eyeballs added, but with the eyelids almost closed. The look of happy peacefulness that follows ecstasy is the face almost completely at rest, as in quiet, happy sleep.

Psychologists have shown what novelists and others who have closely described our everyday life emotions and patterns of behavior have always known: human beings have immensely complex and subtle facial expressions, tones of voice, and touches that communicate our immensely complex and subtle emotions to other human beings. By the time we become adults, our conscious minds are concentrated far more on our verbal forms for communicating emotions, because consciousness is largely specialized for processing verbal behavior. But our vastly more complex subconscious minds are still continually processing and using these vastly complex body-language messengers of emotions to experience others for their own sake (when they are intimates) and to help us decide how others really feel about us, how they will really act toward us, what we can really count on their doing because they are emotionally committed to doing it. We all take it for granted that words can easily lie, but that the body language of emotions, while it can be manipulated too, is far more reliable as signs of our feelings and emotional commitments, so we rely on them as the sources of our most important information about our relations with other human beings. We all know the implications of what one young woman told us: "He always said he loved me and he did all the right things sexually—he was a real sexual technician, right out of the sex manuals. But whenever he said 'I love you,' I looked in his eyes and there was nothing there." If we had asked her what the look of love is, what it was she was looking for in his eyes, she would not have known what to say and, in fact, would probably have thought it bizarre that we would feel the need to ask. She knew subconsciously what the look of love is and she knew how vastly important it is. But, like almost all human beings, she would not know how to express the look clearly in words.

References

Bowlby, John. 1979. *The Making and Breaking of Affectional Bonds*. London: Tavistock.

Ekman, P. 1972. "Universal and Cultural Differences in Facial Expression of Emotion." In *Nebraska Symposium on Motivation 1971*, edited by J.K. Cole. Lincoln: University of Nebraska Press.

_____. et al. 1972. *Emotion in the Human Face*. New York: Pergamon.

Izard, C. E. 1971. *The Face of Emotion*. New York: Appleton-Century-Crofts.

_____. 1980. "Aspects of Consciousness and Personality in Terms of Differential Emotions Theory." Pp. 165-187 in *Emotion*, edited by Robert Plutchik and Henry Kellerman. New York: Academic Press.

Landau, R. 1977. "Spontaneous and Elicited Smiles and Vocalizations of Infants in Four Israeli Environments." *Developmental Psychology*, 13: 389-400.

Morris, Desmond. 1977. *Manwatching*. New York: Abrams.

Plutchik, Robert, and Henry Kellerman, eds. 1980. *Emotion*. New York: Academic Press.

Spitz, R. A. and K. M. Wolf. 1946. "The Smiling Response." *Genetic Psychology Monographs*. 34:57-125.

Stern, Daniel. 1977. *The First Relationship*. Cambridge, MA: Harvard University Press.

Super, C. M. and S. Harkness, 1982. "The Development of Affect in Infancy and Early Childhood." Pp. 1-19 in *Cultural Perspectives on Child Development*, edited by D. A. Wagner and H. W. Stevenson. San Francisco: W. H. Freeman.

44

Power plays an important role in most relationships, but it is particularly important in business organizations. Andersen and Bowman discuss the nonverbal cues of power in professional relationships. The chapter reviews research which examined power and presents conclusions regarding the major factors.

Positions of Power:
Nonverbal Influence in Organizational Communication

Peter A. Andersen
and Linda L. Bowman

Power has been recognized as a crucial construct in the study of human behavior. Bertrand Russell (1938) maintained that "the fundamental concept in social science is Power, in the same sense in which Energy is the fundamental concept in physics" (p. 10). Unfortunately, power has been recognized only recently as an important concept in organizational and applied communication. Tompkins (1984) concluded: "*Rarely is power mentioned* even as a variable in organizational life" (p. 706). Moreover, the role played by *communication* in the creation and maintenance of organizational power has rarely been mentioned until the last few years (Conrad, 1983; Conrad & Ryan, 1985).

Nonetheless, the importance of power in organizational communication is undeniable. Recently, a few excellent essays have shown that communication researchers should incorporate power as a focus of organizational studies (Conrad, 1983; Conrad & Ryan, 1985; Tompkins & Cheney, 1985: Turow, 1985). Tompkins and Cheney (1985) have suggested that power may be the overarching factor in determining the regularities of organizational behavior. In his major work on leadership Burns (1978)

Edited with permission from Andersen, P.A. and L.L. Bowman (in press), "Positions of power: Nonverbal influence in organizational communication." *Journal of Applied Communication Research.*

maintained the hope that human personal obsession with power in the office, bedroom, and corridors be systematically analyzed in the context of human motives, constraints, and resources.

Theory and epistemology in organizational communication have been in flux in recent years. Traditional and quantitative models have been supplemented by a number of interpretive, naturalistic, and critical models (Bantz, 1983; Conrad, 1983; Conrad & Ryan, 1985; Deetz, 1982; Deetz & Kersten, 1983; Putnam, 1982, 1983; Tompkins & Cheney, 1983, 1985). One primary benefit of these developments for organizational communication theory is the restoration of communication as the focus of organizational studies. The purpose of the present article is to demonstrate the important role of nonverbal communication in organizational communication research in general and for organizational power studies in particular. Three theoretical premises and their corollaries provide the basis for a discussion of specific nonverbal actions which form the basis of organizational power.

Premise 1: Organizational power is exercised covertly through deep structures and implicit actions.

Recent research has shown that power lies in deep structures not in surface features such as explicit rules or verbal descriptions. Deep structures are unexamined, preconscious guidelines and constraints on power which are taken for granted by organization members (Conrad, 1983; Conrad & Ryan, 1985; Deetz & Kersten, 1983). The power structure becomes conscious only in relatively rare cases when employees violate the rules of deep structure (Conrad & Ryan, 1985). Usually these structures are not articulated through overt threats and promises, nor are they directly observable or easily measured (Conrad & Ryan, 1985; Tompkins & Cheney, 1985). These influences often produce inaction by organization members (Conrad, 1983). It is important to recognize that these structures consist of implicit rules that rarely reach conscious levels (Conrad & Ryan, 1985; Deetz & Kersten, 1983).

Largely it is through nonverbal actions that implicit, preconscious, power relationships are established and can be studied. Nonverbal communication is subtle, spontaneous, and is usually communicated without conscious awareness as an automatic reflection of underlying feelings (P. Andersen, 1986). Burgoon (1985) maintained that nonverbal communication often operates in an automatic, unmonitored, and "mindless" fashion. Mehrabian (1971, 1981) detailed dozens of studies which show that nonverbal communication is the implicit communication system through which silent power is manifested. This link between nonverbal communication and implicit power structures is a mandate to incorporate nonverbal analyses into studies of managerial and organizational communication.

Premise 2: Uncertainty characterizes organizational power structure.

Formal power structures can be determined by looking at an organizational chart but informal power networks may be both less obvious and more important. Thompson (1967) maintained that complex organizations are characterized by uncertainty and organizational politics which result in autonomy and independence from the formal structure. Thompson (1967) argued that "individuals may maintain or enhance their positions regardless of the official authorized positions they hold. We are thus able to 'explain' those situations in organizations in which it is said there is a 'power behind the throne,' an 'invisible government' or a 'kitchen cabinet'" (pp. 125-126). Hickson, et al. (1971) suggested "organizations are conceived of as interdepartmental systems in which a major task is coping with uncertainty" (p. 217). According to Kanter (1979) bureaucracies are supposed to reduce the uncertain to the predictable and routine, but much uncertainty remains.

As this article will attempt to show, nonverbal communication provides powerful information which reduces uncertainty and both establishes and reveals power structures. Posture, gaze, expression, and position establish and communicate the real power structure of the organization. Mehrabian (1981) maintained,

> The metaphor of power and fearlessness underlies the representation of status. Thus, lower status people assume postures that indicate weakness; they speak softly and are more watchful and tenser in presence of high status others (p. 71).

All human interactions consist of both a report or informational aspect and a command or relationship aspect which is primarily expressed nonverbally (Watzlawick, Beavin & Jackson, 1967). Each communicative act in an organization provides nonverbal cues which establish, over time, the informal power structure of the organization.

Premise 3: Power is dynamic and emerges from relationships not from formal organizational structures and positions.

Experts echo the theme that power is a function of communication relationships not a property of things, individuals, or structure. Burns (1978) argued:

power is first of all a relationship and not merely an entity to be passed
around like a baton or hand grenade . . . it involves the intention or
purpose of both the power holder and the power recipient and hence
it is collective, not merely the behavior of one person (p. 13).

Hickson (1971) likewise argued that "Power is a property of the social
relationship not the actor" (p. 217). Recent approaches view organizational
power relationships as dynamic, changing processes in which employees'
decisions and actions are influenced by memories of their past actions,
their interpretations of the situation, and their projections of future actions
(Pfeffer, 1981; Conrad, 1983). Even "fixed" organizational structures emerge
through communication relationships (Conrad, 1983; Putnam, 1983).

Communication theory and research has established that nonverbal
communication has the primary role in establishing relationships (cf P.
Andersen, 1985; Bateson, 1955; Burgoon & Saine, 1978; Knapp, 1983;
LaFrance & Mayo, 1978; Watzlawick, Beavin & Jackson, 1967). This article
details the numerous nonverbal cues that establish power relationships
in modern organizations, and calls for research which focuses on the
nonverbal communication of power.

Nonverbal Research in Organizational Communication

Traditional organizational communication textbooks rarely mention
nonverbal communication. Laudably, a few texts present such a discussion
but generally without much concern for its theoretical or practical
importance (Goldhaber, 1974; Huseman, Lahiff & Hatfield, 1976; Koehler,
Anatol & Applbaum, 1981): Traditional organizational network research
also lacks nonverbal data (Albrecht & Ropp, 1982). Even the new critical
and interpretive research which focuses on communication, messages,
relationships, and meaning has systematically excluded nonverbal
communication. Recently, researchers and theorists have called for
studying conversation, discussion, discourse, enthymatic structure,
language, language-in-action, metaphors, speech, stories, talk, and
vocabulary with scarcely a mention of nonverbal communication (cf.
Conrad, 1983; Conrad & Ryan, 1985; Deetz, 1982; Deetz & Kersten, 1983;
Fairhurst, Greene & Snavely, 1984; Jablin, 1984; Putnam, 1982; Putnam,
1983; Ragan, 1983; Riggs, 1983; Tompkins & Cheney, 1985; Trujillo, 1983).
Occasionally, researchers deign to recognize nonverbal behavior. For
example, Tompkins and Cheney (1985) suggested that monitoring and
dispensing rewards to subordinates are nonverbal much of the time but
they fail to develop any theory, research strategies, or recommendations
as a result. The present article is consistent with the position taken by

Albrecht and Ropp (1982) who contended that, "For the communication researcher, verbal and nonverbal behaviors of interactants provide core data for analysis" (p. 168).

The Power Domain

The power construct has been studied under a variety of labels which generally reference the same domain of communication including: assertiveness, authority, control, coercion, compliance, dominance, power, social influence, and status. *Power* typically refers to the ability to influence others to do what one wants (Berger, 1985; Henley, 1977; Patterson, 1983). *Status* references one's position in society which generally contributes to power and dominance (Henley, 1977; Patterson, 1983). *Dominance* refers to one's relative position of power in relation to other's (Duran, Jensen, Prisbell & Rosoff, 1979; Patterson, 1983). We view these terms as referencing a single dimension of interpersonal behavior often labeled *Control* (Burgoon & Hale, 1984; Duran, et al., 1979). Next, the various codes of nonverbal communication will be systematically examined to demonstrate the critical role played by nonverbal communication in organizational power.

Physical Appearance

A person's physical appearance communicates at the outset of every interaction and conveys power primarily through attire and physical size. Attire creates first impressions by communicating a number of simultaneous messages. Fowles (1974) maintained, "Our clothes broadcast our sex, our rank, and our up-to-dateness" (p. 348). Formal dress has been found to be an indicant of increased power and control (Brown, 1965; Bickman, 1974; Mehrabian, 1976; Molloy, 1976; Morris, 1977). Mehrabian (1976) asserted that people who select formal dress are tapping the dominance dimension, which may explain why this style of dress persists in the business setting, despite some relaxation of formal dress requirements characteristic of corporations in the past. The suit, in particular, is a symbol of dominance in the organization (Mehrabian, 1976). Molloy, in his best selling book, "Dress for Success," asserted that most authority is transmitted by dark suits. He also claimed that the pinstripe is the most authoritative pattern and that an expensive conservative tie is a vital suit accessory for it symbolizes respectability and responsibility though no evidence for his assertions are provided (Molloy, 1976).

A uniform is a unique form of dress in that it both conceals and reveals status within the group while suppressing other status cues (Joseph & Alex,

1972). The uniform is a certificate of legitimacy and can elicit conformity if it symbolizes authoritative power, as in the case of guard or police uniforms. In a study by Bickman (1974), people more often complied with requests made by an experimenter dressed as a guard than one dressed as a civilian or milkman. Although a uniform affords the wearer a certain authority at times, organization members who work in uniforms generally have lower status than individuals who work in street clothes (Koehler, et al., 1981).

High status dress simultaneously creates perceptions of power and induces conformity. Lefkowitz, Blake, and Mouton (1955), found that when a high status person violated a law, there was a significant increase in the rate of violation by others. Knowles (1973) reported passersby resisted penetrating the boundaries of an interacting social group when the group members wore higher status attire. In an experiment in an uncrowded college library, students fled more rapidly when space was invaded by a well-dressed man than a casually dressed man (Barash, 1973). Although dress provides a channel for expressing individuality, conformity is usually rewarded in a business organization (Scheflen, 1972). Mehrabian (1976) argued that conservative and traditional business dress developed because such attire implied status, respectability, permanence, and trustworthiness. It may be that variation in dress is negatively evaluated as an indicant of instability in the organization setting.

A person's height and physical size is an important component of power and status (Mehrabian, 1972). This attribution may have its roots in the physical advantages that these characteristics gave our ancestors during hand to hand combat (Henley, 1977). The "height is power" phenomenon places short men and most women at a disadvantage; having to look up creates a position of deference (Henley, 1977). Increasing the appearance of physical size can increase dominance (Scheflen, 1972). "Standing tall is in itself a good way of achieving dominance" (Henley, 1977, p. 89). During a confrontation, the act of "standing over another or the more abbreviated displays of height (i.e., raising one's head or brow while looking down) have the effect of 'cutting the opponent down to size' symbolically" (Remland, 1982a, p. 84). Not surprisingly, a slumped posture or a curled up position is submissive as it creates a smaller appearance (Morris, 1977).

Kinesics

Kinesics, communication through bodily movement, gesture, posture, and facial expression has a reciprocal relationship with power.

Posture and Position

Kinesic postures and positions correspond to organizational postures and positions. In general, superiors are more kinesically expansive in both standing and seated positions (Remland, 1982b) than subordinates. One expansive body position is the arms-akimbo position which is more frequently used when addressing a low-status person than a high-status person (Mehrabian, 1968b; Scheflen, 1972). Likewise, Scheflen (1972) noted that individuals who hook their thumbs in their belts are asserting dominance through the same expansiveness analog.

Relaxation is a power cue since higher-status individuals generally are more relaxed. This is probably due to the fact that the powerful can afford to relax, whereas the weak must remain watchful (Prisbell, 1982). Research has shown that when two strangers meet the more relaxed is of higher-status (Mehrabian, 1971; Mehrabian & Friar, 1969). Similarly, among acquaintances Mehrabian and Friar (1969) found that high-status listeners are more relaxed than low-status listeners. Remland (1981) reported that higher status individuals in organizations can behave in a more relaxed and inattentive fashion than those of lower status. The degree of reclining limb asymmetry, and movement are important correlates of high status in contrast to the extremely submissive cues of bodily rigidity and symmetry, like soldiers standing at attention (Mehrabian, 1972, 1976). High status individuals can exhibit limb asymmetry by sprawling or putting a foot up, whereas low status individuals must sit erect (LaFrance & Mayo, 1978; Mehrabian, 1972, 1976). However, Scheflen (1972) suggests that sideways head tilts are submissive postures, whereas holding the head high signals dominance. Mehrabian and Friar (1969) found that closed, as opposed to open, arm positions are associated with higher status, at least for females. Mehrabian (1971) maintained that since standing is less relaxed than sitting, seated positions are high status positions. Finally, people are most relaxed when interacting with a person of low status, moderately relaxed when interacting with those of equal status and least relaxed with a person of high status (Mehrabian, 1968a, 1968b, 1972).

Movement

Research demonstrates that the higher-status persons have access to more locations than lower-status persons (Mehrabian, 1971). Access to managers and executive officers in most organizations is quite limited for most employees, though managers typically have access to their subordinates. Power is also a function of who goes first through a door. Typically the higher-status person precedes another through the door (Goffman, 1967) although this is confounded by age, sex, and physical size. Inconvenience displays are usually performed by lower status persons. Morris (1977) asserts that low-ranking individuals must lower their bodies in the presence of a high-ranked person. However, it is also customary to rise in the presence of a high-status other. This kinesic contradiction may confuse subordinates but can be resolved by placing the high-status person in a seated but elevated position (such as a judge in a courtroom).

Gesture

Surprisingly little research has examined gestural concomitants of power and status. Drawings of men were judged as most subordinate, insignificant, and humble when they show hands behind the back and most powerful when gesticulating (Henley, 1977). Steepling, the gesture of touching the fingertips together in a raised position is perceived as a confident, proud gesture allegedly associated with high-status individuals (Henley, 1977). Pointing at someone is a dominant gesture which often occurs in escalating verbal conflicts (Scheflen, 1972) and communicates disrespect for another's body (Remland, 1981). Henley (1977) suggested that gestures directing another person from a distance are a power prerogative.

Facial Expression

The face conveys emotional states and evaluations better than any other part of the body. Not surprisingly, numerous dominance and submission messages are sent via facial expressions. No simple relationship exists between status and one of the most common facial expressions, the smile. Among both primates and humans, smiling is a submissive gesture often displayed by an animal to appease a dominant aggressor. Women smile considerably more than men, a reflection of their traditionally submissive status. Kennedy and Camden (1983) found that women smiled significantly more than men when taking their speaking turn, evidently as a way to soften the blow of turn-taking as an apology or act of submission. They also found that smiling women were more likely to be interrupted than smiling men. At times, laughing or smiling can symbolize power. Remland (1982a) argued that in adversial proceedings (e.g., courtrooms, task discussions), smiling ridicules the claims of another and suggests their arguments should not be taken seriously. Likewise, sarcastic smiles and disrespectful giggles may be used by a high-status but not a low-status person.

Other facial expressions more clearly communicate power. Scheflen (1972) argued that a protruded jaw is a masculine dominance expression. Likewise, Henley (1977) maintained the jutting chin, along with overhanging eyebrows, frowns, drawn muscles, and the unwavering stare constitute the stern face of authority. Koehler, et al., (1981) mentioned a specific set of facial expressions including the reddened face, furrowed brow, and tightened shoulders, are commonly used by supervisors who are having difficulty refraining from berating a delinquent employee. Exaggerated facial expressions of displeasure such as boredom or disgust emphasize disagreement and disrespect for another individual (Remland, 1982a). Porter and Roberts (1976) concluded that the face is one of the two nonverbal modes of communication of most interest to organizational researchers. Since kinesic displays co-occur with talk during face to face interaction and since such displays may severely modify verbal messages, studies of talk should also examine kinesic behavior whenever possible.

Oculesics

Eye contact or gazing is used to communicate an enormous range of messages including cues of control and power. In one study, recipients of prolonged gazes perceived the looker to be more dominant than recipients of brief gazes (Thayer, 1969). This perception may have early origins, since direct gaze is a dominant act for both primates and in primitive societies as well as in contemporary societies (Burgoon & Saine, 1978; Cook, 1979; Ellsworth, Carlsmith, & Hensen, 1972; LaFrance & Mayo, 1978). Absence of eye contact at key moments in a conversation may signal submissiveness, especially in women. Kennedy and Camden (1983) found that, during a group discussion, women were interrupted significantly more often than men when they did not look at the turn-taker. Mehrabian (1971) claimed that frequent blinking during conversation may imply weakness and submissiveness. Two studies found that dominant people employ more gaze (Kendon & Cook, 1969; Strongman & Chapness, 1968) but Crouch and Koll (1979) failed to replicate this finding. Fromme and Beam (1974) found that high-dominant subjects moved closer when gazed at, while low-dominant subjects moved farther away, though this behavior was more pronounced in males than in females.

Social status is illustrated by who looks at whom. Argyle (1975) stated that individuals who receive gaze are perceived as the most powerful group members. Research has shown that lower-status persons are more likely to look at persons of higher-status (Burroughs, Schultz & Autrey, 1973; Exline, Ellyson & Long, 1975; Exline & Fehr, 1979; Mehrabian, 1971; Mehrabian & Friar, 1969). This pattern is more pronounced if the high-status person shows approval (Efran, 1968; Fugita, 1974). In a study of a military organization, cadets who paid visual attention to low-status persons were rated lower in status (Exline, et al., 1975). One is not obligated to look at a lower status person and may actually lose status by doing so.

Higher-status persons look more when speaking and less when listening than lower-status persons (Exline, et al., 1975; Exline & Fehr, 1979; LaFrance & Mayo, 1978; Patterson, 1983). Apparently the high-status individual has both the ability and prerogative to maintain visual attentiveness while speaking but is not obligated to reciprocate eye contact when listening. These gaze patterns during interactions may severely undercut or augment an individual's power and influence.

Proxemics

Communication through the use of interpersonal space, called prox-emics, is a central status issue in most organizations. Indeed, Porter and Roberts (1976) suggested the way in which people at work use space to convey meaning is one of the two modes of nonverbal communication of greatest interest to organizational researchers. Most of the research on power and proxemics is quite consistent; we provide higher status individuals with more personal space (Dean, Willis & Hewitt, 1975; Mehrabian, 1969). Argyle (1975) reported that "the only direct connection between dominance or status and special behavior is the deference shown to high-status people by keeping at a distance from them" (p. 308). Moreover, as the status differential becomes greater, interaction distances increase even more (Dean, et al., 1975). In organizational communication, Remland (1981) reported that high-status individuals have less accessible territory and more personal space than lower-status individuals. The prerogative to invade others' space clearly lies with people of high power and status. Eisenberg and Smith (1971) wrote that the power to defend one's own territory and the right to invade that of others are clear signs of dominance and prestige.

Another important proxemic variable is the degree of body orientation or angle between two communicators. Mehrabian (1968b) reported that standing individuals maintained a more direct shoulder orientation to a high-status addressee than to a low-status addressee. Body orientation is least direct toward women with low-status and most direct toward disliked men of high-status (Mehrabian, 1968a). Jorgenson (1975) found that equal status dyads assumed a significantly more direct angle of orientation than did discrepant status pairs and low-status pairs assumed a less direct angle of orientation than high-status pairs. Burgoon and Saine (1978) asserted that in group communication, the individual who is faced by most people probably has the most influence.

Tactile Communication

Touch, the most intimate form of nonverbal communication, has the power to repel, disgust, insult, threaten, console, reassure, love, and arouse.

Tactile or haptic behavior functions as a primary indicant of power and status (Prisbell, 1982) and affects relationships within the business organization.

Power and control are communicated through the initiation of touch. Empirically, touchers have been found to be significantly more dominant than recipients of touch (Burgoon & Saine, 1978; Major, 1981; Major & Heslin, 1982; Patterson, Powell & Lenihan, 1986). Likewise, researchers report that higher-status persons more frequently will touch lower-status persons (Henley, 1977; Major & Heslin, 1982). Remland (1981) claimed that this pattern is commonly observed in organizations; superiors touch subordinates considerably more than the reverse. Other tactile behaviors can indicate dominance or submission. Scheflen (1972) stated that direct poking with the index finger is a dominant act, used as a controlling device. In contrast, a person who "cuddles" to the touch of another is perceived as submissive (Henley, 1977). Tactile patterns have been neglected as important but subtle mechanisms of organizational control.

Paralanguage

The study of nonverbal elements of the voice is called paralinguistics or vocalics which include vocal qualities of speech such as pitch, tempo, rhythm, and resonance as well as vocal characterizers (e.g., laughing, yawning) and vocal segregates (e.g., "ah," "uh-huh").

Several studies have found that both social status and credibility can be detected from paralinguistic cues (Harms, 1961; Moe, 1972). Argyle (1975) reported that vocal characteristics associated with higher social status include clearer articulation, sharper enunciation of consonants, and more vocal intonation. One experiment found perceptions of leadership in women to be a monotonic, increasing function of interaction rate (Stang, 1973). Several researchers have reported that power and status is associated with louder speaking (Mehrabian, 1972; Remland, 1982a; Scheflen, 1972). Voices with fast rate, high volume, low pitch, and full resonance carry the sound of authority. Conversely, high pitch is often associated with childlike submissiveness. In their book on organization communication, Koehler, et al., (1981) stated that tone of voice is an important organization variable. When a supervisor is a friend of a subordinate, friendly tones of voice may undermine the perceived importance of a request or command.

One vocalic behavior that has received little attention is laughing. Henley (1977) maintained that laughter is an expression subordinates exhibit to persons higher in status. However, laughing at someone in an awkward situation, or laughing at a superior's *faux pas* is hardly a submissive message. Recently, studies have employed transcripts of conversation without much attention to intonation or paralanguage. Organizational power researchers would be remiss in failing to include vocalic data so easily preserved with audiotape. Since paralinguistic cues can modify, reinforce, undercut, or reverse the meaning of a verbal utterance, these cues mandate increased attention.

Chronemics

Chronemics examines the use and structure of time, and the various meanings attached to it. Our culture is time-conscious; the American slogan "time is money" is indicative of how we treasure time. As with any valued item, the possession of time is correlated with power and status, and is particularly significant in the business organization.

Waiting-Time

While hardly an efficient managerial practice, the act of making a subordinate wait can be used to assert dominance. Insel and Lindgren (1978) maintained that "another psychological dimension to the distress of waiting is the effect of subordination. One who is in the position to cause another to wait has power over him. To be kept waiting implies that one's own time is less valuable than that of the one who imposes the wait" (p. 105). Waiting-time decreases as status increases, so the powerful are provided with luxurious facilities on the rare occasions when they must wait, such as airport V.I.P. lounges (Henley, 1977).

Talk-Time

Power and status also affect the amount of talk-time during an interaction. Dominant individuals will talk more (Kendon & Cook, 1969) and will hold the floor for a greater proportion of the total time than will a less dominant person (Roger & Jones, 1975). High-status persons communicate more frequently and speak longer in group discussion (Hurwitz, Zander & Hymovitch, 1968; Remland, 1981; Stephan, 1952; Weins, Thompson, Matarazzo, Matarazzo & Saslow, 1965). Furthermore, when lower-status individuals do participate, their communication is usually directed toward those of higher-status (Hurwitz, et al., 1968).

Individuals of high-status and those with dominant personalities interrupt more often (Burgoon & Saine, 1978; Henley, 1977; Roger & Jones, 1975; Weins, et al., 1965). This interruption pattern prevails in the business organization, where subordinates may not interrupt a superior and must immediately cede the floor when the superior interrupts (Henley, 1977).

Higher-status people influence the actual speech patterns of lower-status individuals. Koehler, et al., (1981) claimed that subordinates' response latency is shorter, whereas superiors may take their time in answering. Furthermore, utterance duration is affected by the relative status of an interacting dyad with the lower-status person following the lead of the high-status person (Mehrabian, 1968a). Mehrabian (1968a) argued that a subordinate who does not follow the customary low-status pattern will tend to be negatively perceived by a superior.

Initiating or terminating a conversation is a prerogative of the high-status individual (Mehrabian, 1971) who can also dictate the chronemic patterns of the interaction (Burgoon & Saine, 1978). Superiors typically will decide when a meeting will take place, the length of the interaction, and how much time is devoted to each discussion topic (Burgoon & Saine, 1978; Henley, 1977).

Work-Time

Flexibility of work schedule is associated with higher-status in the organization, as it symbolizes control over time. The ability to control the time of others also leads to power. Henley (1977) stated "some people have the power to annex other people's time, and the more they can annex, the more powerful they become; the more powerful they are, the more of other's time they can annex" (p. 49). In a business organization, the time of the high-status person is considered more valuable than that of the low-status person (Koehler, et al., 1981; Remland, 1981). Higher-status individuals have the freedom to waste the time of others while at the same time to expect strict adherence to their own schedules (Burgoon & Saine, 1978; Goldhaber, 1974).

How an employee spends time determines power and status within the organization. Individuals who devote more time, especially spare time, to meetings, to committees, and to developing contacts are more likely to be influential decision makers (Koehler, et al., 1981). Moreover, spending time with the boss increases a subordinate's power even further (Huseman, et al., 1976).

The Organizational Environment

Privileged territories and executive artifacts both determine and maintain organization power. Pfeffer (1981) maintained:

> The provision of social actors with the symbols of power ratifies their power position within the organization and provides them with power because of the symbols (p. 54).

Territories

Organizational behavior is influenced by territorial patterns that promote privilege and project power. As indicated previously, height is associated with power and status. Thus, it is not surprising that the height of an individual's territory symbolizes one's relative importance (Henley, 1977). Low chairs put a person in a subordinate position (Morris, 1977). Conversely, the top floors of high rise buildings are reserved for the executives, with the president or CEO occupying the topmost or penthouse floor (Kanter, 1979; Mehrabian, 1976).

The possession of larger space or territory is both a symbol and a prerequisite of power. Important executives usually have the largest office (Eisenberg & Smith, 1971; Goldhaber, 1974; Huseman, et al., 1976; Mehrabian, 1976; Pfeffer, 1981). Quantity of space is not the only index of power; the elite have *quality* environments as well. The most desirable locations, such as offices with many windows, corner offices, or one next to the company president, signal importance within the organization (Eisenberg & Smith, 1971; Kanter, 1979; Mehrabian, 1976; Pfeffer, 1981). Status is also established by the protective quality of space. Lower-status is indicated by an open work pit or cubicle made from temporary partitions of file cabinets, whereas the "real" walls of an enclosed office blocked by a receptionist's desk provides executive protection from territorial invasion (Goldhaber, 1974; Huseman, et al., 1976; Kanter, 1979).

Executive privacy, while advantageous in many respects, has drawbacks. The inaccessibility of the elite results in loneliness and social isolation (Kanter, 1979; Mehrabian, 1976). Some executives may attempt to overcome isolation by taking strolls through their subordinate's domain, but their unusual presence causes subordinates to become anxious, clam up, feel they're being evaluated, and exhibit avoidance behavior (Mehrabian, 1976). Another detrimental consequence of upper-echelon isolation is that it creates barriers to vital information flow between managers and subordinates. Though Mehrabian (1976) stated that "management consultants are often amazed at how little many senior executives know about fairly significant interoffice matters" (p. 143), organizational researchers have devoted little attention to this important issue.

Group seating patterns can be manipulated to express power. Research has shown that dominant, high-status individuals select the most focal position in a group, particularly the end seat at a table (Heckel, 1973; Sommer, 1967). Highly visible positions also have been positively correlated with increased interaction (Hearn, 1957; Ward, 1968) and provide more control of interaction patterns (Burgoon & Saine, 1978; LaFrance & Mayo, 1978). Persons who occupy focal positions, such as the end seat of a table, were perceived as leaders (Ward, 1968) and were more likely to be selected foreman of a jury in one study (Strodtbeck & Hook, 1961). Followers and individuals who wish to avoid interaction and leadership chose the least focal positions (Hare & Bales, 1963; Lott & Sommer, 1967; Sommer, 1961, 1965).

Artifacts

Long before much empirical research had been conducted on nonverbal communication, the suburban family of the 1950s knew that large houses, boats, and cars were symbols of status. In today's organization, leaders can be identified by the artifacts that accompany their status. Koehler, et al., (1981) suggested organizational status symbols include a special parking place, a high-status company car, and expensive office furnishings. The latest and most expensive pieces of office equipment are power symbols (Pfeffer, 1981), but knowing how to use them suggests a low power rating (Korda, 1983).

Considerable status revolves around possession and use of communication devices such as the telephone. Having more telephones displayed on one's desk than is necessary is a status symbol (Morris, 1977). However, high-status persons do not actually dial the telephones; someone else does that for them. Operating any mechanical device has a tinge of manual labor and a low-status flavor (Morris, 1977). In an age when the telephone is often an environmental invader, a secretary, an answering service or its mechanical equivalent increases an individual's control and dominance (Goldhaber, 1974; Kanter, 1979; Mehrabian, 1976). Indeed, when one executive secretary reaches another executive secretary, high power requires the other executive come on the line first (Morris, 1977). A top executive can manifest special status with a car phone which implies how busy and important he/she is. This is such a power symbol that one phone company markets dummy aerials for phoneless vehicles, a form of dominance mimicry (Morris, 1977).

Briefcases are another organization status symbol (Korda, 1983; Morris, 1977). Bulky briefcases are a sign of low status since subordinates usually attend to more paperwork. Allegedly, slimmer briefcases are higher in status since they only contain vital papers. No briefcase conveys most status, since when you have real power all they want is you (Korda, 1983).

Artifacts and territories are more than organizational ornaments; they function as symbols of organizational power in four ways. First, they are symbols, both to organization members and to outsiders, of the power structure of the organization. Second, individuals who can access high-status territories and possess symbolic artifacts associated with power may rise to more powerful positions in the formal power structure. Third, certain physical objects and spaces may be the actual rewards which maintain the power structure through material reinforcement. Finally, the accouterments of power may produce efficacious self-expectancies that actually predispose an individual to act in a more powerful manner.

Conclusion

In his recent review of social power and communication, Berger (1985) clearly summarized the position of the present article on the importance of attending to nonverbal variables in power research:

> It can be argued that these nonverbal behaviors are more significant in determining the *experience* of power than are variables related to verbal content. One conclusion to be drawn here is that failure to take into account nonverbal behavior in the study of communication and power relationships is to doom oneself to study the tip of a very large iceberg (p. 483).

Hope for a communication theory of organization power will come from an examination of all types of power, formal and informal, expressed through the numerous channels of human communication, verbal *and* nonverbal.

References

Albrecht, T.L., & Ropp, V.A. (1982). The study of network structuring in organizations through the use of method triangulation. *Western Journal of Speech Communication, 46,* 162-178.

Andersen, J.F., Andersen, P.A., & Jensen, A.D. (1979). The measurement of nonverbal immediacy. *Journal of Applied Communication Research, 7,* 153-180.

Andersen, P.A. (1985). Nonverbal immediacy in interpersonal communication. In A. Seigman and S. Feldstein (Eds.) *Multichannel integrations of nonverbal behavior,* (pp. 1-36) Hillsdale, NJ: Lawrence Erlbaum.

_____. (1986). Consciousness, cognition, and communication. *Western Journal of Speech Communication, 50,* 87-101.Argyle, M. (1975). *Bodily communication.* New York: International Universities Press.

Bantz, C.R. (1983). Naturalistic research traditions. In L.L. Putnam & M.E. Pacanowsky (Eds.) *Communication and organizations: An interpretive approach,* (pp. 55-71). Beverly Hills, CA: Sage Publications.

Barash, D.P. (1973). Human ethology: Personal space reiterated. *Environmental Behavior, 5,* 67-73.

Bateson, G. (1955). A theory of play and fantasy. *Psychiatric Research Reports, 2,* 39-51.

Berger, C.R. (1985). Social power and interpersonal communication. In M.L. Knapp and G.R. Miller (Eds.) *Handbook of interpersonal communication,* (pp. 439-499). Beverly Hills, CA: Sage Publications.

Bickman, L. (1974). The social power of a uniform. *Journal of Applied Social Psychology, 4*, 47-61.

Brown, R. (1965). *Social psychology.* New York: The Free Press.

Burgoon, J.K. (1985). Nonverbal signals. In M.L. Knapp and G.R. Miller (Eds.) *Handbook of interpersonal communication,* (pp. 344-390). Beverly Hills, CA: Sage Publications.

Burgoon, J.K., & Hale, J.L. (1984). The fundamental topoi of relational communication. *Communication Monographs, 51*, 193-214.

Burgoon, J.K., & Saine, T. (1978). *The unspoken dialogue: An introduction to nonverbal communication.* Boston: Houghton Mifflin.

Burns, J.M. (1978). *Leadership.* New York: Harper & Row.

Burroughs, W.A., Schultz, W., & Autrey, S. (1973). Quality of argument, leaders, votes, and eye contact in three person leaderless groups. *Journal of Social Psychology, 90*, 89-93.

Conrad, C. (1983). Organizational power: Faces and symbolic forms. In L.L. Putnam and M.E. Pacanowsky (Eds.) *Communication and organizations: An interpretive approach,* (pp. 173-194). Beverly Hills, CA: Sage Publications.

Conrad, C., & Ryan, M. (1985). Power, praxis and self in organizational communication theory. In R.D. McPhee and P.K. Tompkins (Eds.) *Organizational communication: Traditional themes and new directions,* (pp. 235-257). Beverly Hills, CA: Sage Publications.

Cook, M. (1979). Gaze and mutual gaze in social encounters. In S. Weitz (Ed.), *Nonverbal communication: Readings with commentary, Second Edition,* (pp. 77-86). New York: Oxford University Press.

Crouch, W.W., and Koll, M. (1979, May). *The function of eye behavior in signaling dominance and submission in dyadic interactions.* Paper presented at the Eastern Communication Association, Philadelphia, Pennsylvania.

Dean, L.M., Willis, F.N., & Hewitt, J. (1975). Initial distance among individuals equal and unequal in military rank. *Journal of Personality and Social Psychology, 32*, 294-299.

Deetz, S.A. (1982). Critical interpretive research in organizational communication. *Western Journal of Speech Communication, 46*, 131-149.

Deetz, S.A., & Kersten, A. (1983). Critical models of interpretive research. In L.L. Putnam and M.E. Pacanowsky (Eds.) *Communication and organizations: An interpretive approach,* (pp. 147-171). Beverly Hills, CA: Sage Publications.

Duran, R.L., Jensen, A.D., Prisbell, M., & Rossoff, J.M. (1979, February). *The control dimension of interpersonal relationships: Conceptualization, behavioral correlates and measurement.* Paper presented at the annual meeting of the Western Speech Communication Association convention, Los Angeles.

Efran, J.S. (1968). Looking for approval: Effects on visual behavior of approbation from persons differing in importance. *Journal of Personality and Social Psychology, 10*, 21-25.

Eisenberg, A.M., & Smith, R.R. (1971). *Nonverbal communication.* New York: The Bobbs-Merrill Company, Inc.

Ellsworth, P.C., Carlsmith, J.M., & Henson, A. (1972). The stare as a stimulus of flight in human subjects. *Journal of Personality and Social Psychology, 21*, 302-311.

Exline, R.V., Ellyson, S.L., & Long, B. (1975). Visual behavior as an aspect of power role relationships. In P. Pliner, L. Krames, and T. Alloway (Eds.), *Nonverbal communication of aggression* (Vol. 2), (pp. 21-52). New York: Plenum.

Exline, R.V., & Fehr, B.J. (1979) *Person and context in interpretation of gaze behavior.* Paper presented at the Annual Convention of the American Psychological Association, New York.

Fairhurst, G.T., Green, S.G., & Snavely, B.K. (1984). Managerial control and discipline: Whips and chains. In R.N. Bostrom (Ed.), *Communication yearbook 8*, (pp. 558-593). Beverly Hills, CA: Sage Publications.

Fowles, J. (1974). Why we wear clothes, *ETC: A Review of General Semantics, 31*, 343-352.

Fromme, D.J., & Beam, D.C. (1974). Dominance and sex differences in nonverbal responses to differential eye contact. *Journal of Research in Personality, 8*, 76-87.

Fugita, S.S. (1974). Effects of anxiety and approval on visual interaction. *Journal of Personality and Social Psychology, 29*, 586-592.

Fullbright, J.W. (1966). *The arrogance of power.* New York: Vintage Books.

Goffman, E. (1967). *Interaction ritual.* Garden City, NY: Anchor Books.

Goldhaber, G.M. (1974). *Organizational communication.* Dubuque, IA: Wm. C. Brown Publishing Company.

Hare, A., & Bales, R. (1963). Seating position and small group interaction. *Sociometry, 26*, 480-496.

Harms, L.S. (1961). Listener judgments of status cues in speech. *Quarterly Journal of Speech, 47*, 164-168.

Hearn, G. (1957). Leadership and the spatial factor in small groups. *Journal of Abnormal and Social Psychology, 54*, 269-272.

Heckel, R.V. (1973). Leadership and voluntary seating choice. *Psychological Reports, 32*, 141-142.

Henley, N.M. (1977). *Body politics: Power, sex and nonverbal communication.* Englewood Cliffs, NJ: Prentice-Hall.

Hickson, D.J., Hinings, C.R., Lee, C.A., Schneck, R.E., & Pennings, J.M. (1971). A strategic contingencies theory of intraorganizational power. *Administrative Science Quarterly, 16*, 216-226.

Hurwitz, J.L., Zander, A.F., & Hymovitch, B. (1968). Some effects of power on the relations among group members. In Cartwright, D. and Zander, A. (Eds.) *Group dynamics*, (pp. 291-297). New York: Harper & Row.

Huseman, R.C., Lahiff, J.M., & Hatfield, J.D. (1976). *Interpersonal communication in organizations.* Boston: Holbrook Press, Inc.

Insel, P.M., & Lindgren, H.C. (1978). *Too close for comfort.* Englewood Cliffs, NJ: Prentice-Hall, Inc.

Jablin, F.M. (1984). Assimilating new members into organizations. In R.N. Bostrom (Ed.) *Communication yearbook 8*, (pp. 594-626). Beverly Hills, CA: Sage Publications.

Jorgenson, D.O. (1975). Field study of the relationship between status discrepancy and proxemic behavior. *Journal of Social Psychology, 97*, 173-179.

Joseph, N., & Alex, N. (1972). The uniform: A sociological perspective. *American Journal of Sociology, 77*, 719-730.

Kanter, R.M. (1979). How the top is different. In R.M. Kanter and B.A. Stein (Eds.) *Life in organizations*, (pp. 20-35). New York: Basic Books.

Kendon, A., & Cook, M. (1969). The consistency of gaze patterns in social interaction. *British Journal of Psychology, 60*, 481-494.

Kennedy, C.W., & Camden, C. (1983). Interruptions and nonverbal gender differences. *Journal of Nonverbal Behavior, 8*, 91-108.

Knapp, M.L. (1983). Dyadic relationship development. In J.M. Wiemann and R.P. Harrison (Eds.) *Nonverbal interaction*, (pp. 179-207). Beverly Hills, CA: Sage Publications.

Knowles, E.S. (1973). Boundaries around group interaction: The effect of group size and member status on boundary permeability. *Journal of Personality and Social Psychology, 26*, 327-332.

Koehler, J.W., Anatol, K.W.E., Applbaum, R.L. (1981). *Organizational communications: A behavioral perspective*. New York: Holt, Rinehart & Winston.

Korda, M. (1983). Status marks—a gold-plated thermos is a man's best friend. In A.M. Katz and V.T. Katz *Foundations of nonverbal communication* (pp. 164-169). Carbondale, IL: Southern Illinois University Press.

LaFrance, J., & Mayo, C. (1978). *Moving bodies: Nonverbal communication in social relationships* Monterey, CA: Brooks/Cole Publishing Company.

Lefkowitz, M., Blake, R., & Mouton, J. (1955). Status factors in pedestrian violation of traffic signals. *Journal of Abnormal and Social Psychology, 51*, 704-706.

Lott, D.F., & Sommer, R. (1962). Seating arrangements and status. *Journal of Personality and Social Psychology, 7*, 90-95.

Major, B. (1981). Gender patterns in touching behavior. In C. Mayo and N.M. Henley (Eds.) *Gender and nonverbal behavior*, (pp. 15-38). New York: Springer-Verlag, Inc.

Major, B., & Heslin, R. (1982). Perceptions of cross-sex and same sex nonreciprocal touch: It is better to give than to receive. *Journal of Nonverbal Behavior, 6*, 148-162.

Mehrabian, A. (1968a). Communication without words. *Psychology Today, 2*, 52-55.

_____. (1968b). Inference of attitudes from the posture, orientation, and distance of a communicator. *Journal of Consulting and Clinical Psychology, 32*, 296-308.

_____. (1969). Significance of posture and position in the communication attitude and status relationships. *Psychological Bulletin, 71*, 359-372.

_____. (1971). *Silent messages*. Belmont, CA: Wadsworth Publishing Co. . (1972). *Nonverbal communication*. New York: Aldine, Atherton, Inc.

_____. (1976). *Public places, private spaces*. New York: Basic Books.. (1981). *Silent messages: Implicit communication of emotions and attitudes*. Belmont, CA: Wadsworth Publishing Co.

Mehrabian, A., & Friar, J.T. (1969). Encoding of attitude by a seated communicator via posture and position cues. *Journal of Consulting and Clinical Psychology, 33*, 330-336.

Mintzberg, H. (1983). *Power in and around organizations*. Englewood Cliffs, NJ: Prentice-Hall.

Moe, J.D. (1972). Listener judgments of status cues in speech: A replication and extension. *Speech Monographs, 39,* 144-147.

Molloy, J.T. (1976). *Dress for success.* New York: Warner Books.

Morris, D. (1977). *Manwatching: A field guide to human behavior.* New York: Harry N. Abrams.

Patterson, M.L. (1983). *Nonverbal behavior: A functional perspective.* New York: Springer-Verlag.

Patterson, M.L., Powell, J.L., & Lenihan, M.G. (1986). Touch, compliance, and interpersonal affect. *Journal of Nonverbal Behavior, 10,* 41-50.

Pfeffer, J. (1981). *Power in organizations.* Marshfield, MA: Pitman Publishing.

Porter, L., & Roberts, K. (1976). Communication in organizations. In M. Dunnette (Ed.) *Handbook of industrial and organizational psychology.* Chicago: Rand McNally.

Prisbell, M. (1982, May). *Nonverbal communication attributes of power and status in the organizational setting.* Paper presented at the annual convention of Eastern Communication Association, Hartford, Connecticut.

Putnam, L.L. (1982). Paradigms for organizational communication research: An overview and synthesis. *Western Journal of Speech Communication, 46,* 192-206.

Putnam, L.L. (1983). The interpretive perspective: An alternative to functionalism. In L.L. Putnam and M.E. Pacanowsky (Eds.) *Communication and organizations: An interpretive approach.* Beverly Hills, CA: Sage Publications.

Ragan, S.L. (1983). A conversational analysis of alignment talk in job interviews. In R.N. Bostrom (Ed.) *Communication yearbook 7,* (pp. 502-516). Beverly Hills, CA: Sage Publications.

Remland, M. (1981). Developing leadership skills in nonverbal communication: A situational perspective. *The Journal of Business Communication, 18,* 17-29.

Remland, M. (1982a). The implicit ad hominem fallacy: Nonverbal displays of status in argumentative discourse. *Journal of the American Forensic Association, 19,* 79-86.

Remland, M.S. (1982b, November). *Leadership impressions and nonverbal communication in a superior-subordinate interaction.* Paper presented at the annual convention of the Speech Communication Association, Louisville, Kentucky.

Riggs, C.J. (1983). Dimensions of organizational conflict: A functional analysis of communication tactics. In R.N. Bostrom (Ed.) *Communication yearbook 7,* (pp. 517-531). Beverly Hills, CA: Sage Publications.

Rogers, W.T., & Jones, S.E. (1975). Effects of dominance tendencies on floor holding in interruption behavior in dyadic interaction. *Human Communication Research, 3,* 291-302.

Russell, B. (1938). *Power: A new social analysis.* London: George Allen & Unwin.

Scheflen, A.E. (1972). *Body language and the social order.* Englewood Cliffs, NJ: Prentice-Hall, Inc.

Sommer, R. (1961). Leadership and group geography. *Sociometry, 24,* 99-110.

Sommer, R. (1965). Leadership and small group ecology. *Sociometry, 28,* 337-348.

Sommer, R. (1967). Small group ecology. *Psychological Bulletin, 67,* 145-151.

Stang, D.J. (1973). Effect of interaction rate on ratings of leadership and liking. *Journal of Personality and Social Psychology, 27*, 405-408.

Stephen, F.F. (1952). The relative rate of communication between members of small groups. *American Sociological Review, 17*, 428-486.

Strodtbeck, F.L., & Hook, L.H. (1961). The social dimensions of a twelve-man jury table. *Sociometry, 24*, 297-315.

Strongman, K.T., & Chapness, B.G. (1968). Dominance hierarchies and conflict in eye contact. *Acta Psychologica, 28*, 376-386.

Thayer, S. (1969). The effect of interpersonal looking duration on dominance judgments. *Journal of Social Psychology, 79*, 285-286.

Thompson, J.D. (1967). *Organizations in action.* New York: McGraw-Hill.

Tompkins, P. (1984). The functions of communication in organizations. In C. Arnold and J. Bowers (Eds.) *Handbook of rhetorical and communication theory* (pp. 649-719). New York: Allyn & Bacon.

Tompkins, P.K., & Cheney, G. (1983). Account analysis of organizations: Decision making and identification. In L.L. Putnam and M.E. Pacanowsky (Eds.) *Communication and organizations: An interpretive approach*, (pp. 123-146). Beverly Hills, CA: Sage Publications.

――――. (1985). Communication and unobtrusive control in contemporary organizations. In R.D. McPhee and P.K. Tompkins (eds.) *Organizational communication: Traditional themes and new directions*, (pp. 179-210). Beverly Hills, CA: Sage Publications.

Trujillo, N. (1983). "Performing" Mintzberg's roles: The nature of managerial communication. In L.L. Putnam and M.E. Pacanowsky (Eds.) *Communication and organizations: An interpretive approach*, (pp. 73-97). Beverly Hills, CA: Sage Publications.

Turow, J. (1985). Learning to portray institutional power: The socialization of creators in mass media organizations. In R.D. McPhee and P.K. Tompkins (Eds.) *Organizational communication: Traditional themes and new directions* (pp. 211-234). Beverly Hills, CA: Sage Publications.

Ward, C.D. (1968). Seating arrangement and leadership emergence in small discussion groups. *Journal of Social Psychology, 74*, 83-90.

Watzlawick, P., Beavin, J.M., & Jackson, D.D. (1967). *Pragmatics of human communication.* New York: W.W. Norton & Company.

Weins, A.N., Thompson, S.M., Matarazzo, J.A., Matarazzo, R.G., and Salsow, G. (1965). Interview interaction behavior of supervisors, head nurses and staff nurses. *Nursing Research, 14*, 322-329.

Key Terms and Concepts

Muehlenhard, Koralewski, Andrews, and Burdick, *Cues that Convey Interest in Dating*

who should initiate dates   nonverbal cues of interest

Moore, *Nonverbal Courtship Patterns in Women*

females assess	flirting behaviors	ambivalence
quality of mate	courtship readiness	raised eyebrows
gender differences	preening behavior	coy glance
in mate criteria	positional cues	glances and interest
courtship signals	appeal or invitation	

Douglas and Atwell, *Learning to Love*

sounds of love	shifty-eyes	look of sexual
development of senses	shy lover	excitement
look of love	length of gaze	look of ecstacy
importance of feelings	full facial expression	conscious/
eyes	friendly greeting	unconscious
gaze behavior	look of adoration love	

Andersen and Bowman, *Positions of Power*

power	kinesic expansiveness	chronemics
deep and surface	relaxation	waiting-time
structures	access	talk-time
power structure	smile	interruptions
preconscious	jaw	initiating and
nonverbal behavior	exaggerated looks	terminating
uncertainty	of displeasure	conversations
dynamic	direct gaze	flexible work-time
power from	blinking	chair height
relationships	receiving gaze	top floors
status	proxemics	quality space and
dominance	larger spaces	environments
control	invading space	privacy
attire	body orientation	seating patterns
formal dress	initiation of touch	telephone
uniforms	paralanguage status	briefcases
physical size	cues	

Appendix C

Researching Nonverbal Communication

Nonverbal communication presents a unique set of problems for researchers. Most nonverbal behaviors are *unconsciously* performed. At best, we are only slightly aware of them. As a result, questionnaires which ask people about nonverbal communication can only be used to measure people's general traits or characteristics and their reaction to nonverbal messages. The messages themselves must be directly observed.

Observation is no simple task. Many of the most important nonverbal behaviors occur quickly and subtly. A slight change in posture, or a shuffling of the feet, or a quick facial movement can all communicate valuable information which is difficult to observe without technical assistance.

Fortunately, nonverbal research has gotten more sophisticated. Researchers have developed *coding systems* to allow direct observation of certain nonverbal messages and *video technology* has been used to facilitate still other studies.

One of the most important things you can learn from nonverbal research is how you can observe and understand nonverbal messages. Research involves *systematic observation*. These techniques can be used to improve your personal and professional lives. Systems for coding intimacy messages can help you see who likes you. Methods for measuring power can help you assess who is in control at your new job. And so, you can see that in addition to the knowledge this research provides, there is also a practical use to the methods that have been developed.

In this chapter Hecht provides an overview of research
methodology for the study of nonverbal communication. The
chapter summarizes the major approaches to research and
describes basic methods.

45

Methods of Nonverbal Communication Research

Michael L. Hecht

This chapter presents a brief introduction to nonverbal communication
research. After reading the chapter you should have a better understanding of research in nonverbal communication. The chapter is not
meant as a substitute for a full course in research methodology. Instead,
it will introduce you to some of the topics you need to know in order
to understand nonverbal communication.

We conduct research to learn more about nonverbal communication.
You conduct a type of research when you collect information to make
decisions. How do you know if a classmate likes you enough to go out on
a date with you? To answer this question, you might try out a number of
different strategies. First, you might observe the other person while interacting, looking for signs of attraction. How close does this person stand?
Does the person smile at you? Is there mutual eye contact? Second, you
might observe the person interacting with others. Are these interactions
the same as those the person has with you? Third, you might observe
the person's reaction when you mention the idea of doing things together.
Does the person smile when you suggest it would be fun to go to a certain
concert together? Fourth, you might ask other people how this person
feels about you. All these are research strategies. Other everyday research
questions include: How does a sales person know when to try to get the
customer to sign a contract? How do you arrange the furniture in your
room? All of these involve research. More formally, we define research
as: the use of *systematic methods* to answer important *questions*.

Research Questions

Research always starts with a question—without a good question there is no reason to conduct a study. Most nonverbal questions are of three types:

1. *Describe a type of nonverbal behavior.* For example: *What are the different styles of walking?*

Zuckerman, Miserando, and Bernieri were interested in the question, "How can people be present in a situation and avoid interaction?" They described how eye behavior allows people to be together without directly communicating. See Zuckerman, Miserando, and Bernieri, "Civil Inattention Exists—in Elevators," Part 3 (p. 138).

2. *Describe how one type of nonverbal behavior influences another type.* For example: *Do we touch more if eye contact increases?*

Jones wanted to understand how people responded to touch, calling these touch sequences. He had people keep "touch diaries" in which they recorded all of their touches during a day. Jones then identified the most common touch sequences. See Jones, "Communicating with Touch," Part 6 (p. 235).

3. *Describe how nonverbal behavior is related to a type of person or situation.* For example: *Do certain types of people behave in certain ways? Are there differences between men and women in touch? Do people behave differently in different types of environments (in red versus blue rooms)?*

Daly and his coauthors discussed whether men and women differ in their preening behavior. The researchers went to restaurants to observe how many times men and women groomed their hair, straightened their clothes, or looked at themselves in a mirror. See Daly, Hogg, Sacks, Smith, and Zimring, "Sex and Relationship Affect Self-Grooming," Part 2 (p. 87).

People ask questions in order to *describe, explain,* and *predict* nonverbal communication. All research must *describe* behavior in order to study it. We describe body cues by identifying body lean, posture, and mirroring. Can you describe the clothing you are wearing? You might comment on style, color, and material. Is there anything this description has left out? If so, then a better description is possible. Moore was interested in describing flirting behavior. Research assistants observed women in bars and recorded all instances of flirting. The researcher then categorized these descriptions into types of flirting. See Moore, ''Nonverbal Courtship Patterns in Women'' in Appendix B (p. 365).

Research also attempts to *explain* nonverbal communication. These studies tell us how nonverbal behavior communicates. Andersen and Bowman summarized studies which explain how people dominate other people in organizations. These studies tell us how dominance works and allow us to understand this important process. See Andersen and Bowman ''Positions of Power: Nonverbal Influence in Organizational Communication,'' in Appendix B (p. 391).

Finally, research tries to *predict* nonverbal communication. Crusco and Weitzel predicted that tips are increased by touching. They observed touching and tipping in restaurants to test this prediction. See Crusco and Weitzel, ''The Midas Touch: The Effects of Interpersonal Touching on Restaurant Tipping,'' Part 6 (p. 229). Waiters and waitresses can use this information to make predictions about their income! Prediction is the most difficult test because people are so different in their reactions. These wide individual differences among people make predictions very risky.

What Is an Important Question?

How do we know when we have an important question? There are four tests we can apply. First, we can ask if other nonverbal researchers agree it is a good question. If an article is published in a scholarly journal, then other researchers have agreed that the question is at least somewhat important. Scholars such as Thomas Kuhn (1970) argue that this is the most commonly applied standard for judging research.

Second, we can ask how answering the question advances *theory*. Burgoon and Hale discuss Expectation Violation Theory in Part 1 (p. 48). They theorize about the different effects of violating people's nonverbal expectations. We might ask if this theory applies to our expectation of lovers to see if the theory can be extended. This provides a better understanding of both the theory and nonverbal communication.

Third, we can ask if answering the question leads us to other interesting questions for research. Answering the question, ''What are the signs of attraction?,'' allows us to ask what happens if people give off too many signs of attraction. For example, let's assume that increased eye gaze, forward lean, close distances, and touch are all signs of attraction. What happens if someone communicates all of these signs? Or just one of them? Baron (1986) found that too much of a good thing in dress at interviews does not help. Does this apply to attraction messages as well?

Finally, we can ask how answering the question makes us a more effective communicator. The Mehrabian article in Part 5 (p. 203) teaches us how the arrangement of our homes influences communication. This can help us be more effective in home decoration. Not all researchers accept this standard. Ideally, research should pass all four of these tests.

Researchers, therefore, ask and try to answer important questions to describe, explain, and predict nonverbal communication.

Systematic Methods

Good research is systematic. This means that it is planned, organized, orderly, and methodical. Systematic research follows a regular, orderly series of steps in obtaining answers to questions. This allows others to understand how the information was obtained and to repeat the study to see if the same information would be obtained again. Good research is planned from start to finish before anything else occurs. The research plan is like the script for a play or a lesson plan for a class.

Two Approaches to Research

There are two general research approaches: *the grounded approach* and *the hypothesis-testing approach.* Grounded approaches start with a general theory of nonverbal communication. The researcher then formulates overall questions and observes nonverbal communication, obtaining detailed descriptions. Next, the descriptions are examined and organized. Sometimes the descriptions are organized into categories. Look at the Jones study in Part 6 (p. 235). This researcher was interested in understanding how people interpret different types of touch. Assistants described their touch experiences during one day, noting the type of touch and their interpretation of its meaning. Finally, the researcher organized the descriptions into the types of meanings of touch.

The hypothesis-testing approach is different. Here the researcher uses theory to *hypothesize* or make specific predictions about what is expected. Hypotheses are informed guesses about how two or more things go together. The researcher then observes nonverbal communication to see if the predictions are accurate. Daly, Hogg, Sacks, Smith, and Zimring hypothesized that there is less preening in more established relationships. They then observed people in a restaurant and interviewed them about the nature of their relationship in order to test this hypothesis. See Daly, Hogg, Sacks, Smith, and Zimring, ''Sex and Relationship Affect Social Self-Grooming,'' in Part 2 (p. 87).

The main difference between the approaches is how specific the predictions are before the study. In the grounded approach, the researcher has general goals and questions. The specific conclusions emerge out of the study itself and are guided and shaped by what is observed. For example, the researcher might go to parties with the idea of studying attraction and notice that distance, touch, and eye contact play important roles. In the hypothesis-testing approach, the researcher decides beforehand in very specific terms what to look for and examines only the hypothesis. For example, the researcher hypothesizes that touch is an important sign of attraction and observes people at parties to see if (and how) touch and attraction are related.

Focusing on the Individual or the Interaction

Once you have chosen an approach, you decide what you will focus on. Nonverbal communication research typically focuses on either an *individual* or an *interaction*. The difference is who you look at. Researchers who look at the individual study one person at a time, while those who look at the interaction observe interactions between people.

One way of studying *individuals* is to examine how different personality types are expressed through nonverbal behavior. Or the researcher might try to see how people express a certain meaning through voice tone. In Part 2, the Wells and Seigel study of somatotypes (body shape) is an example of this type of research. These researchers showed people pictures of models with different body builds and asked people to guess the model's personality. See Wells and Seigel, "Stereotyped Somatotypes," Part 2 (p. 75). The color table in Part 4 (p. 179) also is based on this type of research. If you showed people models dressed in three different-colored versions of the same outfit, you might get different impressions based on the colors.

Other researchers study the individual by seeing how people form impressions based on nonverbal behavior. Montepare, Goldstein, and Clausen studied people's interpretation of walking styles. They videotaped different walking styles and asked people what emotions they felt were being expressed. See Montepare, Goldstein, and Clausen, "The Identification of Emotions from Gait Information" in Part 2 (p. 78).

Finally, researchers study how people mentally process or understand nonverbal messages. This is also called a *social cognition* approach. Here we are concerned with how the mind operates in organizing nonverbal messages. In Part 4 (p. 155) Gorden, Tengler, and Infante explored how predispositions influence dress. They hypothesized that peoples' cognitive predispositions toward clothing affect their dress and job satisfaction. Since this approach is more recent than the others, we can expect more of these articles in the future. In Part 1 (p. 26), Andersen and Andersen describe a number of cognitive theories.

Other researchers study *interactions* rather than individuals. These researchers examine how people use nonverbal communication in relationships and conversations. The Petronio, Bourhis, and Berquist article in Appendix C (p. 425) shows how to study people as a family. These researchers are concerned about the signs given off by a group of people that communicate they are a family.

This approach is not as frequent as the individual approach because it is more difficult and time consuming. Other researchers study how people coordinate nonverbal behavior with each other. For example, Zuckerman, Miserandino, and Bernieri, Part 3 (p. 138) studied civil in-attention—how two people occupy the same small area without appearing to pay attention to each other.

Still other researchers study how people establish a relationship. Purvis, Dabbs, and Hopper examined how people use facial, eye, and paralinguistic cues to open people up and encourage them to talk. Their article, entitled "The 'Opener': Skilled Use of Facial Expression and Speech Pattern," is in Part 3 (p. 120).

Michael Argyle (1988) discusses these approaches in great detail in his book, *Bodily Communication.*

Methods of Noverbal Research

After determining what to study, the researcher decides how to collect the information needed to answer the question. This is called the *method.* In choosing a method there are a number of decisions the researcher makes. First, the researcher chooses a setting for the study. Some researchers arrange nonverbal communication in an *experiment,* while others study it as it naturally occurs in an *observation.* Second, the researcher decides how to record the behavior and/or the reactions to the behavior.

Experiments

In experiments, the researcher arranges for events to occur and then measures the effects. Researchers arrange nonverbal communication in order to have more control over the situation. If we wait for behavior to happen naturally, there is no telling when or where it will take place. This means the researcher does not have control. If we are studying distance, we can arrange for people to stand 1, 3, and 5 feet apart rather than wait for these distances to occur by themselves. Cash, Cash, and Butters (p. 67) designed an experiment to see if peoples' ratings of their own physical attractiveness is influenced by the attractiveness of other people. In their experiment, subjects first saw pictures of either attractive or not attractive models and then rated their own physical attractiveness. Consistent with the hypothesis, subjects who first saw attractive models rated their own attractiveness lower than those who first saw not attractive models.

Some researchers use a *confederate* to control the situation. A confederate is someone who works for the researcher but whose role is not known to the other participants. Confederates act in a predetermined way to arrange the situation. For example, in a study of distance a confederate can enter a room with a subject, stand either 1, 3, or 5 feet from the person, and talk about a predetermined topic (for example, the university's football team). If we observed naturally-occurring behavior, people may stand 1½, 2¾, and 5⅓ feet apart and talk about different topics at each distance. Then we wouldn't know if the topic or the distance is influencing other behaviors, and the distances would be imprecise.

Sometimes people use videotapes to "arrange" a conversation. The taped conversations will differ in some important nonverbal cue. For example, people may talk quickly on one tape and slowly on a second. The tapes are then viewed by people who give their impressions of the talkers. Gifford, Ng, and Wilkinson videotaped job interviews and showed those tapes to judges who rated the participants. The ratings were then compared to see how the nonverbal behaviors created a certain type of impression. See Gifford, Ng, and Wilkinson, "Nonverbal Cues in the Employment Interview: Links Between Applicant Qualities and Interviewer Judgments" in Part 2 (p. 99).

One way of arranging nonverbal communication that does not work particularly well is to have them act or *role play* a situation. You might take two people who do not know each other and tell them to pretend they are on a date. Then you can observe and see how dates behave. Unfortunately, Jones and Aiello (1979) have shown that having people pretend does not work well because people do not behave the same way when they are not pretending.

Observations

Other researchers prefer to *observe naturally-occurring behavior*. These researchers pick an interactional setting, watch for nonverbal communication to occur, and then record it. Examples of such settings would include the cafeteria, retail stores, living rooms, and parties. The important thing here is that the behavior occurs by itself without the researcher arranging it. The researcher merely records the behavior and its effects. Moore used this style of research in the study of flirting. Two trained observers went to single's bars and observed how women behaved prior to men approaching them. See Moore, "Nonverbal Courtship Patterns in Women" in Appendix B (p. 365). An extended discussion of observation is provided in Mark Knapp's (1978) *Nonverbal Communication in Human Interaction*.

Recording Nonverbal Communication

Regardless of whether the study uses an experiment or an observation, the researcher will still have to *record* nonverbal communication or people's reactions to nonverbal behavior. Recording describes nonverbal communication. When a researcher relates this description to descriptions of other nonverbal behavior, emotions, attitudes, people or situations, we explain and predict nonverbal communication. The three most common methods of recording nonverbal behavior are *surveys, coding systems,* and *field notes.*

Surveys

Most of you are familiar with *surveys.* They have become a common form of gathering information. Surveys use written or oral questions designed to gather information. There are two types of questions: *open* and *closed questions.* The difference is whether or not the survey specifies the type of answer that can be given. Open questions do not specify the type of answer. Examples are: How do you express friendship? What did you find satisfying about this conversation? Newman used open questions to study people's reactions to silence. Videotapes were shown to people who were then asked to describe what they thought the people in the video were feeling and thinking. See Newman, "The Sounds of Silence in Conversational Encounters" in Part 7, (p. 266).

Closed questions provide specific choices for the answers. For example:

> When my friend and I talk I prefer to stand:
> a. 0 to 1 foot apart
> b. 1½ to 4 feet apart
> c. more than 4 feet apart

Closed questions are used in the Andersen and Leibowitz's touch avoidance scale in Part 6 (p. 247) and by Gorden, Tengler, and Infante to study clothing predispositions in Part 4 (p. 155).

The choice of either open or closed questions depends upon a number of factors. Basically, open questions provide more information than closed questions, but are more difficult to interpret.

Surveys can be a useful way of recording nonverbal behavior if certain limitations are kept in mind. First, most people are not aware of nonverbal behavior and, therefore, cannot describe it very well. Asking someone if they leaned forward while talking to someone last week is not effective. It is even less effective to ask people how they *would* behave in a hypothetical or imaginary situation. People are very poor at predicting behavior in anything but the most typical situations (for example, where you will sit in class next time). They are also not very good at explaining why they behaved a certain way because they attempt to rationalize their own behavior.

People can tell the researcher how they interpret behavior, what it means to them, and what they find important. They also can give the researcher information about nonverbal behavior that has taken place very recently, but it may be best to observe and record this directly.

Coding Systems

Coding systems allow the researcher to observe nonverbal communication directly. There are two types of coding systems. The first lists various *types of nonverbal behavior* and the recorder (a person or a machine) just checks off the behavior when it is observed. For example, the researcher might have a checklist for mirroring, touch, eye contact, and close distance (for example, less than 4 feet) to use for observing behavior at a party. Every time the researcher sees one of these behaviors a check is recorded next to the category. If the researcher separates the records for males and females, you will see if sex influences these behaviors. Examples of this type of recording system are provided in this Appendix by Petronio, Bourhis, and Berquist (p. 425) and by Hensley and Taylor (p. 436).

The second type of coding system provides symbols to record specific nonverbal behaviors. One of the first systems of this type was created by Ray Birdwhistell (1970). In his system, when we see a blank face we record —0—. A smile is recorded as ⌣ . Other examples of his recording system are:

Sidewise look	⚭ ⚭
Focus on auditor	⚭ ⚭
Stare	⚭ ⚭
Rolled eyes	⚭ ⚭
Slitted eyes	⚭ ⚭
Eyes upward	⚭ ⚭
Shifty eyes	—⚭ ⚭—
Glare	⚭ ⚭"

A second system was provided by Edward T. Hall (1974). An example of his coding system is:

Body Orientation

This scale describes the orientation of the subjects' bodies to each other, beginning with back-to-back orientation (0) and opening out through side-by-side (5) and right-angle (7) to face-to-face orientation (9). The shoulders are the reference points to observe in deciding orientation. The most common positions for interacting are 5 through 9, although two persons standing "in line" (4) or backed up to each other (0) in crowds will also be aware of and interact with each other to some extent. Be sure that both subjects in an interaction are rated the same on this scale. (See coding Scale opposite.)

Body Orientation

0 -
1 -
2 -
3 -
4 -
5 -
6 -
7 -
8 -
9 -

Other methods of recording nonverbal behavior are presented in Scherer and Ekman's (1982) book, *Handbook of Methods in Nonverbal Behavior Research.*

Field Notes

A final recording method is called *field notes*. Field notes may use one of the previous systems or may just involve going into a setting and writing down descriptions of the observations. It is often best to record the notes while making the observation. If this interferes with the situation (for example, writing notes at a party), then the researcher will record the observations as soon afterwards as possible. These notes will not be as clear or as descriptive as the previous two systems, but they leave the researcher free to observe anything that occurs rather than just what is in the recording system. Sometimes audio tape recorders are used for field notes. Other times researchers use video cameras to record events.

Summary

This chapter provided a brief introduction to nonverbal communication research. Research was defined as the use of systematic methods to answer questions. Three types of questions were identified: questions about one particular type of nonverbal message (for example, what are the types of touch?), questions about how two or more types of nonverbal messages are related to each other (for example, do we establish closer distances in the evening than during the afternoon?), and questions about how nonverbal communication is related to types of people and situations (e.g., do smells have different meanings in Eastern cultures and Europeans cultures?). We also saw that the goals of answering questions were description, explanation, and prediction, and discussed evaluating the importance of questions in terms of their contribution to theory, research, and practice.

Systematic methods were then described. Grounded and hypothesis-testing approaches to research were differentiated based on the specificity of their predictions; hypothesis-testing approaches make specific predictions while ground approaches make more general ones. Next, we considered whether the researcher examined the behavior of the individual or an interaction. Then experiments, where behavior is arranged and controlled by the researcher, were differentiated from observations, where the researcher records nonverbal messages that occur naturally. Finally, we described three methods for recording nonverbal communication: surveys, coding systems, and field notes.

References

Argyle, M. (1988). *Bodily Communication* (2nd ed.). London: Metheun & Co.

Baron, Robert A. (1986). Self-presentation in job interviews: when there can be 'too much of a good thing'. *Journal of applied psychology, 16*, 16-28.

Birdwhistell, R.I. (1970). *Kinesics and Context: Essays on Body Motion Communication*. Philadelphia: University of Pennsylvania Press.

Hall, E.T. (1974). *Handbook for Proxemic Research*. Washington, DC: Society for the Anthropology of Visual Communication.

Jones, S.E., and Aiello, J.R. (1979). A test of the validity of projective and quasi-projective measures of interpersonal distance. *Western journal of speech communication, 43*, 143-152.

Knapp, M.L. (1978). *Nonverbal Communication in Human Interaction*. New York: Holt, Rinehart, & Winston.

Kuhn, T. (1970). *The Structure of Scientific Revolutions*. Chicago: University of Chicago Press.

Scherer, K.R., & Ekman, P. (Ed.) (1982). *Handbook of Methods in Nonverbal Behavior Research*. Cambridge: Cambridge University Press.

46 *Petronio, Bourhis, and Berquist developed a system for identifying families in public places. The system codes nonverbal cues indicating people are together in a family. In this chapter, the system is explained and an application is demonstrated.*

Families in Public Places
But Mom You Promised!

Sandra Petronio, John Bourhis and Charlene Berquist

Goffman (1963; 1971) has written a great deal about behavior in public places. He defines public areas as those where a community has free access. Yet, Lyman and Scott (1970) suggest that while public territory may be openly accessible, the society as a whole typically places restrictions on the types of behavior defined as appropriate within those areas. These restrictions on action form implicit social rules for acceptable behavior in public places. When a family unit enters a public place, members may find it difficult to maintain the typical structure of family interaction patterns and abide by social rules specific to a public territory. For example, the family members often struggle with balancing their private disciplinary techniques while fulfilling the demands of appropriate public behavior. Yet, other types of family patterns are consistently used both in private and in public settings without problems (e.g., the division of labor).

In order to better understand the patterns found among families in public places, an assignment to do an observational study was given to undergraduate and graduate students registered in six family communication courses. These observations took place in both the upper midwest and in the southwest. Approximately 180 observations of families in public places have been conducted since 1984. Most (80%), but not all, of these observations were conducted in shopping malls (Petronio & Bourhis,

Portions adapted with permission from: Petronio, S., and Bourhis, J. (1987). Identifying family collectivities in public places: An instructional exercise. *Communication Education, 36,* 46-51.

1987). The information gathered from these observations is used as the basis for this discussion. Observers were given the following directions:

1. Do not follow the collectivity around the shopping area. Remain in one place and observe the collectivities as they pass you. Following people makes it difficult to write and may upset the people being observed, creating ethical problems.
2. Do not interact with the collectivities. (Note: other research designs may include interviews in order to gather additional information.)
3. Choose an observation location where you are less likely to be seen. If there are two levels, go to the upper level and observe the people below you. If there are corners, stand at the end of one. Choose observational settings in different mall locations (e.g., near department stores, near sporting goods stores, near restaurants).
4. Record "demographic" information including age, gender, race, etc.
5. Describe the observational setting. Note the number of stores in the mall, the day of the week, your location in the mall, how crowded the area is, time of the year (i.e., Christmas shopping) and time of the day.
6. Schedule observations on most days of the week and vary your observations to be conducted in the morning, afternoons and evenings (Petronio & Bourhis, 1987, pp. 49-50).

The present article does not represent systematic, quantitative research. Instead, this paper outlines categories that appeared useful and were consistently found in the unstructured observations conducted by these students. Two parts of these observations are presented: One, a discussion of the way collectivities were identified as family units is offered. This activity was a precursor to observations of family interaction patterns in public. Two, observations of disciplinary actions taken in public between parents and children are presented as well as observations focusing on division of labor between mothers and fathers. These represent important and often occurring patterns found among parents interacting with their children in public.

Part I: Collectivities-as-Families

In order to identify collectivities-as-families, Goffman's (1971) concepts of markers and tie-signs were used. Observers used recording sheets presented in Figures 1 and 2 to identify collectivities-as-families (Petronio & Bourhis, 1987, pp. 49-50). Markers and tie-signs are considered interdependent concepts as will become evident as this discussion progresses. This portion of the presentation is largely based on an article by Petronio & Bourhis (1987). As noted, family collectivities were identified by markers and tie-signs first and secondly observations of family interaction patterns found in public were conducted.

Figure 1
Determining Families in Public Places

Coding Scheme for Markers

	Adult Males/ Adult Females	Adult Male/ Male Child	Adult Female/ Female Child	Adult Female/ Male Child	Adult Male/ Female Child
Hand Hold					
Arm Lock					
Waist Hold					
Hug					
Kiss					
Immediacy					
Verb Exclusivity					
Familial Addresses					

Figure 2

Coding Scheme for Tie-Signs: _____

Wedding Ring
    Male   _____

    Female   _____

Engagement Ring
    Male   _____

    Female   _____

Parental Accouterments

    diapers _____

    bottles _____

    blankets _____

    strollers _____

    toys _____

    baby carrier _____

    others _____

_____

Markers

Markers are behaviors which signify that a relationship exists. These behaviors "mark" or point out that two or more people are associated with each other. Markers require close physical proximity and indicate a relationship between people through types of physical touch or restricted verbal exchange. Immediacy (Mehrabian, 1971), psychological or physical closeness, is a concept that underscores the notion of markers. We assumed that individuals making up a family tend to be in the co-presence of each other in public places, especially if the event is defined as a "family outing." Shopping, going to restaurants, going to parks, state fairs, movies, and the theatre were the types of places observed constituting "family outings." In addition to physical proximity, a baseline criterion, the observers looked for the following behaviors used to communicate a familial relationship: (1) hand-holding; (2) arm-lock; (3) waist-holding; (4) hugging; (5) kissing; (6) presence of children; (7) verbal interaction exclusivity; (8) familial addresses (Petronio & Bourhis, 1987).

As Goffman (1971) points out, holding hands in this culture is an indicator of a significant relationship as are waist-holding and arm-locks. All of these behaviors communicate a willingness to have personal space invaded and therefore are used as a way to identify people who are significant to one another. Hugging and kissing also necessitate invasion of personal space but in a more intimate way. These behaviors are tolerated in public if enacted in a limited fashion. The fact that hugging and kissing are tolerated to some extent may mean that they represent more credible indicators of relational involvement (Petronio & Bourhis, 1987).

The presence of children ranging from infants to adolescents in the company of an adult is used to indicate that the collectivity may be a family. More certainty is gained if the adults enter into the nonverbal behaviors of: (1) monitoring (paying attention to) and/or (2) regulating or controlling the child's behavior. "For non-teenage children, monitoring may be defined as the adult posturing toward and eye-body contact with the child on regular intervals. Regulating behavior may consist of containing the child within a radius around the adult. For teenagers, monitoring is not often employed but the parent does attempt to regulate their behavior" (Petronio & Bourhis, 1987, p. 48) by setting times they should return or disallowing separation.

When the family was in the presence of one another, the observers focused on the frequency with which the individuals directed communicative interaction to each other rather than to non-family members. This exclusivity of verbal interaction marks familiarity and represents another indicator of a family. Yet another verbal strategy is that of familial address.

Familial address is also a marker that communicates a relationship between people. Knapp (1984) suggests that "intimates have some unique speech patterns that distinguish them from non-intimates" (p. 225). Thus, when individuals used nicknames (e.g., Billy, Suzie) and endearments (e.g., dear, sweetheart, honey), they were defined as communicating a bond. In addition, a third indicator was the use of terms reflecting a role relationship (e.g., Mom, Dad, Son, Grandma).

Thus, markers show a relationship between significant others (parent-children, husband-wives, grandparents) in a public setting through allowing personal space invasion by holding hands, arm-locks, waist-holding, hugging, kissing, close proximity of family members, verbal exclusivity and familial addresses. The immediacy of individuals and space invasion thus identifies collectivites as families.

Tie-Signs

Tie-signs also aid the observer in determining whether a group of individuals are related. Tie-signs are social artifacts which communicate the nature of a relationship. Whereas markers are nonverbal *behaviors* which tell us a relationship exists, *tie-signs* are nonverbal artifacts that tell us about the type of relationship. The following are tie-signs used to represent familial relationships: (1) wedding or engagement rings; and (2) parental accouterments. "Separately, each category may not provide credible evidence that the individuals involved have a familial relationship" (Petronio & Bourhis, 1987, p. 48). Hence, to be most effective, these categories were considered in groups or clusters. In addition, to interpret many of these tie-signs, they were evaluated in relationship to the members' immediacy. Therefore, a number of conditions were met over time before observers were confident that they had identified a family.

All societies tend to use social artifacts to symbolize a relationship between individuals (Knapp, 1971). The ring (engagement or wedding) is often worn to communicate the nature of the tie between individuals. When combined with the co-presence of another and the additional evidence of one or more of the markers, there is a cumulative set of information to suggest a familial relationship.

Parental accouterments are artifacts that show a tie between parents and young children. Parental accouterments are those items needed for child care away from the home, including strollers, diaper bags, toys, bottles, blankets, baby carriers, car seats and so forth which are carried to public places to aid the parent in caring for the young child. When an adult was managing these items in the presence of a child or children this was used as a familial indicator.

After the observers were confident that they had accumulated enough information to suggest that they were watching a family, they began to focus on two types of family interaction behaviors: (1) disciplinary actions with children and (2) division of labor activities between mothers and fathers.

Part II: Public Family Behavior Disciplinary Actions

There were several themes that emerged from these observations regarding disciplining children in public places. Our society does not sanction open displays of physical punishment, especially in more recent years with greater attention to child abuse. The parent usually is limited to socially acceptable tactics to control the child's behavior in public. The child's behaviors in need of discipline ranged from disagreements with parents on what to buy while shopping to open temper tantrums resulting from the child not getting what he/she wanted. To achieve an orderly public face or presentation for both the parent and child in dealing with these behaviors, the parents in these observations used either *proactive* disciplinary tactics or *reactive* strategies.

Proactive

Proactive tactics are defined as preventive behaviors that anticipate possible problems in need of disciplinary responses. The parent takes an action before any disruptions occur hoping to reduce the probability the event will take place. The following proactive tactics were observed: (1) talking to the children, thereby keeping their attention. This technique limited the restlessness and opportunity to wander or cause disruptions; (2) physically restraining the child (e.g., holding) was another proactive way to prevent the child from leaving the parent's side; (3) the "goods for services" approach was the third type of exchange and of the three, was the most frequently observed technique. In this exchange, the mother or father promised some type of "goods" such as a toy or an activity (e.g., like riding the horse in front of the store) if the child will behave while in public (the service). This proactive tactic appeared to be less effective than the other two. Observers noted that especially the younger children often forgot they agreed to this contract and acted in a disruptive way regardless of their promise. This often resulted in the parent having to use a reactive strategy in addition to the proactive technique of "goods for service."

Reactive Strategies

Overall, most of the parents tended to use some form of a reactive strategy. Reactive strategies occurred after the unwanted behavior was exhibited in public by the child. The parents used one or more of the following ways to control their child's behavior: (1) silence; (2) denial of shared space; (3) verbal threats; (4) interruptions. We would like to note that very rarely were parents observed physically hitting their children so this was not included as a category.

Silence

Silence was often used by parents in public to communicate disapproval of inappropriate actions to the child. Turk and Bell (1970) note that the use of silence gives a person greater control over the situation. Being silent immediately after the child engages in an inappropriate behavior communicates dissatisfaction and strips the child's power to attract the parent's attention. For example, one little girl was begging her mother for a toy as they walked past a store in the shopping mall. The mother used silence and never acknowledged that the little girl was asking for the toy. By ignoring the demand, the mother did not legitimize the girl's begging. After a while the little girl stopped and they continued to shop.

Denial of Shared Space

The denial of shared space was another tactic used to discipline children in public. For example, in one observation a mother and a three-year-old son were sitting next to each other in a restaurant booth. The child became rambunctious and the mother withdrew the privilege of sitting next to her, ordering the son to sit on the other side. The child was no longer able to share personal space with his mother and by ordering him to sit alone she sent him a message that he was acting inappropriately.

Verbal Threats

Verbal threats were observed in two forms. One, verbal threats to withhold promised goods or activities; two, threats of physical punishment when the parent and child returned to a private place. Usually, these threats were delivered with increasing loudness in the parent's voice. Thus, the threats were administered several times, intensifying the volume each time they were communicated and the parents typically increased the possible negative outcomes to the child.

This type of behavior is similar to the concept of escalation proposed by Watzlawick, Beavin and Jackson (1967). The parents tended to administer the threat first in a reasonable conversational tone. As the interaction progressed and the child did not respond with the behaviors requested by the parent, the parent would administer the verbal threat again, increasing the volume and enhancing the possible negative outcomes. At a point, (usually three times) the child would acknowledge the demand and comply with the parent's desired behavior.

Interruptions

Interruptions by the parent were observed as a disciplinary strategy used more often with older children and when the child disagreed with a suggestion made by the parent. For example, an adolescent girl was observed with her mother shopping for clothes. The mother made several attempts to identify clothing that would be "nice, pretty, go together" but each time the daughter would tell her mother she disliked the choices. While the daughter was telling the mother she hated the things picked out, the mother would interrupt her daughter and point to something else. This strategy appeared to be used as a controlling device, minimizing the potential for escalation into a verbal fight by distracting the daughter from statements of disapproval.

Division of Labor

Division of labor refers to observing the way mothers and fathers divide child care tasks while in public places. The overriding theme in these observations suggests that when mothers and fathers go out with the children, fathers tend to play the "helping role." Fathers seemed to assume the mothers were in charge and responsible; consequently, they engaged in a variety of activities that suggested the mothers were in charge. There were three categories in which division of labor was observed: (1) controlling the child; (2) child maintenance tasks; (3) giving attention.

Controlling the Child

Controlling children in public deals with restricting the behavioral options the child may enact. This category is representative of disciplinary actions, however, in this section we talk about the behaviors mothers and fathers differentially use to control their children.

Generally, these observations showed that mothers were the primary disciplinarian when both mothers and fathers were together in a public setting with their children. The mothers also tended to react more quickly to control the child's behavior than the father. But, it may be that the father's inaction was precipitated by the immediate action of the mother. However, overall the fathers did not frequently participate in disciplining their children when disturbances occurred. The fathers acted disinvolved when the mothers were present. When the mother was away from the father and child shopping in a store, for example, the father would remain with the child until the child would start to be disruptive. At that point, fathers typically sought out the mother to resolve the disturbance.

Child Maintenance Tasks

The fathers usually enacted instrumental tasks such as pushing the stroller whether or not the child was in it, paying for merchandise or food, holding packages and "watching the children" on a short term basis while the mother engaged in some task. The mothers enacted more physically caring and nurturing behaviors such as dressing the children before going outside in the winter months, picking out clothes and food for the children, and monitoring the children more often than the fathers.

Giving Attention

Throughout most of the observations, the mothers tended to give more prolonged attention to the children than the fathers. Mothers spoke to the children more often, particularly young children, they responded more quickly to their needs, and the mothers explained events as well as answered questions more frequently than fathers. The fathers' means of giving attention typically came in the form of play. The fathers would joke, tease or make faces to give the child attention while in a public setting but these behaviors happened more frequently with older children. Overall, fathers seemed to be more attentive to sons. Mothers provided more immediate comfort to their daughters after a frustrating event.

Summary

These observations of families in public places focused first on ways to identify collectivities as family members using markers and tie-signs. Markers assume immediacy or close physical proximity and rely upon identifiers of: (1) hand-holding; (2) arm-lock; (3) waist-holding; (4) presence of children; (5) verbal interaction exclusivity; (6) hugging; (7) kissing; (8) familial addresses. Tie-signs represent social artifacts that communicate the type of relationship which exists between people. Wedding and/or engagement rings and parental accouterments were categories used to symbolize familial ties.

Observations were also made of disciplinary actions taken by parents to control children's behavior. The two major categories of *proactive tactics* and *reactive strategies* represent the way parents dealt with public disturbances by their children. The *proactive tactics* included talking to the child, physically restraining the child and "goods for services." The *reactive strategies* observed were silence, denial of shared space, verbal threats and interruptions. The observers also focused on division of labor concerning child care tasks between mothers and fathers, there are three categories: (1) controlling the child; (2) child maintenance tasks; (3) giving attention.

When families are together in public settings, they must manage the way they interact to fit the rules of appropriate behavior while accomplishing important familial goals, like disciplining their children. These observations have described some of the techniques parents and children use to function as a unit away from the privacy of their homes.

References

Goffman, E. (1963). *Behavior in Public Places: Notes on the Social Organization of Gatherings*. New York: The Free Press.

—— (1971). *Relations in Public*. New York: Harper and Row Publishers.

Knapp, M. (1971). *Nonverbal Communication in Human Interaction*. New York: Holt, Rinehart and Winston.

—— (1984). *Interpersonal Communication and Human Relationships*. Boston, MA: Allen and Bacon.

Lyman, S. and Scott, M. (1970). Territoriality: A neglected sociological dimension. In G. Stone and H. Farberman (Eds.) *Social Psychology through Symbolic Interaction* (pp. 214-226). Waltham, MA: Xerox College Publishing.

Mehrabian, A. (1971). *Silent Messages*. Belmont, CA: Wadsworth Publishing Company, Inc.

Petronio, S. and Bourhis, J. (1987). Identifying family collectivities in public places: An instructional exercise. *Communication Education*, 36(2), 46-51.

Turk, J. and Bell, N. (1972). Measuring power in families. *Journal of Marriage and the Family*, 34, 215-222.

Watzlawick, P., Beavin, J. and Jackson, D. (1967). *Pragmatics of Human Communication*. New York: W.W. Norton & Co., Inc.

The Nonverbal Behavior Analysis Instrument was designed by Hensley and Taylor to study nonverbal behavior in the classroom. The chapter describes how to use the instrument to provide feedback to teachers on their nonverbal behavior.

47

Nonverbal Behavior Analysis Instrument

Robert B. Hensley and Pamela K. Taylor

Student teachers, fresh from a higher education environment, often experience initial difficulty in communicating with school-aged children. Several factors contribute to this problem. Many students in colleges and universities have had limited experience with younger children since they left the elementary and the secondary school themselves. College students' exposure to four years of lectures presented by professors with exceptionally rich vocabularies may pose problems. Still other student teachers experience difficulties in the transition from the role of a student who, basically, consumes information to that of a teacher responsible for leading an instructional sequence.

Undergraduate teacher preparation programs do attempt to address some of these potential problems. However, few provide future teachers with much direct instruction on the nature of the complex teacher/learner interaction that characterizes the public school classroom. Future teachers regularly leave programs eminently well prepared to develop units and lesson plans according to specified guidelines; but, if they fail to understand the dynamics of teacher-learner communication in the classroom, they experience difficulty in successfully implementing these programs. Clearly, there is a case for providing undergraduates with specific information about the nature of communication between teachers and learners.

Knapp (1972) states that more than 65% of our communication is nonverbal. Because of the importance of communication skills for success

Reprinted with permission from: Hensley, R.B., and Taylor, P.K. (1987). Nonverbal behavior analysis instrument. *The Clearing House, 60,* 199-201.

in student teaching, those who supervise student teachers have important responsibilities in this area. They must augment what little treatment this topic gets in the preparation program with presentations and by providing needed counsel to individual student teachers. Some basic descriptions of the dimensions of nonverbal communication will bring this issue into focus.

Kinds of Nonverbal Behaviors

People respond to a variety of nonverbal behavioral cues. These cues take the form of head and limb movements and positioning. Cues manifest themselves in other ways as well. For example, some of the most important cues are observed in facial expressions and in physical proximity of the instructor to the students. Knapp (1972) relates that students within eye contact range of the instructor participate more in class discussions. Eye contact compels attention, and students tend to misbehave less if they know their teacher scans the room regularly. This makes it easier for the teacher to make eye contact and correct the problem without disrupting the class.

In addition, some evidence suggests that facial expressions are universal. That is, they transcend cultural boundaries so that expressions can be read accurately even by people from extremely diverse cultures. As an example, Knapp (1972) notes the cross-cultural similarities of facial expression. He points out that "in several studies with preliterate cultures (New Guinea) which did not have widespread contact with mass media, results, . . . [were] comparable to those found in literate eastern and western cultures" (p. 20). Bull (1983) indicates that even people who are born deaf and blind display the same types of facial expressions as do physically normal people. As noted, facial expressions help people "read" one another. When a person receives positive facial cues, he or she is more likely to continue interacting than if he or she receives negative responses.

Nonverbal Cueing

Teachers who are proficient nonverbal communicators enjoy several advantages over teachers who are not. Depending upon a teacher's nonverbal cues, a learner might feel warmth and acceptance or alienation and rejection. Also, nonverbal communication can strengthen class participation in discussions, curb discipline problems, and motivate students. When teachers use nonverbal cues to help learners feel accepted, learners, in turn, increase their willingness to participate in class.

Facial expressions are an important dimension of nonverbal behavior. A teacher who smiles and asks a question receives more answers than when not smiling. As noted, facial expressions seem to transcend cultural boundaries. Therefore, teachers of multi-lingual or cross-cultural students are able to interact with their students via facial cues.

A second nonverbal dimension, physical proximity, is associated with effective classroom management. Physical proximity can be used to stop a potential problem. Sometimes this is accomplished when the teacher steps in the direction of a learner or group of learners needing attention and/or correction. At other times, actually touching a shoulder or standing in the vicinity of the learner serves to forestall a discipline problem. The strong influence of proximity suggests that learners associate physical distance with psychological distance. Teachers who avoid physical closeness may be seen as uncaring. In contrast, teachers who are less separated physically from learners are seen as more open or friendly. The importance of facial expression and proximity suggest that these dimensions of teacher behavior should receive special attention in the teacher preparation program, particularly during student teaching. The Nonverbal Behavior Analysis Instrument has been designed with this purpose in mind.

Nonverbal Behavior Analysis Instrument

The Nonverbal Behavior Analysis Instrument (see Figure 1) was designed to gather information about teachers' facial expressions and proximity to learners. It is not intended to be judgmental. Rather, it seeks to provide information to the teacher about what he or she did during the observation period. Judgments about what occurred are left to the teacher. This instrument also reveals whether teachers' facial expressions and proximity behaviors were associated with: (1) student gender, (2) student ethnicity, or (3) time of day, and also whether interactions were teacher initiated or learner initiated.

Instructions for Instrument Use

The first section deals with the facial expression the teacher displays. The observer chooses from (1) smile, (2) frown, (3) neutral, or (4) other. If "other" is selected, the observer explains what is observed in the comment section. The second section is concerned with attempted eye contact and physical proximity between the teacher and the student. The observer selects (1) attempted eye contact, (2) proximity (under ten feet), (3) both, or (4) neither. Again the observer will use the comment section

Figure 1
Scoring and Rating Sheets
Record Form

Time of Day _____
Elective or Required Course (Circle one)
Gender of Teacher _____

Facial Expression	Physical	Comments	Gender	Racial/ Ethnic	Type of Interaction

1. A) Smile
B) Frown
C) Neutral
D) Other
	A) Eye contact
	   attempted
	B) Proximity
	   (under 10')
	C) Both
	D) Neither
			A) M
			B) F
				A) Black
				B) White
				C) Hispanic
				D) Oriental
				E) American
				   Indian
				F) Other
					A) SI
					B) TI

Rating Sheet

Response Number	Facial Expression	Physical	Gender	Racial/ Ethnic	Type of Interaction

Rating Sheet
Overall Totals

Expression	Physical	Gender	Racial/Ethnic	Type of Interaction

to explain his or her findings. The third section is the comment segment mentioned previously. This section is utilized for explaining actions in the classroom not covered by the checklist. The fourth section is gender. The observer merely circles the appropriate category of the student involved in the interaction. The fifth section is concerned with racial/ethnic groupings: (1) Black, (2) White, (3) Hispanic, (4) Oriental, (5) American Indian, and (6) other. The final section consists of two choices: SI (student initiated) and TI (teacher initiated). The recorder circles the appropriate category each time an interaction occurs.

In addition to the record form, a rating sheet is provided on which to record the observations. All six categories are included in addition to a column where each interaction is numbered chronologically. At the bottom of each page, a Totals section is provided. On the last page a Ratings Sheet, Overall Totals section, and a final summary section are included, on which observations and comments may be summarized.

Conclusion

This instrument provides feedback to teachers regarding their facial expressions and learner proximity behaviors. By illuminating deficiencies that may inhibit productive classroom communication, educators can become aware of their individual classroom patterns. For example, if a teacher predominantly interacts with white females, this pattern will be revealed by the instrument. Further, the instrument might point out differences associated with such variables as time of day and whether the interaction was teacher or learner initiated. Information of this type can be important to the teacher as he or she plans future instructional activities. If necessary, the teacher can make plans to alter her or his behavior to meet the needs of all learners in the class. In summary, the instrument can help teachers develop conscious control over nonverbal behavior. Nonverbal behavior that is controlled has much more potential to affect learners positively than does behavior that is unplanned, random, and perhaps capricious.

References

Bull, P. 1983. *Body movement and interpersonal communications.* New York: John Wiley & Sons.

Knapp, M.L. 1972. *Nonverbal communication in human interaction.* New York: Holt, Rinehart and Winston, Inc.

Key Terms and Concepts

Hecht, *Methods of Nonverbal Communication Research*

definition of research
3 types of questions
describe
explain
predict
importance
systematic methods
grounded approach
hypothesis-testing
  approach

individual or
  interaction
social cognition
method
experiment
observation
control
confederate
role play
recording nonverbal
  communication

survey
coding system
field notes
open and closed
  questions
coding systems
coding types of
  behavior
coding symbols

Petronio, Bourhis, and Berquist, *Familes in Public Places*

public areas
rules
markers
tie-signs

immediacy
monitoring
regulating

social artifacts
proactive
reactive

Hensley and Taylor, *Nonverbal Behavior Analysis Instrument*

importance of nonverbal communication
nonverbal cuing
proximity
Nonverbal Behavior Analysis Instrument